Legal Theory
and Common Law

Legal Theory
and Common Law

edited by
WILLIAM TWINING

Basil Blackwell

© Basil Blackwell 1986

First published 1986

Basil Blackwell Ltd
108 Cowley Road, Oxford OX4 1JF, UK

Basil Blackwell Inc.
432 Park Avenue South, Suite 1505,
New York, NY 10016, USA

BRITISH LIBRARY CATALOGUING IN PUBLICATION DATA

Legal theory and common law.
1. Common law
I. Twining, William
340.5'7'01   K588

ISBN 0-631-14477-3

LIBRARY OF CONGRESS CATALOGING IN PUBLICATION DATA

Main entry under title:
Legal theory and common law.
1. Common law—Great Britain—Addresses, essays,
lectures. 2. Common law—Addresses, essays, lectures.
3. Jurisprudence—Addresses, essays, lectures.
I. Twining, William L.
KD671.A75L44   1986   349.42   85-26687
ISBN 0-631-14477-3   344.2

Phototypeset by Dobbie Typesetting Service, Plymouth, Devon
Printed in Great Britain by T. J. Press Ltd, Padstow

Contents

Contributors

HUGH COLLINS is a Fellow of Brasenose College, Oxford.

ROGER COTTERRELL is Reader in Legal Theory at Queen Mary College, London.

NORMAN LEWIS is Professor of Public Law at the University of Sheffield.

NEIL MacCORMICK is Regius Professor of the Law of Nature and the Law of Nations at the University of Edinburgh.

DAVID MIERS is Senior Lecturer in Law at University College, Cardiff.

KATHERINE O'DONOVAN is Senior Lecturer in Law at the University of Kent.

BRIAN SIMPSON is Professor of Law at the University of Kent and the University of Chicago.

MARY STOKES is a Fellow of Brasenose College, Oxford.

DAVID SUGARMAN is Reader in Law at Middlesex Polytechnic.

RICHARD TUR is Benn Law Fellow at Oriel College, Oxford.

WILLIAM TWINING is Quain Professor of Jurisprudence at University College London.

CENTO VELJANOVSKI is Lecturer in Law and Economics at University College London.

Table of Cases

1
Introduction

WILLIAM TWINING

Legal theory is currently experiencing a period of expanding interest and diversification. Contacts have been renewed and strengthened with moral and political philosophy, with social theory and with thinkers as diverse as the logician L. Jonathan Cohen and various French structuralists. Some of the interest in intellectual history by political theorists such as Quentin Skinner and J. G. A. Pocock has spread over to the history of legal thought. Detailed textual and contextual study of the work of major figures such as Bentham, Mill, Kelsen, Hegel and Marx is flourishing as never before. Economic analysis of law has spread across nations as well as branches of law; it has, in the process, begun to develop some theoretical sophistication. 'Critical legal studies' have footholds in the United Kingdom and continental Europe as well as the United States.

From time to time fears have been expressed that these developments, however exciting they may be intellectually, tend to widen the gap between legal theory and the academic and practical study of particular branches of law. Such fears can easily be exaggerated: for example, detailed analysis of important concepts used in judicial reasoning continues to flourish; so does applied moral philosophy; there has been an encouraging trend in the direction of comprehensive rethinking of particular fields, as is illustrated by the work of Atiyah, MacNeil and others in contracts, Fletcher and Gross in criminal law, Glendon in family law and a variety of scholars in constitutional and administrative law. This trend has been further stimulated by the deliberate strategy of some leading members of the American Critical Legal Studies Movement to concentrate their energies on developing radical critiques of traditional areas of specialized legal scholarship.

Nevertheless concern about a widening gap between legal theory and particular fields of legal study is not groundless. If one looks at the content of many jurisprudence courses and the literature generated for the student market it is not difficult to see why many students complain that they can see little or no connection between jurisprudence and the rest of the curriculum. Similarly many academic lawyers assert that some debates in legal philosophy or the sociology of law or critical theory have become too 'sophisticated' or 'abstruse' for them to understand. Insofar as such views are held by a significant number of scholars, teachers and students, whether or not they are justified, there is cause for concern.

This book grew out of such concerns. The underlying reasons are complex. No doubt some of the difficulties are an almost inevitable result of specialization within and between disciplines. Doubts about the 'relevance' of theory to practice or to particular studies are endemic. However, in my view, there are some specific features of the current situation of academic law in the United Kingdom that contribute to the problem. At the risk of oversimplification it may be helpful to sketch one interpretation of the historical context.

In nutshell form the story goes as follows:[1] in the heritage of English jurisprudence it was Jeremy Bentham who came nearest to producing a comprehensive legal theory. His Science of Legislation encompassed both systematic study of the law as it is (expository jurisprudence) and systematic evaluation of actual and potential law (censorial jurisprudence) within the framework of a coherent, but controversial, general philosophy that embraced epistemology, ethics and politics. By virtue of a utilitarian's concern with actual consequences, Bentham recognized the relevance of social fact to the understanding of law. But, perhaps because of the age in which he lived, this perception was not backed by a comprehensive social theory of comparable sophistication to his other ideas. Bentham's Science of Legislation was both ahistorical and sociologically naive.

Since Bentham's death in 1832 the dominant strands in English jurisprudence have been, and very largely remain, broadly positivistic, liberal and instrumentalist. However, instead of developing and expanding Bentham's legacy, it was in large part squandered by his successors in jurisprudence. Between the death of Bentham and the advent of Hart mainstream jurisprudence became progressively narrower and less coherent. Austin narrowed down Bentham; the followers of Austin narrowed down Austin, or at least used him eclectically. As David Sugarman explains in his paper (chapter 3) part of this narrowing took the form of the dwindling of interest in censorial jurisprudence, with pragmatic 'common sense' replacing intellectual utilitarianism as the predominant basis for evaluating laws. Between 1900 and 1950 a particularistic, sometimes incoherent, form of analytical jurisprudence dominated English legal theorizing. Whether there was any causal connection, this modified Austinianism fitted quite well with the expository or 'black-letter' tradition of scholarship and teaching that predominated during this period. Jurisprudence was expounded and developed by men who were lawyers first and foremost. Their theorizing kept in touch with law as they perceived it, but it lost touch with developments in philosophy. As MacCormick remarked: 'Lawyers had stopped being interested in philosophy, philosophers in law.'[2]

Both the Expository Tradition and the form of jurisprudence that accompanied it have been the subject of extensive criticism in recent years from a number of different points of view. It is not necessary to rehearse the arguments here. But it is pertinent to observe that, whatever its limitations and weaknesses, traditional analytical jurisprudence had three great strengths. Firstly, it was intellectually rigorous, even though it was not philosophically sophisticated. Secondly, jurisprudence courses often served a valuable function by cutting across different fields of law and by providing a degree of integration of legal study on the basis of broad principle and 'fundamental' concepts. Analytical jurisprudence forced students to explore distinctions, analogies and relationships across doctrinal boundaries in an illuminating way. Thirdly, because of its close relationship to doctrine and because it was taught by lawyers it did not lose touch with bread-and-butter law. It was more abstract than other subjects but it was not abstracted from them.

When in 1952 Herbert Hart was elected to the Chair of Jurisprudence at Oxford the time was ripe for change. Dissatisfaction with the expository approach to academic law was beginning to emerge on a wider scale than previously; there was growing criticism of 'Austinian' jurisprudence, but this lacked a clear theoretical base. 'The Revolution in Philosophy', inspired by Wittgenstein, Ryle, J. L. Austin and others, was in full ferment and its relevance to legal language and lawyers' reasonings was beginning to be perceived by some philosophers. Hart was trained as both a philosopher and a lawyer. His historic achievement was to re-establish close links between jurisprudence and philosophy and to restore Bentham to his rightful place as 'the Father of English Jurisprudence'.

In bringing philosophical perspectives, concepts and techniques to bear on classical questions of jurisprudence Hart was anxious both not to lose his legal audience and to keep in touch with detailed legal analysis. However, partly because of the participation of philosophers, the centre stage came to be dominated by debates that concentrated on the more abstract aspects of Hart's contributions and of legal philosophy in general. To engage in these debates required a philosophical sophistication that most academic lawyers lacked; conversely few of the participants, especially the philosophers, had the detailed legal knowledge and involvement of a Pollock or Goodhart or C. K. Allen.

The new analytical jurists stimulated a revival of interest in legal theory, especially in some fundamental philosophical issues. However, this intellectual excitement met only one of the diverse sources of dissatisfaction with the Expository Tradition. Those who wished for grand synthesizing theory or more realistic or critical approaches to the study of law were still dissatisfied.[3] For the new analytical jurisprudence in practice hardly touched their concerns: Hart himself concentrated for the most part on the questions he had inherited from his immediate predecessors; his leading disciples and critics were interested in normative questions (including issues of applied moral philosophy). But English analytical philosophy of the time was stronger on analysis than synthesis; it had much to say about concepts, language and reasoning, but it had rather less to contribute to understanding the actual operation of laws, the role of law in society and the relationship between law and social change. To the more sociologically minded the least convincing of Hart's claims was the statement that *The Concept of Law* was an essay in descriptive sociology. Moreover, the new analytical jurists were either largely apolitical or, like Ronald Dworkin, they propounded versions of liberalism that were unlikely to satisfy either the left or the right in Britain in a period of political polarization in which it was becoming less and less convincing to claim that law was or could be politically neutral.

Since the mid-1960s academic law in the United Kingdom has expanded, broadened and diversified. Proponents of socio-legal, contextual, critical and economic approaches have all tried to develop alternatives to the dominant expository orthodoxy, with mixed success. They have sought inspiration and help from a bewildering variety of disciplines, intellectual traditions and individual thinkers. The new pluralism in academic law has been matched by a corresponding pluralism in legal theorizing. This has made for excitement but not for coherence.

And it has not always been clear to specialists and students immersed in this
or that piece of technical detail what all this ferment has to do with them.

One of the primary tasks of legal theory is to establish and maintain contact
with developments in neighbouring disciplines.[4] This bridge-building or
'conduit' function takes place at different levels of generality, often in a random
and fragmented fashion. In recent years the main points of sustained contact have
been with English analytical philosophy and, to a lesser extent, with social theory
as propounded by the secular trinity of Marx, Weber and Durkheim. In each
case the strongest links have been established at rather abstract levels. As was
suggested above, the first generation of Hart's disciples and critics have tended
to concentrate on some rather abstract problems of legal philosophy. For somewhat
different reasons, there is also a noticeable gap between the macro-theoretical
ideas that have been imported from social theory and the detailed study of specifics
that represents the mainstream of legal education and scholarship. It is for such
reasons that there is a felt need to cultivate the middle ground.

Against this background it was decided to devote about one-third of the
W. G. Hart Workshop on Legal Theory, held in London in July 1984, to an
exploration of the relations between legal theory and particular legal subjects
or fields of law. This generated sufficient interest to justify extending the exercise
to cover more fields from a variety of perspectives. Five of the contributors to
the original workshop were asked to revise their papers (Lewis, Miers, O'Donovan,
Tur and MacCormick) and several more were invited to write new chapters
specially for this volume. Permission was also sought to include two previously
published papers (by Simpson and Twining) and an unpublished manuscript by
Karl Llewellyn that fitted in with the general theme. This book is the result.
It is intended to be more coherent than a collection of conference papers, but
as an exploratory symposium it does not claim to be either systematic or
comprehensive. It has only been possible to accommodate a sample of topics:
given more space and time I would have hoped to include papers on public
international law, comparative law, legal history, trusts, procedure, labour law,
welfare law and criminology, for example, and a wider range of theoretical
perspectives. The selection was not entirely random. The aim has been to obtain a
reasonable spread of subjects and a diversity of views and to include historical
and analytical treatments that deal with the central theme from different angles.

The instructions to the authors were deliberately quite open-ended: to explore
the relationship between legal theory (or some aspect of it) and scholarship and
teaching in their specialized field of expertise. The selection of topics and authors
was naturally contingent on such factors as availability and expertise. There is
a discernible pattern, some would say bias, in the list of authors: all of them are
more or less dissatisfied with the Expository Tradition in one way or another.
All claim to be critical of 'formalism' . . . but then are we not all anti-formalists
now?[5] They are, however, from significantly different backgrounds. Three of
the contributors, Simpson, Tur and MacCormick, have in other writings been
powerful defenders and practitioners of analytical jurisprudence. Yet in their
papers each is in a different way subversive of significant aspects of mainstream
analytical positivism. Several of us (Twining, Lewis, Miers and to a lesser extent
MacCormick) acknowledge a direct debt to Karl Llewellyn, who is himself

represented here. Veljanovski, whose original training was in economics, claims that micro-economic analysis fits better with legal realism than analytical jurisprudence, yet his outsider's perspective is significantly different in spirit and substance from the Weberian *verstehen* of a Llewellyn (or for that matter a Hart). Like Veljanovski, Roger Cotterrell looks at lawyers' modes of thought from without, as well as from within, as befits someone educated in sociology as well as law; but the perspective of social theory is very different from that of economic analysis.

At least five different contributors (Sugarman, Lewis, Collins, Stokes and O'Donovan) adopt 'critical' perspectives; the affinity is clear, for each explicitly seeks to reveal the inadequacy, as they see it, of important underlying assumptions of 'liberal legal thought' which they variously characterize as 'formalism' (Sugarman), 'liberalism' (Lewis, Collins, Stokes) and 'instrumentalism' (O'Donovan). However, this subversive role of theorizing, articulating and challenging important assumptions of orthodox or traditional legal discourse, is by no means confined to those who overtly ally themselves with current trends in 'critical' studies. All theorists are subversive of assumptions and not all belong to the political left. The boundaries within and outside critical studies are far from clear and here, as elsewhere in jurisprudence, individual writers tend to defy neat classification.

It is hardly surprising that a disparate group of specialists in different branches of law should interpret a fairly open-ended brief rather differently. Each of these essays addresses a particular question or set of questions from an individual perspective. The essays are more diverse than the table of contents suggests. Some are mainly concerned with theoretical aspects of particular fields. Here the authors seem to be asking: what bearing does legal theory have on my subject? Others are at least as much interested in the nature and state of legal theorizing: they are more concerned with what light their special field throws on contemporary legal theory. Richard Tur does both. As was almost inevitable, each essay is selective in that it deals with what the author thinks to be theoretically significant about their subject.

However, there may be more in common between the essays than a first reading might suggest. First, all but the first and last contributions (by Simpson and Llewellyn) were written by British academic lawyers in a specific historical context. All the authors have a shared concern about gaps and dislocations between contemporary legal theory and teaching and research in particular fields. This relates both to the tendency of legal theory to become abstracted and divorced from specialized studies to its detriment and to a sense that theoretical developments have had too little impact on academic treatments of particular subjects. Thus the main unifying theme of the book is a shared concern to move into the middle ground between abstract theorizing and specialized legal studies – in short, to build or repair bridges between the general and the particular in academic law. This, in my view, is a perennial theoretical job of jurisprudence.

There is, however, a puzzle. What is meant by 'theory' in this context? And is there a consensus on this matter among the contributors? When the first drafts of the essays were submitted it seemed to me that the authors had such varied conceptions of theory, both implicit and explicit, that the volume would lack

6	*William Twining*

any coherence. During the process of editing and revision a dialogue developed on this issue among several of us; eventually Neil MacCormick and I decided to try to address it directly in the chapter on the educational rationale of jurisprudence courses (chapter 13). It may be helpful to say something about the question at this stage. In my view, theorizing is an activity directed to posing, reposing, and seeking answers to *general* questions. Legal theory is that part of the discipline of law concerned with all general questions relating to law. This usage is both broad and vague. It is broad in that it encompasses not only the most abstract (philosophical) questions but also less general (middle-order) questions – hence the assertion that cultivating the middle ground is a theoretical task. In this view these questions are of many different kinds (e.g. analytical, empirical, evaluative) and they can be posed at many different levels of generality.[6] The usage is vague, both because it does not specify a precise level of generality or abstraction at which theory begins (how could it?) and because it leaves open widely contested questions about the scope of 'law' and 'discipline', as Roger Cotterrell points out.[7] Some would wish to adopt a narrower conception of legal theory, for example by confining it to questions that are unequivocally or recognizably 'philosophical' or to a range of questions that have traditionally attracted the attention of jurists as being *the* (central) questions of jurisprudence.

In the present context, at least, the breadth and vagueness of this usage are advantageous. A broad vision of legal theory helps us see our subject whole, to locate law in a map of all learning, to spot gaps, biases and imbalances in contemporary treatments, and to identify questions or lines of enquiry that have been more or less neglected or marginalized in our legal culture. The vagueness of this conception of theory helps to emphasize the interrelatedness of general and particular concerns and the artificiality of isolating theoretical from other enquiries. This seems particularly apposite in an exercise devoted to exploring some of the middle ground.

Whether or not other contributors would agree with me, I have no difficulty in accommodating all of their essays within this conception of theory. They have chosen to address a range of questions from a variety of perspectives and at different levels of generality. They have all been selective. But they have all explored aspects of the relationships between their chosen field and more general questions, and as such they are all contributing to legal theory. If the outcome of this exercise is that this book raises, rather than resolves, a number of questions about the nature, scope and functions of theorizing about law as well as about its relationship to specialized legal studies it will have served a purpose.

NOTES

1 This theme is developed in Twining, 'Academic Law and Legal Philosophy: The Significance of Herbert Hart' (1979) 95 *Law Quarterly Rev.* 557.
2 D. N. MacCormick, *H. L. A. Hart* (1981) p. 19.

3 See further Twining, 'Law and Social Science: The Method of Detail', *New Society*, 27 June 1974, p. 758.
4 See below p. 64.
5 See below p. 199.
6 See below pp. 64 and 240-9.
7 See below p. 83-8, cf. 253 n. 5.

2

The Common Law
and Legal Theory

BRIAN SIMPSON

I INTRODUCTION

In England, and in those parts of the world where the English legal tradition has been received, the characteristic type of law is common law, as contrasted with statute law. Common law in this sense has of course been modified by equity, but then equity is just another form of common law. The common law has in its time been given a variety of classifying titles, which reflect different views as to its distinguishing or characteristic feature – for example 'case law', 'judiciary law', 'judge-made law', 'customary law' and 'unwritten law'. Names such as these do not simply provide a neutral description of the common law. They reflect theories as to the nature of the common law, and it would be easy enough to cull from legal writings the expression of very divergent theoretical views of the institution. It seems to me, however, that to date no very satisfactory analysis of the nature of the common law has been provided by legal theory. Indeed, the matter has received remarkably little sustained attention by theoretical writers. What has been the subject of much writing, at least on this side of the Atlantic, has been the doctrine of precedent or *stare decisis*; indeed, a search of the literature for discussions of the nature of the common law tends to locate only accounts of the working of this doctrine, which is itself I suppose 'part of' the common law. To a historian, at least, any identification between the common law system and the doctrine of precedent, any attempt to explain the nature of the common law in terms of *stare decisis*, is bound to seem unsatisfactory, for the elaboration of rules and principles governing the use of precedents and their status as authorities is relatively modern, and the idea that there could be binding precedents more recent still. The common law had been in existence for centuries before anybody was very excited about these matters, and yet it functioned as a system of law without such props as the concept of the *ratio decidendi*, and functioned well enough.

Nor does the common law appear wholly to have altered its character over the years, and a theory of the common law, if it is to seem satisfactory, must cater for this continuity. It must accommodate the common law of the seventeenth as well as the common law of the twentieth century, or at least provide a view of the common law which will serve to explain whatever changes have occurred in the general character of the institution. One such change is indeed the increased importance attached to authority, in particular quoted judicial opinions, in the working of the system. This phenomenon is not peculiar to British Commonwealth courts. American judicial opinions too are heavily buttressed by elaborate reference to authority. But there has developed in modern times no extensive literature attempting to systematize its use or to set out rules of precedent analogous to those produced by English academics or by our appellate courts.

In the sense used here a theory or general view of the common law represents an attempt to provide an answer to the question whether the common law can be said to exist at all – and this has been seriously doubted – and, if so, in what sense. Put rather differently, such a theory will seek to explain how, if at all, statements in the form: 'It is the law that . . . ', such as 'It is the law that contracts require consideration,' can meaningfully be made, when such statements are conceived to be statements of the common law. Such an explanation is essential to the understanding of the workings of the judicial process, which is conducted upon the tacit assumption that the common law (we are not concerned with statute) always provides an answer to the matter in issue, and one which is independent of the will of the court. Put differently the conventions of legal argument embody a belief in the theoretical possibility of a comprehensive gapless rule of law. It is as if lawyers had all been convinced by Dworkin, though none of them have.[1]

What may be called general theoretical propositions of the common law, which are the stuff of legal argument and justification, take a variety of forms. Sometimes they are said to state *doctrines* of the common law (the doctrine of offer and acceptance), sometimes *principles* or *general principles* (the principle of *volenti non fit iniuria*), sometimes *rules* (the rule in *Rylands* v. *Fletcher*), sometimes *definitions* (the definition of conversion), and this is by no means an exclusive list of diversity which is recognized more generously in the language of lawyers than in the writings of legal philosophers. Some attempts have been made to differentiate these concepts; thus Bingham,[2] and more recently Dworkin,[3] have sought to distinguish *rules* from *principles*, and the latter has tried to explain the process of legal decision in problematic cases as involving principles rather than rules. For present purposes these distinctions are not important, and all legal propositions may be considered together, and merely distinguished from propositions which purport only to be *about* the common law. An example would be such a statement as 'The common law does not favour self-help.' Put in a different form, for example like this, 'It is a principle of the common law that self-help is to be discouraged,' this would in my scheme rank as a general theoretical proposition of the common law; it would then purport to state the law, rather than pass an observation about the law. It is primarily with propositions of law that I am here concerned.

In passing it is, however, important to notice that in legal reasoning propositions which are neither propositions *of* law nor propositions *about* law feature prominently. For example, when Devlin J said in the course of his judgment in *Behrens* v. *Bertram Mills*,[4] 'If a person wakes up in the middle of the night and finds an escaping tiger on top of his bed and suffers a heart attack, it would be nothing to the point that the intentions of the tiger were quite amiable,' he was not making a legal observation, but justifying a decision on the law governing liability for dangerous animals by an appeal to common sense. No doubt these non-legal justificatory propositions could be further divided – some for example refer to moral considerations, others to expediency – and they are used to claim for a decision a rationality which is not based upon the artificial reason of the law; though not themselves legal propositions they may be used to support the contention that this or that is the law. In the common law system no very clear distinction exists between saying that a particular solution to a problem is in accordance with the law, and saying that it is the rational, or fair, or just solution. Or, to put the same point in a different way, legal justificatory reasoning does not depend upon a finite-closed scheme of permissible justification, nor does it employ conceptions which are insulated wholly from lay conceptions. The language of the law is not a private language. The legal and extra-legal worlds are intimately associated, not separated in the way in which some legal writing would suggest.[5]

If, however, we confine attention to specifically legal propositions, how are they to be explained? The type of answer given to this question will depend upon the particular theoretical viewpoint adopted, for there appear to me to be a number of different possible conceptions of the nature of the common law. The predominant conception today is that the common law consists of a system of rules; in terms of this, legal propositions (if correct) state what is contained in these rules. Those who put their faith in this conception do not I think mean to adopt the idiosyncratic notion of a rule adopted by Dworkin and by him contrasted with principles. They mean to include his principles, thought of merely as propositions of high generality. I wish to consider the utility of this approach, and to contrast it with an alternative idea – the idea that the common law is best understood as a system of customary law, that is, as a body of traditional ideas of a very varied character received within a caste of experts.

II POSITIVISM AND THE COMMON LAW
AS A SYSTEM OF RULES

The idea that the common law is a set of rules, in some sense forming a system, is intimately associated with the movement known as legal positivism. The sense is unusual in that a set of rules might ordinarily be said to constitute a system if they were all derivative of a single proposition or of a finite set of basic propositions, or perhaps if they could be classified in an ordered way; nothing of this sort is here meant by 'system'. Though purporting to be an empirical observation, this idea is best viewed as a dogma, which derives basically from viewing all law in terms of a model of statute law. In its purest form legal positivism involves two basic assumptions, which will be found, variously elaborated, or sometimes merely covertly or unwittingly adopted, in very many theoretical writings.

The first is that all laws owe their status as such to the fact that they have been laid down. In the curious and archaic language of Austin, laws properly so called are laws *by position*;[6] they are *posited*, set, or prescribed, and human law at least is laid down by humans to humans. Blackstone, though inconsistent in his positivism, thought that municipal law was prescribed by what he called the supreme power in the state,[7] whilst Gray thought that laws were rules of conduct laid down by the courts.[8] Both assumed that laws must have been laid down by somebody or other to rank as laws, and to this extent they were positivists. When in a modern book on the doctrine of precedent Cross wrote, 'Such a rule (one derived from a precedent or series of precedents) is law "properly so called" and law *because it was made by the judges* [my italics], and not because it originated in common usage, or the judges' idea of justice and public convenience,'[9] he is expressing the first basic assumption of positivism. In an uneasily modified form the same assumption is writ large in Kelsen: 'Law is always positive law, and its positivity lies in the fact that it is created and annulled by acts of human beings, thus being independent of morality and other norm systems.'[10] The insistence that all law is positive law originally stood in opposition to the claim that some laws, or all laws, owed their status as such to the fact that they were in accordance with or sanctioned by nature. Pure positivism thus involves the notion that there is only one possible alternative basis for law to that provided by natural law theories.

An obvious point at which difficulty is encountered in maintaining the thesis that all law is posited is when dealing with custom, which common sense would suggest is not laid down; customs, it seems more plausible to say, grow up. Kelsen runs into difficulty over this; though admitting custom as a possible type of law (to be contrasted with statute law) he is at pains to insist that even the norms of customary law, in a system which admits custom as 'a law-creating act', are *positive*. To preserve the dogma the notion of laying down or prescribing law has to be emasculated until it means only that the norms of customary law are the products of acts of will, even though these acts of will are not directed to the making of law at all. 'Since custom is constituted by human acts, even norms created by custom are created by acts of human behaviour, and are therefore like the norms which are the subjective meaning of legislative acts – "posited" or "positive" norms.'[11] This is hardly convincing, but my point is only to illustrate the basic credo.

The second basic assumption is less easy to state with precision. It involves conceiving of law as a finite and comprehensive code. The law, including the common law, is identified with a notional set of propositions which embody the corpus of rules, principles, commands, norms, maxims or whatever, which have, at any given time, been laid down. For present purposes nothing turns upon distinctions between rules, principles, maxims, etc., so this second assumption can be put thus: the law exists as a set of rules, the rules being identical with and constituting the law. Combining these two assumptions of positivism the common law must be conceived of as existing as a set or code of rules which have been laid down by somebody or other, and which owe their status as law to the fact that they have been so laid down. We are to conceive of the common law, somewhat perversely, as if it had already been codified, when we all know it has not. And if communication by words is the manner in which the action of laying down the law takes place, then the words used will constitute the law. In terms of such a model the general theoretical propositions of the common law can be thought of as stating or reproducing rules of the common law, if 'correct', or as putative statements which may or may not be correct.

Around these two basic assumptions cluster various ideas either derived from them or at least intimately associated with them. Thus if all laws are laid down, all laws must have an author, for someone must have performed the act of positing the law. Secondly, there must be some test or criterion for identifying the lawmaker or lawmakers who have authority to lay down the law, or entitlement to do so, for it would be absurd if anyone who cared to do so could lay down law; the primary ground for saying that this or that is the law will be the fact that the right person or group laid it down. Thirdly, if law is by definition laid down, all law must originate in legislation, or in some law-creating act. Fourthly, law so conceived will appear as the product of acts of will, and the law which results as the will of the lawmaker. Fifthly, if laws owe their status to their having been laid down by the right author, it cannot be a necessary characteristic of law that is should have a particular content, for its content will depend upon the will of the lawmaker, who may be devil or angel or something in between – hence the separation of law and morals. And sixthly, if law consists of what has been laid down, then what has been laid down is exhaustive of the law at any given moment. Hence where nothing has been laid down, there is no law. The law is conceived of as in principle a finite system, and this generates difficulties as to whether it is nevertheless comprehensive, in that it nevertheless potentially answers all questions, or whether it suffers from gaps. And, seventhly, unless one admits the possibility of the existence of a number of coexisting common laws, which seems absurd, there must at one moment be one unique and internally consistent set of rules constituting the common law.

This may be called the 'school-rules concept' of law, and it more or less assimilates all law to statute law. In recent times there have been advanced what may be called weaker versions of positivism, which have gone some way towards abandoning the first assumption whilst retaining the second: law continues to be conceived of as a set of rules, but their status as law does not necessarily depend upon their having been laid down. Examples are to be found in the legal theories of Kelsen (who, as we have seen, still maintains that all law is positive in a peculiar sense) and Hart.[12] Such theories, which to me at least seem essentially to belong to a modern civilian tradition, are committed to giving some explanation of how one is to tell whether a putative rule belongs to the club or not. The answer given is that membership depends upon the satisfaction of tests provided by some other higher or basic rule or rules, sometimes called power-conferring rules or rules of competence, in absent-minded conformity to the idea that all laws originate in legislation. Those which qualify are characterized as valid – valid meaning 'binding' or 'existing as a rule of the system' – and the corpus of rules possessing the quality of validity, together with the basic rule or rules (grundnorm, constitution, rule of recognition) constitute the legal system. A legal system is conceived not so much as a functioning human institution, but as an abstract code of rules, systematic only in the peculiar sense that the contents of the code satisfies the tests. Although it might seem consistent with such an approach to admit the possibility that some rules might qualify because of their content (the rule possessing some supposed quality, such as being in accordance with the will of God or the principle of utility) both Kelsen and, less clearly, Hart seem to have in mind criteria dealing with the mode of origin of the rule, or, as Dworkin has put it, with the 'pedigree'[13] of the rule, rather than content. All law is like statute law in that its authority is independent of its content.

As applied to the common law such weak versions of positivism could in principle no doubt cater for the possibility that it consists of rules which are not necessarily of legislative origin, nobody having ever laid them down. Kelsen does not really develop the application of his theory to the common law; he came, of course, from another legal tradition. In his *General Theory of Law and the State*[14] he conceives of law, in the form of general norms, as originating either in custom or in legislation, statutory law and customary law being the two fundamental types of law. Insofar as the common law derives from judicial precedents he apparently conceived of it as statutory; insofar as it is based upon the long practice of the courts it is customary law. Hart, more surprisingly, devotes no more than a small part of *The Concept of Law* to the detailed application of his theory to the common law. But he envisages the possibility that in a complex system the criteria for the validity of rules may include reference to 'customary practice', 'general declarations of specified persons' and 'past judicial decisions', in addition to reference to an 'authoritative text' or 'legislative enactment';[15] such criteria no doubt are included to cater for the common law. Elsewhere he seems to regard the activities of courts as sometimes legislative in character; like Kelsen, Hart perhaps conceives of the common law as a medley of rules of different theoretical character. But in the absence of a rather more full treatment of the subject it is not at all easy to see quite how the common law fits into the scheme of things.

III DEFECTS OF POSITIVISM

But both in its strong and weak forms positivism seems to me to present a defective scheme for understanding the nature of the common law. In its strong form, as presented by Austin, it claims that the common law consists of rules which owe their status as law to the fact that they have been laid down. Now the plausibility of claiming that the common law has been posited – presumably by the judges, there being no other obvious candidates for the honour – turns largely upon the offering of a choice between the devil and the deep blue sea. Austin presented his hearers with the alternative of either agreeing that the common law was laid down by the judges, or believing in the childish fiction (as he called it) that the common law was 'a miraculous something made by nobody, existing I suppose, from eternity and merely declared from time to time by the judges'.[16] Confronted with this crude choice it is natural to prefer the former view.

But difficulties arise if an attempt is made to apply Austin's view to a specific instance. Consider, for example, the rule that parole contracts require consideration (I choose this example because nobody would, I think, deny that this is a rule of the common law). Austin tells us 'there can be no law without a legislative act'[17] and the legislative act here must be a judicial decision, if one is to be found. Now it is well known that this rule has been on the common law scene since the sixteenth century, and some hundreds of reported cases would seem to a historian to be relevant to the understanding of the history and evolution of the rule. There would be no difficulty whatever in citing *authority* for the existence of the rule – that is to say acceptable warrants for the contention that there is such a rule. One might for example cite *Eastwood* v. *Kenyon*,[18] decided some three centuries after the rule had, as we say, emerged, or perhaps *Rann* v. *Hughes*,[19] a little earlier, or perhaps a statement by a modern text-writer. No doubt the best possible authority in this country would be a recent case in the Lords applying the rule. No such case in fact exists, but let us suppose there is a decision, reported in the Appeal Cases for 1970. It would seem to me to be absurd to identify such a case with an act of legislation, conferring the status of law on the rule. For we know that in some meaningful sense the doctrine of consideration has been a feature of the law of contract for centuries before this. The point is that the production of authority that this or that is the law is not the same as the identification of acts of legislation.

Conversely what might plausibly rank as an act of judicial leglislation will not necessarily rank as good authority. Suppose that one was able to find a case, decided say in 1540, where the assembled judges ruled that consideration was necessary in parole contracts, and there was every reason to suppose that this was the first case in which this ruling was given. Not only would it seem wrong to say that the rule derived its status as law today from this antique decision, but the decision would not even rank as particularly good authority for the rule. We may contrast the case of a rule which is of legislative origin – by way of example take that jurisprudential old chestnut, the rule that a will requires two witnesses. Here we can identify the act of legislation which conferred the status of law on the rule as the Wills Act of 1837, and this enactment is the reason why today wills do require two witnesses for effective attestation. The statute appears to be both the only reason and a conclusive reason for saying that this is the law, though if the matter is reflected upon this is only so because of some presuppositions about the relationship of courts to Parliament which are not amenable to the same analysis.

The notion that the common law consists of rules which are the product of a series of acts of legislation (mostly untraceable) by judges (most of whose names are forgotten) cannot be made to work, if taken seriously, because common law rules enjoy whatever status they possess not because of the circumstances of their origin, but because of their continued reception. Of course it is true that judges are voluntary agents, and the way in which they decide cases and the views they express in their opinions are what they choose to decide and express. Their actions create precedents, but creating a precedent is not the same thing as laying down the law. The opinions they express possess in varying and uncertain degree authority, as do opinions expressed by learned writers: that is to say the quality of being viewed as a good reason for saying that what they assert is correct. But to express an authoritative opinion is not the same thing as to legislate, and there exists no context in which a judicial statement to the effect that this or that is the law confers the status of law on the words uttered. It is merely misleading to speak of judicial legislation.

Weaker versions of positivism escape the difficulty involved in the claim that all the rules of the common law are the product of judicial legislative acts. They share however with pure positivism the claim that the law – and this includes the common law – consists of a set of rules, a sort of code, which satisfies tests of validity prescribed by other rules. Such theories suffer from defects which have their source in a confusion of ideals with reality. Put simply, life might be much simpler if the common law consisted of a code of rules, identifiable by reference to source rules, but the reality of the matter is that it is all much more chaotic than that, and the only way to make the common law conform to the ideal would be to codify the system, which would then cease to be common law at all. The myth, for that is what it is, owes its attractiveness to another ideal, that of the rule of law, not men. A wholehearted belief that this ideal is at least partially realizable suggests, wrongly in my view, that law must consist of a set of rules identifiable by a master rule or rules; otherwise how could there be a rule of law?

It is consequently and firstly central to such theories that there exist rules setting out the criteria which must be satisfied by other rules for them to belong to the system. These rules exist either in the sense that they are used and accepted by those concerned – roughly by the caste of lawyers – as the proper way of identifying other rules, or in the sense that they are the necessary presuppositions which make the identification of other rules possible. Either way it seems we must locate these supposed rules by considering the way in which legal propositions are justified, and legal argument conducted. Now it is quite true that in relatively recent times in the long history of the common law growing attention has been devoted, both by the judiciary and by legal commentators, to the formulation of rules governing the use of authorities in legal argument. Such rules constitute attempts to state the proper practice over such questions as what courts are bound by what decisions, how one is to distinguish authoritative statements of law from statements of no authority, what law reports should be used and what difference, if any, it makes if a writer is dead or alive. It is all very theological, with mysteries similar to those which surround the doctrine of papal infallibility.

These rules governing the proper use of authority and the reverence due to it are themselves notoriously controversial. Furthermore, we all know both that the practice of the courts is not at all consistent in these matters, and that judicial views as to the proper thing to do both differ and change: one moment the House of Lords or the Court of Appeal (Criminal Division) or its predecessor is absolutely bound by its own decisions, the next moment it is not. Source rules behave like the smile on the face of the Cheshire cat. Such rules as are advanced are commonly vague, or qualified by escape clauses, the *per incuriam* doctrine for example. The scope of such exceptions may be again controversial. On very many matters no rules can be said to exist at all. For example, what is one supposed to do with a House of Lords decision where they all say different things? And what is the authoritarian pecking order between a decision of the American Supreme Court, dicta by the late Scrutton LJ, and an article by Pollock? There are no rules to deal with conundrums of this sort. Furthermore, arguments to the effect that this or that is the law are commonly supported by reference to ideas which are not specifically legal – expediency, common sense, morality and so forth – as in the example of Devlin J and the errant tiger; they are supported by reference to reason and not authority. And nobody, I think, would claim that rationality in the common law can be reduced to rules.

These familiar facts form the background to the notion of tests of validity, which involves a claim that legal reasoning and justification is governed by rules to an extent which it is not; legal life is far too untidy. Only if it were the case both that the use of authority in the law was wholly rule-governed and that all legal argument was based upon authority would such a theory correspond with reality. Inevitably those who argue for the idea of a master rule either avoid attempting to say, even in outline, what it is or, like Kelsen, make it vacuous ('the constitution must be obeyed') so as to duck the problem.

A second objection to the notion of the common law as a system of rules turns upon the contrast between the essentially shadowy character of the textless common law and the crisp picture of a set of identifiable rules. Consider for example contexts in which a common lawyer might well talk of rules – the rule in *Rylands* v. *Fletcher*,[20] the rule in *Shelley's Case*[21] or the rule in *Hadley* v. *Baxendale*.[22] These I take to be paradigm cases of rules of the common law; to say that the common law consists of rules suggests a system of law in which such rules are the norm rather than the exception. Now one obvious characteristic of these rules is that their text is fairly well settled, though even in the cases where this is so the text is not utterly sacrosanct. The rule in *Rylands* v. *Fletcher* might for example be reformulated or more elegantly stated without the heavens falling; furthermore, there may exist exceptions to these rules which are not included in a statement of the rule. But the general position in the common law is that it lacks an authoritative authentic text; as Pollock put it, the common law 'professes . . . to develop and apply principles that have never been committed to any authentic form of words'.[23] It consequently distorts the nature of the system to conceive of the common law as a set of rules, an essentially precise notion, as if one could in principle both state the rules of the common law and count them like so many sheep, or engrave them on tablets of stone.

IV IS THE COMMON LAW A FICTION?

Indeed, in an important sense, it is in general the case that one cannot say what the common law is, if its existence is conceived of as consisting of a set of rules, and if saying what the law is means reporting what rules are to be found in the catalogue. The realization that this was so led Jeremy Bentham into the most powerful attack ever made upon the idea that the common law could be meaningfully said to exist at all, and it is no accident that this attack was made by a positivist. Although his view of the matter wavered, his extreme and characteristic opinion was that the existence of the common law was 'a fiction from beginning to end', and belief in its existence no more than 'a mischievous delusion',[24] a cover for judicial usurpation of arbitrary power. Of the expression 'common law' he wrote: 'In these two words you have a name pretended to be the name of a really existent object: – look for any such existing object – look for it till doomsday, no such object will you find.'[25] The common law was 'mock law', 'sham law', 'quasi-law', and in consequence the exercise of the judicial function an example of 'power everywhere arbitrary'.[26]

It is instructive to see what drove Bentham into this scepticism. What he perceived very clearly was the existence of an incompatibility between the 'school-rules concept' of law and the thesis that the common law could be regarded as existing in any real sense. His thesis is perhaps most clearly stated in the *Comment on the Commentaries: 'As a system of general rules*, the common law is a thing merely imaginary.'[27] The italics are mine, the point being that Bentham's scepticism leaves open the possibility that in some other sense the predication of existence to the common law might be meaningful. Bentham's scepticism depends mainly upon the fact that rules can only be stated in a language – if somebody asks me to tell him one of the rules of chess I have to *say* something or *write* something in reply. But it is a feature of the common law system that there is no way of settling the correct text or formulation of the rules, so that it is inherently impossible to state so much as a single rule in what Pollock called 'any authentic form of words'. How can it be said that the common law exists as a system of general rules, when it is impossible to say what they are?

Bentham's point reflects, but does not depend upon, the familiar fact that if six pundits of the profession, however sound and distinguished, are asked to write down what they conceive to be the rule or rules governing the doctrine of *res ipsa loquitur*, the definition of murder or manslaughter, the principles governing frustration of contract or mistake as to the person, it is in the highest degree unlikely that they will fail to write down six different formulations of rules or sets of rules. Controversy alone might not matter, but, more fundamentally, there exist no conclusive arguments for saying who is right. And if by some happy chance they all write down (for example) 'killing with malice aforethought', an invitation to explain what *that* means will inevitably produce *tot jurisprudentes quot leges*. Again, we all know that no two legal treatises state the law in the same terms, there being a law of torts according to Street, and Heuston, and Jolowicz, and James, and the contributors to Clerk and Lindsell, and we buy them all because they are all different. And what is true of the academics is true perhaps even more dramatically of the judges, who are forever differing often at inordinate length. When, after long and expensive argument, the Law Lords deliver themselves *ex cathedra* of their opinions – and this is the best we can do – they either confine themselves to laconic agreement or *all say different things, and this even when they claim to be in complete agreement*. It would hardly be worth their while to deliver separate opinions if this were not so. Nor does the common law system admit even the theoretical possibility of a court, however elevated, reaching a final, authoritative statement of what the law is in a general abstract sense. It is as if the system placed particular value upon dissension, obscurity and the tentative character of judicial utterances. As a system of legal thought the common law then is inherently incomplete, vague and fluid; it is a feature of the system that uniquely authentic statements of the rules which, so positivists tell us, comprise the common law cannot be made. This inherent character is a feature of many other valuable social institutions, practices and systems of ideas, expressed sometimes in the opposition of the notion of an art to a science.

Such extreme scepticism as Bentham's seems to me to carry us too far, for at any given moment in time there appear to me to be many propositions of law which would secure general agreement amongst expert lawyers as being correct, and if there are wide differences in the way in which propositions of law are

formulated there is at the same time a very considerable measure of agreement
as to the practical application of the law in actual cases. Viewed as a working
coercive institution the law exhibits a quality of regularity. If the common law
is a fiction from beginning to end, and the exercise of judicial power everywhere
arbitrary, it is difficult to see what explanation can be given of this. Now one
way of explaining the cohesion of thought which seems to explain this regularity
is to say that in spite of a certain degreee of vagueness and uncertainty the source
rules of the common law do not work at all badly. Hart, for example, says: 'the
result of the English system of precedent has been to produce, by its use, a body
of rules of which a vast number, of both major and minor importance, are as
determinate as any statutory rule. They can only be altered by statute.'[28] I doubt
this explanation. If we look back into the history of the common law before there
were doctrines of precedent and articles on the *ratio decidendi* of a case the same
phenomenon – a cohesion of ideas – is to be found; indeed I suspect (though this
is not capable of strict proof) that there was a much greater degree of cohesion
in, say, the fifteenth century than there is today, one aspect of such cohesion
being a high level of controversy surrounding distinctions which appear to those
outside the system as hair-splitting. The explanation for such cohesion cannot
be the use of tests of valid law.

Furthermore, it seems to me that the contemporary rules for the use of authority
in the common law are, as we have seen, vague, uncertain, changing and in any
event incapable of settling the correct formulation of legal rules. Nor does it seem
to me to be true, as positivists must have us believe, that once a rule satisfies
the tests it can only be altered by legislation. The reality of the matter is that
well settled propositions of law – propositions with which very few would disagree –
do suffer rejection. The point about the common law is not that everything is
always in the melting-pot, but that you never quite know what will go in next.
Few in 1920 would have doubted that manufacturers of products were immune
from the liability soon to be imposed upon them, or in 1950 that the House of
Lords was bound by its own decisions. And this is true in English law, which
appears much more cohesive than, say, American law, where legal surprises cause
controversy, but little real surprise.

V THE COMMON LAW AS CUSTOMARY LAW

If, however, we abandon the positivist conception of the common law, in terms
of what other conception can the institution be more realistically depicted and
its peculiar characteristic explained? Positivists take as their basic model of law
an enacted code, but a better starting-point, if we are concerned with the common
law, is the traditional notion of the common law as custom, which was standard
form in the older writers. Hale,[29] for example, divided the law of England into
the *lex scripta* and the *lex non scripta*. The former comprised statutes 'which
in their original formation are reduced into writing, and are so preserved in
their original form, and in the same stile and words wherein they were first
made'. In contrast the *lex non scripta* comprised 'not only general customs, or
the common law properly so called, but even those particular laws and customs

applicable to certain courts and persons'. Blackstone, too, adopted much the same view:

> The unwritten or common law is properly distinguishable into three kinds: 1. General Customs, which are the universal rule of the whole kingdom, and form the common law, in its stricter and more usual signification. 2. Particular customs which for the most part affect only the inhabitants of particular districts. 3. Certain particular laws; which by custom are adopted and used by some particular courts, of pretty general and extensive jurisdiction.[30]

This view of the common law has today fallen almost wholly out of favour, and the reason for this, or at least one predominant reason, is not far to seek. By a custom we commonly mean some practice, such as drinking the health of the Queen after dinner, which is regularly observed and has been regularly observed for some time in a group, and which is regarded within the group as the normal and proper thing to do. It is also integral to the idea of a custom that the past practice of conformity is conceived of as providing at least part of the reason why the practice is thought to be proper and the right thing to do. Clearly the common law as an institution is in part customary in this sense. If, however, one considers general theoretical propositions of the common law – for example the rule against perpetuities, or the doctrine of anticipatory breach, it is perfectly absurd to regard propositions stating such rules and doctrines as putative descriptions of the customary practices of Englishmen. It may be true that such parts of the common law reflect, or are based upon, or are consistent with, ideas and values which either are or once were current in the upper ranks of English society, or in society generally, but this does not make them into customs. Writers such as Hale and Blackstone were perfectly well aware of this point. Thus Blackstone points out that there are some (I suspect he had in mind Sir John Fortescue and Christopher St Germain)[31] who have:

> divided the common law into two principal grounds or foundations;
> 1. Established customs; such as that, where there are brothers, the eldest brother shall be heir to the second, in exclusion of the youngest; and
> 2. Established rules and maxims: as, 'that the king can do no wrong', 'that no man shall be bound to accuse himself,' and the like.[32]

Fortescue, for example, conceived of the law as being derived from principles (*principia*), these being certain universals called maxims, which are not demonstrable by reason; a similar Aristotelian doctrine is found in St Germain, and both writers distinguish these maxims or principles from other grounds of law.[33] Blackstone rejects this distinction as irrelevant to his theme, 'For I take these to be one and the same thing. For the authority of these maxims rests entirely upon general reception and usage; and the only method of proving, that this or that maxim is a rule of the common law, is by showing that it hath been always the custom to observe it.' Hale makes a similar point:

> But I therefore stile those parts of the law, *leges non scriptae*, because their authoritative and original institutions are not set down in writing in that manner,

or with that authority that Acts of Parliament are; but they are grown into use, and have acquired their binding power and force of laws by a long and immemorial usage, and by the strength of custom and reception in the Kingdom.[34]

Thus in characterizing the common law as custom these writers were primarily concerned to make a point about the contrast between the basis for the authority of statute law and that of common law. A proposition derived from statute counts as law because Parliament in the exercise of its lawmaking power has so prescribed – wills require two witnesses because Parliament so provided in 1837. Contracts on the other hand require consideration because as far back as anyone can remember this has been accepted as necessary. As Blackstone puts it,

> in our law the goodness of a custom depends upon its having been used time out of mind, or, in the solemnity of our legal phrase, time whereof the memory of man runneth not to the contrary. This it is that gives its weight and authority; and of this nature are the maxims and customs which compose the common law, or *lex non scripta*, of the kingdom.[35]

Nobody today would, I think, wish to express himself in quite this way. In the first place for the reasons given custom seems an inappropriate term for abstract propositions of law; laws are not customs simply. We need rather to conceive of the common law as a system of customary law and recognize that such systems may embrace complex theoretical notions which both serve to explain and justify past practice in the settlement of disputes and the punishment of offences, and provide a guide to future conduct in these matters. In the second place we are rather more conscious of change in the law – we know for example that although the doctrine of consideration is old, it is not of immemorial antiquity, and that there are recently evolved doctrines too; some come and go, like the deserted wife's equity, and others survive.

With these modifications, however, it seems to me that the common law system is properly located as a customary system of law in this sense, that it consists of a body of practices observed and ideas received over time by a caste of lawyers, these ideas being used by them as providing guidance in what is conceived to be the rational determination of disputes litigated before them, or by them on behalf of clients, and in other contexts. These ideas and practices exist only in the sense that they are accepted and acted upon within the legal profession, just as customary practices may be said to exist within a group in the sense that they are observed, accepted as appropriate forms of behaviour, and transmitted both by example and by precept as membership of the group changes. The ideas and practices which comprise the common law are customary in a more specific sense in that their status is thought to be dependent upon conformity with the past, and they are traditional in the sense that they are transmitted through time as a received body of knowledge and learning. Now such a view of the common law does not require us to *identify* theoretical propositions of the common law – putative formulations of these ideas and practices – with the common law, any more than we would identify statements of the customs observed within a group with the practices which constitute the customs. And this, as it seems to me, disposes of Bentham's main difficulty in admitting the existence of the common law. Formulations of the common law are to be conceived of as similar to grammarians' rules, which both describe linguistic practices and attempt to systematize and order them. Such rules are not simply descriptive in function – they serve also as guides to proper practice, since the proper practice is in part the normal practice. Formulations of such rules are inherently corrigible, for it is always possible that they may be improved upon as accurate statements, or require modification as what they describe changes.

VI THE ACHIEVEMENT OF COHESION IN A CUSTOMARY SYSTEM

It is no doubt impossible in principle to attach precision to such notions as acceptance and reception within the caste of lawyers, and the definition of membership of this group is essentially imprecise. Nevertheless it seems to me that the point made by Hale and Blackstone is correct – that the relative value of formulated propositions of the common law depends upon the degree to which such propositions are accepted as accurate statements of received ideas or practice, and one must add the degree to which practice is consistent with them. Now a customary system of law can function only if it can preserve a considerable measure of continuity and cohesion, and it can do this only if mechanisms exist for the transmission of traditional ideas and the encouragement of orthodoxy. There must exist within the group – particularly amongst its most powerful members – strong pressures against innovation. Young members joining the group must be thoroughly indoctrinated before they achieve any position of influence, and anything more than the most modest originality of thought treated as heresy. In the past centuries of the common law these conditions were almost ideally satisfied. The law was the peculiar possession of a small, tightly organized group, comprising those who were concerned in the operation of the Royal courts; within this group the serjeants and judges, comprising at most about two dozen individuals, were dominant. Legal ideas were transmitted largely orally, and even the available literary sources were, as late as the seventeenth century, written in a special and partly private language. A wide variety of institutional arrangements tended to produce cohesion of thought. The organization of the profession was gerontocratic, as indeed it still is, and promotion depended upon approval by the senior members of the profession. The system of education and apprenticeship, the residential arrangements, the organization of dispute and argument – for example the sitting of judges *in banc* and the existence of institutions such as the old informal Exchequer Chamber – all assisted in producing orthodoxy and continuity. So too did such beliefs as that the common law was of immemorial antiquity, and that if only the matter was considered long enough and with sufficient care a uniquely correct answer could be distilled for every problem.

The combination between institutional arrangements and conservative dogma is well illustrated in Blackstone's description of 'the chief cornerstone' of the laws of England: 'which is general immemorial custom or common law, from time to time declared in the decisions of the courts of justice; which decisions are preserved amongst our public records, explained in our reports, and digested for general use in the authoritative writings of the venerable sages of the law.'[36] Even more striking is this passage from Hale. The context is that Hale is explaining the wisdom of holding jury trials mainly before justices selected from the common law judges, the twelve men in scarlet who sit in Westminster Hall. He says:

> It keeps both the Rule and Administration of the law of the kingdom uniform; for those men are employed as justices, who as they have had a common education in the study of the law, so they daily in term-time converse and consult with one another; acquaint one another with their judgements, sit near one another in Westminster Hall, whereby their judgements are necessarily communicated to one another, and by this means their judgements and their administrations of common justice carry a consonancy, congruity and uniformity one to another, whereby both the laws and the administrations thereof are preserved from the confusion and disparity that would unavoidably ensue, if the administration was by several uncommunicating hands, or by provincial establishments.[37]

In such a system of law as the common law the explanation for the degree of consensus which exists at any one time will be very complex. No *general* explanation will be possible, and this remains true today, except to say that cohesion is primarily an institutional phenomenon. For example, it is very generally agreed today that there are no legal limitations upon the legislative competence of Parliament. The explanation for this is largely connected with the fact that the basic book and the best-written book employed in elementary legal education is Dicey. It is around Dicey that nearby all lawyers study constitutional law. This has been so for a long time now. Dicey announced that it was the law that Parliament was omnicompetent, explained what this meant, and never devoted so much as a line to fulfilling the promise he made to demonstrate that this was so. The oracle spoke, and came to be accepted. Again, a wide measure of consensus is apparent in magistrates' courts on very many points of law. Part of the explanation of this is that all clerks rely on Stone's *Justices' Manual* as a sort of holy writ. Settled doctrines, principles and rules of the common law are settled because, for complex reasons, they happen to be matters upon which agreement exists, not, I suspect, because they satisfy tests. The tests are attempts to explain the consensus, not the reason for it.

To study such a system, whether one is concerned with it at present, or in the past, involves, amongst other things, an attempt to identify what ideas are or were current at any particular period, and what ideas received or acted upon. What is involved is basically an oral tradition, still only imperfectly reduced to published writing. No clearer modern illustration is provided than D.A. Thomas's *Principles of Sentencing*, which published in comprehensive literary form the customary laws of the criminal appeal in England for the first time. The work was indeed a custumal, a *rédaction des coutumes*. As Mr Thomas says with a slight air of puzzlement, 'It is almost true to say that the policies and principles of the Court [of Criminal Appeal and its successor] have developed as an oral tradition among the judges who sit on the Court, and the high level of consistency achieved is all the more remarkable for this reason.'[38] A historian is confined to the use of written sources – records, note books, legal writings, and indeed any document which throws light on the matter; his interest is not limited to a search for authorities. From such sources it is within limits possible to show that the doctrine of offer and acceptance was not a going idea in 1800, though by 1879 when Anson published his book on contract law it had come to be orthodoxy. Opinions as to what ideas were current, and what ideas generally accepted, are necessarily imprecise; there cannot in principle be a catalogue of such ideas, and in any event different and incompatible doctrines and views can coexist. This seems to me to be just as true today as it was in the past. To argue that this or that is the correct view, as academics, judges and counsel do, is to *participate* in the system, not simply to study it scientifically. For the purposes of action the judge or legal adviser must, of course, choose between incompatible views, selecting one or other as the law, and the fiction that the common law provides a unique solution is only a way of expressing this necessity.

When there is disagreement within a customary system there must, if the system is to function, be some way of settling which view should be acted upon – for example for the purpose of directing a jury or determining an appeal. At the level of ideal theory the problem is as it were denied: there is always one uniquely correct solution. At a practical level the problem is solved by institutionalized procedures, and these may take a wide variety of forms, though all will involve vesting a power of decision in some person or persons. In a system which lays claim to rationality – and the common law did – it will be supposed that differences can be resolved rationally by argument and discussion, and that the method adopted to solve disputes at a practical level is in principle capable of producing in general a correct solution to the general question, What is the law? In a tightly cohesive group there will exist a wide measure of consensus upon basic ideas and values as well as upon what views are tenable. Argument and discussion will commonly produce agreement in the end, and so long as this is the case there will be little interest in how or why this consensus is achieved. There is no *a priori* reason for supposing that just because agreement is commonly reached this is because there in fact is a rational way of deciding disputes. When, however, cohesion has begun to break down, and a failure to achieve consensus becomes a commoner phenomenon, interest will begin to develop in the formulation of tests as to how the correctness of legal propositions can be demonstrated, and in the formulation of rules as to the use of authorities – that is to say warrants or proofs that this or that is the law. This is the phenomenon of laws of citation, the most celebrated example of which is the Roman Law of Citations, a constitution of Theodosius and Valentinian of 426 AD.[39]

It has really struck the common law only in the last century. It seems to me to be a symptom of the breakdown of a system of customary or traditional law. For the only function served by rules telling lawyers how to identify correct propositions of law is to secure acceptance of a corpus of ideas as constituting the law. If agreement and consensus actually exist, no such rules are needed, and if it is lacking to any marked degree it seems highly unlikely that such rules, which shift the emphasis from reason to authority, will be capable of producing it. It is therefore not surprising to find that today, when there is great interest in the formulation of source rules in the common law world, the law is less settled and predictable than it was in the past when nobody troubled about such matters. In a sense this is obvious. There is only a felt need for authority for a legal proposition when there is some doubt as to whether it is correct or not; in a world in which all propositions require support from authority, there must be widespread doubt. The explanation for the breakdown in the cohesion of the common law is complex, but it is easy to see that the institutional changes of the nineteenth century, and the progressive increase in the scale of operations, had much to do with the process. In place of the 12 men in scarlet there are now well over a hundred. How far it has proceeded may perhaps be brought home by comparing the current state of affairs with the fact that during the 30 years during which Lord Mansfield presided over the Court of King's Bench it is said that there were only 20 dissenting opinions recorded. In the period 1756–65 not a single decision was given which was not unanimous.[40]

In America, where cohesion broke down some time ago, legal thinkers have toyed with new theories of the nature of the law and of judicial decision either to emphasize this condition, or to rescue the concept of the rule of law despite it.

How then are we to view the positivists' notion of the common law as a body of rules, forming a system in that the rules satisfy tests of validity? We must start by recognizing what common sense suggests, which is that the common law is more like a muddle than a system, and that it would be difficult to conceive of a less systematic body of law. The systematization of the common law – its reduction to a code of rules which satisfy accepted tests provided by other rules – is surely a programme, or an ideal; as such it is an aspect of a more fundamental ideal, that of the rule of law. It is not a description of the *status quo*. It is the ideal of an expositor of the law, grappling with the untidy shambles of the law reports, the product of the common law mind which is repelled by brevity, lucidity and system, and it is no accident that its attraction as a model grows as the reality departs further and further from it. It is, I suspect, a rather futile ideal; the only effective technique for reducing the common law to a set of rules is codification, coupled of course with a deliberate reduction in the status of the judiciary and some sort of ban on law reporting, leading to a redefinition of the distinction between what is law and what is fact. But to portray the common law as actually conforming to this ideal is to confuse the aspirations of those who are attempting to arrest the collapse of a degenerate system of customary law with the reality.[41]

NOTES

This is a revised version of pp. 77–99 of the *Oxford Studies in Jurisprudence* (2nd series, 1973) published by kind permission of Oxford University Press.

1 R. M. Dworkin, 'No Right Answer?', in *Law, Morality and Society* (1977; ed. P. M. S. Hacker and J. Raz) at p. 58.
2 J. W. Bingham, 'What is the Law?' (1912) 11 *Michigan Law Rev.* 1 and 109 at p. 22.

3 R. M. Dworkin, 'Is Law a System of Rules?' in *Essays in Legal Philosophy* (1968; ed. Summers, R.) p. 25 at pp. 34ff.

4 [1957] 2 QB 1 at p. 17.

5 See my 'The Analysis of Legal Concepts' (1964) 80 *Law Quarterly Rev.* 535 esp. at pp. 545 *et seq.*

6 J. Austin, *The Province of Jurisprudence Determined* (1954; ed. H. L. A. Hart) p. xiii.

7 W. Blackstone, *Commentaries on the Laws of England* (1809 edn) p. 44.

8 J. C. Gray, *The Nature and Sources of the Law* (2nd edn; 1948) p. 84.

9 R. Cross, *Precedent in English Law* (1st edn; 1961) p. 23.

10 H. Kelsen, *General Theory of Law and the State* (1961) p. 114.

11 H. Kelsen, *The Pure Theory of Law* (1967) p. 9.

12 H. L. A. Hart, *The Concept of Law* (1961). There are, of course, considerable differences between Kelsen's theory and Hart's. The principal ones are set out in a note at p. 245 of *The Concept of Law.*

13 Dworkin, *op. cit.*, p. 28.

14 See pp. 114 and 149–50.

15 Hart, *op. cit.*, p. 97.

16 J. Austin, *Lectures* (5th edn; 1855) vol. ii, p. 655.

17 *Id.*, p. 216.

18 (1840) II A & E 438.

19 (1778) 7 TR 350, 4 Brown PC 27.

20 1866 LR I Ex. 265, LR 3 HL 330.

21 (1581) I Co. Rep. 936.

22 (1854) 9 Exch. 341.

23 F. Pollock, *A First Book of Jurisprudence* (3rd edn; 1911) p. 249.

24 J. Bentham, *Collected Works*, (1838–43) vol. IV, p. 483.

25 *Id.*

26 *Id.*, p. 460.

27 J. Bentham, *A Comment on the Commentaries* (1928; ed. Everett) p. 125.

28 Hart, *op. cit.*, p. 132.

29 Sir Mathew Hale, *The History of the Common Law* (2nd edn; 1716) p. 22.

30 Blackstone, *op. cit.*, pp. 66ff.

31 Christopher St Germain, *Doctor and Student*, (1530) Dialogue 1 c. 8; Sir John Fortescue, *De Laudibus Legum Anglie* (ed. Chrimes, S. B.; 1942) p. 21.

32 Blackstone, *op. cit.*, p. 68.

33 For the history of this notion see Simpson, 'The Rise and Fall of the Legal Treatise: Legal Principles and the Forms of Legal Literature', (1981) 48 *University of Chicago Law Rev.* 632.

34 Hale, *op. cit.*, p. 23.

35 Blackstone, *op. cit.*, p. 66.

36 *Id.*, p. 73.

37 Hale, *op. cit.*, p. 252.

38 D. A. Thomas, *Principles of Sentencing* (1970) p. xlvi. Typically this book, presented as an essay in description, setting out what the court did, at once achieved a normative status, expounding what ought to be done. A similar function is illustrated by the use of dictionaries to resolve disputes in the game of 'Scrabble'.

39 See F. Schultz, *Roman Legal Science*, (1946) p. 282.

40 See C. H. S. Fifoot, *Lord Mansfield* (1936) p. 46.

41 Since this piece was originally written it has been pointed out to me that the view put forward bears some relationship to ideas developed in a quite different context by T. S. Kuhn, *The Structure of Scientific Revolutions* (1962), Kuhn being concerned to explain radical changes in orthodoxy in the scientific community. There are also analogies, not explored here, with the nature of religious orthodoxy.

3
Legal Theory, the Common Law Mind and the Making of the Textbook Tradition

DAVID SUGARMAN

I THE COMMON LAW MIND: THE NATURE OF THE BEAST

The common law frame of mind continues to overshadow the way we teach, write and think about law. Its categories and assumptions are still the standard diet of most first-year law students; and they continue to organize law textbooks and case-books. Stated baldly,[1] it assumes that although law may appear to be irrational, chaotic and particularistic, if one digs deep enough and knows what one is looking for, then it will soon become evident that the law is an internally coherent and unified body of rules. This coherence and unity stem from the fact that law is grounded in, and logically derived from, a handful of general principles; and that whole subject-areas such as contract and torts are distinguished by some common principles or elements which fix the boundaries of the subject. The exposition and systematization of these general principles, and the techniques required to find and to apply them and the rules that they underpin, are largely what legal education and scholarship are all about.

Its message is reassuring. In any particular situation there is such a thing as the one true rule of law. Students can tease it out from the mass of competing alternatives, once they have learnt the technique. And that technique asserts that law (i.e. case-law) is a unified and internally coherent whole. In this way law is a species of science. It is objective, neutral and apolitical. Knowing the law is largely defined as learning this technique and the basic (overwhelmingly case-law) rules of 'core' subject-areas such as contract, torts and so on. Of course, the claim that law is unified and coherent does not simply depend upon the assertion that the law is ultimately grounded in a small number of general principles. It is also sustained by a battery of distinctions – common law/statute law, law/politics, law/state, law/morality, legal/empirical, technique/substance, form/substance, means/ends, private law/public law, law/history, law/theory – that make it more tenable to regard law as 'pure' and 'scientific'. The common law becomes the nucleus of legal education and scholarship.

Despite the variety of producers and consumers of legal discourse, it is what the judges say and the supposed needs of the legal profession as narrowly defined that have had the greatest magnetic pull over the nature and form of legal education and scholarship. Other aspects that are equally important to understanding law, such as legislation, the operation of law in practice, as well as the history, theory, morality and politics of law, are ignored or marginalized.[2]

The common law mind-frame is also the bearer of an important political message. And that message is that the law (primarily through case-law) and the legal profession (centrally, the judiciary) play a major role in protecting individual freedom; that the rules of contract, torts and constitutional law, for example, confer the maximum freedom on individuals to act as they wish without interference from other individuals or the state. Policing the boundaries within, and between, legal subject-areas constitutes a major foundation of the Rule of Law. In this way, the form as well as the content of the law becomes imbricated within, and synonymous with, our very definitions of individual freedom and liberty, and thereby acquires an additional patina of reverence and universality. The world, as pictured within the conceptual categories of legal thought, is basically sound. It is more or less the best that is realizable. Insofar as a better world is possible, it would not fundamentally differ from the present.

Like any closed model of rationality, it is shot through with self-contradictions, omissions and absurdities, which generations of judges and jurists have sought to repress. For instance, the notion of law as resting upon an objective body of principles founders when we consider that the quest for underlying principles must involve a selection from the sum of principles available and, therefore, a strong evaluative element.[3] Principles are thus inseparable from interpretation and theory which, in turn, are determined by values. Moreover, the logical systematization of positive law is not value-free in the ways assumed by some of its proponents. As Montrose observed:

Austinian analysis and synthesis concealed the employment of ideals of justice in the apparent exposition of what the law is. . . . The task of systematisation . . . both simplifies and idealises. The complexities of actual statements are replaced by generalisations. These, at best, represent but dominant patterns discernible amid the varied pronouncements. More often they are but the writer's views as to what the law ought to be, expressed in language which speaks of principles of what the law is. . . . This is . . . [the] time-honoured practice of juristic legislation. . . . It is, indeed, not very different from the practice of much judicial legislation. . . . Nevertheless, it suffers from the defect which Holmes saw: to adopt his language, no generalisation is worth a straw which is not fully supported by the articulation of the premises on which it depends. Or, perhaps, the language of a recent writer, may be adopted in saying that the visible effect of [legal] education is to enable people to articulate more ingeniously their judgments based on prejudice.[4]

Thus the schizophrenia of the first-year law student: when is it that s/he is supposed to talk about 'law'; and when is it that s/he can talk about 'policy'? We are heirs of this schizophrenia.[5]

There is a growing movement to broaden the study of law beyond the confines of the common law mind.[6] Transcending it, however, is easier said than done. Firstly, for many students and teachers of law, its assumptions, classifications and pedagogy possess a reified logic or inevitability.[7] It is as if the logic and categories of the law make the choices for us and as if we have little say in the matter. This profoundly unhistorical view of legal phenomena de-emphasizes that they are *human* constructs embodying political and moral choices. This dulling of our consciousness inhibits attempts to explore alternatives and even hinders an awareness of the values and assumptions of the common law frame of mind. Of course, it is really we who make the choice. Transcending the common law mind requires that we become conscious of the choices that are made for us by its reified logic and categories; that we recognize that such choices are inherent in all spheres of human conduct; and that we understand that we are capable of making conscious choices without the illusion that those sometimes difficult choices are simply the product of concrete legal rules or categories.

Secondly, whilst an idealized topology of the kind utilized above to describe the logical tenets of the common law mind may provide a basis for a preliminary critique, it really fails to do justice to the richness, complexity and achievements of this tradition, let alone provide a basis upon which an adequate alternative might be constructed. More specifically, it fails to confront the real problems of professional legitimacy, of exposition and pedagogy, of poor funding and mediocre students that characterize just some of the difficulties that have beset academic legal education and scholarship. Insofar as these problems are perennial then the enterprise of rethinking legal education and scholarship will have to confront these prickly issues.

The difficulties referred to stem, in part, from the lack of an adequate intellectual history of modern legal education and thought in England.[8] This essay attempts to demonstrate the value of such a history as a necessary part of the rethinking of specific fields of law within a broadened conception of the study of law.[9] Its specific focus is the constitution of the common law frame of mind within modern legal education and thought, and its archetype, the textbook tradition. This entails analysing the mental and material mechanisms by which legal thought was connected to its intellectual and socio-economic context. Why did the exposition and analysis of existing legal doctrine (what Twining calls the 'Expository Orthodoxy')[10] become the predominant form of legal education and scholarship? Why has it been so difficult to broaden the study of law from within? And why has the standpoint of jurists tended to resemble (but is not reducible to) that of appeal court judges and elite legal practitioners? These are the kinds of questions I hope to address in the remainder of this paper. In particular, the paper attempts to describe how and why the common law mind and the textbook tradition tended to predominate in legal education and scholarship during the seminal period of modern legal education and thought, that is, *c*.1850–1907. I shall refer to this period as the 'classical period'; and the jurists associated with it as the 'classical' jurists. Why the period *c*.1850–1907 is the classical period of modern legal education and thought, and how and why it and its constructs still dominate the ways we think and teach law, is a central concern of this essay.

For reasons of space, several limitations of focus have had to be adopted. Firstly, although legal education and writing appear in a variety of guises my primary focus is university education and scholarship. By way of an exception to this I have briefly discussed the interaction between the new university law texts and the work of the professional law coaches (the so-called 'crammers'). This illustrates the symbiotic relationship between academic and professional legal education and thought. Secondly, I have had to pay only passing attention to the relationship between legal education and thought and their wider intellectual and socio-economic context. Thirdly, this essay is almost exclusively concerned with the construction and reproduction of the dominant tradition of classical legal education and scholarship: namely, the common law frame of mind, in particular, as epitomized by the textbook (expository) tradition. As a result, that body of work which transcended the dominant tradition receives short shrift. This risks portraying legal education and thought as more monolithic than was actually the case.

II THE CENTRALITY OF *c.*1850–1907 AND THE QUEST FOR PROFESSIONAL LEGITIMACY

The role of English universities in legal education is relatively recent.[11] Traditionally, English lawyers have learnt their law by way of apprenticeship. In essence, from the late seventeenth to the mid-nineteenth century formal professional and university legal education were almost non-existent. The impoverished state of English legal education, legal literature and legal science was a recurrent theme of contemporary legal literature.[12] It is not surprising, therefore, that the Select Committee on Legal Education, set up by the House of Commons in 1846, concluded that 'No Legal Education worthy of the name of a public nature, is at this moment to be had in either England or Ireland.'[13] No wonder John Austin opined that 'Turning away from the study of English to the study of Roman law, you escape from the empire of chaos and darkness to a world which seems, by comparison, the region of order and light.'[14]

It was only during the period *c.*1850–1907 that professional law teachers were appointed to universities in any number. For many of these classical legal scholars, the major intellectual task was to transcend the 'chaos and darkness' of contemporary legal education and scholarship and to create a world of 'order and light'. This was also essential if they were to establish themselves as one of the many new professions that arose in the latter half of the nineteenth century. In other words, for Dicey, Bryce, Pollock, Anson, Holland, Salmond and other classical law dons, their desired professional legitimacy in the eyes of sceptical universities and a largely hostile profession required the assertion of a special body of expertise which jurists monopolized. What was this special expertise?

The argument espoused by most classical law dons was that law may appear chaotic but is, in fact, internally coherent. This cohesion derives from the fact that law is grounded upon relatively few general principles. The legal scholar was in a unique position to tease out the general principles underlying the law and impart this sense of cohesion through the teaching of general principles and the systematization of those principles in law textbooks. They were, therefore, uniquely useful to the profession. They showed that the grubby, disorderly world of the court room and law office could, in fact, be regarded as 'science in action'. The law was ultimately governed by principles akin to the laws of natural sciences and was, thus, a subject worthy of a place in the university firmament. Here then was the *raison d'être* of the new professional jurist and university legal education.

Perhaps the most elaborate assertion of this credo was Dicey's highly influential inaugural lecture of 1883, in which he challenged the dominant professional view that law could only be learnt in practice.[15] Central to that challenge was the argument that learning by way of apprenticeship 'inevitably leads to a most incomplete mastery of legal principles' and is 'unsystematic'.[16] It is 'matters of principle rather than matters of detail [that] are the real subject of perplexity to lawyers and to judges'.[17] And this is where the law professor could help:

> [The] . . . proper sphere of professorial activity is to supply all the defects which flow directly or indirectly from a one-sided system of practical training. It is for law professors to set forth the law as a coherent whole – to analyse and define legal conceptions – to reduce the mass of legal rules to an orderly series of principles and to aid, stimulate and guide the reform or renovation of legal literature. . . .
>
> The first duty of a competent teacher is to impress upon himself and his pupils that law can be digested into a set of rules and exceptions, and to make his hearers feel that general, common, normal principles are far more important than what is exceptional, uncommon or abnormal. . . .
>
> [Whole] . . . departments of law can thus be reduced to order and exhibited under the form of a few principles which sum up the effect of a hundred cases, and can thus be understood and remembered. . . .
>
> [Nothing] can be taught to students of greater value, either intellectually or for the purpose of legal practice, than the habit of looking upon law as a series of rules; and further that a school of lawyers imbued with this turn of mind would gradually reduce the whole chaotic mass of legal principles to a clear, logical and symmetrical form.[18]

In his public lecture delivered to Oxford University in 1886, Pollock asked: 'To what end is our study and teaching of law?'[19] And Pollock's answer echoed Dicey's:

> We can guide him [i.e. the undergraduate reading law] to the distinction of that which is accidental and local from that which is permanent and universal. . . .[20]
> [The] lawyer has not reached the height of his vocation who does not find therein (as the mathematician in even less promising matter) scope for a peculiar but genuine artistic function . . . such joy may you find in the lucid exposition of broad legal principles or in the conduct of a finely reasoned argument on their application to a disputed point.[21]

Law, asserted Pollock, was a science. And like Dicey, this seems to have meant little more than that law was clear, rational, internally coherent and systematized. The implication that with a bit of juristic assistance lawyers might resemble mathematicians has its origins in Roman law, Bacon and Savigny.[22] As Savigny's major and highly influential discussion of the jurist's art put it:

In every triangle . . . there are certain data, from the relations of which all the rest are necessarily deducible. . . . In like manner, every part of our law has points by which the rest may be given: these may be termed the leading axioms. To distinguish these, and deduce from them the internal connection, and the precise degree of affinity which subsist between all juridical notions and rules, is amongst the most difficult of the problems of jurisprudence. Indeed, it is peculiarly this which gives our labours the scientific character. . . .[23]

Here, then, was a model of the jurist's function which was enthusiastically embraced. In short, exposition, conceptualization, systematization and the analysis of existing legal doctrine became equated with the dominant tasks of legal education and scholarship.

Other reasons were also urged by classical legal intellectuals to justify their craft. For example, one finds the argument that university legal education would raise 'the tone of the profession',[24] or at least guard it against possible dissipation. In particular, the university law school would constitute an important 'breeder of values' as the Inns of Court had been before them.[25] University legal education and the skills it could provide would help to mediate the 'tedious and distasteful' aspects of practice. If lawyers were to conceive of their work not so much a 'trade' or 'a soulless unsatisfying handicraft' but as 'a science, [which] has, as such, its greatness and perfectability', then they should learn their law at university.[26]

But were legal education and scholarship more than an adjunct to the training of would-be practitioners in the basic skills of their trade? Dicey's defence of university legal education is exclusively couched in terms of the basic technical needs of undergraduates destined for the profession.[27] There is no pretence that wider educational goals are envisaged. This contrasts with the writings of his contemporaries, Bryce and Pollock, who, whilst concerned that university legal education should impart the basic legal techniques, (i.e. teach general legal principles), also asserted that university legal studies were or should be also a liberal education.

Typically, Pollock was the more expansive in his claims. He argued that law was 'the most humane of the political sciences';[28] that law and history are 'allies';[29] and that law and politics are closely connected.[30] Yet for Pollock, too, the major[31] attribute of the new law dons was the ability 'to fix' in the undergraduate's 'mind that there are such things as general principles of law: and that the multitude of particulars in which he must inevitably be versed as a practical student and worker, are not really a chaos. . . .'[32] And it was this which Pollock, in a rhapsodic vein, compared to a painting by Turner, a drawing of Leonardo, 'the full pulse and motion of the orchestra that a Richter or a Lamoureux commands', the virtuosity of a Joachim or 'the flashing sweep of the sabre'.[33]

Twenty-three years after his optimistic inaugural of 1871, Bryce resigned the Regius Chair of Civil Law at Oxford and delivered a more pessimistic assessment of the achievements of the new university law dons.[34] In his legal lectures he had 'usually passed by' the historical and jurisprudential aspects 'because the object of training the intellect of the *cupida legum inventus* seemed more urgent'.[35] And he concluded:

We have accomplished less than we hoped in raising up a band of young lawyers
who would maintain, even in the midst of London practice, an interest in legal
history and juristic speculation. The number of persons in England who care for
either subject is undeniably small, probably smaller, in proportion to the size and
influence of the profession, than in any other civilised country; and it increases
so slowly as to seem to discredit the efforts of the Universities. Of those who have
undergone our law examinations comparatively few have either enriched these
subjects by their writings, or have become teachers among us, or have taken any
part in promoting legal studies elsewhere.[36]

Even law's claims to a liberal foundation had to be adjusted in the light of a
significant concession: that Oxford's classical school was of 'superior value to
even the best arranged Law School, as a part of the education needed to make
a good scholar, a good citizen, and a good Christian'.[37]

Here, as elsewhere, there is the feeling that by the 1890s, if not earlier, the
more vocational aspects of the law dons' legitimacy had gained undisputed
ascendency. In particular, the exposition of general legal principles seemed to
constitute *the* major goal.

Inaugural lectures are often vehicles for the advocacy of one's own specialism.
The criticisms which Dicey and many other classical legal scholars heaped upon
the existing literature undoubtedly echoed, as we have seen, a wider body of
professional opinion. Nonetheless, we must not accept these criticisms at face
value. The writings of some practitioners represented significant attempts to
rationalize, simplify and codify the law in terms of general principles. They
undoubtedly advanced the legal literature; and, of course, they constituted an
important source from which the new law dons constructed their own student
texts – though sometimes, perhaps, their influence was less than scrupulously
acknowledged.

The exposition of law in new student texts was where the classical jurists
excelled. Within the space of about 30 years, a handful of individuals had
transformed the teaching and writing of most of those subjects which then, as
now, were regarded as the core of legal education, as well as several non-core
subjects such as international law and the conflict of laws. And it was this
revolution which jurist after jurist pointed to when advocating the legitimacy
of their newly established profession. No wonder 'the most interesting and,
perhaps, the most important sphere of professorial energy' became the writing
of student law texts.[38]

Dicey was exceptionally frank about the jurists' legislative role in this context.
The new textbook was a kind of 'natural code', a new form of codification. And
it was through them that jurists such as Pothier, Savigny, Kent, Story and
Langdell (in his case-books) had reformed, 'modelled, one might almost say
brought into existence, whole departments of law. . . .'[39] Here was a model – a
model with considerable influence – to which the professional jurist might aspire.

As it happens, the rise of new professional jurists occurred at a unique juncture.
To the extent that the common law had a classificatory system it was rooted in
that irrational (in the Weberian sense) body of rules we call the forms of action.
This, together with the distinction between common law and equity, constituted

the conceptual core of the common law. The collapse of the forms of action, the fusion of law and equity and the unprecedented freedom this afforded textbook writers to reconstitute the common law was freely admitted by jurists and practitioners alike.[40] Here was an unparalleled opportunity for juristic legislation, and the opportunity was not missed.[41]

On the surface, then, the case espoused by the new professional law teachers was substantial. Nor were these the only arguments mustered in their favour. Nonetheless, the intellectual, scholarly and educational confines that inhere in a conception of education and scholarship that ultimately elevates exposition, systematization, conceptualization and the production of lawyers as traditionally conceived as its core, will be self-evident. Here then are the intellectual and pedagogical seeds of a dominant tradition which would tend to marginalize those forms of legal education and thought which sought to transcend the conception of law as an autonomous body of rules. This tendency towards intellectual and social closure was given added impetus by a further desideratum: the classical dons' attitudes towards the judiciary, the legal professions and law reform. Indeed, in one sense, these attitudes substantially undercut the *raison d'être* of the new professional jurist and university legal education. As a result, the niche that they carved out for themselves, *vis-à-vis* the legal professions and the universities, resembled a very narrow ledge. The ways they further trapped themselves within relatively narrow confines are explored in our next section.

III THE NARROW LEDGE: JURISTIC ATTITUDES TO JUDGES, THE LEGAL PROFESSIONS AND LAW REFORM

Persuading the legal profession and the universities to acknowledge the place of university legal education and scholarship called for tact, circumspection and a sense of balance. The legitimacy of the jurist was, of course, asserted. But it was not incongruous with the established provinces of the lawyer and the don. Of course, the strategies available to the classical law teachers were undoubtedly limited. Traditionally, lawyers had not read law at university. The professions and the judiciary had largely managed without them. Why, then, did they need them now? Furthermore, the classical jurists had learnt their law in practice and by reading in chambers. However critical they might be of the profession, the profession had taught them their law and had affected their attitudes. Many maintained direct links with the profession throughout their scholarly careers. In most cases, it is probably not too much to say that they saw themselves as lawyers first and foremost. Several had aspired to practice but had failed. There is certainly something of the judge-denied about Dicey.[42] And they were a highly cohesive group.[43] Nearly all were personal acquaintances for a considerable number of years. They shared, to a remarkable extent, the same social origins, clubs, universities, the sprinkling of practice and similar politics. It was a group unlikely to produce firebrands. All this meant that their response to judges, the legal profession and law reform *vis-à-vis* themselves was likely to prove complex and contradictory. And so it was.

The criticism of learning in chambers is perennial in the discourses of the classical scholars. But usually it is tempered with self-control, respect and a judicious sense of balance. Dicey's oft-repeated censures nonetheless granted much to what could be learnt 'and can be learnt nowhere else than in chambers'.[44]

The law dons sought not to monopolize legal education and scholarship, merely to share it with the profession. What, then, was yielded to the sole competence of the profession? Practitioners were the masters of the relation between law and facts, what was frequently spoken of as the 'empirical' dimension of the law. Thus the linkages between law and daily life were left for the profession. Law dons were masters of the principles of the law not their operation in 'reality'.[45] And 'reality' was usually court-centred.

The sharp divide between law and facts, and law and the empirical, touched the very *raison d'être* of the classical law dons. For their critique of the traditional regime of English legal education and scholarship was pure Weber: the English legal system was peculiarly fact-based, particularistic and unsystematized.[46] The law dons claimed to be able to deliver the profession from this sorry state. To assert that law was principled and internally coherent seemed to require that 'facts' and 'reality' were kept at a safe distance. Facts, fact-collection, 'the empirical spirit' threatened to undermine the very basis upon which the classical law teachers had staked their legitimacy: namely, that law was essentially a simple, unified, coherent whole.[47] From this perspective 'facts' and 'fact-collection' seemed unproblematic and largely peripheral to the concerns of university legal education and scholarship.

But if the jurist's forte was the content of the law, and in particular the exposition and application of its general or universal principles, how did this differ from what, supposedly, only practice and, above all, the decision of the judges could fashion, namely, 'the better opinion' and 'sound judgment'? By claiming the exposition and arrangement of general legal principles as the core of their credentials, the jurists had got themselves in a bind. For these were, after all, the very skills that the traditional oracles of the law – the bar and bench – had claimed for themselves. Even the somewhat narrow province which they asserted as their competence *vis-à-vis* the profession turned out to be problematical. How could jurists maintain their claim to be the devisers and expositors of legal principles without challenging the traditional orthodoxy that vested law-making, 'better opinion' and 'sound judgment' in the bar and, above all, in the bench? One way the province of the jurist was distinguished from that of the judge, counsel and law reformer was by resort to another 'bright light' distinction of classical legal science: the attempted separation of form from substance. Jurists, by an act of conscious self-limitation, refrained from criticizing, let alone meddling, with the *content* of the law. That was for others. Their skills resided in its formal organization; the embellishment of its principles.

The jurists reserved their ire for the confusion and complexity spawned by increasing legislative regulation. Huge tracts of law were governed by a host of statutes partially repealed, partially amended stretching back to time immemorial.[48] Statute law made the view that law was an 'organic and unified system of rules'[49] much more difficult to maintain. The increasing girth of the statute book accentuated uncertainty and subverted 'principle'. In short, the increasing impact of legislation made the need for the renovation of the form of law by jurists and the articulation of its principles even more urgent. It also encouraged jurists to advocate consolidation and even, though less frequently, codification. Now this hostility to legislation was not new to the common law. And some of this enmity was, no doubt, directed at the 'collectivist' aims that seemed increasingly to characterize the statute book.[50] Nonetheless, the problems posed by legislation were real enough.[51] Consolidation, like codification, was not impolitic insofar as it supposedly touched upon the form rather than the content of the law.

But the greater propensity to censure legislation was fuelled by other motives. Legislation evoked Bentham, and Bentham was associated with a radical critique of the common law.[52] For some, at least, of the classical jurists the need to distance themselves from Bentham and Austin on this score (and others) was considerable. Bentham and even Austin were distinguished in that they sought to 'improve and correct' the 'substance' of the law. This is 'different' from the classical scholars' 'interest in scientific amendment of the form of English law'.[53] In that Bentham, in particular, threatened to blow open the dam separating 'form' from 'substance' he was often to receive short shrift. Thus Bryce assures us that the distant efforts of Bentham, Romilly and Brougham 'were chiefly directed to the removal of harsh enactments . . . which defeated the ends of justice. Their modern successors, finding the law purged of its grosser faults, are rather concerned with its reduction into more orderly and systematic shape.'[54] In these ways the classical law teachers seemed complaisant about the content of the law and the activities of the courts relative to their parliamentary counterparts.

The sharply drawn distinctions between form and substance, and between common law and legislation, were accompanied by four further and interrelated dichotomies which additionally preserved the purity and autonomy of the juristic enterprise and the common law itself: namely, the distinctions between law/politics, law/policy, jurisprudence/principles of legislation and is/ought.

These divisions sought to differentiate law from politics, treat the common law as the nucleus of the legal system and elevate the authority of the courts. Legislation had to be marginalized for it threatened the authority of the courts and the assertion that the law was a unified, coherent whole. The legitimacy of the jurist had been pinned to the authority of the common law, rather than the reformism of Parliament. History and legal evolution taught that law adapts itself to changing needs without recourse to extensive legislative intervention. Leaving this supra-human process alone was vital for civilization.

The distinctions between clarification/legislation and is/ought are associated with the writings of John Austin. And it is in his name that it was asserted that jurisprudence, and indeed the scope of legal education, should be devoted to the law as it is rather than as it ought to be. Of course, Austin himself frequently combined the two. Nonetheless, it was not unusual to regard the study of the principles of legislation – 'which discusses the ends or objects of law, and the comparative merits of the different means adopted for attaining them' – as something only the advanced student should encounter. '[It] should certainly come *after* the knowledge of some actual legal system. Indeed, there is much to be said for the plan followed by the University of London, which confines this subject exclusively to those few students who proceed to the higher degree of Doctor of Law'![55]

I have already stressed the deference that was normally shown towards bar and bench, and the desire to be seen to be part of the profession. It was the profession and the production of lawyers to which the classical jurists principally addressed themselves. And in so doing, it seemed natural to imbibe the peculiar etiquette and conventions of the profession. The new student texts were frequently dedicated to judges – the masters of the law – and their authors tended to adopt the professionally circumspect view of what was, and was not, appropriate in a work addressed to the profession. Thus Pollock tells us that he felt obliged to withhold a discussion of the wider goals of his books on contract and torts from the body of the text.[56] And that 'It would not be proper to repeat in a practical law-book' those criticisms of the Employers' Liability Act 1880 which he had 'recorded in a separate note to the report of the Royal Commission on Labour'.[57]

The profession were subtly implicated in, and indeed held out as the real authors of, the new 'scientific' movement in legal thought. Pollock was especially good at this. For example, the first edition of his *Principles of Contract* was dedicated 'To My Master In The Law . . . Sir Nathaniel Lindley [Pollock's pupil-master] . . . One of Her Majesty's Justices of the Common Pleas, I Dedicate the First Fruits of His Teaching.'[58] And in the open letter elaborating upon this dedication, Pollock added that:

> In your [Lindley's] chambers, and from your example, I learnt that . . . the law similarly, is neither a trade nor a solemn jugglery, but a science. . . . To be a fellow-worker with such men as Mr. Justice O. W. Holmes, and in ways which they and you think not unworthy of approval, is at once a privilege and a responsibility.[59]

Pollock was also inclined to emphasize the fact that his major treatises were based upon lectures delivered at the Inns of Court. The implication was that they were unerring, sound and carried the imprimatur of the profession.

In short, jurists merely divined and distilled the best practice or principles of the law, especially those enunciated by 'the great judges', past and present. The jurist was the handmaiden of the wisdom and soundness of the common law as best exemplified in the practice of its great masters. They celebrated its genius in the manner that was representative of the speeches and orations of the profession: 'To Our Lady of the Common Law'. Thus Pollock evokes the 'brotherhood that subsists between all true followers of the Common Law'.[60] And it was this brotherhood which jurists evoked when asserting that the laws of America, the Empire and England were *ad idem* in their essentials.[61]

In other words, the new professional law dons uncritically appropriated much from the culture of the common law: many of the mannerisms, the etiquette, the pedagogy and the 'common sense' of the lawyer. The middle ground that the classical scholars had sought to carve out for themselves, between the profession and the academy, was in substance a very narrow ledge – one which was liable to be overwhelmed at any time by the weight of the culture and narrowly defined interests of the profession.

IV BETWIXT AND BETWEEN CONTINUED:
NEITHER 'HISTORY' NOR 'METAPHYSICS'

Of course, significant efforts were made to transcend the dominant tradition. Bentham, for sure, was no mere expositor: 'I choose', he wrote, 'rather to [study the law by concentrating upon] what it might and ought to be, than in studying it as it is.'[62] Much that he wrote was, therefore, addressed to legislators rather than to the legal profession. Its range (and bulk) were awesome: from moral and analytical philosophy to concrete political reforms, from constitutional codes to panopticon, from economic theory to models of complete legal systems. Bentham's science of law transcended the boundaries separating philosophy, politics, economics, social thought and jurisprudence. Like the parallel work of the Scottish Enlightenment,[63] Bentham's writings were directed at the world of 'public affairs', where political economy was a 'science of legislation', and where the realm of prudent and beneficent legislation was a central concern. In his own country, however, this mighty challenge to the inherited tradition of the common law was largely defanged of its radicalizing potential. How and why did this happen?

Part of the answer lies in the desultory, fragmented and vulgarized ways in which Bentham's ideas reached a wider audience. Establishing an accurate view of his ideas and goals was not a straightforward affair. Much of what he wrote was unfinished; and much remained (and still remains) unpublished. Other hands tampered with his manuscripts: his ideas were simplified and his radicalism was tempered. The confusion has been compounded insofar as many commentators derived their conception of Bentham's leading ideas from his eighteenth-century writings, rather than from his more radical nineteenth-century ones. Then there are the real difficulties which confront Bentham's readers: the pedantic and obscure style characteristic of his middle-period and later writings.

Even in this form, however, they excited concern, not least from lawyers.[64] Bentham's abrasive vitriols ridiculed the sacred cows of English society: religion, the monarchy, the landed and the law. Most unsettling of all, perhaps, Bentham sought to dethrone the traditional 'oracles of the law', the judiciary: within the Bentham canon they would become mere ciphers of a gapless code. In short, the terrain carved out by Bentham simultaneously expanded the province of the jurist whilst diminishing the role, prestige and legitimacy of the profession. The response of the profession was twofold: lawyers either mocked and disowned his 'eccentric' and 'impractical' schemes; or adopted his commitment to clarification, systematization and reform, but in a more guarded, step-by-step fashion.[65]

Other factors also contributed to the attenuation of Bentham's ideas and influence. Consider, for example, John Stuart Mill's discussion of the relationship between Bentham and Austin.

The untying of intellectual knots; the clearing up of the puzzles arising from complex combinations of ideas confusedly apprehended, and not analysed into their elements; the building up of definite conceptions where only indefinite ones existed . . . the disentangling of . . . classifications . . . and, when disentangled, applying the

distinctions (often for the first time) clearly, consistently, and uniformly – these were, of the many characteristics of Mr. Austin's work . . . those which most especially distinguished him. This untying of knots was not particularly characteristic of Bentham. . . . The battering ram was of more importance, in Bentham's time, than the builder's trowel. . . . The urgent thing for Bentham was to assault and demolish . . . unreason. . . . To rescue from among the ruins such valuable materials as had been built in among rubbish, and give them the new and workmanlike shape which fitted them for a better edifice . . . was work for which . . . Bentham had not time. . . . Mr. Austin's subject was Jurisprudence, Bentham's was Legislation. . . .
   [The] subject of his [Austin's] special labours was theoretically distinct, though subsidiary . . . to . . . [that of Bentham]. It was what may be called the logic of law, as distinguished from its morality or expediency.[66]

This passage is illuminating in several respects. It provides additional evidence of how Bentham was safely despatched to a past time when destructive (rather than constructive) work was the order of the day. The present, however, required constructive work. And constructive work was jurisprudence, i.e. 'the logic of the law, as distinguished from its morality or expediency'.[67] In this way one form of juristic enterprise – the analytical approach associated today with Austin and Oxford – became equated with the distinctive province of juristic theorization. In this and other ways legal theory and the jurist's *raison d'être* would frequently become coterminous with analytical philosophy, and therefore estranged from mainstream philosophy and social thought.[68] True, Mill acknowledged that jurisprudence (i.e. of the Austinian kind) was part of a wider subject, legislation, or censorial jurisprudence as Bentham called it; that is, what laws ought to be. But for Mill, as for many lawyers sympathetic to Bentham, logic and contemporary needs dictated that the analytical (expository) task was necessarily prior to (and thus a condition precedent of) censorial jurisprudence. Thus Austinian jurisprudence was afforded the same artificial primacy over censorial jurisprudence that form had been accorded over substance. Of course, expository and censorial jurisprudence so defined were 'theoretically distinct'. Nonetheless, if the province of the jurist (and, therefore, legal theory) were to transcend the confines of the common law frame of mind, the symbiotic or dialectical interaction between these two enterprises required activation and encouragement, rather than partition. In practice, censorial jurisprudence was marginalized; when it was not rendered *ultra vires*, it was perpetually postponed. The fact that it was frequently termed 'legislation' by jurists and others like Mill, testifies to the gulf that existed in their minds between expository and censorial jurisprudence.
   It was Maine, perhaps, more than other single jurists who, echoing Mill, recast in a dogmatic and condescending mould the relationship between Bentham and Austin and, thereby, the province of the jurist:

An important distinction between Bentham and Austin is not as often recognised as it ought to be. Bentham in the main is a writer on legislation. Austin in the main is a writer on jurisprudence. Bentham is chiefly concerned with law as it might be and ought to be. Austin is chiefly concerned with law as it is. . . . [Those] objects are widely different. . . . Almost all of his [Bentham's] more important suggestions have been adopted by the English Legislature, but the process of engrafting on the law what to each successive generation seem to be improvements is in itself of indefinite duration, and may go on, and possibly will go on, as long as the human race lasts. Austin's undertaking is more modest. . . . Jurisprudence, the science of positive law, would if it were carried far, lead indirectly to great legal reforms by dispelling obscurities and dissipating delusions, but the investigation of the principles on which the direct improvement of substantive legal rules should be conducted belongs, nevertheless, not to the theorist on jurisprudence but to the theorist on legislation. . . .

Bentham was in truth neither a jurist nor a moralist in the proper sense of the word. He theorises not on law but on legislation; when carefully examined, he may be seen to be a legislator even in morals.[69]

Bentham's *oeuvre*, however, was not confined to censorial jurisprudence. Ironically, it was Bentham himself who exalted definition, precision and systematization as *the* hallmarks of a modern legal science. He distinguished this from the traditional common law frame of mind typified by Blackstone.[70] Now Bentham's characterization of Blackstone (and, thereby, the common law mind) as the antithesis of his own conception of legal science was more problematic than he acknowledged.

For Blackstone had likewise sought to overcome the 'very immethodical arrangement'[71] of previous legal writers. . . . But whereas Blackstone had been satisfied to polish, and perfect the conventional 'technical' arrangement of English law, Bentham countered by unveiling his rival (if not quite antithetic) conception of a 'natural arrangement' – a systematic classificatory structure presenting the contents of a legal system in the most intelligible manner possible, and at the same time providing a slight but comprehensive sketch of what (the law) *ought to be*. . . .[72] Bentham believed himself now equipped with 'a complete . . . plan of a complete body of the laws', the model for a legal system in which 'there are no *terrae incognitae*, no blank spaces; nothing is at least omitted, nothing unprovided for'.[73,74]

In short, Bentham's dream of a complete and comprehensive body of laws (what he termed a *pannomion*) was in some respects a continuation of, rather than a decisive break with, orthodox legal thought. The ideal of a 'natural' legal arrangement was at the core of the hegemonic assumptions that sustained both Blackstone and Bentham. Bentham's exaggeration of the logical element in law was a commonplace idealization within the discourse of the common law; and it could be used to vindicate a more traditional conception of the jurist's art. It was a common hostility towards natural rights and metaphysics[75] and the subsumption of legal science with scientific rationality which led radical Bentham and conservative lawyers to be perceived as inhabiting diverse ends of the same spectrum.

Indeed, for some commentators, the continuities were more striking than the discontinuities. Hazlitt's famous assessment, for instance, treated Bentham as a 'jurist' first and foremost: 'his forte is, arrangement', albeit of a more systematic and rational kind and on a grander scale than hitherto.[76] Hume follows Hazlitt, though he is more sensitive to Bentham's originality:

As Hazlitt suggested, very few of the ideas that he [Bentham] took up . . . were wholly new. He found them in the thinking of his contemporaries, as part of the climate of opinion. . . . Bentham reached . . . [his] conclusions ahead of most of his contemporaries. But many of them might have worked to the same point, for they shared his assumptions about sovereignty, individualism and legal modes of social control. What enabled him to get ahead of them was his greater readiness to accept the challenge of those ideas, his unequalled willingness to work within their terms, and his unequalled tenacity in following through an argument to its conclusion however distant that might be from its original starting point. . . .

[In] important respects, [Bentham was] a representative as well as a creative thinker. . . .[77]

Yet it would be wrong to characterize the common law frame of mind as wholly concerned with rationality (in the Weberian sense).[78] Bentham's extreme rationalism could repel as well as attract. To understand the ambivalence that Bentham generated within many a lawyer we must perceive how the common law frame of mind straddled a contradictory field of discourses. A tendency towards scientific rationality was yoked to an irrational belief in the spontaneous, piecemeal, unconscious continuity of the law. The law was a residue of immutable custom.[79] This is the ancient constitution that was central to England's national identity and the protection of individual freedom. In this aspect of common law culture, Whiggish notions of continuity had been allied to a Burkean conservative tradition, with its veneration of age-old institutions. Thus scientific rationality was forever being mediated, refracted and sustained by an omnipresent irrationality: therein lies the peculiar rationality of the common law mind.[80] As Maitland put it, 'under the fostering care of . . . [the Inns of Court] English jurisprudence became an occult science and its professors "the most unlearned kind of most learned men"'.[81] Thus lawyers could, with seeming effortlessness, eulogize the haphazard, particularistic, unsystematic evolution of the common law; and trumpet its intrinsic rationalism. Like a magnetic field, the history of English legal thought and education has experienced the perpetual pull and push of these competing poles. As a result, the common law mind was forever betwixt and between. It required a little of history and metaphysics. But it could only continue to maintain its complex equilibrium by keeping history and metaphysics at a safe distance, which usually meant allied to the present needs of the profession. It was Maitland who brilliantly discerned the ways in which the common law required a pseudo-historical and a pseudo-theoretical tradition as distinct from a fully fledged one:[82]

[The] practical necessity for a little knowledge is a positive obstacle to the attainment of more knowledge and . . . what is really required of the practising lawyer is not . . . a knowledge of medieval law as it was in the Middle Ages, but rather a knowledge of medieval law as interpreted by modern courts to suit modern facts. . . . The more modern the decision the more valuable for his purposes. That process by which old principles and old phrases are charged with a new content, is from the lawyer's point of view an evolution of the true intent and meaning of the old law; from the historian's point of view it is almost of necessity a process of perversion and misunderstanding. . . . I do not say that there are not judgments and text-books which have achieved the difficult task of combining the results of deep historical research with luminous and accurate exposition of existing law . . . but the task is difficult. The lawyer must be orthodox otherwise he is no lawyer; an orthodox history seems to me a contradiction in terms. . . .

[It] is easier for a Frenchman or a German to study medieval law than it is for an Englishman; he has not before his mind the fear that he is saying what is not 'practically sound', that he may seem to be unsettling the law or usurping the functions of a judge.[83]

The constitution of the knowledge base of the profession and the relationship between professional knowledge, professional organization and lay persons was anchored in a profoundly anti-historical and anti-metaphysical epistemology. The conceptual categories of the common law were in this sense a profound obstacle to the broadening of legal education and scholarship from within. Bentham's critique of Blackstone's (and orthodox legal science's) dependence upon irrationality (in the Weberian sense) detailed the role and importance of irrationality within the culture of the law.[84] But the seeming success of the Benthamite revolution obscured the extent to which the culture of the common law remained crucially dependent upon a complex blend of rationality and irrationality.

Other factors hastened the relative neutralization of Bentham's alternate enterprise.[85] For example, John Stuart Mill's critique of Benthamite utilitarianism undoubtedly sapped Bentham's reputation. In essence, Mill sought to enlarge utilitarianism so that it embraced those features of social and political life that Bentham had allegedly neglected: the historical, the sociological, the broader, moral aspects of human nature and 'feeling', and the reconciliation of majority rule with the protection of minorities.[86] If this critique had been applied to the province of jurisprudence then it might possibly have inaugurated an even richer and more subtle juristic canvas than that bequeathed by Bentham. But this was not to be. Curiously, Mill spared utilitarian legal theory the censure and reappraisal that characterized his critique of Benthamite social and political thought.[87] Legal theory was treated differently from other moral sciences. Indeed, it was not, it seems, a 'moral science';[88] and, therefore, no real attempt was made to work out the consequences of his emphasis upon the sociological, the historical and the moral for the nature and functions of legal theory. The reasons for this separation of law from what today would be termed the social sciences would seem to be the following. For Mill the crux of jurisprudence was the abstraction and analysis of those core, universal legal principles that grounded all legal systems; that is, those principles that 'do not depend on the accidental history of any' particular legal system or society.[89] Thus, as we have seen, Mill defined the tasks and practical value of jurisprudence as pre-eminently philosophical. First and foremost, it should be analytical and particularistic. Legal theory, so defined, did not need to be relativized and historicized. Indeed, it was necessarily dependent upon a profoundly unhistorical and unsociological epistemology. Thus the common law frame of mind was ratified and legitimated.

The eclipsing of Bentham by Mill was hastened by other factors. For some, Benthamism became synonymous with the atomistic and hard-hearted features of early-nineteenth-century political economy and industrialization. The authoritarian and social-control implications of his social-reform proposals, notably his plans for prisoners, paupers and the poor law, were also a source of hostility. And, as we have seen, Bentham (and Austin) were pigeonholed as representatives of 'analytical' legal thought; and thereby counterpoised against the increasingly influential historical schools of Germany and England. In this context, therefore, it is not wholly surprising that the Bentham of Dicey's *Law and Public Opinion* is a 'hero in a non-event'.[90]

As Collini observes, whilst Mill welcomed the historicist luminance that Maine shed over Bentham and Austin, he feared 'that the new fashion for historical research would be at the expense of, or at least would divert attention from, the immediate tasks of reform. . . .'[91] And he goes on to cite Mill's objection that the efficacy of the historical perspective 'is continually perverted into an attack on the use of reason in matters of politics and social arrangements. . . .'[92] Mill had good reason for concern. The historical school, notably (but by no means only) Maine, had wedded history to a defence of individualism and the *status quo*. What should have been a liberating force sustaining radical reforms was prone to paralyse the present by means of the past. Maitland discerned the dangers most clearly. In a letter to Dicey he wrote:

> I have not for many years past believed in what calls itself historical jurisprudence. The only direct utility of legal history . . . lies in the lesson that each generation has an enormous power of shaping its own law. I don't think that the study of legal history would make men fatalists; I doubt it would make them conservatives. I am sure that it would free them from superstitions and teach them that they have free hands.[93]

For many jurists, the major antidote or alternative to the analytic, utilitarian tradition of Bentham and Austin was historical jurisprudence. To some extent this happened as early as the 1820s, although it probably reached its apogee during the period c.1880–1914. But it will be clear that it could never sustain a conception of legal theory and the juristic enterprise which really challenged the common law frame of mind.

The narrowing of Bentham was also abetted by one of his most dedicated followers, John Austin. Austin was not unsympathetic to censorial jurisprudence. But the bulk of his energies were expended upon expository (analytical) jurisprudence. Austin's jurisprudence gave explicit as well as implicit support to the prioritization of expository jurisprudence over censorial jurisprudence. For many, therefore, Austin legitimated both the conflation of analytical jurisprudence with legal theory and the narrowing of the jurist's province to exposition, systematization and the analysis of concepts. Austin replaced Bentham as 'the true founder of the Science of Law', and 'the spokesman of his generation'.[94] Thus Buckland recalled that in his youth 'Jurisprudence meant . . . Austin. He was a religion.'[95] But it would be wrong to assume that Austin swept all before him. For example, Austin's static and unhistorical deductions were tellingly ridiculed by Maine, Bryce and Pollock. Nonetheless, Austin's legal critics did not fundamentally challenge the juristic enterprise he symbolized. For all their efforts to historicize the province of jurisprudence, their central concerns and epistemology were essentially orthodox and Austinian. The quest for fundamental legal notions and their clarification and arrangement was, at best, relativized rather than repudiated.

What happened to Bentham was also to befall Austin. Friends and foe alike tended to narrow his ideas. The writing and publication of Austin's work was haphazard and incomplete as well as vulgarized by editors and interpreters. His best-known work, *The Province of Jurisprudence Determined*,[96] was intended as a tentative preface to his larger *Lectures on Jurisprudence*.[97] But over 30 years separated their publication. The *Lectures*, reconstructed by Austin's widow from his notes, appeared only in 1863. Few commentators read the *Province*, the *Lectures* and his *The Uses of the Study of Jurisprudence*[98] together. It was Austin's avowedly narrower and preliminary *Province* which received most attention.

Sarah Austin tells us that her husband 'had long meditated a book embracing a far wider field. . . .'[99] Its subject was to be the principles and relations of jurisprudence and ethics. 'I intend', wrote Austin, 'to show the relations of positive morality and law . . .'[100] This book never materialized. He left behind him a body of work whose form and substance did not fully reflect his juristic ambitions. Nonetheless, Austin's *Lectures* were deemed too elaborate for most readers. They were substantially abridged into popular 'student editions'.[101] It was through these truncated versions that most students experienced Austin and jurisprudence. His discussion of the bearing of morality on law and the relationship between positive law, divine law and utility were expunged from these editions. Above all, Austinian jurisprudence was taken as the most sophisticated defence of the common law credo that the law of the land was the measure of justice.[102] In analytical jurisprudence as in historical jurisprudence there was a tendency to equate the good with the existent: the law (and English society) had become normative concepts.[103]

Maine's influential critique of Austin had done much to license this narrowing. For instance, Maine cautioned readers of Austin that 'the most serious blemish in the "Province of Jurisprudence Determined" was Austin's discussion of the relations between the law of God, the law of nature and the theory of utility.' Maine could barely conceal his irritation at the incursion of metaphysics (or, worse still, natural law) in an avowedly jurisprudential treatise. The 'identification, which is their object', wrote Maine

> is quite gratuitous and valueless for any purpose. . . . I much doubt whether such an enquiry would have seemed called for in a treatise like Austin's. Taken at its best, it is a discussion belonging not to the philosophy of law, but to the philosophy of legislation. The jurist, properly so called, has nothing to do with any ideal standard of laws or morals.[104]

Just how narrowly Austin and jurisprudence could be conceived is evidenced by the dictum of Austin's most successful editor, Jethro Brown, who in 1916 wrote:

> Justice, as a concept in jurisprudence, is conforming to law – if not conformity to established rules of law, or to the spirit of law in its totality, then according to a law which the judges make and apply retrospectively.[105]

This interpretation of Austin was fortified by the most successful jurisprudence textbook of the classical period, Holland's *Jurisprudence*.[106] Holland's text applied classical legal scholarship's enthusiasm for systematization, conceptualization and exposition in a manner which was dogmatic, narrow and pedantic. On Holland's death, a colleague summed up his achievements thus:

> He [Holland] once referred to himself as 'impelled by, a . . . morbid hatred of disorder'; and it is true that the whole bent of his mind was towards orderliness and simplification. . . . [Holland's text was] . . . perhaps the most successful book on jurisprudence ever written. [It appeared in thirteen editions during the author's long lifetime.] Substantially Holland's doctrine was that of Austin, but he made it less vulnerable by discarding many of Austin's crudities and inconsistencies, and was more persuasive because he wrote in a style which, though sometimes slightly pedantic . . . is far more attractive than that of Austin; and in all essentials he maintained the same doctrine through the forty-four years of the book's successive editions. . . . It is indicative of his serene confidence in the strength of the position he had adopted that in the . . . [last] edition he hardly refers to any criticism more recent than that of Sir Henry Maine.[107]

The last edition of Holland's *Jurisprudence* was published in 1924. He defined jurisprudence as a 'formal science of positive law'. The function of his book was 'to set forth and explain those comparatively few and simple ideas which underlie the infinite variety of legal rules'.[108]

By the end of the classical period, legal theory, legal history, private law and public law were dominated by similar criteria of relevance, which simultaneously served to separate them from one another, whilst recasting them in an analogous fashion.

V LANGUAGES OF RECIPROCITY AND CONFLICT

Thus in the period *c.*1850–1907 we can detect the constitution of a common consciousness – some sort of consensus about the underlying form of classical legal thought and the respective provinces of the juristic elite and the legal elite (including the bench); and that this consensus was largely shared by and constructed in collaboration with their American and German counterparts. In this sense it was a truly international enterprise.

Nonetheless, there were major disagreements at the levels of general and particular jurisprudence. At the level of general jurisprudence, for instance, did people obey the law principally because they feared the threat of state-imposed sanctions? What was the relationship between law and morality? And how should we theorize the personality of trade unions, corporations and the state? At the level of particular jurisprudence, controversy raged around numerous questions: should company directors be liable for negligent as well as fraudulent misstatements? What was the ambit of strict liability in the law of torts with particular reference to the decision in *Rylands* v. *Fletcher*?[109] Should combinations of employers and employees be subject to legal immunities? And to what extent could and should the doctrine of consideration in the law of contract be reduced 'to strict logical consistency'?[110]

Moreover, the space afforded to classical legal scholarship and its underlying structure did not spring fully dressed from the heads of Dicey, Pollock, Langdell and Holmes. The title of this essay is a self-conscious attempt to align my work with that body of intellectual and social history and social thought which stresses that history is 'an active process, which owes as much to agency as to conditioning'.[111] The ideological hegemony of the common law mind is not satisfactorily portrayed in terms resembling familiar models of 'one-dimensional control in which all sense of struggle or contradiction is lost'. [112] Far from desiring to convey an impression of *stasis*, I want to stress the reciprocal and symbiotic nature of the relationship between the respective elites within legal education and thought and the legal profession. It was an implicit social contract about social and cultural relationships whose boundaries were constantly being probed.[113] It exemplified a genuinely dialectical dynamic to which all interested parties contributed.

I have already touched upon the ways in which this dynamic interaction occurred – notably the ways in which classical legal scholars accommodated themselves to the conventional mores of the common law; and the influence of the new student texts upon the form and content of the law. But this theme requires greater elaboration. Whilst classical law teachers often conceived of themselves as 'barristers without portfolio'[114] they were far from being marionettes. I have already quoted the lament of Bryce that English lawyers seemed peculiarly uninterested in, and scornful towards, jurisprudence, legal history, comparative law and Roman law. Pollock and Maitland did not conceal their bitterness on this score. For instance, Pollock wrote:

> If the Inns of Court (that is, their present anomalously constituted governing bodies) took anything like an adequate view of their duty to the profession and the public, these things would not be left to the private enterprise of a few scholars, some of them (to their praise and our shame be it said) neither lawyers nor Englishmen. Not the least curious of our nineteenth century sights . . . is Professor Vinogradoff of Moscow discovering Bracton's notebook in the British Museum, amid the profound indifference of English lawyers.[115]

And so it was beyond the confines of Lincoln's Inn, the Temple and Westminster Hall – to Germany, principally, and also to America, as well as to Roman law – that classical jurists looked for their models and for their inspiration and erudition.[116] And yet, taking the longer view, one might say that they turned out to be false gods. Of course, the real and substantial achievements that were effected by English scholars in Roman law, legal science and legal history are almost inconceivable without the impressive historical and legal scholarship of Germany. Nonetheless, this legacy was ultimately double-edged. It was both historical and anti-empirical; its association of law and mathematics rendered law as a supra-historical reified logic; and its obsession with systematization, internal coherence, legal reasoning, the form of the law and its corresponding de-emphasis of the content and values of the law and its operation in practice was likely to reinforce rather than subvert the common sense of the common law mind.[117] Continuity and consensus were inferred rather than demonstrated. Ultimately its politics – sustained, in part, by a strong, reassuring, evolutionist strain – were complaisant and conservative. And the same might be said of the influential writings of American writers such as Langdell, Ames and Holmes (at least in some of his moods). Paradoxically, therefore, the important influence of German and American scholarship was simultaneously to open and to close doors. Or, rather, insofar as they opened doors the additional space they afforded to conceptions of legal science that sought to explore the historical contingency of the law, rather than ratify that dominant tradition of the common law which asserted that law was 'autonomous but sensitive', was severely limited. What this points to is the existence of a consensus about the basic goals, methods and ends of legal science, a frame of mind which spanned the dominant traditions of legal thought in Germany, the United States and England – and which was mutually supportive. It is an interesting quirk of history that, at about the same period when the highly systematized Pandectist model of law was being appropriated and built upon by law teachers in England, it was under attack in Germany. The so-called 'free' and 'interests' schools of thought associated with the name of the jurist Ihering criticized the Pandectist's elevation of systematization as an end in itself. This critique prefigured many of the American Legal Realist criticisms of legal formalism and 'mechanical jurisprudence'.

The new legal scholars not only exhibited their independence by looking abroad. Despite the distinction between form and substance, they could be outspoken and candid in their criticisms of the decisions of the courts. And this plain speaking on occasions extended to acknowledging that judges and jurists 'made' law. Nonetheless, the admission of judicial or juristic creativity was relatively rare. Moreover, the legitimate province of the jurist was still problematic. In other words, the identity and standpoint of the jurist were subject to a pattern of struggle: of confrontation and riposte, action and reaction, dispute and 'resolution'. One of the clearest examples of this pattern was the juristic response to the House of Lords' decision in *Derry* v. *Peek*.[118] The directors of a tramway company stated in the prospectus that they had the right to use steam power: in fact, they had not the right and knew they had not, but they expected to get it. They had acted honestly but unreasonably. In effect, the Court of Appeal extended the law by holding that the absence of reasonable grounds for believing a statement to be accurate is sufficient to ground liability for fraud. However, the House of Lords reversed this decision. Negligent misstatements were insufficient of themselves to give rise to liability in fraud.

Pollock had welcomed the Court of Appeal's decision and both in public and in private he waged war against the decision of the House of Lords. Even before it was fully reported, he published a substantial critique of their Lordships' decision.[119]

It will some day, probably before long, be necessary to inquire how far the opinions of Lord Bramwell and Lord Herschell contain a necessary *ratio decidendi*, or are binding on the Court of Appeal and other subordinate authorities.

There exist, however, many courts administering the Common Law, but not bound by the decisions of the English courts; and before such courts a recent decision of the House of Lords is, of course, freely open to criticism. The purpose of this paper is to show that the grounds assigned to *Derry* v. *Peek* . . . are erroneous in law, and ought to be disregarded by every tribunal which is at liberty to disregard them.[120]

Pollock's remarks did not go unchallenged. For in the very next issue of the *Law Quarterly Review* Pollock's colleague at Oxford, Anson, not only defended the decision of the House of Lords, but admonished Pollock's critical tone:[121]

I cannot think it desirable that an appeal should be addressed to all courts . . . to disregard a decision of the House of Lords if they can, to elude it if they cannot. . . .

To admit enquiry into the reasonableness of a belief admitted to be honestly entertained, might be gratifying to legal practitioners, or to the jurist who likes to contemplate rules of law through a golden haze of equitable possibilities. It could not be satisfactory to anyone who is likely to be asked to give an opinion . . . nor indeed to those who believe the Common Law, as it stands, to be a monument of practical common sense.[122]

In a footnote Pollock inserted to Anson's essay, he rather lamely explained that his call to disregard or elude the decision of the House of Lords was directed chiefly at American courts![123] Pollock continued to use all the strategies of counsel to denigrate the decision, to suggest exceptions, limitations, ways of distinguishing it, as well as to illustrate its monstrous potential, without actually saying that it was wrong – at least in public. He detailed how some judges had 'unconsciously sought to narrow or cut down the effect of *Derry* v. *Peek*'. [124] Pollock was well satisfied. In 1893 he wrote to Holmes that: 'My enemy *Derry* v. *Peek* has not been so much as cited in court here – certainly nothing like a judicial discussion.'[125]

Of course, it is extremely difficult to measure the impact of Pollock's condemnation of *Derry* v. *Peek*. As the decision itself makes clear, the judiciary were by no means unanimous on the role of equity and negligence-based liability in this area. Parliament, with exceptional speed, had expressed its disapproval.[126] What can be claimed is that the history of *Derry* v. *Peek*, and of several other leading cases, illustrates the complex and symbiotic relationship between judicial and juristic lawmaking – a creative partnership that has received insufficient attention to date. The subsequent history of *Derry* v. *Peek* bears this out. On the whole, its ambit was cut down by the courts. In 1914, the Lord Chancellor, Viscount Haldane, decided (in spite of the House being bound by its own decisions) that the decision should be further restricted.[127] And Haldane consulted with Pollock on the ways this might be done:

Haldane asked me last week to a tobacco talk of *Derry* v. *Peek* and the possibility of minimising its consequences. The Lords are going to hold that it does not apply to the situation created by a positive fiduciary duty such as a solicitor's, in other words, go as near as they dare to saying it was wrong, as all Lincoln's Inn thought at the time.[128]

But taking a broader view of the classical period in public, at least, it was Anson rather than Pollock who seemed to represent the dominant view of the permissible scope of juristic criticism. We have already seen how and why the identity and standpoint of jurists came to be 'dependent to an extraordinary extent on what . . . [were] considered to be the needs of present and intending practitioners'.[129] We have also seen that the student law textbook – the expository tradition – was a major cause and effect of this identification with the needs and standpoint of the profession. In that sense the relationship between law dons and the judges was consensual in form. Nonetheless, it was also conflictual in character, as the different languages of Anson and Pollock testify. And by the end of the classical period (that is, by *c*.1907) the language adopted by Anson tended to prevail. By the end of the classical period the expository tradition and the jurists' highly arbitrary and circumscribed conception of identity and standpoint had hardened; it had almost become a dogma. In the concluding section I want briefly to allude to some of the variety of forces that sustained or were sustained by the predominance of the textbook tradition and the highly restrained notions of juristic identity and relevance that it epitomized. Given the space available, the analysis that follows is no more than a thumbnail sketch of phenomena I hope to treat in more detail elsewhere.

VI UPHOLDING AND PROLONGING THE TEXTBOOK TRADITION

Vulgar Austinism[130] also reflected and possibly sustained the slow rise of legal formalism, as the dominant mode of judicial discourse, which paralleled the rise of classical legal education and science. In my view, the rise of legal formalism had a greater influence upon academic legal education and scholarship than *vice versa*, in part because extra-legal considerations were probably more important in explaining the adoption of legal formalism.[131] This is illustrated by the House of Lords' 'self-declaration of infallibility' in 1898.[132] The rise of legal formalism must have appeared to some jurists and lawyers as if the judiciary had endorsed vulgar Austinism. It was as if their Lordships had adopted the somewhat circumscribed definition of the legitimate criticism of the judiciary which Anson had espoused in connection with juristic commentaries. In other words, both academia and the bench had adopted parallel discourses which rendered the criticism of case-law more, rather than less, difficult. In such an intellectual climate, broadening the study of law had become a task of colossal proportions.

A further feature of this unseasonable climate was the translation of that tradition of Hobbes–Locke–Blackstone which had elevated the judiciary as *the* guardians of individual freedom into the language of classical legal thought which found its most influential form in Dicey's *An Introduction to the Study of the Law of the Constitution*.[133] There are three aspects to this development. Firstly, it was part of a wider body of thought, a boundary theory of law and state, which treated the state as a legal framework within which people are secured a certain space, guaranteed by the judiciary, to fulfil their private desires.[134] Secondly, the autonomy and authority of the judiciary had become the grundnorm of the English constitution and the medium through which individual freedom was constituted. The preservation of the rule of law was dependent upon the guaranteed autonomy of the judiciary. This reconciled the sovereignty of Parliament and the rule of law. Thus to contradict or criticize the decisions of the courts came close to impugning the authority of the law and the rule of law itself. In effect, Dicey had posited the maintenance of the judiciary's authority as the highest value in the legal universe. Thirdly, in an increasingly democratic society, the legitimacy of the state was, in part, articulated through its claims to judicial independence and the Rule of Law. Arguably, the English state became increasingly dependent upon an autonomous legal profession and legal system in order to legitimize itself. In this way, the legal profession and legal system constituted the state.[135] One consequence of this was that the state was, therefore, extremely reluctant to interfere in what was perceived as the province of the profession. Codification and the reform of the legal profession (notably the bar) and of legal education all suffered as a result.

But if we are to understand the dominance and tenacity of the expository tradition, we must also look beyond the realm of academic law. In particular, the development of modern legal education and scholarship can only be fully understood in the context of the parallel developments of the metamorphosis of university education in England[136] and the renaissance in the professional education of lawyers. The great university reform movement of 1850-1914 forced Oxford and Cambridge to become secular institutions. Within Oxbridge the dons were divided about the purpose of education. By 1914 a particular conception of education had emerged victorious. This conception of education rested upon the following beliefs. Firstly, that teaching rather than research was the primary aim of the university. Secondly, that regular and extensive examinations constituted the major means of assessing undergraduates. Finally, that the job of the university was to provide a 'liberal education'.[137] However, a 'liberal education' was somewhat narrow, 'exactness within a narrow range', as Sir John Seeley described it.[138] It aimed not at breadth but at highly specialized excellence. Clearly, this definition of education was unlikely to encourage a broad conception of legal education and thought.

Other aspects of university education at Oxbridge undoubtedly hindered the development of legal education. During the classical period, classics at Oxford and mathematics at Cambridge dominated the curricula. Nearly all the available scholarships to students were in those fields. As a result, the best students tended to read classics or maths. Those reading law had a maximum of two years' legal studies as they were still required initially to immerse themselves in either classics or maths. All this discouraged students from reading law, especially good ones.[139] In fact, in the race between the new disciplines such as the natural sciences, law and history, law lost out in terms of student numbers and the resources it attracted.

Furthermore, the demise of the 'men of letters' tradition and the professionalization of academic disciplines undoubtedly fragmented scholarship and learning into narrow, divided camps. Professionalization and examinations encouraged a 'disciplinary tribalism'[140] and a strenuous effort to claim the objectivity of the expert specialist. All this helped to legitimize the classical law dons' stress upon legal exposition and their effort to differentiate this from questions of history, politics, interpretation and values.

Oxbridge's importance in law stemmed from the fact that, numerically speaking, it dominated the production of law graduates.[141] Only in the 1950s did London University join it as a significant producer of law graduates. The hegemony of Oxbridge and, more recently, London was further enhanced by their domination of the production of law teachers. Thus the form of education and scholarship offered at Oxbridge and, more lately, London are of special importance in explaining the dominance of the expository tradition.

But what of London University and the provincials that slowly emerged from the second half of the nineteenth century onwards? Most of the London colleges and certainly those in the provinces were created in part as reaction against Oxbridge. They asserted the vocational, professional and technological nature of their education. Provincial law schools were largely the creation of the provincial law societies. With very little state expenditure on higher education, only in this way could provincial universities establish law schools. As a result, these law schools were highly sensitive to the needs of the profession and for many years, the bulk of the tuition at provincial law schools centred around preparation for the Law Society's own examinations, rather than for their own law degrees.

Furthermore, until the 1960s a significant proportion of provincial law school staff were part-time practitioners, largely unsympathetic towards and untrained in law in any broad sense. The inadequate resources available to higher education especially in the period prior to the rise of the new universities in the post-Robbins period[142] meant that, even if somebody desired to teach or undertake a broadened conception of legal education and scholarship, the resources available to fund such work were meagre. In short, the dominant tradition of classical legal education and scholarship had the pre-eminent merit of being cheap. Thus there were the real financial limits on broadening legal education and thought.[143] The actual number of institutions, students and therefore teachers teaching law were relatively small and grew relatively slowly until about 1960. It is only since the 1960s that an enormous expansion in institutions teaching law and thus in the number of law teachers has taken place. Until then this monolithic quality undoubtedly discouraged pluralism in education and thought.[144]

In this context, the recurrent references to the dearth of student texts and the need to produce them take on an additional dimension. The circumstances in which the classical jurists found themselves seemed to require textbooks that conceived of the law as unitary and principled and which verged on the 'dogmatic'. Pedagogically, their ultimate *raison d'être* was *simplicity* of exposition, orientation and standpoint. They did their best to ignore the 'exceptions' and 'aberrations'; they concentrated upon the principles and 'the general part' of the law. They emphasized 'the best law', that is, they were highly selective in the cases they cited and deliberately eschewed the enumeration of numerous authorities which was the hallmark of practitioner texts. Many student texts were organized in numbered paragraphs or as codes subdivided into numbered rules – though this practice was by no means exclusive to elementary texts. One of Anson's innovations was to place case names 'where I thought they would be most conspicuous – in the margin';[145] and this fashion was taken up in other elementary texts. Of course, there were gradations of simplification. Pollock's great treatises were headier fare. Nonetheless, even these sought to project the law in an uncomplicated fashion which stressed that the law was derived from a small number of basic principles. The medium was the message. And the message was essentially about simplicity, and also through simplicity a celebration of the law as general principles, leading cases, judges and lawyers. Above all, perhaps, its message was about what the average student and lawyer was deemed to 'bear and wear'.[146]

Clearly, the form and substance of the new student texts, especially when seen in the context of the growth in university examinations, lent themselves to what has become the dominant form of legal pedagogy: the teaching of law as a simple set of rules; that examinations test the ability to resolve legal problems by reference to certain 'pat' answers; and that law texts and teaching are 'vocational' (albeit in a peculiarly narrow and artificial sense) and examination-orientated. But further impetus for this conception of law, legal education and legal scholarship came from beyond the universities. We must briefly explore the complex interrelationship between university and professional education and scholarship.

The testing and training of the legal professions was in a sorry state for most of the nineteenth century. Mandatory examinations for the bar were not established until 1872.[147] The Solicitors Act of 1860 introduced preliminary and intermediate examinations (the latter was taken halfway through articles) in addition to a final examination.[148] In essence, this left the legal education of most solicitors and barristers in the hands of the private law coaches, the crammers.

The crammers are the great, unsung anti-heroes of modern legal education and scholarship.[149] Beyond London, Manchester, Liverpool and parts of Yorkshire, the Law Society provided no formal education for articled clerks. Crammers were, therefore, an essential lifeline for most would-be solicitors who worked in the provinces. Crammers also filled the demand for texts specifically designed for examination candidates. They attracted considerable numbers of students; and a high proportion of those excelling in the Law Society's examinations. 'Of 394 awarded First Class Honours at The Law Society examination from January 1900 to June 1939 inclusive, 337 were Gibson and Weldon students.'[150] By 1883, seven-eighths of the candidates sitting Law Society examinations did not attend a single one of the Society's lectures, and less than 3 per cent attended the whole. The Law Society's lectures were not viewed as sufficiently practical or examination-orientated. From 1893 the Law Society started to copy the methods of Messrs Gibson and Weldon, but numbers continued to remain relatively small.

In sum, throughout most of the classical period the bulk of lawyers acquired their conceptions of law, legal scholarship and legal education from crammers not universities. Clearly, this has an important bearing on the profession's attitude to these subjects. Moreover, the crammers' pedagogy – their notions of relevance and identity – undoubtedly percolated upwards into the lecture halls of the universities. The new provincial university law schools significantly drew upon the methods of the crammers in their efforts to provide the vocational education required by intending solicitors. They also employed a number of crammers on their staffs. Crammers were also significant both as coaches and as the authors of texts designed for candidates taking the external LLB of the University of London.

52   *David Sugarman*

The success and tenacity of cramming in legal education (academic and practitioner) undoubtedly undercut the legitimacy and worth of an academic legal education in the eyes of lawyers and would-be lawyers; and thereby served to intensify the divide between the academic and vocational, theory and practice. The dominance of cramming and its pedagogy over the profession, and its imbrication within university legal education, undoubtedly rendered the task of broadening legal education more difficult.

There is also an interesting and complex relationship between the materials produced by crammers and the new university student textbooks. By the late nineteenth century certain books and allied aids produced by crammers were largely watered-down versions of the classic student texts produced by the new university law dons. Indeed, mini-versions of, or notes to, classic texts were produced by law coaches often with the approval of the relevant law don.[151] The simplifications and spoon-feeding of some of the university textbooks was thereby intensified and vulgarized in these aids for students and practitioners. It was through these 'nutshells' that many lawyers glimpsed at Dicey, Pollock and Salmond. These were the Harriet Martineaus of legal scholarship. On the one hand, the new academic texts represented a 'scholarly' alternative to the crammers' aids. On the other hand, the standpoint and relevance of the academic texts was sufficiently proximate to the crammers' texts for the former to be viewed as a more elevated and somewhat more elaborate form of crammer.

The dominance of the expository tradition was also sustained because of the relative dearth of mediums through which scholarly work could be published.[152] The tiny number of publishers who specialized in law books were preoccupied with the needs of practitioners or intending practitioners. Standard texts by Pollock, Anson, Kenny, Salmond and Dicey, as well as numerous practitioner works, were edited and updated under new hands but largely retained their old form and values. Thus the influence of many classic academic and practitioner works have persisted long after the deaths of their original authors. Like the forms of action, their authors may be buried but they still rule us from their graves. This practice, together with the existence of only one major academic legal periodical throughout the classical period,[153] surely inhibited innovative scholarship and education.

There are many extra-legal factors and parallels that seem to me to be important but which considerations of space do not allow me to consider. These include the tenacity of positivism as the dominant paradigm in the social sciences of England, and the fear of collectivism and of the breakdown of ordered government that haunted several key classical jurists.[154]

But I should like to conclude by way of three paradoxes. Firstly, several of the classical jurists *simultaneously* assisted in the construction of a liberal legal science (with its elevation of the expository tradition) *and* demonstrated that its foundations were built on sand. Buckland poured scorn on the notion that law was grounded upon universal principles. It was 'doubtful whether any claim of universality is maintainable or useful', he said.[155] His critique was directed at the ways jurists asserted the unity of the law without subjecting those assertions to empirical assessment. Despite Pollock's repeated emphasis upon law as science, following Holmes, he also attacked the attempt by writers such as Ames to reduce legal rules to 'strict logical consistency. That quest is . . . misconceived. Legal rules exist not for their own sake, but to further justice and convenience. Reasonableness, no doubt, is the ideal of the Common Law . . . [Nevertheless] the field of reason . . . includes many things outside strictly logical deduction.'[156] Indeed, his preoccupation with reasonableness and the need to harmonize law and morality has a strong natural law quality about it. These natural law tendencies were not limited to Pollock. Although it has been rarely acknowledged, aspects of Austin's work can be seen as a conscious attempt to construct a bridge between utilitarianism and natural law.[157] Moreover, the vulgarization of Austin's thought has obscured his efforts at empirical speculation (as in his discussion of political sovereignty), just as it has clouded the fact that his ideal curriculum for a law school acknowledged the importance of the science of legislation, and what today we term 'the social sciences', as well as the analytic.

Maine exposed the double-talk that characterizes legal discourse, which disguises change, manufactures continuity, resorts to strange fictions and invents spurious 'traditions'.[158] He was also sensitive to the ways the common law mind exaggerated the logical and universal elements in law:

> The tendency of German juridical opinion, shows that we are in danger of over-estimating the stability of legal conceptions. . . . I am not sure that even such juridical thinkers as Bentham and Austin are quite free from it. They sometimes write as if they thought that, although obscured by false theory, false logic, and false statement, there is somewhere behind all the delusions which they expose a frame-work of permanent legal conceptions which is discoverable by a trained eye, looking through a dry light, and to which a rational Code may always be fitted. . . . [This] position is certainly doubtful, and possibly not true. . . . [Legal] notions . . . are perishable. . . . [Even] jurisprudence itself cannot escape from the great law of Evolution.[159]

Maitland, the greatest of the classical jurists, who stood firmly outside the dominant tradition, repeatedly emphasized the dogmatic, anti-historical and present-minded qualities of the expository tradition.[160] One of the reasons why Dicey is endlessly fascinating and perplexing is that despite his efforts to eschew politics, history and the 'empiric', he nonetheless showed that an inquisitive mind cannot be contained within the narrow confines of an autonomous conception of legal scholarship.[161]

Secondly, despite the deficiencies of the classical tradition, the classical period appears more cosmopolitan, more sensitive to foreign learning, theory and history and more overtly concerned with the relationship between law and society relative to what followed. Its frank acknowledgment of judicial legislation and its occasionally outspoken criticisms of case-law seem to verge on the disrespectful. Of course, several major figures transcended the dominant tradition after *c*.1907. Nonetheless, their marginalization and relatively small numbers within university education, at least until the 1960s, is clear.

Thirdly, the direct and immediate influence of the classical law dons over the legal profession was relatively slight. The vast majority of lawyers continued to learn their law beyond rather than within the academy. The ancient prejudices against the academic lawyer seem to have survived. The profession's refusal to acknowledge its indebtedness to doctrinal writers was symbolized by that bizarre rule of judicial etiquette which only permits the citation of authors who are deceased. On the other hand, a few jurists, notably Austin, Maine, Dicey and Pollock, exerted a powerful and unprecedented influence on law and state. The nature and character of law as an academic discipline, the boundaries that separate it from other disciplines, and the elevation of certain topics and techniques as the core of legal education and scholarship, with the subordination or driving into silence of others, was largely the product of a revolution in legal education and thought that occurred in the period *c.*1850–1907. This period was truly the classical or golden age of English legal scholarship. And it was in this period that academic lawyers, in partnership with the courts, fundamentally reconceptualized the form and content of English law. Here were the true codifiers of modern law. The clarity and precision that they imposed upon a chaotic common law was not inconsiderable. But their importance transcended immediate professional concerns. A new constitutional bulwark was created where only the sovereignty of Parliament and an 'unwritten constitution' were supposed to exist. Moreover, juristic categories were a vital ingredient of the educated person's conception of state, society and politics.[162] Legal thought was constitutive of consciousness.[163] The law in the cases and on the statute book, distilled and reconstituted in the new student law texts, operated like a language, naming and claiming wider areas of social life, belief, action, intention and subordinating or driving into silence others. For example, legal categories created social identities: school children, women and young persons, the family, ages or kinds of 'responsibility', the 'public' sphere, the 'private' sphere, etc., etc. The relative deference of the jurists, the largely invisible practices of lawyers and the declaratory theory of precedent have tended to obfuscate the role of lawyers, judges and jurists as translators and creators of one of our most important political and social discourses. In short, they are conceptive ideologists.[164]

> But although on . . . occasions their views may seem to have served functions which could properly be described as 'ideological', there is nothing to be gained by treating them collectively as an entity which could be reduced to ideology. Nor, though some of the assumptions now appear remote and the ambitions bizarre, is it easy to feel that the intellectual problems involved and the strategies available for coping with them were so purely a matter of time and place that they can confidently be dismissed by a methodologically more sophisticiated age. It is not, after all, only the poor and inarticulate who may stand in need of being rescued from the enormous condescension of posterity.[165]

NOTES

This essay draws upon a larger work in progress on the history of legal education, legal thought and legal scholarship in England *c.*1800–1980. Other aspects of this research have appeared in: Sugarman, 'The Legal Boundaries of Liberty: Dicey, Liberalism and Legal Science' (1983) 46 *Modern Law Rev.* 102; D. Sugarman, 'Law, Economy and the State in England, 1750–1914: Some Major Issues' in *Legality, Ideology and the State* (1983 ed. D. Sugarman) pp. 245–9; and D. Sugarman and G. R. Rubin, 'Towards a New History of Law and Material Society in England, 1750-1914' in *Law, Economy and Society: Essays in the History of English Law, 1750-1914* (1984; ed. G. R. Rubin and D. Sugarman) pp. 77-83 and 99-110.

I am grateful to Rick Abel, Harry Arthurs, Peter Fitzpatrick, Bob Gordon, Morton Horwitz, Dick Risk and William Twining for invaluable encouragement; to David Flaherty, whose legal history seminars at the University of Western Ontario provided an excellent opportunity to test out some of these ideas; to John Dinwiddy, for helpful comments on section IV of this essay; to William Twining, for unstinting editorial support; and to the American Bar Foundation and the British Academy, for generous financial assistance in the preparation of my research. None of them is responsible for my errors and omissions.

1 Readers will, I hope, appreciate that what I have constructed is an 'ideal-type', that is, 'a "model" based on the ideas of many writers but not found in any one of them in this integrated form and with such a clear statement of implications': R. Bendix, *Max Weber: An Intellectual Portrait* (1959) p. 274; and see *id.*, pp. xx and 271-81. This model is based on historical materials. One of the functions of this essay is to document concrete examples of the ways these notions were constructed and became part of the taken-for-granted assumptions which bound together the elite fractions within the legal professions: lawyers, judges and law teachers. Some of the limitations of this ideal-type are also indicated in the text.

There is a growing body of work (largely North American) which has brilliantly illuminated some or all of the features of the common law frame of mind in Anglo-American legal science. Key works to which I am greatly indebted include: P. S. Atiyah, *The Rise and Fall of Freedom of Contract* (1979); G. E. White, *Tort Law in America* (1980); L. Friedman, *Contract Law in America* (1965); B. Abel-Smith and R. Stevens, *Lawyers and the Courts* (1967); C. H. S. Fifoot, *Judge and Jurist in the Reign of Victoria* (1959); R. Cocks, *Foundations of the Modern Bar* (1983); G. Gilmore, *the Death of Contract* (1974) and *The Ages of American Law* (1977); F. H. Lawson, 'Doctrinal Writing: A Foreign Element in English Law?' in F. H. Lawson, *Selected Essays*, vol. I (1977) p. 207; Gordon, 'J. Willard Hurst and the Common Law Tradition in American Legal Historiography' (1975) 10 *Law and Society Rev.* 9, 'Historicism in Legal Scholarship' (1981) 90 *Yale Law J* 1017, (book review) (1981) 94 *Harvard Law Rev.* 903, 'Legal Thought and Legal Practice in the Age of American Enterprise, 1870-1920' in *Professions and Professional Ideologies in America* (1984; ed. G. L. Geison) p. 70 and 'Critical Legal Histories' (1984) 36 *Stanford Law Rev.* 57; M. J. Horwitz, *The Transformation of American Law, 1780-1850* (1977) and 'Lectures in American Legal History Since 1890' (unpublished, 1976); D. Kennedy, 'Toward an Historical Understanding of Legal Consciousness' in *Research in Law and Sociology*, vol. 3 (1980; ed. S. Spitzer) ch. 1 and 'The Structure of Blackstone's Commentaries' (1979) 28 *Buffalo Law Rev.* 205; McCurdy, 'Justice Field and the Jurisprudence of Government-Business Relations' (1975) 61 *J American History* 970; R. Stevens, *Law School: Legal Education in America from the 1850s to the 1980s* (1983); Schlegel, 'American Legal Realism and Empirical Social Science' (1980) 28 *Buffalo Law Rev.* 459 and (1981) 29 *Buffalo Law Rev.* 195; Chase, 'The Birth of the Modern Law School' (1979) 23 *Am. J Legal History* 329; P. Stein, *Legal Evolution* (1980); J. W. Burrow, *Evolution and Society* (1966) and *A Liberal Descent* (1981); J. G. A. Pocock, *The Ancient Constitution and the Feudal Law* (1957) and *Politics, Language and Time* (1971); and S. Collini, D. Winch and J. Burrow, *That Noble Science of Politics* (1983).

2 See Twining, 'Some Jobs for Jurisprudence' (1974) 1 *Brit. J Law and Society* 151-6.
3 Cf. R. Dworkin, *Taking Rights Seriously* (1979).
4 Montrose, 'Return to Austin's College' (1960) *Current Legal Problems* 9.

5 M. J. Horwitz, 'Lectures of American Legal History Since 1890' *op. cit.*

6 For a valuable attempt to think through such a project within the general reform of legal education and scholarship, see *Law and Learning: Report to the Social Sciences and Humanities Research Council of Canada by the Consultative Group on Research and Education in Law* (1983).

7 See Singer, 'The Legal Rights Debate in Analytical Jurisprudence from Bentham to Hohfeld' (1982) *Wisconsin Law Review* 975.

8 But cf. Sugarman, (book review) (1980) 7 *Brit. J Law and Society* 297, 'Theory and Practice in Law and History: A Prologue to the Study of the Relationship between Law and Economy from a Socio-Historical Perspective' in *Law, State and Society* (1981; ed. B. Fryer *et al.*) p. 70, 'Law, Economy and the State in England, 1750-1914: Some Major Issues' in *Legality, Ideology and the State* (1983; ed. D. Sugarman) p. 213, and *op. cit.*

9 On the role of intellectual history within this project, see Twining *op. cit.* (1974) pp. 161-4, and chapter 4 below, 'Evidence and Legal Theory'.

10 Twining, 'Academic Law and Legal Philosophy: the Significance of Herbert Hart' (1979) 95 *Law Quarterly Rev.* 558. On the continuing influence of the textbook tradition within English legal education and scholarship see Hart, 'Dias and Hughes on Jurisprudence' (1958) 4 *J Society of Public Teachers of Law* (N.S.) 149; Twining, *op. cit.*, n. 2, pp. 149-74, 'Is Your Text-Book Really Necessary?' (1970) 11 *J Society of Public Teachers of Law* (N.S.) 81, 'Treatises and Text-books' 12 *id.*, 267; Lawson, *op. cit.*; Fifoot, *op. cit.*, pp. 27 *et seq.*; Milton (book review) (1981) 44 *Modern Law Rev.* 735; Sugarman, 'The Legal Boundaries of Liberty' *op. cit.*, p. 102; and Harlow, 'A Treatise for Our Times?' (1984) 47 *Modern Law Rev.* 487.

11 See generally Abel-Smith and Stevens, *op. cit.*, pp. 63-76, 165-86 and 349-76; Fifoot, *op. cit.*; and F. H. Lawson, *The Oxford Law School, 1850-1965* (1968).

12 For example, see *The Law Times*, vol. I, 1843, p. 215; *The Westminster Review* 1833, p. 69; *Law Journal*, vol. 35, 1900, p. 354; *Westminster Gazette* 1833, pp. 67-9; C. G. Addison, *Wrongs and their Remedies* 2nd edn; 1864) p. vi; C. G. Addison, *The Law of Contracts* (5th edn; 1862) pp. vi-viii.

13 *Report from the Select Committee on Legal Education*, PPX (1846) p. 1.

14 J. Austin, *Lectures in Jurisprudence* (5th edn; 1885) p. 58.

15 A. V. Dicey, *Can English Law Be Taught At The Universities?* (1883).

16 *Id.*, pp. 10-11.

17 *Id.*, p. 10.

18 *Id.*, pp. 18, 20-1.

19 F. Pollock, 'Oxford Law Studies' (1886) 2 *Law Quarterly Rev.* 453.

20 *Id.*, pp. 54-5.

21 *Id.*, p. 463.

22 F. Schulz, *History of Roman Legal Science* (1946); F. Bacon, *Essays (1597 and 1612), Advancement of Learning* (1605 and 1623) and *Proposition Touching the Amendment of the Law* (1616); F. C. von Savigny, *Of The Vocation of Our Age for Legislation and Jurisprudence* (1831; ed. and trans. A. Hayward). The mathematical or geometric ideal was one of the hallmarks of the rationalist movement's efforts to extend scientific rigour to the moral sciences including law: see further J. Mill, *Essay on Government* (1820); Mill, 'Austin on Jurisprudence' (1863) 118 *Edinburgh Rev.* 449; and Grey, 'Langdell's Orthodoxy' (1983) 45 *University of Pittsburgh Law Rev.* 16-27.

23 Savigny, *op. cit.*, pp. 38-9.

24 J. Bryce, 'The Academic Study of the Civil Law' (1871) in his *Studies in History and Jurisprudence* (1901) vol. II, p. 500.

25 See generally W. R. Prest, *The Inns of Court Under Elizabeth I and the Early Stuarts 1590-1640* (1972); J. H. Baker, 'The English Legal Profession, 1450-1550' in *Lawyers*

in Early Modern Europe and America (1981; ed. W. R. Prest) pp. 34–5; D. Duman, *The English and Colonial Bars in the 19th Century* (1983) pp. 184, 194–5.

26 Bryce, *op. cit.*, p. 21. The arguments echo Blackstone.

27 See Dicey, *op. cit.*

28 Pollock, *op. cit.*, p. 454.

29 F. Pollock, *English Opportunities and Duties in the Historical and Comparative Study of Law: An Inaugural Lecture* (1883) pp. 11 and 29.

30 *Id.*, p. 14.

31 Pollock, *op. cit.*, n. 19, p. 454.

32 *Id.*, pp. 454–5.

33 *Id.*, p. 463.

34 J. Bryce, 'Valedictory Lecture' (1893) in Bryce, *op. cit.*, p. 504. See also F. W. Maitland, 'Law at the Universities' (1901) in *The Collected Papers of Frederic William Maitland*, vol. III (1911) p. 419.

35 Bryce, *op. cit.*, n. 34, p. 515.

36 *Id.*, p. 518.

37 *Id.*, p. 519.

38 Dicey, *op. cit.*, p. 22.

39 *Id.*, p. 24.

40 *Id.*, p. 17; F. Pollock, *Principles of Contract* (1st edn; 1876) p. v; *The Law of Torts* (4th edn; 1895) p. 2; F. W. Maitland, 'Historical Note on the Classification of the Forms of Personal Action' in Pollock, *id.*, p. 522, and *The Forms of Action at Common Law* (1948) p. 81.

41 See n. 40.

42 See R. Cosgrove, *The Rule of Law: Albert Venn Dicey, Victorian Jurist* (1980) ch. 2.

43 See generally N. Annan, 'The Intellectual Aristocracy' in *Studies in Social History* (1955; ed. J. H. Plumb) p. 241; and C. Harvie, *The Lights of Liberalism* (1976).

44 Dicey, *op. cit.*, p. 6.

45 *Id.*, p. 7.

46 Weber's celebrated discussion of the irrational nature of the English legal system relative to its continental counterparts is in M. Weber, *Economy and Society*, vol. 2 (1968; ed. G. Roth and C. Wittich) pp. 721–5, 784–808, 889–92 and 976–8. See generally A. Kronman, *Max Weber* (1983) pp. 120–4; and Sugarman, 'Weber, Modernity and "the Peculiarities of the English": On the Rationality and Irrationality of Law, State and Society in Modern England' (forthcoming).

47 See Bryce, *op. cit.*, n. 24, 494.

48 See, for example, *id.*, pp. 489–90; Bryce, *op. cit.*, n. 34, p. 511; Pollock, *op. cit.*, n. 29 p. 10; Stephen and Pollock, 'Section Seventeen of the Statute of Frauds' (1884) 1 *Law Quarterly Rev. 1;* A. V. Dicey, *Law and Public Opinion in England During the 19th Century* (2nd edn; 1914) pp. 396–8; F. Pollock, *A First Book of Jurisprudence* (6th edn; 1929) pp. 354–63; Sir W. Markby, *Elements of Law* (4th edn; 1889) ss. 57–9, 78, 93; W. R. Anson, *Principles of the English Law of Contract* (1st edn; 1879) pp. vi–vii; 'The Franchise Bill' (1884) 1 *Law Quarterly Rev.* 25; C. Morazé, *The Triumph of the Middle Classes* (1966) p. 94.

49 Bryce, *op. cit.*, n. 24, p. 499.

50 The *locus classicus* is, of course, Dicey, *op. cit.*, n. 48.

51 See, for example, Manson, 'Tinkering Company Law' (1890) 6 *Law Quarterly Rev.* 428.

52 For an important discussion of Bentham's radicalization see Dinwiddy, 'Bentham's Transition to Political Radicalism 1809–10' (1975) 36 *J. History of Ideas* 683. See also Dinwiddy, 'Early-Nineteenth-Century Reactions to Benthamism' (1984) 34 *Transactions of the Royal Historical Society*, 5th series, 47.

58   *David Sugarman*

53 Bryce, *op. cit.*, n. 24, p. 479.
54 *Id.* See also Markby, *op. cit.*, ss. 194-5.
55 Clark, 'Jurisprudence: Its Use and Its Place in Legal Education' (1885) 1 *Law Quarterly Rev.* 205-6.
56 F. Pollock, *The Law of Torts* (4th edn, 1895) p. ii.
57 *Id.*, pp. ix-x.
58 F. Pollock, *Principles of Contract* (1st edn; 1876).
59 F. Pollock, *Principles of Contract* (4th ed.) pp. iii-v.
60 Pollock, *op. cit.*, n. 56, p. v.
61 *Id.*; and Sir F. Pollock, *The Expansion of the Common Law* (1904) pp. 1-24. On the ideological aspects of 'Americomania' see Tulloch, 'Changing Attitudes Toward the United States in the 1880s' (1977) 20 *Historical J* 825.
62 J. Bentham, 'A Comment on the Commentaries' in *A Comment on the Commentaries and A Fragment on Government* (1977; ed. J. H. Burns and H. L. A. Hart) p. 310.
63 See I. Hont and M. Ignatieff (eds), *Wealth and Virtue* (1983); D. Winch, 'The System of the North: Dugald Stewart and his Pupils', in Collini, Winch and Burrow, *op. cit.*, ch. 1; Stein, *op. cit.*, ch. 2; K. Haakonssen, *The Science of a Legislator* (1981).
64 See, for example, Dinwiddy, *op. cit.*, n. 52 (both articles).
65 See *id.*
66 Mill, *op. cit.*, pp. 440-1.
67 *Id.*, p. 441. See also, Mill, 'Bentham' (1838) *London and Westminster Rev.* 467. The latter is interesting because whilst it characterizes Bentham as predominantly destructive and practical, it also acknowledges, in ways that are absent in Mill's review of Austin, that Bentham's *method* was particularistic, i.e. in a sense, analytical. For a critique of Mill on Bentham, see H. L. A. Hart, *Essays on Bentham* (1982) Introduction and chap. 5.
   A shrinking back from recognizing Bentham's analytical prowess is evidenced by the way his best-known work, *An Introduction to the Principles of Morals and Legislation*, has usually been treated as a work of moral philosophy, and by the tendency for its more analytical chapters to be neglected, therefore generating a distorted view of the character of the work as a whole: see H. L. A. Hart, 'Introduction' to J. Bentham, *An Introduction to the Principles of Morals and Legislation* (1982; ed. J. H. Burns and H. L. A. Hart).
   It has been observed that if Bentham's *Of Laws in General* (1970; ed. H. L. A. Hart) had appeared in print somewhat earlier than it did, the notion of J. S. Mill and others that Bentham's *forte* was destruction and legislation, not jurisprudence, would have had to be considerably modified: see, for example, Hart, *Essays on Bentham, op. cit.*, p. 108.
68 See Twining, *op. cit.*, n. 10, pp. 557-80.
69 Sir H. S. Maine, *Lectures on the Early History of Institutions* (4th edn, 1885) pp. 343-5, 400.
70 Bentham, *op. cit..*, n. *passim*.
71 W. Blackstone, *Commentaries on the Laws of England* (1826 edn) vol. 3, pp. 265-6.
72 Bentham, *op. cit.*, n., pp. 415-17.
73 J. Bentham, *Of Laws in General* (1970; ed. H. L. A. Hart) pp. 233 and 246.
74 D. Lieberman, 'From Bentham to Benthamism' (1985) 28 *Historical J* 205; and see generally pp. 203-5.
75 Within and beyond the law, an antagonism towards natural rights and metaphysics was, in England, sustained through their association with natural law, continental thinking, France's despotism, centralization, potentially revolutionary doctrines and *a priori* thought.

76 W. Hazlitt, *The Spirit of the Age* (World Classics Edition, 1960) pp. 5–6, cited in L. J. Hume, *Bentham and Bureaucracy* (1981) p. 9; see also Hume, pp. 9–10, 15 and 85.

77 Hume, *op. cit.*, pp. 10 and 237.

78 On Weber's notion of rationality, see R. Brubaker, *The Limits of Rationality* (1984).

79 See further Pocock, *op. cit.*; also 'Burke and the Ancient Constitution' in his *Politics, Language and Time* (1971), and *The Machiavellian Moment* (1975) pp. 9–30, 340–1 and 345–8.

80 This theme is further explored in Sugarman, *op. cit.*, n. 46.

81 'Outlines of English Legal History' in *The Collected Papers of Frederic William Maitland*, vol. II (1911; ed. H. A. L. Fisher) p. 483.

82 See generally P. B. M. Blaas, *Continuity and Anachronism* (1978) pp. 248–62.

83 'Why the History of English Law is Not Written' in *The Collected Papers of Frederic William Maitland*, vol. I (1911; ed. H. A. L. Fisher) pp. 490–3. See generally Gordon, 'Historicism in Legal Scholarship', *op. cit.*, *passim*, and 'J. Willard Hurst', *op. cit.*, *passim*.

84 See Lieberman, *op. cit.*, pp. 203–5.

85 Bentham's increasing political radicalism and his association with republicanism also encouraged lawyers to scale down his ideas and distance themselves from him: see generally Dinwiddy, *op. cit.*, *passim*. Also F. Rosen, *Jeremy Bentham and Representative Democracy* (1983).

86 See, for example, Mill, *op. cit.*, n. 67. See further, R. J. Halliday, *John Stuart Mill* (1976) ch. 2; A. Ryan, *J. S. Mill* (1974) chs 2 and 4; D. Winch, 'The Cause of Good Government: Philosophic Whigs versus Philosophic Radicals', in Collini, Winch and Burrow, *op. cit.*, ch. 3; S. Collini in *id.*, ch. 4; J. Burrow, *Evolution and Society* (1966) ch. 3; W. Thomas, *The Philosophic Radicals* (1979) ch. 4.

87 See Ryan, *op. cit.*, p. 101.

88 In the sense of comprehending the study of politics, political economy and society: see Collini, *op. cit.*, pp. 147–8.

89 Mill, *op. cit.*, n. 22, p. 444; and see pp. 442–6.

90 Lieberman, *op. cit.*, 200.

91 Collini, *op. cit.*, p. 147.

92 *Id.* at n. 54.

93 Cited in C. H. S. Fifoot, *F. W. Maitland, A Life* (1971) p. 143.

94 S. Amos, *The Science of Law* (1874) p. 4. Again, it was Maine who played an important role in this process: see, for instance, Maine, *op. cit.*, p. 343.

95 W. W. Buckland, *Some Reflections on Jurisprudence* (1945) p. 2.

96 (1832).

97 *Lectures on Jurisprudence or the Philosophy of Positive Law* (1863), 2 vols.

98 *On the Uses of the Study of Jurisprudence* (1863).

99 J. Austin, *Lectures on Jurisprudence or the Philosophy of Positive Law* (4th revised edn, by R. Campbell; 1879) vol. I, p. 16; see generally pp. 16–18.

100 *Id.*, p. 18.

101 For example, J. Austin, *The Student's Edition, Lectures on Jurisprudence* (abridged by R. Campbell; 1920) and W. J. Brown, *The Austinian Theory of Law* (1906).

102 Austin's own words, taken out of their wider context, aided this interpretation.

103 Cf. E. A. Purcell Jr, *The Crisis of Democratic Theory* (1973), ch. 14 on America as a normative concept within American legal thought.

104 Maine, *op. cit.*, pp. 369–70.

105 Brown, 'The Jurisprudence of M. Duguit' (1916) 32 *Law Quarterly Rev.* 181.

106 *The Elements of Jurisprudence* (1st edn; 1880).

107 Brierly, 'Sir Thomas Erskine Holland' (1926) 42 *Law Quarterly Rev.* 475.

108 Holland, *op. cit.* (13th edn; 1924) p. 1.

109 (1868) LR 3 HL 330.
110 F. Pollock, *Principles of Contract* (9th edn; 1921) p. xi.
111 E. P. Thompson, *The Making of the English Working Class* (1968 edn) p. 9. See generally P. Abrams, *Historical Sociology* (1982) pp. ix–xviii.
112 R. Johnson, 'Three Problematics' in *Working-Class Culture: Studies in History and Theory* (1979; ed. J. Clarke *et al.*) p. 230 (as a criticism of Althusser).
113 My emphasis upon languages of reciprocity and conflict was suggested by Joyce, 'Languages of Reciprocity and Conflict' (1984) 9 *Social History* 225. See also W. Sewell Jr, *Work and Revolution in France* (1980) and G. S. Jones, 'Rethinking Chartism' in his *Languages of Class* (1983) ch. 3.
114 A. W. B. Simpson, 'The Survival of the Common Law' in *Then and Now, 1799–1974* (1974) p. 64.
115 (1885) 1 *Law Quarterly Rev.* 118–19.
116 For a valuable study of the influence of Roman law and the German historical school on classical legal thought see Stein, *op. cit.*, esp. chs 3–5. Other relevant works are collected in Sugarman and Rubin, *op. cit.*, pp. xliv–xiv, n. 289. The importance of the German historical school on English historical thought is brilliantly conveyed by C. E. McClelland, *The German Historians and England* (1971) and J. W. Burrow, *A Liberal Descent: Victorian Historians and the English Past* (1981).
117 See Stein, *op. cit.*, pp. 61–7 and 87–8. See generally J. W. Burrow, *Evolution and Society* (1966) pp. 137–78 and 'The Village Community and the Uses of History in Late 19th Century England' in *Historical Perspectives* (1974; ed. N. McKendrick) pp. 255–84; and J. Burrow and S. Collini in Collini, Winch and Burrow, *op. cit.*, ch. 7.
118 (1889) 14 App. Cas. 337.
119 Pollock, '*Derry* v. *Peek* in the House of Lords' (1889) 5 *Law Quarterly Rev.* 410.
120 *Id.*, p. 410.
121 W. R. Anson, '*Derry* v. *Peek* in the House of Lords' (1890) 6 *Law Quarterly Rev.* 72.
122 *Id.*, pp. 72 and 74.
123 *Id.*, p. 72, n. 3.
124 Pollock, (1892) 8 *Law Quarterly Rev.* 7.
125 *Holmes–Pollock Letters* (2nd edn; 1961), vol. I, p. 49.
126 In the Directors' Liability Act 1890.
127 See *Nocton* v. *Ashburton* [1914] AC 932.
128 *Holmes–Pollock Letters, op. cit.*, p. 215.
129 Twining, 'Some Jobs', *op. cit.*, pp. 151–2.
130 On the vulgarization of Austin's ideas, see W. L. Morison, *John Austin* (1971) ch. 5; and section V of this essay.
131 See J. P. Dawson, *The Oracles of the Law* (1968) pp. 88–95; R. Stevens, *Law and Politics* (1979) chs 2 and 3.
132 Dawson, *op. cit.*, p. 91, discussing *London Street Tramways Co. Ltd* v. *LCC* [1898] AC 375.
133 A. V. Dicey, *An Introduction to the Study of the Law of the Constitution* (1885).
134 See Sugarman, 'The Legal Boundaries of Liberty', *op. cit.*, pp. 106–8.
135 See T. Johnson, 'The State and the Professions' in *Social Class and the Division of Labour* (1982; ed. A. Giddens and G. Mackenzie) p. 186.
136 See generally A. J. Engel, *From Clergyman to Don* (1983) and S. Rothblatt, *The Revolt of the Dons* (1968). See also W. H. G. Armytage, *Civic Universities* (1955); Michael Sanderson (ed.), *The Universities in the 19th Century* (1975); and J. W. Anderson, *English Education, 1789–1902* (1930).
137 See S. Rothblatt's outstanding study of changing notions of liberal education, *Tradition and Change in English Liberal Education* (1976).

138 Quoted in M. Sanderson's excellent 'Introduction' to Sanderson *op. cit.*, p. 7.
139 See, for example, Bryce, *op. cit.*, n. 34, pp. 519–23.
140 The phrase is John Burrow's, *A Liberal Descent, op. cit.* p. x - although it is not used in this context.
141 The figures and a more detailed analysis will appear in Rick Abel's forthcoming book on English lawyers, to be published in 1987 by Basil Blackwell. Also see Abel, 'The Decline of Professionalism?' (1986) 49 *Modern Law Rev.* (January issue).
142 *Report of the Committee on Higher Education* (1963; Cmnd 2154; Chairman Lord Robbins).
143 See Twining, 'Some Jobs', *op. cit.*, pp. 151-2, and 'The Benson Report and Legal Education: A Personal View' in *Law in the Balance* (1982; ed. P. A. Thomas), pp. 200-4 and 210.
144 Abel, *op. cit.*
145 W. R. Anson, *Principles of the English Law of Contract* (1879) p. vii.
146 I have borrowed this phrase from Stefan Collini in Collini, Winch and Burrow, *op. cit.*, p. 167, who uses it in the context of discussing Bagehot's writings. The reference to M. McLuhan's *The Medium is the Message* (1967) was also suggested by Collini, *id.*
147 See further Abel-Smith and Stevens, *op. cit.*; Cocks, *op. cit.*; and D. Duman, *The English and Colonial Bars in the 19th Century* (1983) pp. 16, 22, 24, 59 and 78–86.
148 See further H. Kirk, *Portrait of a Profession* (1976) ch. 3.
149 See *id.*; and P. Leighton 'An Unwelcome Legacy?' (1984) *Topical Law* 41; also R. H. Kersley, *Gibson's, 1876-1962* (1973).
150 Kersley, *op. cit.*, p. 3.
151 For example see J. F. Mannooch, *An Analysis of Sir Frederick Pollock's, Law of Torts, For Students* (1st edn; 1911); E. L. Burgin and E. G. M. Fletcher, *The Students' Conflict of Laws, Being an Introduction to the Study of Private International Law based on Dicey* (3rd edn; 1937); I. G. Briggs, *Notes on Pollock's 'Contracts'* (1937). Salmond recognized the need for a watered-down version of his treatise on torts: see J. W. Salmond, *A Summary of the Law of Torts* (1912).
152 Twining, 'Some Jobs', *op. cit.*, pp. 151-2 and 161. See also the Society of Public Teachers of Law, Working Party on Law Publishing, *Working Papers* (1976-7).
153 The *Law Quarterly Review* founded in 1884.
154 On the latter, see Sugarman, 'The Legal Boundaries of Liberty', *op. cit.*, pp. 109-10.
155 Buckland, 'Difficulties of Abstract Jurisprudence' (1890) 6 *Law Quarterly Rev.* 445.
156 Pollock, *Principles of Contract* (9th edn; 1921) pp. x-xi.
157 Cf. Dinwiddy, 'Utility and Natural Law in Burke's Thought: A Reconsideration' (1974-5) 16 *Studies in Burke and His Time* 108-9.
158 See, for example, H. S. Maine, *Ancient Law* (1861) pp. 80-1.
159 Sir H. S. Maine, *Early Law and Custom* (1901) pp. 360-1. I am grateful to Geoffrey Samuel for drawing this passage to my attention.
160 See Maitland, *op. cit.*, n. 83, *passim.*
161 As Dicey's most cogent critic acknowledged: see Sir I. Jennings, *The Law and the Constitution* (1st edn; 1933). See also Sugarman, 'The Legal Boundaries of Liberty', *op. cit.*
162 This is one of the key themes of Collini, Winch and Burrow *op. cit.* See especially S. Collini, 'A Place in the Syllabus: Political Science at Cambridge', in *id.*, ch. 11.
163 For a valuable explication of this perspective see Gordon, 'Legal Thought', *op. cit.*, *passim.* See also Sugarman, 'Theory and Practice', *op. cit.*, pp. 95-6; Sugarman and Rubin, *op. cit.*, pp. 121-2 and the material in n. 444a.
164 See M. Cain, 'The General Practice Lawyer and the Client' in *The Sociology of the Professions* (1983; ed. R. Dingwall and P. Lewis) ch. 5; and Gordon, 'Legal Thought', *op. cit.*, *passim.*
165 S. Collini in Collini, Winch and Burrow, *op. cit.*, pp. 376-7.

4
Evidence and Legal Theory

WILLIAM TWINING

One way of looking at jurisprudence is as the theoretical part of law as a discipline.[1] In this sense, it is synonymous with legal theory, but it is broader than legal philosophy. One's view of the nature and role of legal theory depends upon one's view of the discipline of law. In this context general definitions are not very helpful. Just as law as a social institution shades off and overlaps with other social phenomena in extraordinarily complex ways, so law as a subject cannot and should not have rigid boundaries that segregate it from other disciplines. For certain purposes, in some contexts, lines have to be drawn; but as often as not precise definitions and sharp boundaries do more harm than good. In relation to other disciplines, the study of law is a complex, varied and amorphous part of a general intellectual enterprise, the direct end of which is the advancement of knowledge and understanding. As a practical matter there has to be a rough division of intellectual labour; there need to be specialized institutions, and individual specialists. But when these artificial boundaries become institutionalized or rigidified, the theorist has a much more important role to play in subverting divisions and building intellectual bridges than in settling lines of demarcation.

Academic law can also be seen as the intellectual and scholarly branch of law-related activities in the real world – whether it is related to the concerns of professional lawyers or of other specialized participants in legal and law-related social processes; or to the unspecialized and enormously diverse concerns of non-specialists who become involved in such processes. Here again specialization has its uses: one does not expect, for example, many judges or solicitors or policemen or plaintiffs to be academic experts in jurisprudence or indeed in most fields of law. But one function of legal theorizing is to break down institutional barriers, habits of action, or ways of thought that divide off the academic from the applied, theory from practice, the law in books from the law in action.

Law is a fascinating, complex, important and pervasive phenomenon in society. Professional legal practice is a quite varied and influential form of specialized activity which is by no means coextensive with the law in action. The discipline of law is also wide-ranging, varied, amorphous and important. It is potentially enormously interesting, even if in practice it is sometimes made unforgivably boring.

If one looks at law as a discipline in these terms, it is hardly surprising that its relationship both with other disciplines and with the world of affairs is perennially problematic. Such problems are close to the core of the concerns of many legal theorists – whether they proceed by agonized introspection, over-confident assertion (usually reading one part as the whole), eye-catching polemics, grand theorizing or patient reflection about quite small questions. The primary task of the jurist is to study the assumptions underlying legal discourse; many of those assumptions lie at key points of contact between the world of learning and the worlds of practical affairs.

This kind of perspective on law as a discipline may seem almost banal, yet it has many implications and ramifications. Here let me just pick out a few quite simple points for brief comment. First, on this view, the notion of an autonomous discipline or a pure science has, at most, a very limited place. Understanding law is dependent on understanding much else besides. If there are general aspects of legal discourse or action that are characteristic or unique, they are a relatively small part of the enormously complex phenomena, practices and ideas that make up the subject of law. For example, many legal skills such as interpreting rules or determining facts or negotiating or justifying decisions in legal processes involve practical reasoning and basic human skills that are of enormously wide application. Everyone interprets rules; everyone weighs evidence; everyone is involved in negotiations; everyone applies rules to facts. Lawyers and jurists sometimes speak as if they are the only people who do such things. To concentrate on the characteristic or the peculiar or the unique – to treat such elements as 'the core' in a strong sense – involves not only leaving out much that is equally important to understanding; it also involves risks of distortion – as is clearly illustrated by approaches to evidence that concentrate on the artificial rules. If the direct end of any discipline is understanding, isolating the peculiarly legal or treating law as a subject apart is very often inimical to that end. In this view, the study of law is dependent on other disciplines; such notions as a pure science of law or law as an autonomous discipline are dangerous, even if in a very few narrow contexts they might be defensible.

Because of its intimate connections with the world of affairs – with legal practice and the law in action in a broad sense – nearly all legal discourse is strongly participant-oriented. This is true, even in its theoretical aspects. Its main audiences are actual or intending participants with concerns related directly or indirectly to their own activities. These participants are very varied and so are their concerns. Legislators, judges, barristers, solicitors, bailiffs, caterers, prostitutes, bureaucrats, bandits, tenants, pressure groups and revolutionaries are all producers and consumers of legal discourse. The activities and products of academic law as an enterprise – teaching, research, writing, and theorizing – are inevitably influenced by these varied concerns. The response is often *ad hoc* and unsystematic – witness the biases and imbalances in legal literature. But the gravitational pull is persistent and strong. This is a fact of considerable significance in interpreting our received heritage of legal theorizing. For many of our leading jurists have treated one kind of participant as their primary audience or target: for example, Bentham addresses his model legislator; Holmes's bad man is an ordinary office lawyer thinly diguised; much of Karl Llewellyn's work and Ronald Dworkin's universe have appellate court judges as their main focus; much critical legal theory is primarily directed at dissentient insiders and outsiders.

This view of law is pluralistic in a descriptive sense. Here pluralism is not some indecisive form of evasion or fence-sitting; it is quite compatible with strong commitment to particular values, positions, postures or strategies. Rather it is an acknowledgment of the variety and richness of our subject, the multiplicity of perspectives and levels at which it can be approached and the limited capacity of any of us to obtain more than an occasional glimpse of the whole.

So much for law as a discipline. Jurisprudence can be viewed as the theoretical aspect of that discipline – that is, it is concerned with general questions about and assumptions underlying all kinds of legal discourse, including both law talk and talk about law. One way of looking at legal theorizing is as an activity directed to a variety of tasks all of which are directly concerned with understanding. These tasks occur at various levels and require different kinds of knowledge, skills and aptitudes. They can be characterized in various ways and the list could be quite long. For present purposes – with particular reference to problems of theorizing about evidence – a brief restatement of the tasks might go as follows:

(1) Intellectual history, that is the systematic study and criticism of the heritage of legal thought and critical study of the work of individual thinkers.
(2) High Theory, that is to say the exploration of fundamental general questions related to the subject-matter of law as a discipline, such as questions about the nature and functions of law, the relations between law and justice, or the epistemological foundations of different kinds of legal discourse. This is the particular sphere of legal philosophy.
(3) Middle-order theorizing, prescriptive as well as descriptive; in particular:
  (a) the development of general hypotheses about legal or law-related phenomena capable of being tested by empirical methods; and
  (b) the development of prescriptive working theories for various kinds of participants in legal processes, such as prescriptive theories of legislation, adjudication and legal reasoning.
(4) The conduit function, that is to say the systematic exploration at a general level of the relationship between law and at least the more general aspects of all other disciplines relevant to law. This is approximately equivalent to Julius Stone's view of jurisprudence as 'the lawyer's extraversion'.[2]
(5) The integrative or synthesizing function, that is to say, the task of exploring and articulating frames of reference which provide a *coherent* basis for law as a discipline, for legal discourse generally and for particular parts of it.[3]

The list is incomplete and there are many overlaps. But this formulation helps to bring out a number of points that are worth stressing in the present context.

First, legal theory in this broad sense encompasses a great diversity of questions. These questions arise from quite different concerns at different levels in varied contexts; appropriate responses to such questions are correspondingly diverse. Confusion of levels and conflation of questions foster the kind of artificial polemics to which jurisprudence is particularly prone. This way of mapping legal theory is, I think, more helpful and far less misleading than classifications in terms of 'schools' and 'isms' and 'ists'.

Secondly, this kind of map is a safeguard against the error of treating one part as if it were the whole. The most common version of this error today is the tendency to treat legal philosophy as coextensive with legal theory. It is unduly narrow, and impoverishes the discipline of law, to equate jurisprudence with legal philosophy or to treat philosophical questions as being the only, or the primary, worthwhile concern of every serious jurist. Questions which one kind of philosopher or another would treat as philosophical questions occupy a special place in legal theorizing. These are questions about the most general and, in a loose sense, the most fundamental assumptions of legal discourse. Such questions stand at the centre of legal theory; they also represent a critical point where boundaries between disciplines break down. For questions about justice or the nature of law or rights or reasonings, for example, are shared by philosophers, political theorists, social scientists and jurists on an almost equal footing. However, there are many general questions about law which also deserve to be treated as theoretical questions, but which are not peculiarly or exclusively philosophical. Prescriptive working theories for participants (e.g. a theory of appellate advocacy or judging); middle-order theories about legal phenomena (for example, a cross-cultural theory of litigation or dispute settlement) or a theoretical framework for a particular field of law or an area of legal discourse (such as a theory of contract or of criminal law) are examples of theorizing and theories which belong to jurisprudence, but fall outside, or at least go beyond legal philosophy – though they all, of course, have philosophical dimensions.

This view is not anti-philosophical. But it does strongly suggest that overconcentration on legal philosophy – on the more abstract problems of legal theory – may lead to the neglect of some other functions of legal theorizing, such as the construction and criticism of middle-order theories, of working theories for participants, and the devising of mapping theories, that is coherent frames of reference for law-as-a-discipline and for particular sectors thereof.

The theory of evidence provides a concrete illustration of this general view of law-as-a-discipline, and of the role of theorizing within it. It highlights one kind of theorizing which is particularly important at a time when established conceptions of academic law are being challenged and attempts are being made to construct or develop coherent alternatives. The emphasis will be on the integrative function – that is on mapping connections between different lines of enquiry and constructing coherent frames of reference; but the other main tasks of legal theorizing are also involved. Evidence scholarship has a rich, but extraordinarily homogeneous, intellectual heritage; there are numerous and rather complex connections with other disciplines, notably logic, epistemology, historiography, psychology, forensic science and forensic medicine. Much of our stock of existing theories takes the form of advice to particular participants, notably triers of fact, trial lawyers, detectives and, of course, Bentham's legislator. Some fundamental philosophical questions, not conventionally seen as having jurisprudential relevance, are central. And, I shall suggest, a theory of evidence and proof needs to be set in the context of – indeed it almost necessarily presupposes – a middle-order theory of litigation and like processes.

What follows then is a brief sketch of what might be involved in attempting to develop a coherent approach to the study of evidence and related matters within a conception of law as a discipline that is much broader than the orthodox rule-dominated, expository tradition of academic law. It is a case study of one way of trying to broaden the study of law from within in respect of a particular field or topic.

THE PROBLEM STATED

In the orthodox view, evidence is the means of proving or disproving facts, or of testing the truth of allegations of fact, in situations in which the triers of fact have no first-hand knowledge of the events or situations about which they have to decide what happened. Typically, decisions on disputed questions of fact are decisions to be taken in situations of uncertainty. In a broader view, that I shall develop later, 'evidence' is *information* from which further information is derived or inferred in a variety of contexts for a variety of purposes.

Most legal discourse about the subject of evidence is centred on the rules of evidence. The leading textbooks and treatises expound the rules and explore their rationales; public debate has tended to concentrate on the reform or conservation or codification of the rules – although there have been some significant moves away from this narrow perspective in recent years.[4] Most specialized writing about evidence by lawyers for lawyers reveals the same rather narrow range of questions and concerns. Nearly all courses on evidence are devoted almost exclusively to the rules; they are based almost entirely on appellate cases, statutes and secondary writings based on these sources. The most important arena in which problems of evidence and proof arise in practice is in the contested trial, but records and reports of trials are hardly ever looked at in courses on evidence – let alone made the object of systematic study. Yet the cases of Alger Hiss or Sacco and Vanzetti or Roger Tichborne or Alfred Dreyfus are potentially rich materials for law study, as important and as susceptible to disciplined analysis as *Hadley* v. *Baxendale* or *Donoghue* v. *Stevenson* or *D* v. *NSPCC*.[5] There is relatively little empirical research on the operation and impact of the rules. In short, the predominant conception of the field of evidence, by judges and practitioners as well as by scholars, teachers and students, is a rather clear case of the dominance of the expository or blackletter tradition. The subject of evidence is typically treated as being coextensive with the law of evidence.

This is strange for a number of reasons. First, the scope and practical importance of the rules of evidence have generally declined over the years. If Bentham had had his way there would have been no rules of evidence to study, but the subject would surely have remained an important part of the study of law.

Secondly, the dominant academic view of the law of evidence is that it is but a series of not very coherent exceptions to a general presumption of freedom of proof – that is an absence of formal rules. A variant of this view, often attributed to Thayer, was recently expressed by Professor Heydon as follows:

> The rules of evidence state what matters may be considered in proving facts and what weight they have. They are largely ununified and scattered, existing for disparate and sometimes conflicting reasons: they are a mixture of astonishing judicial achievements and sterile, inconvenient disasters. There is a law of contract, and perhaps to some extent a law of tort, but only a group of laws of evidence.[6]

Thirdly, there are quite well-established enclaves of study of problems of proof and proving in forensic contexts that have not been assimilated into the study of evidence within the discipline of law. The whole field of forensic science, psychological studies of eyewitness identification and the recent debate about probabilities are obvious examples. They are well-established lines of enquiry that have no settled place within the study of law. They float fragmented in a void, detached from any larger subject and from each other, randomly colliding or sailing past each other like meteorites.

Fourthly, there is a remarkable series of abortive attempts from Bentham through Wigmore to the present day to produce general theories of evidence that integrate the logical and the other aspects into a coherent whole. Almost without exception, they have failed to become established as standard ways of approaching the subject. There is a legacy of broad theories, but they have been largely forgotten.[7]

Fifthly, even within the expository tradition, it has been recognized as very dangerous to isolate evidence from procedure and procedure from substantive law. Yet evidence scholarship has done just that – quite systematically. The motives for this separation have quite often been worthy – to search for underlying principles, for example, or to simplify and to codify the rules of evidence. The result has been an extreme form of isolation that has left much evidence discourse largely unaffected by intellectual developments elsewhere.

This critique of the predominant mode of evidence discourse provides a basis for a preliminary statement of the problem of rethinking the field: if current treatments tend to be narrow, fragmented, artificially isolated from contiguous fields, unempirical and, above all, incoherent, then an adequate alternative needs to be comprehensive, coherent, realistic, empirical, contextual and sufficiently well integrated that the relations between different lines of enquiry are clearly mapped. This suggests that there is a need for a broad synthesizing or mapping theory that meets these standards.

INTELLECTUAL HISTORY

This general formulation of the problem will do as a start; but it requires refinement through more detailed probing. One way of doing this is through intellectual history – one of the standard tasks of the theorist.

There are, of course, many ways of approaching and justifying intellectual history. In the enterprise of rethinking a field, at least three perspectives are particularly helpful. One can look at past writings as a resource – as a treasury of particular questions, answers, concepts, arguments, errors, and so on. By reviewing the heritage of past work in the field as a whole, one can form some judgment of its strengths and weaknesses, spot imbalances and distortions, false trails and non-questions, as well as acceptable answers and other achievements. One can, in short, take stock and map out the current state of our collective knowledge, ignorance and disagreements. Communing with one's predecessors – at least those who seem worthy of attention – is also one of the most fruitful ways of clarifying one's own views. Criticism is, *inter alia*, a mode of self-definition. Such communion is also a powerful antidote to *hubris* – not least in the field of evidence, which is peopled by giants: Bentham, James and John Mill, Fitzjames Stephen, Thayer, Wigmore and a host of substantial figures who might have been treated as stars in a less rich tradition.

The stock of literature about or relevant to judicial evidence is vast. It includes not only the primary and secondary specialized legal literature of many jurisdictions, but also a wealth of spasmodically interacting writings from other disciplines. A full-scale intellectual history of this heritage would have to deal with classical, medieval and modern rhetoric; with the emergence of probability; with developments in psychology, forensic science and forensic medicine. These are all central. One also needs to identify possible parallels and connections with such fields as decision theory, information science, historiography and the sociology of knowledge.

Here I shall confine my remarks to something much narrower: specialized literature on judicial evidence in the Anglo-American tradition. This includes a mass of cases scattered throughout the law reports; an equally bulky and almost totally neglected accumulation of trial records and secondary accounts of such proceedings – a potentially rich source both for studying the law of evidence in action and of raw material for exercises in analysing mixed masses of evidence; in England, an unruly jungle of statutory bits and pieces; in other common law jurisdictions, a series of interesting attempts at codification – from the Indian Evidence Act 1872; various American codes, of which the most important is the Federal Rules of Evidence; and, looking to the future, a draft Canadian Code of Evidence that the late Sir Rupert Cross praised as being the best of the lot.[8] These statutory fragments and codes have almost all been preceded by public debates which have at least two notable characteristics: one is their repetitiveness – for example, the points of disagreement and arguments advanced in recent debates in England about the CLRC Report of 1972 and the Police and Criminal Evidence Act 1984 have many familiar echoes in the pages of the *Edinburgh Review* and other journals as far back as the 1820s.[9] A second characteristic has been that apart from a few hiccoughs, the trend has been almost entirely in the direction of the reduction of the scope and importance of the exclusionary rules – a stumbling trek in the direction indicated by Bentham, who favoured their total elimination. The trend is clear; whether it represents the march of progress towards rationality is much more debatable. In this instance, it is typically conservative proponents of law and order who claim to have reason on their side.

The secondary literature on evidence – despite its extent – represents only a tiny portion of this vast heritage. My own researches have been largely confined to this sector, which is more than enough for one individual. It is extraordinarily rich and has attracted some of the best legal minds, of whom Bentham, Wigmore and Thayer are the outstanding figures.[10]

All five functions of legal theorizing are amply represented in the specialized secondary literature on evidence. Bentham, Wigmore and others addressed directly fundamental philosophical problems of epistemology and logic. Bentham and Wigmore again tried to provide broad synthesizing theories which, *inter alia*, indicated important points of connection with other disciplines. Wigmore's *Science of Judicial Proof* represents the most systematic attempt to integrate the logical, psychological and scientific dimensions of proof within a single conceptual framework.[11] This was sufficiently flexible to accommodate at least some specific advances in those subjects over a period of some 40 years. The central concern of both writers was to advance largely middle-order working theories for participants – but different participants. Bentham's *Rationale* is consistently addressed to the legislator and, only indirectly through him, to the trier of fact. Wigmore's *Science* purports to adopt the standpoint of the trial attorney in court. The historical development of the law of evidence and of writings about it was treated at length by Thayer, Wigmore and Holdsworth. Rather surprisingly, not much detailed history of this kind has been done since.[12]

The weakest part of this heritage is on the empirical side – there is very little sustained work either at the level of empirical middle-order theorizing or in respect of detailed factual research. I shall return to this later. The relevant point here is that most of the functions of theorizing have been attended to in the past in respect of evidence, but almost no work of significance was done in the 50 years before the late 1970s. Thus it is not true that we have no tradition of theorizing about evidence; rather it is the case that this tradition has been almost entirely forgotten, at least until recently. Few evidence scholars have drawn on Bentham's *Rationale* or Wigmore's *Science of Judicial Proof* or the heritage of classical and modern rhetoric. Thus *Cross on Evidence*, the most influential contemporary English work in the field, contains only one citation of a theorist (Gulson), the most casual of references to Bentham and no reference to Wigmore's *Science* or even to his general theory of proof.

The most striking feature of this received tradition of evidence scholarship is how homogeneous it is. Nearly all of the Anglo-American writers from Gilbert to Cross have shared essentially the same basic assumptions about the nature and ends of adjudication and about what is involved in proving facts in this context.[13] There is undoubtedly a dominant underlying theory of evidence in adjudication, in which the central notions are truth, reason and justice under the law. It can be restated simply in some such terms as these: the primary end of adjudication is rectitude of decision, that is the correct application of rules of substantive law to facts that have been proved to an agreed standard of truth or probability. The pursuit of truth in adjudication must at times give way to other values and purposes, such as the preservation of state security or of family confidences; disagreements may arise as to what priority to give to rectitude of decision as a social value and to the nature and scope of certain competing values – for example, whether it makes sense to talk of procedural rights or to recognize a privilege against self-incrimination. But the end of the enterprise is clear: the establishment of truth.

There is also a broad consensus about means. Proving is seen as essentially a rational process, involving the weighing of the probative force of evidence relevant to specific allegations of fact. The primary difficulties involved are seen as practical rather than theoretical: it may be difficult to find or manufacture evidence, it may be difficult to get it before the trier of fact; it may be difficult to assess its reliability or to know how to decide when the evidence is incomplete or unreliable – hence the elaborate apparatus of burdens, presumptions and standards of proof which are essentially rules for or aids to decision in situations of uncertainty. But, by and large, the underlying assumptions as to what is involved are treated as if they are unproblematic. There is a world of fact independent of our beliefs about it; experience is the basis of belief; making inferences from evidence and reasoning about disputed questions of fact involve a straightforward application of ordinary common sense or practical reasoning; this in turn assumes a shared stock of knowledge in society – a sort of cognitive consensus – and a general ability on the part of most adult members of society to make rational judgments about issues of fact on the basis of their 'general experience' – what Jonathan Cohen calls a general cognitive competence.[14]

In short, nearly all Anglo-American writers seem by and large to have adopted, either explicitly or by implication, a particular ontology, epistemology and theory of logic. All of these are closely identified with a particular philosophical tradition, that is English empiricism, as exemplified by Locke, Bentham and John Stuart Mill. Evidence scholarship and theorizing have been characterized by a series of long-running debates and disagreements – for example, about the scope and justifications of exclusionary rules of evidence. These have almost invariably taken place within a framework of shared philosophical assumptions or by the almost systematic ducking or begging of difficult philosophical questions.[15] Thus most disagreements have not been seen as stemming from philosophical differences, except perhaps in relation to defenders and opponents of utilitarianism. The dominant tradition of evidence discourse has largely taken for granted a set of assumptions that bear the hallmark of the eighteenth-century enlightenment – what may be termed optimistic rationalism: one seeks the truth by observation and reason and if one seeks long enough the truth will out – most of the time.

Thus a stocktaking of our heritage of specialized scholarship and theorizing about evidence suggests the following: a clear and straightforward theory of proof integrated with a rather simplistic normative truth theory of adjudication. A collection of relatively sophisticated concepts and distinctions in respect of such matters as rationality, relevance, standards of proof and presumptions. A broad consensus among specialists that any deviation from a presumption in favour of freedom of proof requires justification; a lack of consensus about what constitute good justifications, with the result that there is a rich, but confusing body of literature on the rationales and practical utility of those particular deviations that make up the surviving laws of evidence in a given jurisdiction.

The great bulk of this heritage of specialized evidence scholarship has been normative rather than empirical. We have little systematic knowledge about the psychological processes of 'weighing' evidence, about the actual operation and impact of the rules of evidence, about the probative value of most kinds of evidence in respect of particular kinds of probanda or about how information is actually processed and used at different stages of litigation and like processes. Moreover, much of this specialized tradition is uncontextual – the tendency has been to concentrate on events in the courtroom in contested jury trials, rather than on what happens to information at every stage in a great variety of different processes and arenas. The Rationalist Tradition *is* simplistic; much of specialized evidence discourse postulates *one* law of evidence, *one* type of process, *one* kind of enquiry, and a single purpose or end to litigation. There is, moreover, no sustained concern to explore the implications of adopting more sceptical postures or a different conception of rationality.

Obviously, these sweeping generalizations are subject to exceptions and caveats. Here I want to develop the last point briefly: the essentially unsceptical nature of the Rationalist Tradition of evidence scholarship seems to contrast rather sharply with the tone of much contemporary writing on judicial processes.[16] This other body of literature is much more varied than the literature on evidence. It includes attempts to develop some middle-order empirical theories of dispute-settlement or litigation (e.g. Black, Abel, Griffiths);[17] it includes normative design theories of adjudication (e.g. Bentham); participant working theories (such as Llewellyn's Grand Style of Judging or Fuller's theory of rational adjudication)[18] and a vast agglomeration of contributions, written from a variety of perspectives, at different levels of generality by people from a wide range of disciplines. There is a strain of scepticism that runs through much of the literature that is strikingly absent from writings on evidence. Rabelais's Judge Bridlegoose throws dice to decide cases (a precedent followed in 1983 by Judge Alan Friess in New York);[19] trials are referred to as forensic lotteries or degradation ceremonies or licensed battles or conveyor belts. Some of the main survivals of the law of evidence, such as technical safeguards for the accused, have been attacked from the right as sacred cows[20] and from the left as harmful or useless obfuscating devices.[21]

This is not the place to examine these different kinds of scepticism in all their rich variety. What is striking is the extent to which we have two contrasting intellectual traditions that have developed largely in isolation from each other, although they deal with extensively overlapping subject-matter. The one is homogeneous, isolated, normative and optimistically rationalistic. The other is diverse and interdisciplinary; some of it is based on empirical research and much of the writing is sceptical, at least in tone. The aspirational rationalism of the evidence scholars is rooted in assumptions that belong to the eighteenth-century enlightenment; the more sceptical or realistic writers on judicial processes seem to be more the heirs of late-nineteenth-century and early-twentieth-century thought – of Croce, Collingwood, Freud, Mannheim, Marx and Weber.[22] Yet the potential incompatibilities between the two traditions may not be quite as fundamental as might at first sight appear; the rationalism of evidence writers is modified by some important caveats: for example, the pursuit of truth in adjudication is often subordinated to other values; their concern is with approximations to truth, with standards of proof expressed in terms of probabilities, rather than certainties; and the kind of reasoning involved is the 'soft logic' of open-system reasoning with regular acknowledgment that deductive reasoning and strict mathematical reasoning have limited scope in practice. Similarly few, if any, of the iconoclastic writers about judicial processes prove, on examination, to be genuine philosophical sceptics; many explicitly deny that they are 'extreme relativists'; in criticizing particular institutions the same writers often invoke the very standards of aspirational rationalism; and few, except in moments of rhetorical exaggeration, deny that truth, reason and justice are core concepts in any plausible prescriptive theory of adjudication.

The Rationalist Tradition of evidence scholarship has also been very largely isolated from other relevant but diverse fields, such as forensic medicine, forensic psychology, probability theory, epistemology and decision theory. In each case, the extent of interaction and the nature of the relationship is rather different.

For example, psychologists working on eyewitness identification have tended to accept rather uncritically some of the unsceptical assumptions of the Rationalist Tradition, even though the general tendency of much psychological work in this area is sceptical of the reliability of eyewitness testimony.[23]

PHILOSOPHICAL DIMENSIONS

A theory of evidence has to confront a number of questions that are clearly philosophical and so belong to the philosophy of law in a narrow or strict sense. As Bentham saw more clearly than most, questions about proving the truth of allegations about past facts are directly related to fundamental issues of ontology and epistemology. Is there a world of fact independent of our beliefs about it? Are warranted judgments about the truth of allegations of fact about objects and events in the real world possible in principle? What is the basis for such judgments? Professor Postema has recently shown that there is an intimate historical and analytical connection between Bentham's theory of fictions and his theory of evidence.[24] Bentham's ideas on evidence are founded on his epistemology and ontology: and his work on evidence may well have stimulated some of his later thoughts on logic and fictions. Closely related to these concerns is the persistent tradition of scepticism and relativism in philosophy; but as I have already indicated, just as few legal theorists are either fully fledged or solely specialist philosophers, similarly few legal sceptics are genuine philosophical sceptics.

A significant recent development has been a resurgence of interest in philosophical problems of probabilities and proof. This has been stimulated by Jonathan Cohen's work in the logic of induction and the series of lively controversies that this has provoked.[25]

These examples by no means exhaust the connections between philosophy and the theory of forensic evidence. A striking feature of these particular examples is that the points of contact are with areas of philosophy that are not commonly perceived as being central to jurisprudence. In recent years the most sustained connections between jurisprudence and philosophy have related to ethical, political and conceptual problems and to the nature of reasoning about disputed questions of law. The theory of evidence is also concerned with practical reasoning – mainly about disputed questions of fact; its links with probability theory, epistemology, historiography and the philosophy of science are relatively unfamiliar to lawyers.[26] Thus the resurgence of interest in this area involves extending the range of questions that may properly be regarded as central to the philosophical sector of jurisprudence. It is particularly welcome that there is a growing recognition that it really does not make much sense to confine the study of 'legal reasoning' or 'lawyers' reasonings' to disputed questions of law – another example of the narrowing influence of the expository tradition. Out of this may develop a much broader and richer perspective on questions about the nature of practical reasoning in legal discourse. Justifying, arguing towards and appraising decisions on questions of fact, questions of sentencing, assessment of damages, parole and many other important decisions in legal processes involve a complex mixture of philosophical issues about the nature of practical reasoning and of other kinds of questions about the nature of legal processes; these in turn raise interesting and relatively neglected questions about the interrelationship between forms and styles of reasoning and different kinds of practical decisions. For example: To what extent do modes of reasoning accepted to be appropriate to questions of law, questions of fact and questions of sentencing exhibit the same logical structure? To what extent do contextual factors generate different criteria of relevance and of appropriateness? – and so on.

MIDDLE-ORDER THEORY

If the appropriateness of modes of reasoning about questions of fact or other important reasonings in legal processes is to a greater or lesser extent dependent on the contexts of the decisions involved, we need to try to understand something about these contexts. Here I should make an admission. When I started on my work on the theory of evidence I defined the topic as 'theoretical aspects of evidence and proof in adjudication'. The reference to 'adjudication' signalled that I was mainly concerned with decisions on disputed questions of fact by adjudicators, that is judges, juries and other third-party triers of fact. I realized, although not clearly enough, that there must be an intimate relationship between a theory of legal evidence and a theory of adjudication – that adjudicative decisions on questions of fact take place in the context of what are commonly referred to as adjudicative or judicial processes and that the notion of these processes is problematic. As my work progressed, this organizing category came to seem less and less satisfactory. The reasons for this are too complex to retail here, but one can put the matter in simplified form as follows:[27] terms like 'adjudicative process' and 'judicial process' are misleading insofar as they distract attention from the truism that adjudicative decisions are always preceded and succeeded by a series of other decisions – such as decisions to prosecute or to sue; not to settle; to plead not guilty, to appeal and so on. It is an accepted part of the study of so-called judicial processes that adjudicative decisions cannot be understood in a vacuum. They need to be seen as one stage – which is usually not reached in practice – in a complex form of social process that we know as legal process or litigation. The interaction between adjudicative decisions and events that precede and succeed them is so complex and so intimate that it is perilous to study them in isolation. Strictly speaking it is misleading to speak of adjudicative or judicial *processes*, as if these are something other than *stages* in some longer process. Similarly the same bit of information may start as a clue (or lead) in the process of detection, be transmuted, possibly transformed, into potential evidence (e.g. in the form of a deposition or a written confession) and play a role in a whole variety of decisions, before it is presented – perhaps in a new form, if at all – directly to the trier of fact as evidence. The same bit of information may subsequently have a role to play at later stages, for example, in sentencing and parole; again it may appear in different forms at these stages.[28] A theory of evidence, in this view, needs to give an account of how information is or may be processed and used at all the important stages in the process, and not just at the adjudicative stage. In short, a contextual approach pushes one to substitute for evidence and proof in adjudication, as an organizing concept, something like the processing and use of information in litigation.[29] The prospect of thus broadening the scope of the enquiry is rather daunting; but it may be the best way of avoiding some of the distortions, omissions and artificialities of the more traditional modes of discourse.

One can elaborate this point briefly by returning to Bentham. One of the strengths of his theory of evidence, as with so much of his jurisprudence, is that it is closely integrated with many other aspects of his thought, and the connections are pretty clearly indicated. Thus his theory of evidence is part of his general theory of adjective law (including procedure and judicial organization) which in turn fits into the framework of the constitutional code. This in turn is but one part of his 'pannomion' – or complete body of laws – which in turn is founded on utility. Within his theory of evidence the interconnections between procedure, substantive law and the logical, psychological, epistemological and scientific aspects of proof are all fairly clearly sketched. Their place in his grand design is also clearly mapped. Bentham's theory of adjective law is *par excellence* an example of a design theory, that is to say it is an integrated body of recommendations addressed to the ideal legislator for the design of a body of institutions, procedures and laws in accordance with utility. His *Rationale of Judicial Evidence* has, with some justification, been called his masterpiece.[30] It is remarkable that it has been almost forgotten in this century. It still repays careful study. But, for my purposes, it has proved to be seriously deficient. Setting aside particular points where it is outdated or Bentham's judgments were idiosyncratic or distorted by his passions, one can single out three main limitations. First, it involves a direct and all-too-consistent application of the principle of utility in a way which reveals both the intellectual power and the unacceptable consequences of unmodified utilitarianism. He is dismissive of the presumption of innocence and other safeguards, he places too much faith in publicity as the main safeguard against the abuse of power, and he is even prepared to condone a limited use of institutionalized torture.[31] While his analysis reveals very clearly the intellectual weaknesses of some of the arguments that have traditionally been advanced by civil libertarians, his lack of concern for the protection of the innocent and his dismissal of central ideas of due process as mere sentimentality cannot, I think, be explained away merely as miscalculations that can be adjusted within utilitarianism. My personal attitude is one of respectful ambivalence and, on some issues, Bentham seems to me to be best regarded as a worthy enemy.

Secondly, Bentham's theory is, in essence, very simple. The direct end of procedure is the correct application of substantive law to true facts in accordance with utility, subject to preponderant vexation, expense and delay. The truth of allegations of fact is to be tested by ordinary methods of common-sense reasoning within a framework of free proof. The simplicity and coherence of the theory give it enormous clarity and persuasive force – but it is too simple. Even in his day, I think that it was unrealistic to try to postulate a set of institutions designed simply to serve a single direct end. His model of the Natural System of Procedure – despite its attractions – smacks more of Rousseau than Bentham.

In any society and especially in modern industrial society, institutionalized litigation has to cope with a variety of demands, often conflicting, in an enormous range of types of case raising a great variety of types of problems, involving in respect of evidence, proof of many different kinds of fact by a multiplicity of means. For example, I do not think that straightforward implementation of law and enforcement of rights are the only desired or desirable outcomes of litigation. Compromise, termination of conflict, redistribution of goods, focusing of public attention, political or legal change and many other ends for which litigation is in fact used are sometimes justifiable ends and need to be accommodated in institutional design.[32] At best, Bentham's theory is one possible ideal-type for certain kinds of standard cases.

Thirdly, Bentham's theory is solely an aspirational, prescriptive – in some aspects Utopian – theory.[33] It is part of a tradition that has made almost no attempt to advance knowledge and understanding of the actual operation and effects of legal processes empirically. Even an adequate design needs to be based not only on a clear normative theory, but also on a realistic and differentiated appreciation of how things work in practice and of what is feasible. A middle-order empirical theory of litigation, and of the processing and uses of information within it, may contribute not only to better designs, but also to a better understanding of social processes and phenomena, including law. The study of evidence needs to be empiricized and here Bentham's work is of only limited value. In this respect we are likely to obtain more help from elsewhere.

PARTICIPANT WORKING THEORIES

Bentham's prescriptions were addressed to the legislator and through him to the judge in the form of instructions about the weighing of evidence. Some of his advice is also relevant to others; but there are clearer examples of participant working theories. The most prominent of these is Wigmore's *Science of Judicial Proof*, which is directly relevant to the trial lawyer in court and almost equally valuable for him in preparing for trial and for all who are involved at the stages of investigation or in the processes of collecting, recording and manufacturing evidence.[34] Wigmore provides a framework for accommodating the findings of forensic science and psychology as they bear on assessing the probative force of various kinds of evidence in respect of different probanda – ranging from the probative force of fingerprints in proving identity to what the 'science' of his day had to tell us about the influence of gender, race and age on the veracity of witnesses – almost nothing. This aspect of his work seems to the modern reader to be both old-fashioned and naive, but his application of some simple methods of logic to the analysis and organization of complex, mixed masses of evidence is of lasting value and deserves to be better known. In my own teaching, I have been getting students to undertake detailed analysis of complex trial records using a modified version of Wigmore's method; Professors Anderson and Ewald of the University of Miami have been using the same scheme for injecting an element of analytical rigour into teaching the elements of trial court practice[35] and Professor David Schum, a psychologist at Rice University, has used Wigmore's theory as the basis for some impressive theoretical and empirical work about how triers of fact actually reason from evidence in simulated trials.[36] It is hoped that some of this work will be made available in a form that will be of immediate practical value, not least in the direct teaching of some important practical skills.

Nearly 90 years ago Oliver Wendell Holmes said: 'for the rational study of the law the black-letter man may be the man of the present, but the man of the future is the man of statistics and the master of economics'.[37] It is only relatively recently that this theme has been taken up by Sir Richard Eggleston and a number of others, who have emphasized how a basic grasp of elementary mathematics and statistics is an essential part of the equipment of the practitioner in handling evidentiary matters even in contexts in which formal statistical analysis cannot be openly or directly applied.[38] The trial lawyer may be able to pick up without formal training some of the general lessons that psychologists have to teach or what he needs to know about forensic science and medicine; but ability to analyse and evaluate evidence is as important and fundamental a part of the intellectual discipline of law as ability to analyse and argue about rules.[39]

So far I have reported to you a few, highly selective impressions and conclusions arising from some research into the history of specialized writings on evidence. The main conclusions that emerge from this part is that there is a vast range of different kinds of questions that are worth asking in respect of evidence; that our stock of answers to these questions is fragmented and uneven; and that perhaps the first need is for a broad coherent framework that would map the relations between a range of different lines of enquiry that seem to converge and interact in complex ways in the context of the study of what Bentham called 'judicial evidence'. In short, what is needed is a synthesizing or mapping theory. One possible perspective, to which I am personally attracted, is to look at questions about evidence and proof as questions about the processing and uses of information in the context of the total process of litigation, broadly conceived. This, I think, would at least provide the prospect of mapping and co-ordinating different approaches and specialized lines of enquiry in a way that would meet at least some of the criticisms of the underlying theory of the Rationalist Tradition, while preserving such notions as truth, reason and justice as core concepts.

Many standard topics would look quite different from that perspective. To take but one example, the problem of eyewitness identification. In the orthodox view, as exemplified by the Devlin Report and notorious cases such as George Davis, Luke Dougherty and Oscar Slater, the problem of misidentification is perceived as a problem of *unreliable evidence* in contested jury trials.[40] The perceived evil is that there is a risk of wrongful conviction and imprisonment of a few persons accused of serious crime – perhaps six to a dozen a year in England. If, however, one adopts a total process model of litigation, one is concerned with the processing and uses of information at every stage in criminal and other proceedings. From this perspective the problem of misidentification has to be redefined quite radically. Identification statements are seen not merely as *evidence* presented to a jury, but as *information* that performs a variety of functions in a series of *decisions*: decisions to investigate, to arrest, to interrogate, to hold an identification parade, to confess or to plead guilty – to mention the most obvious criminal examples. In criminal proceedings, the *mischiefs* of misidentification are all of the substantial harms suffered by victims (i.e. objects of false identification statements). They extend beyond wrongful conviction to include all the vexations and expenses of being subjected to legal proceedings – the financial, psychological and other evils of being suspected, harassed, interrogated, arrested, threatened with prosecution, cautioned, or even tried and acquitted. The category of victims of misidentification statements is correspondingly enlarged. Vandals, demonstrators, football supporters and juveniles are likely to outnumber the alleged murderers, professional thieves and robbers who have occupied centre stage in the traditional debates. Problems of misidentification are seen to arise in other proceedings and arenas; and the nature of the problem, as well as its scale, looks rather different.

All of this has implications for research as well as reform. For example, most psychologists have by and large accepted rather uncritically the orthodox definition of the problem – as concerning unreliable evidence in contested jury trials. As a result they have concentrated on a rather narrow range of issues and, in particular, on that ungainly device, the identification parade – often with a distorted view of its importance and its actual functions in practice: they tend to see it solely as an evidence-manufacturing device, overlooking the fact that it may serve to eliminate suspects, to lead to closing a case for lack of evidence or to securing the co-operation of a suspect by persuading him that the game is up.

The example of misidentification suggests that a mapping theory can do more than merely provide a coherent framework for charting relations between traditional questions and established lines of enquiry; it may also identify new or neglected questions or suggest that old ones were misposed. And this may lead both to different lines of enquiry and to new perceptions of connections with established enclaves of knowledge that had not previously been seen to be relevant. However, suggesting that a different perspective may provide a more coherent and suggestive framework for approaching a field such as evidence falls far short of advancing a general theory of evidence. A mapping theory charts relations between lines of enquiry and raises questions; a general theory purports to provide answers to such questions.

Here I wish to sound a note of caution. In an epiphanic moment in my adolescence my father, quite matter of factly, asked me: 'What are flowers for?'; he hardly paused for an answer. If I were asked today, 'What is a theory of evidence for?', it would be tempting to make some grand utilitarian claims: to organize a mass of divergent material; to guide practice; to generate hypotheses; to restructure courses; to devise new institutions; to reorient or update public debate; to provide a rationale for conservation, reform or radical action. A fully worked-out theory of evidence might modestly or immodestly contribute to all these ends. But I am reminded of a famous introductory lecture at University College by A. E. Housman in 1892, in which he effectively mocked shortsighted and mundane justifications of science as missing the point. He concluded that 'the true aim of science is something other than utility. . . . Men who have risen, if you call it rising, from barge boys to millionaires have not risen by their knowledge of science.'[41]

I am much of Housman's mind. I would also carry his scepticism a little further. Jurisprudence is often presented – especially to students – as a bewildering and diverse collection of refined products called 'theories' as if it were a sort of motley exhibition of mud-pies or sandcastles – of alleged 'schools' and 'isms' – which they are invited to peruse, evaluate, admire or destroy. Of the many fallacies involved in this mud-pie image of theorizing two need to be laughed out of court: the first is the fallacy of treating all theories of or about law as comparables and rivals – indeed to treat them as more or less solid things like mud-pies. The second is to assume that the only positive outcome of theorizing is the manufacture of theories. The activity of theorizing is much more varied than that. Some jurists do produce collections of answers that are tangible enough to be praised for their elegance or their explanatory power or to be used for target practice. But that is only one of many ways of advancing understanding.

It is tempting to move from a critique of past theories to a bold clarion call proclaiming the need for a new theory. My remarks on evidence could be interpreted as a call for a Brand New Theory of Evidence for the Modern Age. But this is also too neat and too simple. In sketching one possible way of developing a different perspective on evidence and information in litigation, I have been suggesting that legal theorists have a constructive role to play in building bridges, sculpting syntheses or hatching theories. The study of evidence also reminds us that all such structures are built on shifting sands. We may have to wait many years for a new theory of evidence to emerge, probably as the work of many minds; if it does, however useful or illuminating it may be, it will not be difficult to show up the flimsiness of its foundations, whatever its particular form and content. Meanwhile, there is one further job for the jurist to undertake in his daily work – to examine critically the underlying assumptions of all legal discourse and to question established ways of thought, especially those that are becoming entrenched. One task of the theorist is to pick away at all assumptions, including his own. Whether he adopts the role of court jester or the Innocent in *Boris Godunov* or the child in the story of the Emperor's clothes or any other form of hired subversive – his first job is to ask questions and, with the greatest respect to the greatest of our gurus, to let the consequences take care of themselves.

NOTES

1 This is an abbreviated version of an inaugural lecture, delivered at University College, London on 2 June 1983 and published in (1984) 47 *Modern Law Rev.* 261. It is reprinted here with minor revisions by kind permission of the editor of the *Modern Law Review* and Sweet and Maxwell Ltd. The intention of this paper is to restate and develop in general terms a number of themes that have been explored at greater length in a series of writings over 12 years. The view of legal theory and its place in the discipline of law is advanced in (1) 'Some Jobs for Jurisprudence' (1974) *Brit. J Law and Society* 149 and (2) 'Academic Law and Legal Philosophy: The Significance of Herbert Hart' (1979) 95 *Law Quarterly Rev.* 557 and (3) 'The Great Juristic Bazaar' (1978) *J Society of Public Teachers of Law* (NS) 185. A programmatic statement of the need for rethinking the field of evidence is set out in (4) 'Good-bye to Lewis Eliot' (1980) *J Society of Public Teachers of Law* (NS) 9; the intellectual history of Anglo-American evidence theorizing and scholarship is explored in detail in (5) 'The Rationalist Tradition of Evidence Scholarship' in *Well and Truly Tried* (1982; ed. Louis Waller and Enid Campbell) p. 211; (6) *'Theories of Evidence: Bentham and Wigmore'* (1985); and (7) 'Some

Scepticism about Some Scepticisms', I (1983) *J Law and Society* 137, II (1984) *J Law and Society* 285; the educational implications are examined in (8) 'Taking Facts Seriously' in (1984) 34 *J Legal Education* 22; and particular applications of this perspective are developed in (9) 'Identification and Misidentification: Redefining the Problem' in *Evaluating Witness Evidence* (1983; ed. S. Lloyd-Bostock and B. Clifford) p. 255; (10) *Analysis of Evidence* (with Terence Anderson, teaching materials) (1984); (11) 'Anatomy of a Cause Célèbre: The Evidence in Bywaters and Thompson' (Earl Grey Memorial Lecture, Newcastle (1982)); and (12) 'Debating Probabilities' (1980) 2 *Liverpool Law Rev.* 51. I am particularly indebted to the Social Science Research Council for a personal research grant which provided the opportunity to work on theoretical aspects of evidence and proof full-time during 1980-1. For ease of reference these works will be cited hereafter in the following form: *op. cit.*, n. 1, no. 3 at p. 187.

2 Julius Stone, *Legal System and Lawyers' Reasonings* (1964) p. 16.

3 See further, *op. cit.*, n. 1, nos 1 and 2.

4 E.g. *Report of the Royal Commission on Criminal Process* (1981; Cmnd 8092).

5 See further, *op. cit.*, n. 1, nos 9-12.

6 J. D. Heydon, *Cases and Materials on Evidence* (2nd edn; 1984) p. 3.

7 *Op. cit.*, n. 1, nos 5 and 8.

8 E.g. R. Cross, *Evidence* (5th edn; 1979) p. 4.

9 Discussed in *op. cit.*, n. 1, no. 6.

10 For an historical overview, see *op. cit.*, n. 1, no. 5.

11 J. H. Wigmore, *Principles of Judicial Proof* (1913, 1931); the third edition was entitled *The Science of Judicial Proof* (1937), but this change was of no intellectual significance.

12 For references to historical writings on evidence since Wigmore, see Wigmore 1, *Treatise* (Tillers rev.; 1983) §8.

13 *Op. cit.*, n. 1, no. 5. The most notable exception is the Scottish writer James Glassford, whose An Essay on the Principles of Evidence and their Application to Subjects of Judicial Inquiry (1820) adopted an holistic rather than an 'atomistic' approach to the evaluation of evidence. Glassford's work is discussed by M. A. Abu Hareira *A Holistic Approach to the Analysis and Examination of Evidence in Anglo-American Judicial Trials*, (1984), unpublished doctoral thesis, University of Warwick.

14 L. Jonathan Cohen, 'Freedom of Proof' in *Facts in Law* (1983; ed. W. Twining) p. 1 at pp. 6 *et seq*. Cohen also uses the terms 'cognitive capacity' and 'cognitive ability' in this context.

15 *Op. cit.*, n. 1, no. 7.

16 *Id.*

17 See esp. J. Griffiths and D. Black in D. Black (ed.), *Towards a General Theory of Social Control* (1984) and Abel, 'A Comparative Theory of Dispute Institutions in Society' (1973) 8 *Law and Society Rev.* 217; cf. Griffiths, 'The general theory of litigation - a first step' (1983) 5 *Zeitschrift für Rechtssoziologie*, Heft 2.5.145.

18 K. N. Llewellyn, *The Common Law Tradition: Deciding Appeals* (1960); L. Fuller, *The Principles of Social Order* (1981; ed. K. Winston) at pp. 86 *et. seq.*; R. Summers *Lon. L. Fuller* (1984).

19 *New York Law Journal* 17 April 1983.

20 E.g. Cross, 'The Right to Silence and the Presumption of Innocence - Sacred Cows or Safeguards of Liberty?' (1970) 11 *J Society of Public Teachers of Law* (NS) 66.

21 E.g. D. McBarnett, *Conviction* (1981), discussed *op. cit.*, n. 1, no. 7.

22 See generally H. Stuart Hughes, *Consciousness and Society* (1958).

23 See *op. cit.*, n. 1, no. 9.

24 G. Postema, 'Facts, Fictions and Law: Bentham on the Foundations of Evidence' in *Facts in Law, op. cit.*, p. 37.

25 Esp. L. Jonathan Cohen, *The Probable and the Provable* (1977). For a bibliography of the recent debates see *Facts in Law, op. cit.*, at pp. 156–7.

26 This is less true of continental Europe where there is considerable interest in questions of epistemology and the philosophy of science.

27 See further *op. cit.*, n. 1, nos 7 and 9.

28 The question how far information and evidence can be appropriately individuated into 'bits' and how far it is safe to talk of 'the same bit' at different stages in a process are important issues that need further exploration.

29 On the use of 'litigation' as an organizing category see Griffiths, *op. cit.*

30 Mary Mack, *Jeremy Bentham: An Odyssey of Ideas* (1962) p. 3. See *op. cit.*, n. 1, no. 6.

31 See further W. and P. Twining, 'Bentham on Torture' in *Bentham and Legal Theory* (1973; ed. M. James) p. 39; Twining, 'Why Bentham?' (1984) 8 *The Bentham Newsletter* 34.

32 In *Scotch Reform* Bentham said: 'Another mode of termination is by what is called a *compromise*: which, being interpreted, is *denial of justice.*' 5 *Works* 35 (ed. Bowring) discussed in *op. cit.*, n. 1, no. 6. The nature of litigation has, of course, changed radically since Bentham's day; for example, trials have become much longer and more complex than in 1800; much more emphasis is put on documentary evidence; techniques of preserving evidence and of discovery have changed beyond recognition; various kinds of discretions of adjudicators have been much enlarged. Bentham would have approved, of some, but not all, of these developments. But his simple model of the adjective law as being directed solely to the efficient enforcement of substantive law does not fit the varied purposes, functions and types of modern litigation in its broadest sense.

33 See however, H. L. A. Hart, *Essays on Bentham* (1983) p. 37n.

34 *Op. cit.*, n. 11, discussed in *op. cit.*, n. 1, no. 6.

35 See further *op. cit.*, n. 1, no. 10.

36 See especially Schum and Martin, 'Formal and Empirical Research on Cascaded Inference' (1982) 17 *Law and Society Rev.* 105 and references there. In my view, the work of Schum and his associates represents one of the most significant contributions both to the theory of evidence and to empirical research in the field in recent years.

37 'The Path of the Law' (1897) 10 *Harvard Law Rev.* 457, 469.

38 R. Eggleston, *Evidence, Proof and Probability* (2nd edn; 1983); David W. Barnes, *Statistics as Proof* (1983). See further, bibliography, *op. cit.*, n. 25.

39 This notion is developed in *op. cit.*, n. 1, no. 8.

40 *Id.*

41 A. E. Housman, 'Introductory Lecture', University College, 1892 (1933 reprint) p. 8.

5
The Law of Property and Legal Theory

ROGER COTTERRELL

What can legal theory offer to the understanding of contemporary property law? This paper seeks to suggest some answers to this question. But the analysis of property and property law is used here primarily to illustrate a view of the nature of legal theory and of some of its applications. So this paper is more concerned with outlining and illustrating a conception of legal theory than with unravelling contemporary problems of the property law field. Nevertheless it attempts to show how theory may help to clarify some of these problems.

Property law provides a particularly interesting field within which to explore the relationship between legal theory and legal doctrine. In the traditional view at least,

> the law of property, and more especially the law of real property, presents in almost every respect a marked contrast to the rest of the law. . . . It is logical and orderly, its concepts are perfectly defined, and they stand in well recognised relations to one another. . . . Above all, this part of the law is intensely abstract. . . . The various concepts had, and still have, when properly understood, a very necessary relation to the economic facts of life, but once created and defined they seem to move among themselves according to the rules of a game which exists for its own purposes. . . . More than anywhere else we seem to be moving in a world of pure ideas from which everything physical or material is entirely excluded.[1]

Property law offers richly stocked and highly developed fields of doctrine in which to test legal theory's claim to aid the understanding and interpretation of legal ideas.

However, when we move from the traditional core of property law – real property – to its expanding periphery where rights to many new, or newly recognized and debated, forms of wealth are in issue the image of property law as a game played according to known and well-tried rules seems less appropriate. Even the nature and purposes of the game itself may be seriously in issue. The meaning of the term 'property' or the utility of invoking it as a basis of legal intervention and as an organizing concept for legal doctrine may seem increasingly questionable. Furthermore, even in the traditional core doctrinal areas of rights in land, fundamental questions about the appropriate objects of legal protection have re-emerged in Anglo-American law in recent years to remind us that property law is the basic legal expression of the nature of economic life in all its aspects. Here, as in all other areas of law, doctrine has to be understood in relation to the social context in which it gains its significance as a mode of regulating behaviour.

Legal doctrine in the property field thus has a formidable 'rational strength'. At the same time its central social and economic importance in changing Western societies creates tensions within it which appear increasingly serious. If we are to understand both the power of doctrinal abstractions in this area and their limits – when social, economic or other pressures break through them and force us to revise or discard them – we need aid from outside legal doctrine itself. We need methods of interpreting it and showing the wider context in which its characteristics and problems are formed. Legal theory may provide the means. But what kind of legal theory?

In the following sections an attempt will be made, first, to outline a conception of legal theory which may be of service in this context; secondly, to identify some general contemporary problems in the property law field as they present themselves in ordinary legal analysis; and thirdly, to consider how legal theory may provide aid in understanding the nature and causes of these problems.

THEORY AND DOCTRINE

What kind of legal theory can provide a means of interpreting legal doctrine in the ways suggested above? It would seem to need to be theory which is both 'inside' legal doctrine as lawyers[2] comprehend and use it, understanding the manner and techniques of lawyers' interpretation of doctrine in legal reasoning and discourse, and also 'outside' it, understanding its significance in the wider society beyond the limited professional world in which it is typically formed. In this writer's view, therefore, the kinds of enquiries which have typified analytical jurisprudence even in its broadened modern forms need to be set in (and substantially modified by) a wider theoretical context drawing on social theory. The theoretical study of legal doctrine and legal institutions – if it is to add significantly to the lawyer's perception of doctrine and institutions – needs to be set in the context of a wide theoretically informed view of the nature of societies: of their structure and of the conditions and forms of stability and change in them.[3]

This necessarily involves a rather complex and uneasy relationship between legal theory – which on this view needs to integrate a wide variety of kinds of enquiry within a unified framework of explanation – and claims regarding law as an autonomous discipline. Legal theory is described by William Twining, in the course of a valuable attempt to set out an integrative conception of theory, as 'the theoretical part of law as a discipline',[4] but immediately problems arise with this formulation since everything turns on what is meant by 'law as a discipline'. Twining remarks that law cannot and should not have rigid boundaries which segregate it from other disciplines. The study of law is asserted to be 'part of a general intellectual enterprise, the direct end of which is the advancement of knowledge and understanding',[5] and this is surely correct. Nevertheless, he claims that one of the tasks of legal theory is to help to make the discipline of law more coherent and integrated and another is to connect law as a discipline with other disciplines relevant to it.[6] At the same time it is said that the notion of an autonomous discipline or pure science of law 'has, at most, a very limited place'.[7] On the one hand, the idea of law as the basis of a distinct discipline is asserted; on the other, it seems to be substantially denied.

Twining seems to use the term 'discipline' in an extremely loose sense. But what is typically implied by those who talk of the discipline of law is an important element of *uniqueness* and a significant intellectual *autonomy* in lawyers' methods of analysis. Lawyers do plainly engage in quite distinctive forms of practice and it is often very important to professional legal practice to adhere to the idea of an autonomous science of law.[8] But a rigorous legal theory should treat the claims made in favour of 'pure' legal method as part of its subject-matter, as matters to be examined and explained. When law is asserted to be a discipline without an exact specification and elaboration (in comparison with other disciplines, practices and forms of analysis) of what it is which makes legal analysis autonomous or unique in some respects, the assertion has all the flavour of an ideological pronouncement: an assertion that legal questions can be answered by asking other legal questions; that law consists of 'lawyers' issues'; that legal knowledge is somehow self-standing; that the epistemology on which it is founded needs no examination, being expressed satisfactorily in well-understood and taken-for-granted lawyers' traditions of thought and practice. In my view legal theory should not merely replicate legal ideology and its taken-for-granted certainties. It should analyse and explain legal ideology so as to help towards a better understanding of the social significance of legal ideas.[9] Thus it is more appropriate for legal theory to treat law as a *field of experience* than as a discipline; a rather heterogeneous subject of study centred on a variety of types and problems of regulation potentially involving a wide diversity of practices, techniques, modes of thought and forms of knowledge. The boundaries of this subject are, of course, fixed by its focus on the institutions and practices which we choose to specify as legal, a choice which must itself be theoretically justified.

It follows from the postulate that law is a field of experience – of modes of thought and action and of forms of knowledge and practice – that the theoretical problem of identifying the field of law is not that of finding some inherent or natural 'essence' of law, for example in terms of fundamental legal values, principles or concepts; or in terms of a certain logical structure of normative systems; or of distinctive formal patterns of authority. It is that of marking out an intelligible area of empirically analysable social phenomena. Thus the task of conceptualizing 'law' is more like that of defining, say, 'urban problems' in urban sociology, or 'medicine' in medical sociology, or 'transport' in transport economics, or 'the public sector' in public sector economics. Since law, on this view, is an aspect of society, the empirical theory required both to identify it as a field of study and to provide fundamental guidance in understanding the most general features of that field is necessarily social theory. But it is important to stress that identifying a field of experience is not necessarily the same as identifying a 'discipline'.

Legal theory can thus best serve the need for better understanding of the nature of law by an agnosticism about law's disciplinary claims. It follows that it can make no commitment to make law more 'coherent' or 'integrated' as a discipline. However, by seeking to explain the conditions shaping the development of contemporary law, it may perhaps suggest how far such aims are feasible. But its sole essential commitment ought to be to better understanding of the nature of law, and this requires that it refuse to ally itself unconditionally with the interests of any particular type of participant in legal processes (lawyer, legislator, judge, policeman, litigant, etc.). Since this commitment involves continually trying to transcend the partial perspectives on law of these various participants, it may, as Professor Twining suggests, help to break down barriers dividing off 'the academic from the applied, theory from practice, the law in books from the law in action'.[10] But it is very important to see this as a possible by-product of legal theory, not as one of its functions, for these barriers are – in a variety of forms in a variety of contexts – part of the world of law which theory should seek above all to understand and explain.

Legal theory cannot ignore or dismiss participants' perspectives. But neither is it very useful to adopt a despairing relativism, assuming that all such perspectives are of equal worth. Some perspectives on law are more comprehensive, better informed and more rigorously thought through than others. They are better able to understand rival perspectives and explain, interpret or incorporate them, revealing their assumptions and limitations. Legal theory should, if it is to be a sustained contribution to the deeper understanding of law, constantly aim for a unifying perspective which incorporates and transcends limited participant perspectives. Even if such an aim may never be realized, to reject it as an aim is to condemn the study of law to the incoherence of a babel of voices drowning out each other; an incoherence which must become more hopeless as the study of law expands its tolerant 'pluralism' to give a hearing to a continually widening range of participant views on law.

This is true no less at the level of what Twining calls 'high theory'[11] than at the level of day-to-day involvement in legal affairs. Of course Rawls and Durkheim, for example, as 'high theorists' of law in society from different intellectual traditions do have something in common, although not nearly as much as, say, Weber and Hayek. But one must surely recognize that radically different kinds of feats are being attempted by different writers in this pantheon of high theory. Some are apparently creating theory to demonstrate the purity of legal discourse, others constructing value systems for Western democracy, others attempting to provide a basis for the systematic study of social behaviour. Still others are trying combinations of these and other aims. An integrative legal theory cannot ultimately be satisfied with collecting all these writers' products somewhat indiscriminately together in an undifferentiated general category as high theory or legal philosophy. A writer's answers to the questions he has set himself cannot be condemned by reference to the findings of another writer concerned with quite different questions. However, all the high theorists of legal theory share a concern with the fundamental question of the nature of law. This common focus may allow us to test the adequacy or significance of the *questions* asked by one theorist by reference to the findings of another theorist of perhaps quite different orientation.

It might be said, for example, that Durkheim makes explicit some of the sociological assumptions on which a theory of justice such as Rawls's ultimately rests; or that Kelsen's pure theory is, in part, an elaboration and rationalization of one particularly important type of legal thought among the several types which Weber links with particular political, social and historical conditions in his massive picture of legal and social history. Such linkings of contrasting theorists are contentious and used here only as tentative illustrations. The point, however, is that an attempt to link such very different kinds of theory by such means may ultimately be necessary to clarify the scope and place of each, to make possible an identification of its limitations and explanatory power by broadening the perspective within which it is considered.

Where do these considerations leave us in determining the utility of legal theory in the analysis of legal doctrine? Theory should aid the lawyer not, it seems to me, by joining with him in his own kind of participation in law; not by helping his rationalization of doctrine by means of improved classifications and definitions. Theory should attempt to put the lawyer's analytical problems into a wider perspective by showing the nature of legal doctrine as it appears in a broader view than that which the lawyer's immediate professional concerns dictate. This broader view comes from the attempt to explain *why* doctrine has a particular form and content at a given time and place, what forces – not just within the legal professional environment but within the social and political environment as a whole – have acted to produce this situation, what consequences follow from it for other aspects of society beyond those to which the lawyer's immediate concerns directly relate, what social forces are acting to bring about doctrinal change, and what directions of doctrinal change appear likely in the light of this analysis. Every one of these enquiries denies the claims of a pure science of law and of law's disciplinary autonomy. They operationalize the assumption that the only real aid to understanding which theory can offer the practising or academic lawyer (or any other legal participant) is a framework of thought in which to extend the necessarily partial perspectives derived from his specific form of involvement with law. In what follows an attempt will be made to apply some of these ideas in discussion of aspects of property law.

ASPECTS OF PROPERTY: PROBLEMS IN THE ORGANIZATION OF LEGAL DOCTRINE

For lawyers, classification of legal doctrine is part of the enterprise of rationalizing legal rules and ideas; organizing the complexity of law as doctrine in ways which make it manageable as a body of knowledge and predictable in its consequences. The classification of a body of law as 'property law' may serve to identify either the legal doctrine relating to a particular area of problems or situations in economic and social life (so-called fact-based classification) or a body of doctrine defining rights or duties or legal arrangements of a kind distinct from those encompassed by other areas of doctrine (a classification founded on the distinctiveness of doctrinal arrangements and devices). Lawyers' doubts about the coherence of property law as a field are founded on uncertainty as to whether either of these modes of classification is presently adequate to provide a basis for rationalizing doctrine. Inevitably the two modes are related. But it is the latter of them which attracts most attention in legal writing.

It is of interest that some American commentators write of the 'death of property'[12] in much the same way that others have heralded the demise of contract.[13] It is suggested that the variety of current usages of the category of property is such that lawyers could dispense with the term 'property' altogether without losing anything in legal analytical clarity.[14] At the heart of this claim is the assertion that the notion of 'thing ownership' – the notion that property rights can be understood as rights against other persons in relation to things – has become incoherent and with it the basis of property itself, since so-called property rights now exist also in relation to benefits far too intangible or diffuse to be considered 'things'.[15]

Charles Reich's much discussed 1964 essay on the 'new property'[16] highlighted the increasing importance of numerous forms of 'wealth' extending beyond the orthodox categories of private property and embodied in franchises, occupational licences, job security, government contracts, social security benefits and numerous other forms of benefit entitlement often dependent on government guarantee. It argued not that these should be recognized as giving rise to rights and duties of the same nature as those associated with traditional forms of private property, but that their modern importance showed the inadequacy of existing legal conceptualizations. It argued that changes in the bases of wealth in modern society had made existing property law thinking too limited in scope to encompass many of the most fundamental modern forms of wealth or entitlement on which most citizens depended, and that, as a result, they lacked adequate legal protection, especially from arbitrary seizure or cancellation by government.

How far can these ideas be applied outside an American context? The context in which Reich's thesis was raised and has subsequently been much discussed includes the 'takings' and 'due process' clauses of the United States Constitution which specifically refer to 'private property' or 'property' and protect it from being 'taken for public use without just compensation'[17] and the owner of property from being deprived of it 'without due process of law'.[18] Debates in American legal literature in recent years on the scope of property and the recognition of 'new property' rights in government largesse naturally reflect the entrenched constitutional significance of the 'property' label which carries particular protections for those rights to which it can be attached. The line between property and non-property is constitutionally important. In at least some of the 'takings' cases it has been drawn by using the 'thing-ownership' conception of property.[19] Yet, it is argued, the concept of property in general legal use has been transformed by pragmatic extensions from a Blackstonian 'physicalist' notion of dominion over 'the external things of the world'[20] to an entirely abstract conception of the protection of value – which can exist in such forms as trademarks, trade secrets or business goodwill. At the same time the nature of these objects of property is such that absolutist concepts of property rights as unfettered dominion have appeared obviously unsuitable in relation to them. Thus it is claimed that while the concept of property has been extended in numerous ways to encompass increasingly significant forms of wealth – and arguments around the Reich thesis rage over its further extension – the attribution of property rights no longer allows reliable predictions of the kind of protection which will be granted by the law.[21] Hence the term property no longer identifies a coherent field of legal rights and duties. Property is 'dead' as a result of having been worked to death in indiscriminate legal application.

In the English context the matter may appear somewhat differently. For one thing, the constitutional significance of the property label is largely absent.[22] The thing-ownership conception of property can be treated as perhaps no more than a dispensable motif in legal analysis. Hohfeld is often credited with firmly establishing in Anglo-American legal thought the 'bundle-of-rights' conception of ownership which explicitly displaces legal concern with a relationship between the individual property-holder and the thing constituting the object of property, and sees property essentially as a cluster of jural relations between persons by which entitlements are fixed. Given this viewpoint the object of property, the 'thing' in relation to which rights exist, often ceases to be of much interest in legal analysis. But viewing matters in a broader comparative perspective of legal history and development there may be dangers in putting too much emphasis on the contrast between Blackstone's mid-eighteenth-century pronouncements on property in terms of 'things' and Hohfeld's twentieth-century 'revolution' in legal thought as marking fundamental changes in the nature of doctrine or its interpretation. The Hohfeldian approach can be used to illuminate property conceptions in extremely diverse legal systems and its relevance is in no way restricted to modern law.[23] Furthermore it seems clear that English law has for centuries been thoroughly familiar with the notion that the most abstract of entitlements can be encompassed by property law. 'The realm of medieval law is rich with incorporeal things. Any permanent right which is of a transferable nature, at all events if it has what we may call a territorial ambit, is thought of as a thing that is very like a piece of land'.[24] The need to think in terms of things hardly prevented the elaboration of abstractions, so it appears. Throughout much of English legal history the most concrete of assets – land – has been thought of in terms of the abstraction of estates; and the notion of incorporeal property has its roots in ancient and primitive societies.[25] Wolfgang Friedmann notes, in sharp contrast to the agitated discussion in much of the American literature, that 'as has always been inherent in the common-law concept of property, and as is increasingly recognized in the civilian legal systems, property is not confined to the control of "things", but extended to the whole field of legitimate economic interests and expectations'.[26]

On this view what is of particular interest is to compare the longstanding flexibility of Anglo-American approaches to property with the struggles of some civilian systems – particularly the German – to transcend the rigidities of legal definitions associating property only with corporeal things, and to overcome problems associated with the inheritance of Roman law notions of *dominion*. And what is perhaps most salutary for comparative lawyers is the recognition that, despite widely different doctrinal traditions of common law and civil law systems, the protection of 'legitimate economic interests and expectations' has been substantially achieved irrespective of these differences, though the rules providing this protection may be classified differently (and not necessarily as rules of property law) in different systems.[27] There is a considerable danger in exaggerating the actual practical effects of doctrinal differences between modern legal systems, and also in overestimating the extent, significance or suddenness of changes in legal thought.

In the realm of intellectual property law the legal concept of 'property' itself as applied to this field finds little place in contemporary discussion despite the rapid development and important practical problems of doctrine in the area. It would seem that broad general concepts defining a 'legal essence' of property can be dispensed with in the practical business of constructing protection for a variety of interests out of a range of pragmatically developed bodies of doctrine relating to such as copyright, patents, confidential information and trademarks. A common-sense 'fact-based' classification seems, at least for the present, adequate to define this field. All this is consistent with the pragmatic approach of Anglo-American common law to conceptualization. Where English judges have felt the need to theorize in doctrine about the nature of property in general they have often taken a fairly robust approach, tailoring their view to the circumstances of its application in the instant case and occasionally using a concept fully wide enough to embrace the 'new property' and much more besides. Thus Malins VC remarked in 1869 in *Dixon* v. *Holden*: 'What is property? One man has property in lands, another in goods, another in a business, another in skill, another in reputation; and whatever may have the effect of destroying property in any one of these things (even in a man's good name) is, in my opinion, destroying property of a most valuable description.'[28]

Where then do the doctrinal difficulties lie? We can identify at least three areas of doctrinal problems which seem of general importance within the property law field at present and, although they are closely related, it is convenient to outline each of them in turn.

Identifying Objects of Property

One area of difficulty arises from the need, despite the flexibility of legal approaches referred to above, to identify clearly in doctrine the assets which modern property law protects. Although there is nothing very new about the 'new property' and nothing new at all about the importance of incorporeal property in law, the range of types of incorporeal property has expanded greatly since the nineteenth century and has assumed greatly increased economic importance. Even the use of the concept of 'thing-ownership' as a mere motif of property law has seemed increasingly unrealistic in legal experience because it seems irrelevant to doctrine relating to forms of wealth which seem to be coming to occupy centre stage in economic life. The name given to the 'bundle of rights' identified in some property claims, for example 'copyright' or 'patent' or 'trademark', is the only name we use to refer to the asset protected, whereas in more traditional property forms we could distinguish, for example, the estate in land from the land itself. But there remains an apparent need – if we are to continue to think in terms of property in these kinds of cases – for a focus of entitlement, an identifiable asset around which rights can crystallize.

Sometimes it is not easy to see what this can be. According to Anglo-American law, copyright protects not ideas but the form of their expression, yet it may often be hard to separate the latter from the former,[29] or to identify unambiguously the relevant form – as, for example, in protection of computer software.[30] It is often said that it is the labour embodied in the creation which founds the right to protection but English copyright law has tended to provide protection for the commercial entrepreneur rather than the creator as such, given the absence of any clear concept of 'author's right' of the continental type.[31] Thus it seems most appropriate to treat the *result* of the labour as being protected. But what exactly is this? German writers describe it as 'the fabric of the work determined by its substance and form'.[32] The complex nature of creativity and originality has to be explored, since what is actually being protected is the embodiment of ideas.

Certainly, in many cases this causes no problems. Earlier English law found no difficulty in manipulating extremely nebulous property forms. Only when we seek to *generalize* about the nature of property and related areas can serious difficulties arise, for English courts have understandably been reluctant to adopt a general principle that something as hard to define as knowledge itself can be considered property.[33] But as technological or marketing ideas, design innovations and state-of-the-art techniques, trademarks, market information and many kinds of data resources, etc., are recognized as increasingly important forms of *wealth* in contemporary societies – often more important than the material things which have been the traditional focus of property law and which are now increasingly produced by means of, or are dependent on, these modern forms of wealth – the future of property law as a coherent field of doctrine may depend on its capacity to analyse them convincingly as (objects of) 'property'. One problem seems to be to define clearly the proprietary interest protected in such a way as both to facilitate and justify the protection to be provided by law. As will appear, this problem is ultimately not so much a technical–legal one as a social one.

Identifying Rights as Property Rights

A second and closely related area of doctrinal problems concerns the distinction between property rights and other rights. Insofar as property law extends to cover numerous forms of incorporeal property existing merely because the law defines them as identifiable wealth, property means only what the law says it is *in a particular context*. Thus, as Vandevelde points out in relation to American law, we cannot predict the kind of rights which will exist for a property owner merely by virtue of their categorization as *property* rights. They vary extensively with the type of property.[34] The point applies equally to English developments. Of course different kinds of property, such as real and personal, have always been associated with different kinds of rights. But any attempt to assimilate property rights in different fields of property law seems increasingly difficult. Nowadays, the diverse fields of property law – and, again, particularly intellectual property law – show fundamentally differing principles at work determining the nature of property rights. For example, the Plant Varieties and Seeds Act 1964[35] defines the unique rights of an owner of a plant variety at the same time as it creates this special type of property.

But again it is important to make clear what exactly is new in these developments and what is not. Just as property law has for centuries protected assets hard to think of as things, so it has long accepted a great variety of types of property right. The change that has occurred in relation to property rights as in relation to property assets is a change in the relative social significance of different property forms. As more abstract forms of property asset have become of central economic importance so the diverse kinds of property right associated with them have assumed increasing importance in legal doctrine. The problem of the diversity of property rights is moving from being a peripheral problem of property law doctrine to a central one.

Thus if the categorization of rights as property rights is to be of continuing value in legal doctrine it is necessary to identify what, if anything, such rights have in common in modern law. Some literature emphasizes the right of exclusion, in some sense, as central to the property-holder's position,[36] other writing explores the position of the property-holder as regards claims by or against third parties,[37] or the kinds of remedies given by law to protect property.[38] On another view property rules uniquely create entitlements which can be taken from the holder only if he agrees and at a price which he negotiates.[39] These possible identifications of the nature of property rights cannot be discussed here. What is important is merely to note that the matter remains one of controversy and is important to the coherence of property law as a field of doctrine.

Use Value and Exchange Value

A third area of problems affecting the coherence of property law doctrine concerns the relationship between exchange value and use value as matters for protection by property law. The nature of this relationship has re-emerged as an issue of great difficulty and importance. It has received more discussion in English writing on property law than have the two previously mentioned problem areas[40] but, as will appear, it turns out to be closely related to them.

Typically, modern property law has focused its attention particularly on the protection of rights to exchange value, that is, on the property-holder's right not only to use his property asset but also to deal freely with it as a commodity in legal transactions by which he can exchange it or some part of it for money or some other commodity. In English land law the simplification of conveyancing is recognized as the guiding principle behind the 1925 real property legislation. The legal estates constructed to facilitate the realization of exchange value are the central pillars of the law around which other interests are arranged. The importance of the trust for sale and the associated doctrine of conversion; the doctrine of overreaching in the law of strict settlements; the relationship of legal and equitable rights under a trust – all these are badges of the centrality of exchange value among the objects of protection in property law. Rights recognized by law as mere rights of use without exchange value have, in general, not been treated as proprietary rights. Although this is a tendency of the law rather than an absolute principle the general orthodox position is that a proprietary right must be 'definable, identifiable by third parties, capable in its nature of assumption by third parties, and have some degree of permanence or stability'.[41]

However, recently in numerous contexts assertions have frequently been made before English courts of the need for much more extensive protection of use value alone by means of property rights. The cases have usually involved a conflict between a claimed right of an occupier to remain on land and the claim of exclusive control asserted by the holder of a legal estate in the land. In many recent cases English courts have given protection to the occupier even against a third-party assignee of the legal estate and even though, on orthodox analysis, the occupier possesses no more than a licence to occupy the land.[42] A claim that some years ago would have been recognized as, at best, contractual or involving other rights, founded on reliance in good faith, solely against the original holder of the legal estate, is now increasingly recognized as involving proprietary rights enforceable against third parties. Sometimes the occupier's rights are protected by imposition of a constructive trust on the holder of the legal estate, but a variety of formulations and remedies is used.

These developments should also be seen in the context of an extensive growth, over a longer period, of legislative protection of use value especially through landlord and tenant legislation creating, for example, the 'status of irremovability' of the holder of a statutory tenancy which is non-assignable and therefore lacks exchange value.[43] Also important has been the statutory protection of rights of occupation of the matrimonial home.[44]

Developments such as these create doctrinal uncertainties about the nature of property rights in general and about the legal policy which provides the rationality of their protection. Statutory developments, such as Rent Acts protections, can often be rationalized by property lawyers as the intrusion of public law principles in a private law area. The uncertainties resulting from this intrusion may thus be seen as inevitable and attributable to a familiar and well-understood cause, the clash of social policy and planning considerations and private rights. But the registration of seemingly irreconcilable conflicts between protection of use value and protection of exchange value *within* private law doctrine is harder for many lawyers to accept. In *Williams & Glyn's Bank* v. *Boland* Lord Scarman made the opposing practical considerations in one such instance explicit: on the one hand, the convenience and efficiency of conveyancing promoted by clarity of legal title and the absence of encumbrances on title; on the other, social justice in the protection of a person occupying the land on the faith of a prior agreement or understanding from eviction by a third party obtaining the legal estate.[45] In other cases the problem has been to construct a form of property right primarily to protect use or occupation which would achieve justice without attracting a range of unintended consequences from the applicability of pre-existing property law rules or else undermining those rules.[46]

Finally, it should be noted that the greater attention to rights of use as distinct objects of protection by property rights has emerged in an era when law has increasingly restricted some important use rights of property-holders,[47] for example through planning and pollution controls. In a wider context we can thus speak of a fragmentation, not only of ownership (as orthodox English property law commentary has always asserted), but of the very concept of property right itself. Hence the connection with the more general problem, already discussed, of identifying property rights as such.

THE RELEVANCE OF THEORY

Lawyers require little or no aid from legal theory to produce immediate practical case-by-case solutions to doctrinal difficulties such as those discussed above. Conceptual organization of doctrine of the kind offered by much analytical jurisprudence is likely to be no more than *ex post facto* rationalization of pragmatic legal solutions arrived at in the practical business of deciding cases and legislating to meet immediate perceived regulatory needs. Lawyers' lack of concern for general analysis of the nature of 'property' in the rapid contemporary doctrinal development of intellectual property law illustrates the point. So does the seemingly free and easy approach, noted above, to recognition and specification of rights as 'property rights'. Lawyers systematize and generalize doctrine as seems necessary and possible for the task in hand. Broad concepts give way where necessary to the demands of the moment. And sometimes such concepts seem unhelpful or irrelevant to the solution of pressing doctrinal problems.[48]

How then can theoretical analysis be used in the ways suggested in the earlier sections of this paper to aid understanding of the problems of property law doctrine discussed above? Legal theory can aid the lawyer's understanding by attempting to explain how such doctrinal problems have arisen and what conditions and causes have contributed to them. We should, indeed, as Durkheim suggested, treat *certain* aspects of doctrinal change as an index, a reflection, of wider social change outside the professional milieu of law. But the reflection may, and often will, be distorted in complex ways. Many characteristics of legal doctrine are to be explained in terms of the effects of this narrow professional milieu; and doctrine can, of course, bring about change as well as reflect it. A complex set of interactions between ideas and behaviour is involved.

The problems of contemporary property law which this paper has identified can, when set in a wider context, be arranged in a kind of circle. Property law in capitalist society has been concerned, above all, with identifying and protecting assets which are economically valuable as objects of commerce. The orthodox emphasis on exchange-value protection suggests this but it is reflected more generally in what Charles Donahue has described as the tendency in property law towards the agglomeration in a single legal person of the exclusive right to possess, privilege to use, and power to convey the object of property,[49] an agglomeration which makes possible the unfettered employment of property assets as capital. Thus, at the same time as the law has recognized an ever widening range of commercially valuable assets as objects of property, it has shown a preference for making rights in such assets as complete as possible so as to facilitate economic transactions and the security of capital.

The increasing importance of what we might call knowledge-assets – objects of intellectual property – as wealth has caused serious difficulties for this orthodox approach to property law. The difficulty of recognizing these fully and unambiguously as property-assets and of giving anything like absolute rights in them has been a social rather than a technical-legal difficulty. Insofar as forms of information are to be protected as private property, law is faced with the idea, deeply rooted in contemporary Western societies, that freedom of information is socially valuable. There are fundamental ideological problems in pushing too far the notion that knowledge can be privately owned and controlled. These problems are aggravated by the fact that, unlike the master's secrets which the apprentice of the past took a solemn oath to keep, modern knowledge-assets are typically owned or controlled by large corporations whose moral claims to such assets may seem less obvious than those of the human creator of knowledge derived from personal skills and experience.

In part the proliferation of *limited* property rights, and the more general fragmentation of the concept of 'property right', are a consequence of the problems involved in adapting property law to provide protection for the immense wealth which knowledge-assets represent in contemporary society. The limitation of scope of property rights in these assets has resulted from a *social* judgment that they can constitute property-assets to a strictly limited extent. It may well be, therefore, that the widespread attempts to assert 'new property' rights, and proprietary rights to use or enjoy assets held by others – including those recognized in the English cases and legislation on occupiers' rights – have been strongly, if indirectly, promoted by the disorienting effects on the concept of property which have been brought about by more general changes in the basis of wealth.

Thus property forms appropriate to protect the traditional forms of wealth of the 'haves' – the relatively economically powerful – encounter difficulties as forms of wealth change. As legal forms adapt to protect these new forms of wealth, new claims to property brought by the 'have-nots' (those holding relatively few orthodox property entitlements) seem to become plausible because a claim that, for example, social welfare entitlements or a job may be property[50] is, *prima facie*, no less convincing than that forms of knowledge can be protected as property. It might be argued that in both cases the success of the claim should depend on the degree of security which, according to a judgment of justice or social policy, a private expectation (obtained lawfully by grant or agreement) of income should be given by law when it cannot adequately be protected by contract or other personal rights. Indeed, Bruce Ackerman's analysis of recent developments in American constitutional adjudication on property rights suggests that these developments probably necessitate just such an approach in which the analysis of inherent doctrinal characteristics of 'property' is superseded by adjudication on an explicit policy basis.[51]

But the circle of problems is completed – and revolves without resolution – because any such rationalization and entrenchment in doctrine of this diversity of property forms further prevents the clarity of property rights which capitalist economic activity requires – the first problem in the circle.

The schematic character of the general line of analysis sketched above makes essential the caveat that it is intended merely to indicate directions for further theoretical enquiries. But it suggests that what theory can contribute perhaps most importantly to the lawyer's immediate tasks of analysis of doctrine is an assessment of how fundamentally rooted in wider social changes are the doctrinal tensions which he observes. That in itself may suggest whether piecemeal doctrinal changes are likely to resolve the perceived difficulties or merely to displace them temporarily, or shift them to another area of the law. And, while legal theory as understood in this paper cannot properly dictate moral or political choices, it may, by clarifying the nature of doctrinal problems, indicate where these choices lie and how fundamental in their consequences they may be.

In the teaching of property law these considerations have a special relevance. Land law, perhaps more than any other area of legal doctrine, is frequently taught as an exercise in technicalities.[52] The technical 'rational strength' of doctrine in this area, distilled from the accumulations of legal pragmatism over long centuries, encourages this. But the matters discussed in this paper suggest that particular social/historical conditions lie behind the central technical problems of doctrine. Further, once the sociological factors shaping doctrine and its problems are recognized it becomes possible to understand more clearly the moral and political issues which arise in this broader legal context. Theoretical analysis, by showing law as an aspect of social life, should confront the student of law with the moral choices and dilemmas which 'law-as-technique' and legal ideology disguise or deny. Nevertheless, it is necessary to insist: legal theory exclusively serves no particular constituency. Its perennial responsibility is not primarily to improve legal education, legal practice or legal services. It is simply to promote understanding of the nature of law.

As for the present tasks of theory in this area several related areas of study suggested by the discussion above seem important. One of these concerns the relationship discussed in much of the social scientific, philosophical and historical literature on property[53] between property and *power*. This is a matter which warrants much more analysis. The concept of property in law is a device by which law guarantees relations of power while disguising their nature. In private law, power is not normally recognized directly in legal doctrine as an attribute of an individual which he can wield over another. This is because the fundamental principle of general equality before the law of all citizens is inconsistent with any such general recognition. The property form allows the attributes which give an individual power over another to be *separated* from him in legal doctrine as an asset which he owns. The attributes, facilities, capacities and resources which give some persons power over others become 'things' – objects of property – which can be conceptualized in law as distinct from their holder. In property law, therefore, the situation is not that persons are recognized as having power over others but that power resides in the property which they own – in the things which are conceived by law as distinct from them and to which they are connected by legal rights acquired in various possible ways which, as far as legal doctrine is concerned, are equally available to all. Looking at matters in this way suggests why the problem of defining modern types of property-asset in legally convincing ways may be more than just a minor technical problem for legal doctrine. If the property form provides a particular framework for the exercise of power which is ideologically significant, changes both in the kinds of assets recognized by law and in the kinds of property rights so recognized may have very important consequences for legal ideology.

Closely connected as another area for further enquiry is the relationship between popular lay conceptions of property and lawyers' conceptions. This is something which has been extensively considered speculatively in the American literature.[54] But the foregoing discussion of social problems in adapting the property form to secure a convincing legal recognition of knowledge-assets indicates an importance in enquiring into lay conceptions of property which is quite distinct from the considerations involved in the constitutional debates of the American writings. Thus if, as suggested above, the property form disguises and guarantees power by means of the specific relationship established in ideology between the person, on the one hand, and the thing owned, on the other, the thing-ownership conception of property cannot be dismissed as insignificant quite as easily as modern Hohfeldian legal analysis suggests. The conception may be of great social or ideological significance, even if of limited value as an aid to lawyers in solving technical problems in doctrine. Ackerman argues that the thing-ownership conception is, indeed, fundamental to lay conceptions of property.[55] If this is so it may well be that ideology sets important limitations on the scope of legal doctrinal innovation in the property law field.

Analysis of the ideological significance of the property form may help in understanding the persistence of two distinct and apparently competing doctrinal traditions in Western property law: the continental Romanist conception of property as *dominium* over things (single owner having absolute entitlement to a distinct asset) and the common law conception of fragmentation of ownership (no *dominus* but many possible kinds of property entitlement held by different people in relation to a single material source of wealth). It may be suggested that *technically* the common law conception is more appropriate to encompass the changing forms of wealth which have emerged in Western societies since the beginnings of capitalist development, and to provide extremely flexible and sophisticated devices for their deployment and protection. On the other hand, the Romanist conception of *dominium* which serves to crystallize ownership in terms of a distinct, identifiable asset owned (*res*) and a distinct, more or less absolute owner (*dominus*) provides a means of clearly distinguishing property rights from personal rights. In this way it creates the clear separation of owner and owned which, it has been suggested above, is perhaps fundamental to some major *ideological* effects of the property form. That continental systems have sought to modify Romanist tradition in many ways to create considerable flexibility in property conceptions reflects the problem of meeting technical demands on legal doctrine. Equally, the tensions in common law property doctrine identified in this paper suggest that ideological aspects of law may set limits on its technical capabilities.

What lies behind all of these suggestions for further enquiries is the belief that in the area of property doctrine, as in so many other areas of legal thought and analysis, theory can probably achieve most by contributing towards an understanding of the ideological foundations and effects of the law – the wider, taken-for-granted currents of thought and belief in society to which legal ideas are related and to which they contribute. The idea of property has often been associated, not only in a long tradition of political theory but also in popular conceptions, with broad notions of liberty. The orthodox conception of property as the unfettered freedom to do as one will with lawfully held objects of wealth, whatever the social effects of so doing and irrespective of the claims of the property-less to a share in the resources of life, supports a conception of liberty as the freedom to exercise property-power for the accumulation of profit without any limits except those created by the opposed property-power of others. One consequence of the extensive challenges to the orthodox legal conception of property which this paper has discussed may be a more widespread recognition that liberty as an ideal in contemporary conditions must mean not the liberty of property-power but the liberty of *property-security* in which the diffusion of guaranteed entitlements to the use of resources necessary for personal welfare is recognized as the basis of genuine freedom. Thus tensions in legal doctrine in this area may promote ideological change in various ways as well as reflecting it.

NOTES

1 F. H. Lawson, *The Rational Strength of English Law* (1951) p. 79.
2 Generally in this paper I use the term 'lawyers' to refer to both practising and academic lawyers. Since the central concern of discussion throughout the paper is with legal doctrine and its problems and consequences, this linking of legal practitioners and law teachers in a single category is intended in this context to identify a range of legal 'participants' who have a particular shared professional/intellectual concern with the integrity of legal doctrine – its coherence, clarity, rationality and utility as a body of knowledge and as a basis of practice. In many other contexts it would, of course, be important to distinguish typically different concerns of legal academics and practising lawyers, as well as of sub-groups within each of these two broad, ambiguous and overlapping categories.
3 The conception of legal theory sketched in the following paragraphs is elaborated in Cotterrell, 'English Conceptions of the Role of Theory in Legal Analysis' (1983) 46 *Modern Law Rev.* 681; and in *The Sociology of Law: An Introduction* (1984).
4 Twining, 'Evidence and Legal Theory' (chapter 4 above) p. 62.
5 *Id.*, p. 62.
6 *Id.*, p. 64.
7 *Id.*, p. 63. For a response, see below p. 253.
8 See Cotterrell, *The Sociology of Law, op. cit.*, ch. 6.
9 *Id.*, pp. 120 *et seq.*; Cotterrell, 'Legality and Political Legitimacy in the Sociology of Max Weber' in *Legality, Ideology and the State* (1983; ed. D. Sugarman) pp. 84 *et seq.*
10 Twining, *op. cit.*, p. 62.
11 *Id.*, p. 64.
12 T. C. Grey, 'The Disintegration of Property' in *Property* (1980; ed. J. R. Pennock and J. W. Chapman).
13 G. Gilmore, *The Death of Contract* (1974).
14 Grey, *op. cit.*, p. 73.
15 See e.g. Vandevelde, 'The New Property of the Nineteenth Century: The Development of the Modern Concept of Property' (1980) 29 *Buffalo Law Rev.* 325.
16 Reich, 'The New Property' (1964) 73 *Yale Law J* 733. Reich's paper has had very considerable influence and its central thesis has been regarded as path-breaking. The modern importance of 'new property' rights is, however, stressed by Thurman Arnold in his *The Folklore of Capitalism* (1937) pp. 121-2. See also Lynn, 'Legal and Economic Implications of the Emergence of Quasi-Public Wealth' (1956) 65 *Yale Law J* 786.
17 US Constitution Amend. V, cl. 4.
18 US Constitution Amend. V, cl. 3; Amend XIV, sec. 1.

19 *Penn Central Transp. Co.* v. *New York City* (1978) 438 US 104; Grey, *op. cit.*, p. 72.
20 W. Blackstone, *Commentaries on the Laws of England* (15th edn; 1809) vol. II, p. 2.
21 Vandevelde, *op. cit.*
22 Cf. *Belfast Corp.* v. *O. D. Cars Ltd* [1960] AC 490, interpreting the provision regarding the taking of property without compensation under the Government of Ireland Act 1920, s.5(1).
23 Hoebel, 'Fundamental Legal Concepts as Applied in the Study of Primitive Law' (1942) 51 *Yale Law J* 951; Hallowell, 'The Nature and Function of Property as a Social Institution' (1943) 1 *J Legal and Political Sociology* 115.
24 F. Pollock and F. W. Maitland, *The History of English Law* (1968 edn) vol. II, p. 124.
25 Lowie, 'Incorporeal Property in Primitive Society' (1928) 37 *Yale Law J* 551; Hoebel, *op. cit.*
26 W. Friedmann, *Law in a Changing Society* (2nd edn; 1972) p. 117.
27 F. H. Lawson, 'Comparative Conclusion' in *International Encyclopedia of Comparative Law*, vol. VI (1975) ch. 2.
28 (1869) LR 7 Eq. 488 at p. 492.
29 See e.g. the remarks in the American case of *Nichols* v. *Universal Picture Corp.* (1930) 45 F 2d 119 at p. 121.
30 Ulmer and Kolle, 'Copyright Protection in Computer Programs' (1983) 14 *International Rev. Industrial Property and Copyright Law* 161; A. Wilson, 'The Protection of Computer Programs under Common Law - Procedural Aspects and United Kingdom Copyright Law and Trade Secrets' in *The Legal Protection of Computer Software* (1981; ed. H. Brett and L. Perry) pp. 80 *et seq.*
31 W. R. Cornish, *Intellectual Property* (1981) pp. 297-8; Dworkin, 'The Moral Right and English Copyright Law' (1981) 12 *International Rev. Industrial Property and Copyright Law* 476.
32 Ulmer and Kolle, *op. cit.*, p. 181.
33 *Boardman* v. *Phipps* [1967] 2 AC 46; and see Hammond, 'Theft of Information' (1984) 100 *Law Quarterly Rev.* 252; Cornish, *op. cit.*, pp. 289-90 on confidential information as property.
34 Vandevelde, *op. cit.*
35 As amended by the Plant Varieties Act 1983.
36 E.g. M. Cohen, *Law and the Social Order* (1933) p. 46.
37 E.g. Alexander, 'The Concept of Property in Private and Constitutional Law: The Ideology of the Scientific Turn in Legal Analysis' (1982) 82 *Columbia Law Rev.* 1545.
38 Grey, *op. cit.*, p. 72.
39 Calabresi and Melamed, 'Property Rules, Liability Rules, and Inalienability: One View of the Cathedral' (1972) 85 *Harvard Law Rev.* 1089.
40 See e.g. Simmonds, 'The Changing Face of Private Law: Doctrinal Categories and the Regulatory State' (1982) 2 *Legal Studies* 257.
41 Lord Wilberforce in *National Provincial Bank Ltd* v. *Ainsworth* [1965] AC 1175 at p. 1248.
42 See e.g. Moriarty, 'Licences and Land Law: Legal Principles and Public Policies' (1984) 100 *Law Quarterly Rev.* 376.
43 G. C. Cheshire and E. H. Burn, *Modern Law of Real Property* (13th edn; 1982) pp. 455-6.
44 Matrimonial Homes Act 1983.
45 *Williams and Glyn's Bank Ltd* v. *Boland* [1981] AC 487 at pp. 509-10.
46 See e.g. *Binions* v. *Evans* [1972] ch. 359; *Re Sharpe* [1980] 1 WLR 219; *Lyus* v. *Prowsa Developments Ltd* [1982] 1 WLR 1044.
47 See e.g. Friedmann, *op. cit.*, pp. 102 *et seq.*

48 See e.g. D. Harris, 'The Concept of Possession in English Law' in *Oxford Essays in Jurisprudence* (1961; ed. A. G. Guest).

49 C. Donahue Jr, 'The Future of the Concept of Property Predicted from its Past' in *Property* (1980; ed. J. R. Pennock and J. W. Chapman).

50 Reich, *op. cit.*

51 B. A. Ackerman, *Private Property and the Constitution* (1977).

52 A laudable attempt to provide a student textbook escaping from this pattern is K. J. Gray and P. D. Symes, *Real Property and Real People* (1981) which in expounding doctrine seeks to look at, *inter alia*, 'the underlying ideology of property law' (p. 7). Despite there being much of value in the book's discussions its theoretical content is inadequate to enable it to do more than scratch the surface of the most fundamental issues surrounding real property doctrine. Thus the models of *Gemeinschaft* and *Gesellschaft* social relations are the fundamental, and almost the sole, tools of theoretical analysis employed. Property law as a whole is seen as expressing social relations of *Gesellschaft*. Such new developments as the decision in *Williams and Glyn's Bank v. Boland* are interpreted as a reaffirmation of *Gemeinschaft* values. All this carries us a little way, but not far. First, it does not explain why such values are being reaffirmed in such a context. Secondly, the concepts of *Gemeinschaft* and *Gesellschaft* are used to epitomize 'the policy motivations which underlie the case law' (p. 364) rather than to provide a basis for understanding the nature of the social relations which law regulates. Hence these snippets of social theory are used only to elaborate the rhetoric of the law, not to pierce it by means of theoretical analysis.

53 Cohen, *op. cit.*; Philbrick, 'Changing Conceptions of Property in Law' (1938) 86 *University of Pennsylvania Law Rev.* 691; K. Renner, *The Institutions of Private Law and their Social Functions* (1949); E. B. Pashukanis, *Law and Marxism: A General Theory* (1978); Reich, *op. cit.*

54 Ackerman, *op. cit.*; Alexander, *op. cit.*

55 Ackerman, *op. cit.*

6
Public Law
and Legal Theory

NORMAN LEWIS

When addressing my first-year public law students I explain to them that only two substantial problems stand between them and a mastery of the course. The first is to provide a satisfactory definition of law and the second a definition of the public sphere. All else is plain sailing. These two problems will occupy my undivided attention during the course of this essay. Only one qualification perhaps needs to be added before I proceed in earnest. It is that I must circumscribe the rather bald statement about the public sphere.

I have long taken the view that 'constitutional law' is what stands at the heart of the public lawyer's concerns. Administrative law is almost certainly a misnomer, being no more than a treatment of the informal or perhaps rather less formal workings of the public machine. Its uncritical adoption fails to perceive that it is normally used to encompass certain unspecified and untheorized empirical problems of the administration. Its fairly discrete identification in American federal law is understandable given the legislative history of the past 50 years or so and the theoretical unwillingness of American constitutionalists to admit of patterned intrusion into the conduct of 'private' business. Even so the mood has changed detectably in recent years and constitutional lawyers recognize regulation to be an issue examined in and around the Oval Office too.[1] It is, in my view, the 'search for the constitution' which represents the important exercise to be conducted,[2] and this is merely another way of saying that a discussion of the public hemisphere involves an analysis of the legitimation foundations of the British polity.[3]

In recent years there has been considerable discussion of the problem of 'deregulation' or even 'delegalization', which, for all it says about political ideology, is terribly misleading in its normally stated terms.[4] If one adopts an expanded concept of law which argues that 'law-jobs' are socially necessary phenomena and coterminous with organized life itself, then all the problems of delegalization or deregulation are relegated to matters of legitimation. Who has and who should have the authority to act in what way? It is ultimately a moral question; or to put it another way: a constitutional question. Discussions of the public/private divide have become quite fashionable in recent years, even if little of the zealous courtship of the fashion has taken place in Britain.[5] This is an important matter which has received less attention than it might have done in

Britain given the clear evidence of the compenetration of the state/society or public/private divide in the last 100 years.[6] Its somewhat belated entrance on to the constitutional agenda is yet another reminder that constitutionality is the key issue for discussion. This is because we cannot simply arbitrate a definition of what is public and what private. Either there are transcendentally defined areas of privacy and social space or there are cultural and historical definitions or assumptions. In either case the demarcation of constitutionally correct or incorrect conduct is more than conventional, if I might use a philosophical term in this setting. The criteria for identifying the constitution, just as the criteria for identifying 'law', are not, however, always a matter of clear articulation in most British legal scholarship. To these matters I shall direct some little attention.

A PROBLEM OF DEFINITION

Traditional treatments of constitutional or public law are, on the whole, pretty baffling in terms of the presuppositions on which they are based. Usages tend either to be conventional, with the conventions hidden or not spelled out, or fundamentally inarticulate. This tends to apply both to the use of the term 'law' and to the intellectual strategy to be adopted in seeking to map out or chart an anatomy of some unspoken version of constitutionality. Let us take but one example, hastily expressing the caveat that it is, in this respect, no better or worse than most constitutional texts.

In his *Constitutional Conventions*, Geoffrey Marshall[7] makes a number of statements, some of which I find broadly acceptable and some highly contestable. What is significant, however, is the lack of any obvious epistemological tack, or perhaps I should confine myself here to saying that the book is based upon fairly elusive theoretical foundations. Thus,

> the Constitution is unwritten, or to put it more accurately, it includes a large number of non-legal conventional rules. . . . It could be said that in general they are rules of *non-legal accountability*.[8] (emphasis added)

Elsewhere we are informed that although conventions do not always modify legal powers, their major purpose is 'to give effect to the principles of governmental accountability that constitute the structure of responsible government'.[9] To the trained eye it is manifestly the case that the inarticulate basis of his usage of the term 'law' is crudely Austinian. Not, of course, that this is spelled out, but no other interpretation seems possible. It is, naturally, perfectly in order to adopt Austinian definitions, though how one seeks to explain contemporary phenomena in light of them is a matter of some little puzzlement, at least to the present writer. Nor, I think, would it be unfair to say that such definitions are these days rarely accepted uncritically by most scholars who address the issue directly and openly. Over and above this particular problem, however, we find that the notion of 'accountability' has been smuggled into the debate without being 'unpacked'. There is, in fact, some lively literature addressing this issue and it would have been helpful to know precisely what notion of accountability was being adopted, since it would have given us some insight into the author's own concept of constitutionality. All that appears from the text is that the constitution is unwritten, it is loosely associated with the rule of law (another highly problematic concept),[10] and is apparently associated with 'responsible' government. Given that the presuppositions upon which these items have been based have not been disclosed, it is not clear whether the 'answers' arrived at are satisfactory or not. It is unclear since we do not know what questions are being posed. I shall wish to pursue this matter a little further, but before doing so I want to make it clear that in calling for clearer theoretical definition I have no particular author in mind. Suffice it to say that I can find no current scholarship in and around the field of constitutional or public law that seems adequate in this respect.

In developing this theme I want unashamedly to hijack a stimulating essay written at the outset of the Second World War. It is R. G. Collingwood's *An Essay on Metaphysics*[11] and, although its grander theoretical core is controversial in itself, it is highly enlightening about the knowledge 'claims' which inform much intellectual debate in Britain. He was not, at the time, speaking to lawyers or legal scholars in particular, but he nevertheless encapsulates a great deal of what I would wish to say about legal and constitutional scholarship, had I the eloquence.

Collingwood attacks, *inter alia*, intuition as a basis of scientific thinking and labels the genre, which we should immediately recognize, as 'realism' or 'intuitive realism'. This has, I should hasten to add, nothing at all to do with the school of legal realism which held sway in the United States earlier this century. It is worth quoting Collingwood at length:

> In . . . unscientific thinking we hardly know that we are making any presuppositions at all. Because of their tangled condition, the thoughts which come up out of the bottom of our minds present a deceptive appearance of 'immediacy'. I find myself thinking 'That is a clothes line', and if I merely reflect on this thought without analysing it I decide that what has happened is this: I have been confronted with something which in itself, quite apart from what anybody may think about it, just is a clothes line: and being a clever fellow I have just 'apprehended' that clothes line or 'intuited' it, for what it really is, a clothes line. And if I never think at all except in this quite casual and unscientific way, I shall always be content to believe this is all that knowledge can ever be: the simple 'intuition' or 'apprehension' of things confronting us which absolutely and in themselves just are what we 'intuit' or 'apprehend' them as being.[12]

He goes on to argue that every thought we possess arises from a presupposition and that scientific or orderly thinking deals with things in their logical order, putting what is presupposed before what presupposes it and that ultimately we are faced with absolute presuppositions which are largely historical truths and which are not themselves capable of affirmation or rebuttal. Now this perhaps represents some kind of philosophical pragmatism and as such may be challenged by others but what it succeeds in doing is causing us to chase our data, observations, sense-experiences, call them what we will, back to their logical starting-points so that we can decide whether this is a race we wish to enter or not. This intuitive realism does seem to be what so many lawyers and writers on the constitution rely upon and although it is not necessarily the same thing as scientific positivism, there are clear signs of association. In this respect it is worth dwelling on what Collingwood has to say about what he calls positivistic metaphysics but what we may simply call positivism.

Positivism, as Collingwood describes it, is the name of a philosophy (*sic*) greatly favoured in the nineteenth century which, in its English form, is identified closely with J. S. Mill. For adherents to this philosophy the process of enquiry fell into two stages. First, facts were ascertained; then they were classified. The ascertaining of facts was work for the senses; the business of thought was to classify them. A concept was, therefore, the same thing as a class of facts which were of course 'observable' and thus a concept was valid only if the facts of which it was a class were observable. An 'hypothesis' then was an expectation of observing facts of a certain kind under certain conditions. What, asked Collingwood, was wrong with such a position? First, he disputed that 'facts' were observed merely by operation of the senses. Psychology, he reminds us, had been founded centuries ago on the recognition that through our senses we undergo feelings rather than observe facts: 'Here positivism ignored the whole history of modern thought and reverted in a single jump to a long-exploded error of the Middle Ages.'[13]

The second defect which he detected was the maintenance of the belief that every concept or notion was a class of observable facts. This amounted to arguing that scientific thought has no 'presuppositions', which is another way of saying, it seems to me, that facts are theory-neutral. If the function, then, of thought is to classify observed facts, there must be facts available for classification before thought can be set to work. If facts are so readily available then there is clearly no need to presuppose anything; one simply begins the task of classification. This would only be tenable according to Collingwood if the work of observing facts were done by the senses without any assistance from the intellect. But since this is demonstrably not the case, the process in which the exercise takes place involves numerous presuppositions. Such presuppositions are not in his view generalizations about matters of fact and do not await verification.

I shall say just a little more about this argument before attempting to locate it firmly within the title of this essay. It will do us no harm at all to spend a little time on 'second-order' issues. When Galileo 'discovered the path of scientific progress' he did so by rolling a ball down an inclined plane. Instead of first making observations and then asking what they proved, he first framed hypotheses and then devised experiments to test them. Similarly with the early Greeks' achievements in geometry. The feature common to these two discoveries in Collingwood's view was that people gave up the attempt to construct a science by arguing from their observations of things they discovered under their noses, and set to work instead by asking questions and demanding answers to them. To quote a lawyer in this context might be naughty but nice. It was Bacon, Collingwood reminds us, who had insisted that the science of nature develops when man begins 'putting nature to the question', extorting from her an answer to the questions he chose to ask, instead of contenting himself with noting down whatever she elected to reveal. Kant had taken care to acknowledge his debt by using a quotation from Bacon as the motto of *The Critique*.[14]

It is the asking of the questions then with which we must concern ourselves. The 'ranging of the mind in search of its prey is called asking questions,' says Collingwood. The science we have depends in substantial measure upon the questions we put to nature, as in 'what will happen to x in relation to y in closed conditions?' Within that framework, as he argues, modern science has many achievements to its credit, but one should be careful not to claim too much. One concluding quotation is impossible to resist; 'If all you want is to congratulate yourself on having the kind of science that you have, you may do so. If you want to congratulate yourself on having the best of all possible kinds of science, that is not so easy; for nobody knows what all the possible kinds would be like.'[15] For 'science' read 'legal scholarship' and the Collingwood detour should begin to make sense. Unless we argue for some transcendental version of knowledge based upon humankind as necessarily a particular kind of animal (a favourite candidate is perhaps 'rational purposive' man/woman)[16] and if we take Collingwood's point about 'intuitive realism' and 'positivism' then we owe it to scholarship and the intellect to expose our 'presuppositions', starting-points, hypotheses, call them what we will.

A perennial subject of controversy has been whether the natural and the social world should be interpreted according to common 'scientific' criteria and I shall, as a mere journeyman in these matters, not presume to enter the debate but to say only that the social world presents the self-same problems of interpretation identified by Collingwood in the larger setting.[17] The nature of the 'presuppositions', the epistemology, if we like, of modern social theory, has been highly contested in recent times but it would probably be fair to say that various versions of what we might usefully label philosophic 'pragmatism' have tended to dominate. Crudely put, these 'knowledge' claims are that the presuppositions, especially the 'absolute presuppositions' which are the starting-point for enquiry, are to some degree or another culturally or historically determined. Kuhn's writings have been highly influential in this respect and his description of 'paradigm shifts' in the way people theorize about the social world belongs generally to that stream of what I have labelled 'pragmatism' (to counterpose it to 'empiricism' and to 'transcendental' theories of various sorts) which may broadly be conceived of as claims that theories of social science at least are the products of particular societies. The broad assumption is that there is in principle some kind of sociological and/or historical explanation which will tell us why certain ways of viewing the world have predominated at one time, and others at another.[18]

Be all this as it may, our problem as lawyers, constitutionalists, political scientists *et al.* is essentially the same as those which have been outlined. We cannot work around the areas of 'law' or of 'constitutionality' as if facts were theory-neutral and might be taken for granted. We need to worry around the issues of how to characterize 'facts', what we are to say about them and what we are to see in them. It is for this reason that we should be concerned at *the outset of our enquiries* with conceptual questions which 'require from us an account of the proper things to say and think about the facts, or, in an older jargon, an account of how we should conceive them'.[19] This being said, let us return to our first problem.

A PROBLEM OF DEFINITION: LAW

I have already touched upon the point that much of traditionalist writing has assumed a concept of law which is Austinian or neo-Austinian. It is, at best, some version of a *Gesellschaft* form whose central components include that it is rule-based, that it is the bearer of encashable rights and duties, and normally that the rules which matter are those which have a particular pedigree; in Britain, statutes of the realm and the decisions of the common law courts.[20] That is a position which it is possible to adopt with some degree of logical consistency, but how it relates to questions about the nature of consitutionality is more than a little puzzling. Indeed, even some of the better work in public law in recent years has fallen foul of a failure to relate issues of constitutionality to a clear concept of law.[21] Our 'nature' then needs to be put to the question. There are a number of ways in which this could be done, but I shall speak to two only, though they are related in my mind at least by one strong bond. That bond is constituted by Karl Llewellyn's law-jobs theory, which I have long held to be the single most important contribution to the sociology of law in the last 50 years.

The law-jobs theory is well known, though not as well known as it deserves to be, and I shall not wish to speak to it at length, not least because I have done so elsewhere.[22] Even so, some brief background description is called for.

The law-jobs theory posits that in every group, high or low, from a scout-troop to the United Nations, certain jobs need to be collectively performed in the interests of cohesion and stability:

> And when one looks to see, it is plain enough what the great and basic job is, on which the institution of law and government is focused. It is the job . . . of becoming and remaining and operating as *enough* of a unity . . . to be and remain recognizable *as* a group or *as* a political entity or *as* a society.[23]

Llewellyn's claim amounts to the fact that institutions for performing the law-jobs, variously and not consistently numbered, are 'socially necessary' constructs and in this respect he has much in common with Talcott Parsons's classic theory of social organizations.[24] Another way of putting the same claim is that Llewellyn here is using 'essential' or 'real' definitions. A 'real' definition purports to capture the essence of either the thing or the concept defined, and at first glance looks remarkably like a mere tautology, but need not be if the status of *a priori* knowledge is regarded as such that conceptual truths and conceptual relations are capable of being expressed in terms of the necessities to which human action is subject.[25] It has to be said, however, that although Llewellyn expressed himself in the language of real definitions he sometimes seemed to act as if the law-jobs were simply empirical generalizations. The latter would of course have forced him to examine anew his 'absolute presuppositions', but either way we should find no difficulty in accommodating his theory. I shall return to this larger matter shortly. First, however, and briefly, let us touch upon the jobs themselves.

Within the context of 'the great and basic job' of maintaining social cohesion, a number of 'ideal-type' subcategories emerge. These are the law-jobs of:

(1) The disposition of the trouble case. This amounts to the fact that procedures for grievance-resolution are a necessary feature of group life.
(2) Preventive channelling. For like reason all social systems require procedures of varying degrees of subtlety for the avoidance of disputes.
(3) The constitution of groups. This is the requirement for arrangements or procedures for the establishment of 'constitutional' authority. Whose say is to count?
(4) Goal orientation. This refers to the institutions for securing that a group or social system examines its overall direction and *raison d'être*. It will almost certainly conflate procedural and substantive issues.[26] I should add, if briefly, that the law-jobs are self-evidently distributed in (even) Western societies among the legislative, judicial and administrative processes. This fact alone is of enormous potential for the study of our constitutional and public law, but there are others and they should be regarded as even more weighty. In particular, Llewellyn has often been accused of providing a value-neutral theory of law and legal systems, but closer examination shows this to be not quite the case.

Although a rudimentary description of the law-jobs theory leaves out of account the moral component, this is to dwell only on the 'barebones' aspect of the enterprise. Yet it is clear that, however underdeveloped, legitimation issues did figure in Llewellyn's thinking; hardly surprising given his clearly expressed admiration for Weber. Llewellyn's shorthand for the moral dimension of law was 'questing', meaning that the procedures and institutions for performing the socially necessary jobs had to be harnessed to the belief-system of the group or social system.[27] In short, Llewellyn's theory, properly unpacked, makes law co-terminous with 'legitimate institutional power'. Now, law defined as legitimate institutional power can be defended in a number of different ways and I should say a word about this matter before looking at the implications of adopting this concept as the one informing the answer to the first problem posed at the outset of this essay.

First, it may be that we should wish to define law as 'morally legitimate power', though if this were transcendentally defended it would not be a question simply of what we wished, but rather what we should be forced to contend.[28] If, for instance, purposive rational action has to be attributed to all human beings lest they be treated as less than human, then at least the hard core of legal meaning becomes a matter which goes considerably beyond cultural choice or any other form of convenient pragmatism. The best of these arguments are extremely attractive and exceedingly difficult to refute.[29] However, without prejudice to the status of this position, I shall adopt a different, more 'pragmatic' stance. I shall instead, *à la* Collingwood, ask a question of Western political systems in general and the British polity in particular; viz., *if* I were to regard law as being coterminous with legitimate institutional power, what would I find within our systems of governance? Or to put it another way, what would be distilled if I *immanently* examined and logically counterposed traditional legal assumptions, including the highly normative concept of legal autonomy? What would I produce if I were to seek an empirical description of legitimate institutional power? The answer, I believe, is that I should find courts performing 'law-job One', I should find quangos performing law-job One, I should find ombudsmen and local authority subcommittees, tribunals and disciplinary committees also engaged in the same functional activity. The framework and the context would not always be identical but, all things being equal, they would all be exercising influential power, would all be engaged in decision-making and would all be acting 'legitimately' in that they would all in manners, variously loose and tight, be *entitled* to do what they were doing. A matter not entirely without interest is that similar talents and skills would be required in each of those contexts, thereby making the nature of the undertakings and activities so closely related as logically to separate them out from the activities of other actors in the public social world.

This is obviously an argument not confined to any single one of the law-jobs, but, since the 'disposition of the trouble case' is so close to the heart of traditional legal thinking, it serves my argument perfectly well to use it most extensively for illustrative purposes. I shall find, I know, that the law-jobs, broadly conceived as ideal-types, will be performed within the whole apparatus of public (to say nothing of private) power. I know that because (regardless of their being real or essential definitions, or partaking of the character of 'synthetic *a priori*' knowledge) they have always been there when I have looked, and Western systems of governance would have to change dramatically for me to find my observations confounded. But of course I have been asking for evidence of 'legitimate public power', and naturally I should find different materials with my concept of law so defined than if I defined it in some other way. If I did not define it at all but merely 'intuited' it then I should properly be accused of sleight of hand and of producing untutored confusion.

Moreover, looking for legitimate institutional power will cause me to unearth things which would be readily and immediately classifiable as 'legal' by the intuitionists, by those with a disguised *Gesellschaft* or neo-Austinian concept – but I shall unearth other things as well. I shall be observing the behaviour of governmental advisory committees as well as that of land-use planning enquiries; I shall be observing the behaviour of local authority management subcommittees as well as that of the county court, but then I should have to, given the question I have put to 'nature'. What seems more to the point, however, is to ask for the manner of the question being put to 'nature' by those who only observe the county court and statutory enquiry. What is their unifying theme? What are their presuppositions? I am entitled to know, but I am not always told. If, moreover, I was to seek the presuppositions of those many scholars, not least those operating in the field of constitutional law, and to track them to their lairs, I feel sure that together we should have a most entertaining time in relating those presuppositions to the public empirical world which we inhabit.

Let me summarize this argument. Most usage of law in the constitutional texts has been undeveloped or unexplicated. It is, however, for the most part a product of the English tradition, dominant perhaps ever since the appearance of Bentham's *Fragment*, of contesting the validity of natural law or morally informed theories of law in favour of value-free descriptions of an undefined or largely undefined 'legal' world. When definition is forthcoming (e.g. Austin, Hart, Kelsen) its 'absolute presuppositions' are elusive or highly contestable at both the prescriptive and descriptive levels.

If, on the other hand, we are to equate law with legitimate institutional power, our analysis of the modern world, at least from one particular sharp focus, will have considerable explanatory potential. Furthermore, there is every reason why we should adopt this formulation. First, it is a real or essential definition which, therefore, genuinely transcends historical conditions, and secondly, whatever the inclinations of others, there can be few more important enterprises *per se* for the constitutional scholar than to map out legitimate institutional power.[30]

THE PUBLIC DOMAIN:
ANOTHER PROBLEM OF DEFINITION

To identify 'the public domain' is, of course, to define a major constitutional concern. It is to locate the pulse of authoritative, legitimate decision-making, even if it leaves open the question of what manner of decision-making is in turn legitimate.

The classical liberal theory of the British constitution is expounded by Dicey, who, with others of his time, detected a clear cleavage between the public and private spheres. The public was restricted to the election of an assembly, whose task was to create the conditions and the context for private ordering to take place. Those conditions and contexts might be marginally contested, but periodic adjustments and accommodations would ensure that the two spheres rarely commingled.

I have argued elsewhere[31] that such a distinction was untenable when it was first made and has become totally unsustainable over the longer period. These vital arguments I shall pass over for present purposes but several matters require some elaboration. The constitutional settlement of the seventeenth century has left us with a Parliament which claims legislative omnicompetence in spite of the promises contained in the Bill of Rights. In other words, notwithstanding the post-Second-World-War importance of the European dimension, there is no 'reserved' constitutional business. I should, if pressed, argue for an irreducible private sphere on other grounds,[32] but I would not be engaging in an immanent critique of the state of the nation were I to do so. This is, in fact, what I shall be primarily concerned to analyse in this section. What will I find if I turn the legitimation/ideological claims of the British system of governance in on themselves and subject them to scrutiny for their degree of logical fit and correspondence with the empirical world? The fact is that Parliament in uncontested constitutional theory may legislate as it wishes. The constraints of a *substantive* nature, are considered to reside in the procedural imperatives of our constitution – or, as I have argued elsewhere,[33] the legitimation foundations of the British state are comprised in the procedural features of the 'rule of law' as understood post-1689. Some further explanation is necessary.

The twin pillars of the constitutional settlement came, over a period of years, to mean the omnicompetence of an elected representative Parliament whose promises to the people were supervised by the courts of common law. This is to collapse together a number of intricate strains which I address in the work referred to above. However, in short, a democratically elected and recallable assembly was seen to be supervised according to strong principles of legal autonomy. The promises of which the courts were public trustees, however, were only those of a very general sort; *viz.*, that 'legislative commitments' would be honoured (thus the canons of statutory interpretation and, of course, *ultra vires*) and that public agents would not act in an openly dishonourable fashion (the Wednesbury test for reasonableness, estoppel and other, relatively minor, impedimenta).[34] No *principes généraux du droit* confined the administrative machine which has come to be Parliament's agent and no specific body of public law has emerged to give special definition to the nature of the public compact. Nevertheless, both reliance on the courts and the right to elect the omnicompetent assembly give force and meaning to two incontestable legitimation principles, these being the reverse faces of the same constitutional coin. It should be remembered that I am here engaging only in an 'immanent' critique of our constitutional fundaments; that is to say that I am simply examining the internal logic of constitutional ideology and pitting it against empirical (political) reality.

The two principles which are at base of our polity are openness and accountability. This will surprise many, but it should not. Let us take openness first: all the major ideological underpinnings of constitutional discourse entail, presuppose, openness as a systemic characteristic. This statement is equally true of all the collective phenomena to which we have long clung and to which we have long paid homage; to 'democracy', to 'legal autonomy' and to the 'rule of law'. Let me address them briefly in turn.

Democracy is a highly contested notion,[35] but let us settle for the narrowest, most consensual variety. Let us settle for representative democracy based on universal suffrage and recallability with the representative owing mere judgment and nothing to delegate status. The elective, the choosing, exercise depends entirely for its meaning upon selecting between alternatives, upon exercising preference and judgment. It is, again, a 'real' or 'essential' definition. To choose presupposes knowledge about alternatives and knowledge cannot at heart be ignorant. Inferences may be ignorant but the raw material for choosing must not be contaminated. This is not, of course, to *describe* the behaviour of British public life, it is rather to characterize its essential nature; it is to unpack its claims and expose them to whatever real world it finds.

Legal autonomy too, we shall discover, depends upon beliefs which transcend any particular moments. It is the notion that a disinterested, non-partisan, cadre of specialists shall contest arbitrary conduct, shall hold the mighty to their tryst with the public, with citizens, and shall honour their formally announced pledges. This too can only rationally be conducted in an atmosphere of calculation and measurement, of information as opposed to concealment. Again, we speak to the characteristic rather than the actual nature of autonomy.

Since the rule of law in Britain has come to mean a fusion of these two phenomena, it should hardly surprise that it too presupposes an open society. The Diceyan version, it will be recalled, depended *centrally and crucially* upon the existence of generalizable rules known in advance, so that the civic pre-ordering of affairs could be rationally undertaken. Substitute 'the rule of legitimate institutional power' for 'the rule of (undefined) law' and the consequence of knowing in advance how that institutional power proposes to address civic affairs is an unalloyed belief in open government, freedom of information *et al.* The argument seems to me to be closed; the logical implication of recognizing the collapse of the highly dubious notion of the separation of powers and the fact of the extended administrative state is that its conduct, policies and programmes should be known, probably in advance. If the state does more than issue rules (i.e. 'legal' norms) then other manifestations of institutional power need public declaration as surely as statutes of the realm or judicial pronouncements in open court.

ACCOUNTABILITY: A BRIEF SURVEY

The literature on accountability, with the exceptions already noted, is for the most part impoverished. This, in my view, is primarily because it is normally conjured out of the air or smuggled into debate without reference to its authorizing presuppositions. It is true that in recent years some attention has been paid to problems of accountability in a middle-range, systems or meta-policy kind of fashion. Forms of vertical and horizontal, *ex post* and *ex ante*, accountability have been usefully discussed but these are ultimately only of value where they can be related to a larger criterion or principle.

Having espoused the concept of openness through an examination of immanent constitutional beliefs, we are thereby already carried some way towards accepting a minimalist version of accountability. This is because predicating openness as a central belief carries with it the necessary entailment that conduct thereby illuminated shall in some way be judged; that it shall be examined to see in what sense it passes muster. That judgment was originally, in earlier periods of our history, made according to criteria of financial stewardship, and whereas that continues to be of crucial significance, the basic transformation from representative government to representative *democratic* government has fundamentally altered civic expectations. The account to be rendered must now, if choosing is the accompaniment of visibility, be capable of evaluation by citizenry and Parliament alike.

Let us limit ourselves to the latter since our primary constitutional axiom is that of parliamentary sovereignty or omnicompetence. Parliament, on this view, is representative of the voter as franchise-holder from time to time. If the elective exercise is to be meaningful, public power has to be accountable to Parliament, whose members can then be judged by their constituents. Now, whereas the quality of and the mechanism of account may properly be regarded as contingent matters, they must be such as to satisfy Parliament ultimately that it is in a position to make a rational assessment of publicly exercised power. Leaving aside for a moment what constitutes (legitimate) publicly exercised power we have now advanced the argument considerably.

The role of the constitutional lawyer in particular thereby becomes clearer. It is to examine the empirical map of public power and the institutions of its exercise to see how far an account, the opportunity to judge public conduct, is in fact rendered to Parliament. This exercise will not be further treated here, but suffice it to say that were such an examination to be currently conducted, it would be impossible to resist the conclusion that procedures of accountability are markedly deficient, regardless of what a proper restorative balance might look like.

LEGITIMATE PUBLIC POWER

I have explained that no attempt will be made here to plead for a reserved sphere of private life (though it may be argued that a belief in the individual physical liberties is part of our civic expectations) and that parliamentary omnicompetence will be taken as axiomatic. I have elsewhere made a detailed defence of the argument that, since power is now exercised through rather than by Parliament, we may safely speak not only of parliamentary omnicompetence but also of executive delegated omnicompetence. Parliament operating as it does within a complex system of welfare capitalism mediated to a considerable extent by external factors must act primarily through its agents.[36] Within British traditions such agents (except where their conduct is specifically prohibited) will be wielding legitimate public power.

The argument from now on is relatively simple, if instructive. The agents of Parliament are simply all those whom it appoints, directly or indirectly: ministers, civil servants, quasi-government, quasi-non-government, the nationalized industries. In short tracing legitimate public power becomes largely an (empirical) mapping exercise which, of course, we are entitled to do relatively unimpeded if openness is at the heart of our polity. The activities of the agents or 'public actors', not least the way they exercise their discretion, the way they make, unmake or fail to make policy – these should be a major focus for investigation. This way we include the whole of 'legitimate public power' – legislation, contract, concessions, grant, remission, franchise. All relationships acted out in Parliament's name, even inferentially, drop into the sack. That way the networks and webs of government fall to be examined by the constitutional lawyer. Not merely the formal manifestations – the statutory duty to consult, the quango, the advisory committee – but the informal and semi-formal arrangements which we may characterize as modes of policy intervention.

One of the styles of policy intervention in recent times most remarked upon, at least by political scientists, is the phenomenon known generically as corporatism.[37] The fact that it is a phenomenon rarely remarked upon by lawyers must say something about the theories upon which they operate. Presumably it is fairly difficult simply to 'intuit' or 'merely apprehend' corporatism, pluralism, *ex parte* negotiations with interest groups and the like. It seems, however, relatively straightforward to comb the social science texts and the journalistic prose, to say nothing of publications emanating from government, and to identify styles and concepts of policy intervention once put on enquiry. An immanent critique based upon close examination of the rule of law, however, will reveal such patterns and processes. An immanent critique is one which *par excellence* puts questions to 'nature'. It says, 'If these are your claims, your ruling principles, are you being true to them? If not, what do you wish to do about it?' It will usually reveal central contradictions between legal and constitutional ideology (the grain beneath the rule-of-law stone) and political actuality.

One more issue concerning legitimate public power may be identified, not least because it is normally ignored in legal scholarship. It is the issue of non-decision-making. Perhaps the central failure of the 1970s' infatuation with discretion in legal circles was that it did not work programmatically on K. C. Davis's observation that the decision not to act/not to prosecute was an issue of outstanding vitality to the conduct of public business. A literature of a political-science sort exists in relation to non-decision-making, to not pursuing particular regulatory programmes, to the fact of patterns of familiarity which shape the political agenda, the terms of public debate and the like. It has not been programmatically addressed by public lawyers who ought to be engaged in the profession of constitutional architecture. Indeed, to my knowledge, few if any of our colleagues have attended to the American literature on judicial review of agency/administrative/policy inaction or failure to implement or prosecute policies.[38] The failure to take timely or effective action can scarcely be underestimated, whether it relates to allowing the Stock Exchange to conduct its affairs without governmental interference or the trade union movement to organize without respecting democratic formulae,[39] yet it merits scarcely a mention in the constitutional texts. This range of inaction, of non-decision-making, is barely addressed in institutional terms, is outside the contemplation of orthodox legal scholarship, unsurprisingly given its positivistic traditions. Yet, when the accountability call comes, it ought to figure most prominently on the roll of public concerns. Bringing 'studied failure to act' to book is merely one, if vital, strand of the web of public power legitimately approved by our governmental practices. It needs attention and would respond effectively to the appearance of new institutions and formulae for genuine accountability. Sir Douglas Wass, in his 1983 Reith Lectures[40] canvassed the idea of a Standing Royal Commission to examine matters of constitutional concern and this, no doubt, could make a valuable contribution to the issues under discussion. My own feelings, developed elsewhere, are that a more systematic and intricate approach to these problems is required, but at least Sir Douglas has initiated a lively debate.[41]

CONSTITUTIONAL HIGHLIGHTS

My search for legitimate institutional power has led me through an immanent critique of ruling ideology to deep-seated expectations about openness and accountability which in any event are logically necessary in a free society which sets its store by a wish to treat citizens equally. Furthermore, the axiom of parliamentary sovereignty, set against a map of actual decision-making in the 'public' realm, reveals that delegated executive 'omnicompetence' is a legitimate feature of our constitutional system and practice.

The natural implication of this state of affairs is that the constitutional lawyer sets about the task of charting the institutions and processes of actual public power, in the first place to describe what he sees. In the second place, the contradictions revealed between actuality and constitutional claim should lead to a reassessment of the constitutional machinery of government with a view to restoring meaning to the underlying principles which inform rule-of-law ideology. If that were attempted there is little doubt in my mind that new expectations would be engendered which in turn would lead to newer demands for institutional delivery systems. The logic of an immanent critique is, after all, the setting in train of a dialectic process.[42]

I have not chosen here to speak at length about the institutional implications of exposing and relating constitutional claim and reality. Even so, a signpost might be erected if only to defend myself against charges that what has gone before is mere aridity. Perhaps the salient feature of British governmental practice is its pursuance of networked, 'twilight' decision-making; its classification of interests as 'insiders' and 'outsiders' and its obsession with *ex parte* dealings. With due respect to the need for confidentiality in sensitive areas of public activity, the constitutional response must surely be to bring public business into the sunlight. Freedom of information is, of course, a precondition of this exercise and it is now an idea whose time has surely come. Nonetheless, in and of itself, it will do little to meet constitutional promise and will need considerable buttressing by tailored democratic devices. We could begin, however, by thinking about Government in the Sunshine Legislation, by paying attention to the US Federal Advisory Committees Act 1974 and evaluating the sophisticated transatlantic studies of the *ex parte* and lobbying problem.[43] Were we to do so we should have begun to canvass a more contemporary role for a reawakened judiciary whose potential for liberating participative discourse in the policy-making process has scarcely been tapped. The judiciary, not necessarily as presently constituted, are 'the least dangerous branch' and legal autonomy is a moral heritage to be prized. These two are capable of underwriting a system of constitutional law which recognizes the need for a responsive set of institutions directed to producing, as Richard Stewart has said, a 'surrogate political process'.[44] Ask questions of our public 'nature' and we might all be pleasantly surprised at some of the answers we received. Intuitive realism belongs to the darker ages of legal analysis.

NOTES

1 See e.g. Pierce and Shapiro, 'Political and Judicial Review of Agency Action' (1981) 59 *Texas Law Rev.* p. 1175.

2 See the most illuminating book carrying this title by Nevil Johnson (1977).

3 The literature on legitimation is enormously rich, though most of it can be traced back to Weber. For a recent influential treatment see J. Habermas, *Communication and the Evolution of Society* (1979).

4 See e.g. Lewis and Harden, 'Privatisation, De-Regulation and Constitutionality: Some Anglo-American Comparisons' (1983) 34 *N Ire. Legal Q* p. 207, and the same authors, *De-Legalisation in Britain in the 1980s* (1984).

5 See for example, the symposium on the issue in (1982) 130 *University of Pennsylvania Law Rev.* p. 1289, and Lewis and Harden, *De-Legalisation in Britain, op. cit., passim.*

6 For one of a number of very good treatments, see G. Poggi, 'State and Society under Liberalism and After' in *The Development of the Modern State* (1978).

7 G. Marshall, *Constitutional Conventions* (1984).
8 *Id.*, p. 1.
9 *Id.*, p. 18.
10 Though see I. Harden and N. Lewis, *The Rule of Law and the British Constitution* (1986). Perhaps the best treatment of the thorny problem of accountability is B. Smith and D. Hague, *The Dilemma of Accountability in Modern Government* (1971) esp. ch. 14 by E. L. Normanton.
11 R. G. Collingwood, *An Essay on Metaphysics* (1940).
12 *Id.*, p. 34. I am grateful to Deryck Beyleveld for drawing my attention to this quotation and introducing me to Collingwood's work.
13 *Id.*, pp. 144-5.
14 *Id.*, pp. 238-9.
15 *Id.*, pp. 37 and 254-5.
16 For an impressive modern treatise on this theme see A. Gewirth, *Reason and Morality* (1978).
17 For a general view of the problems see A. Ryan, *The Philosophy of the Social Sciences* (1970), and W. G. Runciman, *A Treatise on Social Theory*, vol. 1 (1983).
18 See particularly T. S. Kuhn, *The Structure of Scientific Revolutions* (1962). Pragmatist theories are, in the language of philosophy, 'incommensurable'; cf. transcendental rationalism for which see M. Hollis, 'The Limits of Irrationality', in *Rationality* (ed. B. Wilson 1974) pp. 214-20.
19 Ryan, *op. cit.*, pp. 4-5.
20 See for a broad description of *Gesellschaft* and competing legal forms E. Kamenka and A. Tay, *Beyond Bourgeois Individualism: The Contemporary Crisis in Law and Legal Ideology in Feudalism, Capitalism and Beyond* (1975; ed. E. Kamenka and R. S. Neale), p. 127.
21 See the otherwise admirable work of my colleague Tony Prosser, 'Towards a Critical Public Law' (1982) 9 *J Law and Society* 1, where he identifies the problem without coming to any very firm conclusion.
22 'Towards a Sociology of Lawyering in Public Administration' (1981) 32 *N Ire. Legal Q*, 89, *De-Legalisation in Britain*, *op. cit.*, and Harden and Lewis, *op. cit.*
23 'Law and the Social Sciences Especially Sociology' (1949) 62 *Harvard Law Rev.* 1286. The law-jobs theory is treated at various places by Llewellyn but the most rigorous exposition is to be found in 'The Normative, the Legal and the Law-Jobs' (1940) 49 *Yale Law J* 1355.
24 T. Parsons, *The Social System* (1951).
25 See e.g. M. Hollis, *Models of Man* (1977) esp. ch. 3.
26 A somewhat lengthier treatment can be found in 'Towards a Sociology of Lawyering', *op. cit.*
27 See 'The Normative', *op. cit.*, p. 1399.
28 What we would have to do in fact is to conflate two things: the 'real' definition of law as socially necessary for normative integration, and the attribution of a particular, necessary, moral identity to the basic norms themselves.
29 The best in my view are Gerwirth, *op. cit.*, and Beyleveld and Brownsword, 'Law as a Moral Judgement vs Law as the Rules of the Powerful' (1983) 23 *Am. J Jurisprudence* p. 79.
30 This raises the important issue of the separation between law and politics for which see *De-Legalisation in Britain*, *op. cit.*, pp. 5-7.
31 *Id.*, pp. 7-13.
32 See Gewirth, *op. cit.*, esp. pp. 213, 242 and 275.
33 See Harden and Lewis, *op. cit.*, esp. ch. 2.

34 *Id.*
35 See *Id.*, ch. 2.
36 See *Id.*, *passim.*
37 See e.g. G. Lembruch and P. C. Schmitter (eds), *Patterns of Corporatist Policy-Making* (1982). A. Cawson, *Corporatism and Welfare* (1982), and M. Harrison (ed.) *Corporatism and the Welfare State* (1984).
38 See e.g. Stewart and Sunstein, 'Public Programs and Private Rights' (1982) 95 *Harvard Law Rev.* 1195, and Lehner, 'Judicial Review of Administrative Inaction' (1983) 83 *Columbia Law Rev.*, p. 627.
39 See esp. L. C. B. Gower, *Review of Investor Protection*, Report Part I (1984; Cmnd 9125).
40 D. Wass, *Government and the Governed* (1984).
41 Harden and Lewis, *op. cit.*, part III.
42 See e.g. Trubek, 'Complexity and Contradiction in the Legal Order' (1977) 11 *Law and Society Rev.* 529.
43 See e.g. ACUS, *A Guide to Federal Agency Rulemaking* (1983).
44 Stewart, 'The Reformation of American Administrative Law' (1975) 88 *Harvard Law Rev.* 1667.

7
Legal Theory and the Interpretation of Statutes

DAVID MIERS

> the interpretive function may be said to be the central function of a legal system.
>
> *Talcott Parsons*[1]

Interpretation is a central feature of social life, while the interpretation of statutes constitutes an increasingly significant part of the professional life of judges[2] and of those who advise public and private persons about their legal rights and duties. The shared experience and familiarity with interpretation in these and other contexts have not, however, been accompanied by agreement as to its constituent properties; sharp and profound differences of opinion as to what it entails continue to be voiced, for example, in social theory, historiography, literary criticism and various branches of philosophy.[3] The persistent and perplexing uncertainties that are addressed within and between these and other disciplines likewise continue to constitute the stuff of our disagreements about the theory and practice of statutory interpretation. Does a coherent account of interpretation presuppose a theory of adjudication and/or legislation? Is there a single right answer to every question of statutory interpretation and, if not, what does that tell us about the enterprise? What are the values and the limits of reliance upon the judicial interpretation of statutes for developing more general descriptive (and prescriptive) accounts of interpretation? Do the various 'rules' of statutory interpretation comprise anything beyond, at best, an innocuous set of propositions that can be pressed to justify alternative outcomes to points of dispute or, at worst, a sinister rhetoric that obfuscates and mystifies the operation of bias and prejudice? What is, and what ought to be, the relationship between the formulation and the interpretation of legislation, and can one of these enterprises be made 'better' (and in whose judgment) without adjustments to the other? And what is meant by 'interpretation', 'the intent of the legislature' or even a 'text'?

Some of these questions have only recently been canvassed in the literature; others are more familiar. They are all, however, constant reminders of the importance, firstly, of distinguishing between the who, the what and the why of interpretation and interpretive practices and, secondly, of resisting the seductive tendency to criticize the practice without first constructing an adequate account of how problems of interpretation arise and why the practices that ordinarily resolve them are not dispositive in some cases. Failure to attend to these matters encourages a misplaced scepticism.

Of course we can be sceptical about the capacity of contemporary interpretive practices to facilitate even a measure of predictive efficiency, let alone to be dispositive of a majority of questions of statutory interpretation. Likewise, we can be sceptical about their capacity to constrain the exercise of judicial discretion, to contribute to the realization of some conception of rational adjudication or about the possibility of constructing anything better; but it is important to begin by clarifiying *who* is being sceptical about *what* aspects of interpretive practice, for what purpose and to what degree.[4] A first task for legal theory is to isolate and to formulate the matters that require clarification.

Statutory interpretation is important to legal theory *inter alia* because descriptions of interpretive practice as applied to statutes are evidence against which theories or explanations of, for example, judicial process or adjudication can be tested;[5] but what of the contribution of legal theory to our understanding of these practices? Legal theory continues to be troubled by a tension between two, apparently rival, conceptions of what is to be regarded as the authoritative source of meaning when interpreting statutory provisions.[6] One conceives the statutory *text* as an object capable of bearing meaning independent of the interpreter (and, indeed, of the author's possible intentions) which is in large measure self-interpreting. Within a formalist tradition, such a conception encourages a belief in the determinacy of the text and in the validity of attending primarily to its linguistic components as the best (and in extreme versions, the only) method for elucidating the 'meaning' that this conception asserts is contained within the text. The second regards the *interpreter* as being the appropriate object of study,[7] whose discretion to create meaning is considered to be more or less constrained by a variety of factors (of which the canonical terms of the text are but one). In extreme versions, this conception would relegate to the waste bin, almost entirely, any potential in the text for constraint beyond the cynical use by the judiciary of such formulations as 'the plain words of the statute' to rationalize previously arrived-at decisions. Thus, and allowing for the hyperbole of those who have just rediscovered the light bulb, two commentators sympathetic to the main tenets of the critical legal studies movement write of its attitude to interpretive practices:

> Legal doctrine not only does not, but also cannot, generate determinant results in concrete cases. Law is not so much a rational enterprise as a vast exercise in rationalization. Legal doctrine can be manipulated to justify an almost infinite spectrum of possible outcomes. Moreover, a plausible argument can be made that any such outcome has been derived from the dominant legal conceptions. Legal doctrine is nothing more than a sophisticated vocabulary and repertoire of manipulative techniques for categorizing, describing, organizing, and comparing; it is *not* a methodology for reaching substantive outcomes.[8]

Leaving aside for the moment the epistemological assumptions implicit in these two positions,[9] it is clear that in their extreme versions neither represents the mainstream treatment of statutory interpretation within Anglo-American legal theory. Nevertheless each represents a *starting-point* which can subsequently be compromised, on the one hand, by a concession to the observable fact that statutes do frequently delegate to judges (and other interpreters) the task of giving specific content to open-ended expressions or that words do have a penumbra of uncertainty, and on the other, by a recognition that whatever cosmetic functions they may perform, the exact words of the text are taken seriously by judges and that failure to attend to them routinely results in criticism, or that words do bear, in given contexts, a core of settled meaning.

Thus standard treatments of the (judicial) theory and practice of statutory interpretation in this country have observed that such rules, approaches, canons, aids and presumptions concerning interpretive practice as have been generated by the judiciary continue to be neither systematic nor dispositive.[10] The absence, in particular, of priority norms for resolving conflicts between them means that confidence in the predictive value of these practices remains low.[11] While some writers have interpreted recent *dicta* advocating a purposive approach to interpretation as an attempt by the judiciary to assimilate to one set of rational and consistent propositions the old triumvirate of literal, golden and mischief rules,[12] it is difficult to argue that these *dicta* explicitly constitute a comprehensive and agreed set of interpretive practices.[13] This remains so even when they are read together with the more substantial accumulation of *dicta* recorded in textbooks on statutory interpretation that indicate how specific issues are to be approached. It is arguably the case that the development of a comprehensive set of interpretive practices is neither a desirable objective for the judiciary, nor in any event a feasible one.

Given the freedom that they enjoy under the present regime, it is difficult to see why judges should want to initiate radical changes in their practices. In much the same way as they have deliberately not formulated rules for 'discovering' the *ratio decidendi* of a case,[14] judges have in this context consistently allowed themselves scope for determining what constitutes good interpretive practice. The judicial interpretation of statutes has traditionally been characterized by a high degree of tolerated indeterminacy as to what amounts to acceptable practice. Recorded deviations are relatively rare, as they are in the analogous context of dealing with precedent.[15] The critical responses to them typically reaffirm the generally understood boundaries; they do not ordinarily bring very much greater definition to what does amount to acceptable practice.[16]

Were radical change desirable, its feasibility must be doubted. A comprehensive set of interpretive practices presupposes the following minimum conditions. Agreement, firstly, as to the classification of statutes and their individual provisions or as to the purposes of interpretation (and leaving aside the possibility of such agreement for the purposes of drafting and enactment). Agreement, secondly, as to how problems of interpretation are to be identified and formulated and as to what constitute authoritative and cogent arguments apt to resolve them. Thirdly, the construction of a set of priority rules for resolving conflicts both within and between each of these subsets of interpretive activity. All of these pose a range of difficulties for a prescriptive theory of the (judicial) interpretation of statutes that purports to be dispositive even of a majority of issues of statutory interpretation.[17] A more moderate set of aspirations for developing good interpretive practice need not, however, regard them as insuperable.

Notwithstanding these various features of contemporary interpretive practice, standard treatments of the judicial interpretation of statutes emphasize that its indeterminancy, though tolerated and inevitable, is bounded. It is a social fact that judges (and other interpretive communities) do recognize and routinely act upon a set of constraints (which includes the specific terms of the statutory text) that have meaning for them and which foreclose some interpretations. By contrast with what has been characterized as the 'nihilism' of the critical legal studies movement, this standard treatment does postulate that 'objective interpretation' is both a meaningful and possible epistemology.

> Objectivity in the law connotes standards. It implies that an interpretation can be measured against a set of norms that transcend the particular vantage point of the person offering the interpretation. Objectivity implies that the interpretation can be judged by something other than one's own notions of correctness. It imparts a notion of impersonality. The idea of an objective interpretation does not require that the interpretation be wholly determined by some source external to the judge, but only that it can be constrained. To explain the source of constraint in the law, it is necessary to introduce two further concepts: one is the idea of disciplining rules, which constrain the interpreter and constitute the standards by which the correctness of the interpretation is to be judged; the other is the idea of an interpretive community, which recognizes these rules as authoritative.
>
> The idea of objective interpretation accommodates the creative role of the reader. It recognizes that the meaning of a text does not reside in the text, as an object might reside in physical space or as an element might be said to be present in a chemical compound, ready to be extracted if only one knows the correct process; it recognizes a role for the subjective. Indeed, interpretation is defined as the process by which the meaning of a text is understood and expressed, and the acts of understanding and expression necessarily entail strong personal elements. At the same time, the freedom of the interpreter is not absolute. The interpreter is not free to assign any meaning he wishes to the text. He is disciplined by a set of rules that specify the relevance and weight to be assigned to the material (e.g., words, history, intention, consequence), as well as by those that define basic concepts and that established the procedural circumstances under which the interpretation must occur.[18]

A critic can question the ideological assumptions that inform these constraints, and may in particular cases demonstrate that they are question-begging, mutually inconsistent or otherwise incompatible with other generally held values which the legal system or the political morality of a society purport to advance, but to understand *how* they are employed and *why* they have significance for the interpretive community under scrutiny, it is necessary to comprehend *what* they assert to be good interpretive practice.

> So even if all justifying reasons in law never function as more than ostensibly justifying reasons to cloak decisions always motivated upon other grounds, the only possible way of establishing that would be by reasonably exhaustive study and analysis of what are, on any view, at least *ostensibly* justifying reasons. So we may as well get on with it, to see what turns up.[19]

As has already been suggested, all of these various conceptions of interpretation expressly or impliedly assume some position as to the possibility of objective knowledge. In this respect, a theoretical study of statutory interpretation as an intellectual activity raises profound and difficult issues. It is only in recent years that the competing epistemologies generated within, for example, social and linguistic theory, have been seen to have any relevance to what are analogous concerns in legal theory.[20] Being matters of 'high theory', these issues properly belong within legal theory's treatment of statutory interpretation and, as recent controversies indicate, can illuminate aspects of the epistemological assumptions made by these various conceptions. But there is also a place for 'middle-order' theory which emphasizes, for example, the development of frames of reference that provide a coherent basis for legal discourse generally and for particular parts of it, such as statutory interpretation.[21] Middle-order theorizing may also include the development of prescriptive working theories of interpretation and associated activities such as legal reasoning or adjudication.

It is perhaps here that legal theory can lay to rest the persistent view that 'academic' discourse is of marginal relevance to the 'practical' problems of statutory interpretation. An atheoretical stance asserts that interpreters can simply get on with the business of interpretation – of responding directly to the text either unencumbered, except in a minority of cases, by any assumptions about their role or the function of interpretation, or in the absence of any systematic procedures for diagnosing and resolving problems of interpretation. Certainly the interpretation of statutes has its mundane aspects. It ordinarily involves decisions (which have to be made, like it or not) about the scope of statutory words or the relationship between a statutory provision and another authoritative source of law which do not directly raise questions, for example, about the 'intention of the legislature' or about preferred theories of adjudication. But this does not mean that statutory interpretation is easy or that it can exist as a routine intellectual activity in the absence of assumptions about the interpreter's standpoint and about his conception of good practice: 'there is no practice without theory, however much that theory is suppressed, unformulated or perceived as "obvious"'.[22]

It may be that legal theory has failed to show practitioners how it can be relevant to issues of statutory interpretation; the traditional concentration on conceptual questions is some way removed from such issues as whether the word 'bar' in s.75(5) of the Licensing Act 1964 denotes a counter over which intoxicating liquor is served or the room containing that counter.[23] But as Lord Diplock's speech in *Carter* v. *Bradbeer* clearly demonstrates,[24] there is a place for middle-order theory in statutory interpretation. It would be a poor reflection on legal theory if it could not construct a coherent account of that activity which would be of value to professional interpreters.

A connected task is to get behind the assertion sometimes made that statutory interpretation is an 'art' and is for that reason not susceptible to analysis.[25] If by this is meant that statutory interpretation is substantially a matter of experience, then that is of course so; but that does not mean that the abilities of a seasoned campaigner to formulate issues of statutory interpretation accurately and quickly and to construct arguments apt to resolve them (or to counter opposing arguments) are ineffable. After many years' experience, professional interpreters may well speak of a 'feel' for what constitutes good interpretive practice or of their ability to identify a 'fit' between one statutory provision and another; but such metaphorical talk should not be allowed to disguise discernible and describable intellectual processes.

Beyond these aspects of high and middle-order theorizing, other tasks for legal theory suggest themselves.

(1) The development of a sociology of legislation which, while examining at large the formulation, implementation and impact of legislation, looks in particular at the interpretation of statutes by all those, including judges, who undertake that job.

(2) Analysis of the ways in which interpretive practice could be 'better' which recognizes the force of different actors' conceptions of 'good' practice.[26]

(3) Assuming interpretive practice could be 'better', an analysis of the desirability of reform and, in particular, its potential impact upon other practices such as legislative drafting.

(4) Further exploration of the similarities and dissimilarities between the interpretation of case-law rules and statutory rules,[27] and of statutory rules and other rules (trusts, wills, international conventions, contracts and the like) intended to have legal force.[28]

The issues that have been raised in the foregoing paragraphs are central to the theory and practice of statutory interpretation; some have received greater attention than others within legal theory, but there is certainly no shortage of items to make up its agenda. One of these items concerns the potency of the analogy between interpretation in legal and in non-legal contexts, in particular, literary contexts. There is a current resurgence of interest in this analogy, prompted in part by theoretical developments within literary criticism. The following section considers the implications and value of this analogy for our understanding of interpretive practice as it applies to statutory provisions.

INTERPRETATION IN LEGAL AND LITERARY CONTEXTS

There is an enduring attraction in drawing analogies between the interpretation, on the one hand, of statutes and, on the other, of literature, music and such other products of the imagination.[29] Both enterprises apparently involve the construction of 'meaning' from the interaction of three objects of study: a text or other object displaying signs having meaning within a given context, an author whose 'intended' meaning is supposedly represented by the text, and an interpreter who at some later point in time seeks to give a 'meaning' to the text which usually, but not always, is intended to be congruent with what the author intended. So the familiar problems of statutory interpretation are replicated in the interpretation of literature or music. Texts do not always yield single right answers in particular cases but their signs are compatible with competing interpretations in respect of which the applicable norms supply no agreed order of priority. Neither do texts always appear exactly to represent the intentions of the author as gleaned from other sources within the text or indeed from outside it. Interpreters may disagree as to whether the intentions of the author are either 'available or desirable'[30] as a guide to interpretation and may likewise disagree as to whether, if at all, changes over time in linguistic, social or other values should be relevant to present interpretation. It would be possible to cite many instances from legal discourse that reflect these similarities;[31] for present purposes we may note the quite striking similarities in the way in which law and literature have characterized some of their main theoretical assumptions about interpretation and about the relationship between the author, the text and the interpreter.

A powerful, and for many years, the dominant conception of critical practice within literature was 'expressive realism'. 'This is the theory that literature reflects the *reality* of experience as it is perceived by one . . . individual, who *expresses* it in a discourse which enables other individuals to recognise it as true.'[32] Belsey observes that one implication of this theory is that 'the text is seen as a way of arriving at something anterior to it'.[33] This could as well describe the basic constitutional principle of statutory interpretation that requires a judge to read the words of the section in order to discover what Parliament's intention was. Likewise, the problems normally associated with the question whether, and to what extent, recourse should be allowed to parliamentary and pre-parliamentary texts as evidence of that intention are equally well characterized in this criticism of expressive realism:

> Difficulties which have emerged include the problem of access to the idea or experience which is held to precede the expression of it. What form does it take? Do ideas exist outside discourse? Is the idea formulated in one discourse (a letter or a diary) *the same* as an idea formulated *in different words* in another discourse (a literary text)?[34]

Echoes of legal rhetoric can also be found in one of the most important critiques of expressive realism, new criticism. In its original version, new criticism denied altogether the relevance of the author to critical practice; its insistence upon the words of the text as being the uniquely authoritative source of meaning has its counterparts in often repeated judicial and other *dicta* about the role of the interpreter.

Both these conceptions (and their variants) of the relationship between the text, its author and the interpreter share the assumption that each constituent is autonomous and that a main task for theory is to reconcile and accommodate the conflicts that arise between them. This is precisely the same assumption that is made in connection with statutory interpretation, and which results in the tension within legal theory described earlier. Recent developments in literary criticism challenge this epistemological position, and thus have significant implications for theoretical accounts of statutory interpretation. Dworkin, among others, has relied on some of these developments as a way of coming to terms with the seemingly intractable alternative between meaning lying in the plain words of the statute or in the efforts of a (relatively) unfettered interpreter; between objectivity and subjectivity in interpretation. Though of importance, Dworkin's use of literary theory to develop his own position on interpretation and its relationship to his theory of adjudication is not uncontroversial. Likewise, the value of drawing analogies from literary theory for the purpose of improving interpretive practice in statutory interpretation demands careful consideration.

Interpretive Communities in Theory

To put the matter shortly, it is argued that texts do not exist independently of the interpreter, but that it is the interpretive practices of the community (legal, musical, literary, etc.) to which he belongs that themselves constitute the text.[35] To start one's enquiry by asking whether it is the judge or the statutory words that constitute the authoritative source of meaning is to beg a number of critical questions about the independence of the objects of study (readers, texts) and about the validity of interpretive strategies designed to rationalize a subjective decision or to discover a meaning contained in the section. This is the orthodoxy; to the contrary it is argued that interpretive strategies do not post-date the text but are logically prior to it and constitute it.

> Interpretive communities are made up of those who share interpretive strategies not for reading (in the conventional sense) but for writing texts, for constituting their properties and assigning their intentions. In other words, these strategies exist prior to the act of reading and therefore determine the shape of what is read rather than, as is usually assumed, the other way around.[36]

Literature (and statutes) are therefore conventional categories created by the interpretive strategies to which the relevant communities subscribe; but this creation is not without its constraints. Paraphrasing Fish, the act of recognizing a set of words as a statutory text is not constrained by something in the text, nor does it issue from an independent and arbitrary will; rather, it proceeds from a collective decision as to what will count as a statutory text, a decision that will be in force only so long as a community of readers or believers continues to abide by it.[37] Thus all the phrases concerning the supremacy of Parliament in the matter of certain sets of words having been promulgated under a given set of rules, and all the other rules of statutory interpretation with which lawyers are familiar and to which judges constantly resort, constitute the interpretive strategies of these communities, which in turn constitute what will count as a statutory text. Interpreters, no less than the texts which their strategies constitute, are themselves constituted by conventional ways of thinking.

According to this thesis, disagreements between those who believe that the text is the sole authoritative source of meaning (be they characterized as textualists or formalists) and those who believe that other sources of meaning may be authoritative (contextualists, realists) or between 'literal' and 'liberal/mischief/ purpose' approaches to interpretation are in theory not disagreements about *how* to interpret a text, but about *what* constitutes the text.

Suppose we are debating whether judges should formally be allowed to consult the commentary that accompanied a Law Commission's draft Bill, which was itself enacted verbatim, in order to assist them to ascertain the meaning of the statutory words. We would be wrong to describe this as a debate about how to interpret a text, since that presupposes the separation of text and interpreter which the thesis denies. We would, instead, be debating whether the Law Commission report constitutes part of the text to be interpreted. The textualist's arguments that we should recognize only the statutory words appear to derive *from* the nature of the text (the expressed will of Parliament); in fact their function is to provide support *for* his conception of the text. Likewise the contextualist's arguments that we should attend to these other sources of meaning rest on beliefs about the relationship between a text and its surroundings 'that bring into existence the very text for whose existence they had called'.[38] Meaning is not 'there' in the text, awaiting discovery; nor are interpreters 'free' in the sense that they can choose any interpretation unsupported by reasons authenticated by the interpretive community of which they are, for a given interpretive purpose, members. The key is to stop thinking about interpretation as an activity *in need of* constraint (that of the text or of some intellectual or other mechanism internal to the interpreter), but to think instead of 'interpretation as a *structure* of constraints which comes complete with its own internal set of rules and regulations, its list of prescribed activities which is also, and at the same time, a list of activities that are proscribed'.[39]

Under this thesis, issues about objectivity versus subjectivity in statutory interpretation cease to have any significance since they are no longer autonomous theoretical positions about what constitutes the authoritative source of meaning. Judges (and other interpreters) are not neutral in their standpoint, but articulate or assume a collection of values and preferences (which may be the subject of disagreement within the membership of their interpretive community) which necessarily means that they do have an interest in *how* and *why* they interpret statutes (after all, it is precisely *how* they interpret statutes that contributes to the recognition of their interpretive practices as constituting a discrete interpretive community). But by the very same token, their interpretations are not subjective 'because they do not proceed from an isolated individual but from a public and conventional point of view'.[40] Interpretive practice ceases to be a matter of reconciling distinct elements each capable of bearing 'meaning' and each pulling in different directions. No interpretation can be formulated within an interpretive community with regard to any given dispute that is not already posited by that community's interpretive strategies. While this does not guarantee that either the strategies themselves or their application to particular issues will be uncontroversial, it does guarantee that neither is whimsical, capricious or arbitrary. And while their application to particular cases may be controversial, this does not mean that there are never clear cases nor better answers.

Explicit discussion of interpretation does not figure prominently in Dworkin's initial development of his theory of adjudication, though it is clear from 'Hard Cases' that he considered statutory interpretation at least to be subsumed by it.[41] His treatment of interpretation has since become more expansive, both because his recent writing draws in part upon the developments in literary theory summarized above and because he conceives law more broadly as an interpretive concept: 'legal practice is an exercise in interpretation not only when lawyers interpret particular documents or statutes, but generally'.[42]

In 'No Right Answer',[43] Dworkin likened statutory to literary interpretation in that there is no independently demonstrable answer to such a question as 'did David Copperfield have a sexual affair with Steerforth?' any more than there is to the question whether, for example, the medical induction of an abortion by a nurse under the direction of a doctor constitutes the termination of a pregnancy 'by a registered medical practitioner' within s.1(1) of the Abortion Act 1967.[44] While it is theoretically possible that within the given enterprise there is no single right answer to questions of this kind Dworkin argues that for all practical purposes the enterprise can and will support one answer which, in broad terms of 'fit' with all other relevant parts of the enterprise, is in this preferred sense 'right'.

In 'Law as Interpretation' Dworkin takes this further.[45] He argues that as between the theoretical possibility of the 'text' being insufficiently 'dense' to support one 'right' answer, and the apparent freedom of the interpreter (a judge) to create one, the act of interpretation takes place within a 'chain enterprise' that limits the freedom of the interpreter to ascribe any meaning other than that which is 'right' within the enterprise. Under this conception, all participants (interpreters) in the enterprise beyond the initial participant (author, draftsman) who is 'free' from constraint, are progressively more constrained by the interpretations their predecessors have ascribed to the text. In a developed legal system, the scope for ascribing 'other' interpretations may in particular cases be reduced to vanishing point; sometimes there will be room for disagreement. Of course it is not easy to work out what the legitimate (that is, congruent with what the enterprise now entails) interpretation will be, but it remains the judicial task to attempt this.

> Each judge must regard himself, in deciding the new case before him, as a partner in a complex chain enterprise of which these innumerable decisions, structures, conventions and practices are the history; it is his job to continue that history into the future through what he does on the day. He *must* interpret what has gone before because he has a responsibility to advance the enterprise in hand rather than strike out on his own. So he must determine, according to his own judgment, what the earlier decisions come to, what the point or theme of the practice so far, taken as a whole, really is.[46]

This responsibility should, in turn, take place against the backcloth of some political morality which supplies the best explanation of the individual practices and of the enterprise taken as a whole.

On the face of it, Dworkin's argument has affinities to that developed by Fish and others, and seems to reflect one common understanding of legal interpretation. Interpreters are engaged in an enterprise which generates its own criteria for judging whether particular propositions about aspects of that enterprise are 'true'. Of course it is not the enterprise itself (being an abstraction) that actually generates these criteria, but its officials. However, their discretion is bounded by their duty to advance the enterprise (and in so doing create more, and more refined, criteria) consistent with some principles that best account (within a liberal democracy) for what has happened so far. In this sense truth is relative to the enterprise.

But Fish's thesis is much stronger than this.[47] He argues that these criteria do not only supply the basis for judging decisions made within and about the enterprise, but constitute the enterprise itself. And because these criteria both define and exhaust the enterprise, an interpreter cannot both be a participant in that enterprise and at the same time exercise his discretion in a way that does not advance the enterprise. When Dworkin argues that a judge must render decisions that generate a better institutional fit or that advance the 'chain enterprise' with which he is concerned, rather than 'strike out on his own', Fish argues that it is simply not possible for him to 'strike out on his own' and still be subscribing to the interpretive community of which he is, in virtue of his beliefs, a member.[48] If the judge *can* produce an interpretation that is different from that of his fellow judges, that is because his interpretation is *already possible* (albeit not wholly agreed upon) within the judicial community. In such a case, it is open to the judge to persuade others within the community (and using the accepted strategies, albeit they may also be controversial) to accept 'his' interpretation, which is not 'his' in the sense of being wholly a product of his own imagination, but 'his' in the sense that he is marshalling arguments to support an interpretation already permitted within that community. These interpretations cannot be demonstrated to be right or wrong against some independent source because there is none; there are only the reasons generated within the community which persuade its members to preferred readings of the text. If there are 'other' criteria, such as some theory of political morality as proposed by Dworkin, these are already part of the rhetorical baggage of the community:

> it is neither the case that interpretation is constrained by what is obviously and unproblematically 'there', nor the case that interpreters, in the absence of such constraints, are free to read into a text whatever they like. . . . Interpreters are constrained by their tacit awareness of what is possible and what is not possible to do, what is and is not a reasonable thing to say, what will and what will not be heard as evidence, in a given enterprise; and it is within those same constraints that they see and bring others to see the shape of the documents to whose interpretation they are committed. . . . In searching for a way to protect against arbitrary readings (judicial and literary), Dworkin is searching for something he already has and could not possibly be without.[49]

In seeking to outflank the division 'between those who believe that interpretation is grounded in objectivity and those who believe that interpreters are, for all intents and purposes, free',[50] Dworkin assumes the very epistemological separation between text and interpreter that his argument seeks to transcend.

Dworkin's conception of law as interpretation, though still being developed, is controversial in other respects. Of particular relevance to the theory and practice of statutory interpretation is his treatment of judicial interpretation as the paradigm. Though confined to a numerically small number of cases, the judicial interpretation of statutes casts a long shadow over statutory interpretation generally. Insofar as other interpreters may wish to predict the outcome of disputed points of interpretation, it is wholly apt to attempt descriptive accounts of the beliefs and practices to which the judiciary subscribe and which constitute the interpretive community of which they are members.[51] Insofar as some other interpreters may perceive judicial interpretation as a model to be emulated, it is also appropriate to attempt prescriptive accounts of the form and substance of these beliefs and of the practices that they generate and sustain. But it is certainly misleading to suggest either that descriptive accounts of judicial interpretation will also be sufficient to describe all other instances of statutory interpretation, or that what is prescriptively desirable for the judiciary ought also to be so for other interpretive communities.

The confusion of the judicial interpretation of statutes with statutory interpretation more generally and of participant with observer status (though an individual can be a participant in one community and an observer of another) is apparent both in other accounts of statutory interpretation and in accounts of such other subjects of interpretation as case-law rules, precedents and *rationes decidendi*.[52] These confusions arise largely from a failure to distinguish relevant standpoints and stages in a process of decision-making. These distinctions in turn generate sets of beliefs and practices that are both at variance with (though they may overlap) judicial interpretation and constitute different interpretive communities. Within our legal system judicial decisions interpreting statutes have legal priority over the decisions of other interpretive communities and may be enforced against members of those communities otherwise unwilling to comply with them. But while these aspects of interpretive authority and compulsion require analysis and pose some particular difficulties, they do not exhaust interpretive activity in law, whether generally or in the particular case of statutory interpretation.

Interpretive Communities in Practice

What value do these various arguments have for the way in which judges and other interpreters practise interpretation, or for the way in which we read statutes and cases interpreting them or teach students about statutory interpretation?[53] Can they help in any way to determine whether an aircraft hangar filled with fire pumps and synthetic rubber is a 'repository',[54] or whether the re-enactment in a consolidation Act of the *ipsissima verba* of the repealed provision means that Parliament has approved the earlier judicial interpretation of these words?[55]

> There are two answers to this question. The first is to point out that the question itself assumes that in order for something to be interesting, it must affect our everyday experience of [statutory interpretation]. . . . the fact that a thesis has no consequences for practical criticism is damning only from a parochial point of view. The other answer to the question is institutional, as it must be. The elaboration of this position is something that matters because the issues it takes up are considered central to the institution's concerns. The status of the text, the source of interpretive authority, the relationship between subjectivity and objectivity, the limits of interpretation – these are topics that have been discussed again and again; they are basic topics . . .[56]

and, as such, require constant theoretical attention. Propositions and assumptions about the epistemological basis of statutory interpretation clearly need to be addressed and evaluated at a theoretical level, but, as has already been indicated, theoretical endeavour can properly take place at a number of levels, and can help us to understand and to develop good interpretive practice. There is, I think, some force in the practitioners' traditional criticism of legal theory's contribution to understanding in this context. Even if we discount the possibility of interpretive practices being determinative of issues of statutory interpretation, insufficient attention has been paid (though things are changing) to developing, so far as is possible, systematic analyses of the strategies and procedures that comprise interpretive practice. These analyses can be encouraged by drawing analogies between interpretation in legal and literary contexts, but the limitations of such an exercise should not be overlooked.

While it is tempting to see parallels between expressive realism and new criticism on the one hand, and orthodox judicial views on the intention of Parliament and the supremacy of the statutory text on the other, the chronology of the changes in the way in which these two disciplines have characterized the relationship between text, author and interpreter does not correspond and so it would be wrong to see in these different characterizations a historical development reproduced (though they may reflect similar concerns) in both enterprises.

Secondly, to draw these analogies is to imply a similarity in what is to be interpreted. Paraphrasing Gray, the assertion that a statute ' "must be interpreted like any other book" is based upon the fallacy that all books are to be interpreted alike, and begs the question, "to what class of books does [a statute] belong?" '[57] Legislation does, after all, have aims different both from non-legal texts and from other legal texts intended to have the force of law. Insofar as legislation is principally addressed to public bodies (what may be called government talking to itself), it defines and gives legitimacy to the structure, composition, powers, obligations and financing of such institutions as nationalized industries, other public corporations and administrative agencies. Insofar as legislation is principally addressed to individuals and to private organizations, it defines or alters the legal significance of their actions, or of their relationships with one another or with the state. Legislation deals with issues of the first economic, political and social importance and, most important of all, can be used to coerce the unwilling to comply with its directions.[58] In all these respects the interpretation of legislation assumes a significance qualitatively different from the question whether *Hamlet* is to be interpreted as farce or tragedy. Jackson makes this point well:

> But here, the analogy [with literary interpretation] breaks down. David Copperfield and Steerforth are not, despite the fiction of the discussion, real persons; the determination of whether or not David has a homosexual affair with Steerforth has no possible impact *outside* the sphere of literary discourse. No real person will be happier or richer by virtue of the outcome. But the litigants in a courtroom are real people. The determination of whether one of them has a right or not has a considerable impact outside the sphere of legal discourse; one of them will assuredly be the happier or the richer by virtue of it. . . . Real cases are not the same as fictional cases; the judge has a responsibility to people as well as to the system of principles and rights. Dworkin's system provides an excellent model for classroom legal discourse, where people's lives do not depend on it. But there is a distinction between adjudication and interpretation: the former is an exercise in the relationship between

(literary or legal) propositions; the latter is an exercise in the relationship between such a system and people's lives.[59]

Of course the interpretive practices of judges and others can be shown to involve similar concerns to those of Shakespearean scholarship, and there are other non-legal texts such as the Bible having a prescriptive dimension that require interpretation. But while we may acknowledge that the notion of interpretive communities can illuminate the perennial problems of statutory interpretation, we should not lose sight of the differences between the *function* and the *impact* of interpretation in legal (and specifically statutory) contexts and non-legal contexts.[60] Moreover, we must surely be careful not to assume uncritically theoretical positions taken from other disciplines that are themselves controversial.[61]

In my opinion, a principal virtue of talk about interpretive communities is that it underlines the importance for legal theory of analysing *routine* interpretation. The few hundred cases involving points of statutory interpretation that reach the higher courts are almost always atypical; they are precisely the cases in which the interpretive practices within the community fail to generate a preferred reading. What we should be examining first is not how these controversial cases are resolved, but why the practices that routinely and effectively dispose of the vast majority of issues of statutory interpretation fail to persuade the relevant members of the interpretive community of the 'rightness' of one preferred reading in this instance. 'Hard cases' are the cutting edge: they illustrate and test how far the practices that are routinely applicable ('easy cases') take us; but we need first to identify and analyse why it is that easy cases *are* dispositive of issues of statutory interpretation. The test of interpretive practice is not whether it can reduce the number of aberrant cases to nil, but whether, in the majority of disputes, litigated or not, interpretive communities share an understanding about the cogency and validity of particular arguments and acknowledge the results to which they lead. Textbooks on statutory interpretation (and the relevant parts of legal theory) have traditionally concentrated on the *pathology* of statutory interpretation; we would do better if we began by analysing how conditions of doubt *typically* arise and how they are *typically* resolved. It is not especially helpful to ask for better interpretive practices (or simply to complain about literal or purposive interpretation leading to the wrong result) until we have some idea of the nature of particular problems of interpretation which these practices are designed to resolve.[62]

Consideration of routine interpretation raises a substantial agenda for research in legal theory, involving *inter alia* the themes that are addressed in *How to Do Things with Rules*.[63] The concept of interpretive communities developed by Fish and others underlines the importance of these themes. It encourages us to analyse and to formulate generalizations about the practices of *particular* interpretive communities; and not to take one important community as comprising the whole interpretive enterprise. These generalizations may take the form of diagnostic models of conditions of doubt arising in statutory contexts and of typologies of what, for particular communities, constitute 'good justificatory arguments'.[64] At a different level, another object of middle-order theorizing is to formulate a set of intellectual procedures for tackling problems of interpretation. This may involve such eminently 'practical' matters as formulating procedures for identifying what rules and what word(s) are to be interpreted and recognizing and arranging specific arguments for and against competing interpretations.[65] Underlying all these and their related endeavours is an insistence on constant clarification of standpoint and the beliefs that constitute it. To achieve these objectives legal theory will need to draw upon such related disciplines as social or linguistic theory to elucidate, for example, the functions of an interpretive enterprise and the role of rhetoric within it[66] and the use of such key concepts as 'intention',[67] 'text' and 'context'.

One aspect of the agenda for legal theory thus involves attempts to construct systematic and rational accounts of interpretive practice as displayed by the judiciary, of which Bennion's impressive 'code' of statutory interpretation is a particularly good example.[68] Nevertheless, a fully rounded analysis of statutory interpretation needs to take account of the interests of such interpreters as Holmes's Bad Man, or the bigamist Henry Allen,[69] a tax consultant devising new avoidance schemes or Parliamentary Counsel devising new clauses in a Finance Bill to counter them, and of the range of standpoints that can constitute other interpretive communities. Judicial interpretation is important, but it is not coterminous with law as an interpretive concept.

NOTES

1 The issues discussed in this chapter, particularly those concerning interpretation in legal and non-legal contexts and the desirability of studying the characteristics of routine interpretation may be seen in part as a restatement and in part as a development of the approach to interpretation followed in W. Twining and D. Miers, *How To Do Things With Rules* (2nd edn; 1982).

2 See, e.g., Lord Hailsham LC, *Johnson* v. *Moreton* [1980] AC 37, p. 53.

3 See, e.g., P. Winch, *The Idea of a Social Science* (1958); B. Wilson (ed.) *Rationality* (1977); R. Bernstein, *The Restructuring of Social and Political Theory* (1978); E. Carr, *What is History?* (1969); C. Belsey, *Critical Practice* (1980); M. Polyani, *Personal Knowledge* (1974), and H. Gadamer, *Philosophical Hermeneutics* (1970). An exploration of linkages between theory in these disciplines and some of the themes of this paper is Twining, 'Some Scepticism about Some Scepticisms' (1984) 11 *J Law and Society* 137 and 285. Their more particular application to statutory interpretation is considered in Abrahams, 'Statutory Interpretation and Literary Theory: Some Common Concerns of an Unlikely Pair' [1979] *Rutgers Law Rev.* 676 and J. White, *When Words Lose Their Meaning* (1984).

4 See Twining, *op. cit.*, pp. 142-3.

5 See, e.g., R. Stevens, *Law and Politics* (1979), who uses changes in the senior judiciary's attitudes towards statutory interpretation to substantiate and illustrate his account of the exercise by the House of Lords of its judicial function; especially pp. 333, 342-4, 357-8, 475-6, 564 and 576-7.

6 See Abrahams, *op. cit.*, and also J. Stone, *Legal System and Lawyers' Reasonings* (1964) pp. 29-34, 289 and 348-54.

7 Bishop Hoadly's famous remark, 'whoever hath *absolute authority* to interpret any written or spoken laws, it is *he* who is truly the *law-giver* to all intents and purposes, and not the person who first wrote or spoke them,' is a classic instance of this conception. More

130   *David Miers*

recent examples are J. Willis, 'Statute Interpretation in a Nutshell' (1938) 16 *Canadian Bar Rev.* 1, and J. Griffith, *The Politics of the Judiciary* (1st edn 1977). Concentration on the interpreter is also encouraged by the conception of statutory interpretation as an instance of the delegation of legislative power. See in particular Jaffe, 'An Essay on the Delegation of Legislative Power' (1947) 47 *Columbia Law Rev.* 359, and Payne, 'The Intention of the Legislature in the Interpretation of Statutes' [1956] *Current Legal Problems* 96, especially p. 105.

8 Hutchinson and Monahan, 'Law, Politics and the Critical Legal Scholars: The Unfolding Drama of American Legal Thought' (1984) 36 *Stanford Law Rev.* 199 at p. 206. While there are some important criticisms that the critical legal studies movement can make of the liberal rationality of such writers as Dworkin, Hart and Rawls, and more particularly of the rules of statutory interpretation (see Gordon, 'Critical Legal Histories', *id.*, pp. 113-16), its underlying premise seems either wholly unoriginal (see Johnson, 'Do You Sincerely Want to Be a Radical?', pp. 248ff.) or to deny altogether the possibility of occupying any critical position other than one which treats legal discourse as a sham. By denying any critical stance other than its own, the critical legal studies movement makes impossible the development of any standards by which alternative explanations of legal discourse could be judged. But this position is surely fundamentally flawed. The critical legal studies movement posits assumptions about the world (social contingency and the contradictions between individual and collective interests) which are regarded as insuperable (see Kennedy, 'The Structure of Blackstone's Commentaries' (1979) 28 *Buffalo Law Rev.* 205, at pp. 212-13), and make illusory the possibility of regarding legal (or any other) discourse as being meaningful except as a device for maintaining the hegemony of those that practise it. But it is logically impossible to deny altogether the epistemological basis of all other critical positions without simultaneously making some assumptions about the epistemological basis of one's own. Either the assumptions that the critical legal studies movement posits about the world apply equally to itself, in which case it is self-defeating, or it has changed the nature of its assumptions about the world (so as to facilitate the possibility of its own position), in which case it is self-contradictory. 'The project of radical doubt can never outrun the necessity of being situated; in order to doubt *everything*, including the ground one stands on, one must stand somewhere else, and that somewhere else will then be the ground on which one stands.' Such infinite regress could only be halted if one could stand free of any ground whatsoever, but once one takes a view about anything, one is presupposing what constitutes the perspective from which that view is taken. (S. Fish, *Is There a Text in this Class* (1980) p. 360. See also D. Lyons, *Ethics and the Rule of Law* (1984) ch. 3).

9 One task for legal theory is to explore how 'knowledge' about statutory interpretation in Anglo-American jurisprudence comes to be socially established as 'reality'; see P. Berger and T. Luckmann, *The Social Construction of Reality* (1966).

10 E.g., Davies, 'The Interpretation of Statutes in the Light of their Policy by the English Courts' (1935) 35 *Columbia Law Rev.* 519; Frankfurter, 'Some Reflections on the Reading of Statutes' (1947) 47 *Columbia Law Rev.* 527; R. Pound, 'Interpretation of Statutes' in *Studying Law* (2nd edn; 1955; ed. A. Vanderbilt) p. 529; Marsh, 'The Interpretation of Statutes' (1966-7) 9 *J Society of Public Teachers of Law* 416; The Law Commissions, *The Interpretation of Statutes* (1969; HC 256); J. Harris, *Legal Philosophies* (1980) ch. 12; R. Dias, *Jurisprudence* (5th edn; 1985); D. Lloyd *Introduction to Jurisprudence*, (4th edn; 1979) pp. 863-77; R. Cross, *Statutory Interpretation* (1976); and R. Dickerson, *The Interpretation and Application of Statutes* (1974).

11 K. Llewellyn, *The Common Law Tradition* (1960) p. 373, argued that the normative ambiguity displayed by these 'rules' of interpretation was inevitable 'so long as we

and the courts pretend that there has been only one single correct answer possible. Until we give up that foolish pretense there must be a set of mutually contradictory or conflicting *correct* rules on How to Construe Statutes: either or any available as duty and sense may require. Until then, also, the problem will recur in statutory construction as in the handling of case law. *Which* of the technically correct answers (1) *should* be given; (2) *will* be given – and Why?'

12 See Cross, *op. cit.*, pp. 42-3; Lloyd, *op. cit.*, p. 865; and E. Driedger, *The Construction of Statutes* (1974) p. 67. These authors rely on *dicta* of Lord Reid in *Pinner* v. *Everett* [1969] 3 All ER 257, *Maunsell* v. *Olins* [1975] AC 373 and *Jones* v. *DPP* [1962] AC 635, and of Lords Diplock and Simon of Glaisdale in *Maunsell* v. *Olins* and *Carter* v. *Bradbeer* [1975] 1 WLR 1204.

13 Twining and Miers, *op. cit.*, pp. 335-8.

14 *Id.*, p. 276.

15 Three notable instances, all of which involve various degrees of rebuke to deviance practised by Lord Denning, are the remarks of Lord Simonds in *Magor & St Mellons RDC* v. *Newport Corp.* [1952] AC 189, of Lord Diplock in *Davis* v. *Johnson* [1979] AC 272 (also involving deviant interpretations of the doctrine of precedent) and Lord Scarman in *Shah* v. *Barnet LBC* [1983] 1 All ER 230.

16 In *Hadmor Productions* v. *Hamilton* [1982] 2 WLR 322, Lord Diplock does emphatically assert that reports of parliamentary proceedings are a 'no go' area for judicial purposes. This was prompted by Lord Denning's explicit reliance on *Hansard* in the Court of Appeal judgment; but compare Lord Hailsham's reference to covert use, 418 *HL Debs*, col. 1345 (26 March 1981).

17 See D. Miers and A. Page, *Legislation* (1982) pp. 201-10. Few suggestions have been made to classify statutes for interpretive purposes; none of those that have (e.g. W. Friedman, in *Law and Social Change in Contemporary Britain* (1951) pp. 239-65) have been in any way developed. Lord Evershed, 'The Impact of Statute on the Law of England' (1956) 42 *Proc. Brit. Academy* 247, saw as a matter of 'surpassing importance' the question whether there can and ought to be 'some change in the method or character of the judicial function so far as it is concerned with the interpretation of the enacted law' (pp. 261-2). None of his suggested reforms, which included statutory statements of principles to be applied when a judge is interpreting, and a classification of legislation with corresponding rules of interpretation, have, however, attracted agreement among those officially involved in interpretation. On the contrary, they have provoked serious disagreement, as the debates on Lord Scarman's two Interpretation of Legislation Bills in 1980 and 1981 demonstrate; see 405 *HL Debs*, cols 276-306 (13 February 1980) and 418 *HL Debs*, cols 64-83 (9 March 1981).

18 O. Fiss, 'Objectivity and Interpretation' (1982) 34 *Stanford Law Rev.* 739 at p. 744.

19 N. MacCormick, *Legal Reasoning and Legal Theory* (1978) p. 16.

20 See, e.g., Goodrich, 'The Role of Linguistics in Legal Analysis' (1984) 47 *Modern Law Rev.*, 523.

21 See W. Twining, 'Evidence and Legal Theory' (chapter 4 above) p. 64. Books such as Maxwell, *The Interpretation of Legislation* (12th edn; 1969) or *Craies on Statute Law* (7th edn; 1971) attempt to state the 'present clear law' whose underlying structure it is the task of descriptive legal theory to elucidate. It is also the task of legal theory to formulate generalized or provisional rules, even though their application to specific cases cannot be simply described; J. Harris, *Law and Legal Science* (1979) ch. 5.

22 Belsey, *op. cit.*, p. 4.

23 *Carter* v. *Bradbeer* [1975] 1 WLR 1204.

24 *Id.*, pp. 1205-7.

25 See, e.g., Silving, 'A Plea for a Law of Interpretation' (1950) 98 *University of Pennsylvania Law Rev.* 499; Sneed, 'The Art of Statutory Interpretation' (1983) 62 *Texas Law Rev.* 665.

26 Miers and Page, *op. cit.*, pp. 196-210. Describing the report of the Law Commissions, *op. cit.*, as constituting the first serious debate in modern times on the role of the judiciary in statutory interpretation, Stevens, *op. cit.*, pp. 410-12, argues that governments since 1969 found it too threatening to existing conceptions of the political balance between the judiciary and the legislature and have for this reason preferred the more traditional views expressed in the report of the Renton Committee, *The Preparation of Legislation* (1975; Cmnd 6053). The reception accorded to Lord Scarman's Bills, both of which were based on the Law Commissions' report, amply bears out Stevens's analysis.

27 Llewellyn, *op. cit.*, p. 371; W. Twining, *Karl Llewellyn and the Realist Movement* (1973) pp. 239-41; and more generally on the relationship between legislation and case law, Lord Evershed, 'The Judicial Process in Twentieth Century England' (1961) 61 *Columbia Law Rev.* 761; Munday, 'The Common Lawyer's Philosophy of Legislation' (1983) 14 *Rechtstheorie* 191; Atiyah, 'Statute Law and Common Law' (1985) *48 Modern Law Rev.* 1; and E. Wambaugh, 'How to Use Cases and Statutes' in *Studying Law, op. cit.*, p. 537.

28 See, e.g., M. McDougal, H. Lasswell and J. Miller, *The Interpretation of Agreements and World Public Order* (1967); Wambaugh, *op. cit.*; Dias, *op. cit.*, p. 225; J. Gray, *The Nature and the Sources of the Law* (1921) p. 174; and Edwards, 'Interpretation of Legal Documents' (1979) 20 *Jurimetrics* 174.

29 E.g. Frank, 'Words and Music: Some Remarks on Statutory Interpretation' (1947) 47 *Columbia Law Rev.* 1259.

30 One theory of literary criticism, new criticism, particularly denies that the author's intentions are in any way accessible or relevant to the interpretation of the text he has written, since the qualities the interpreter is seeking - unity, clarity, consistency, integrity - are properties not of the author, but of the text; see W. Wimsatt, *The Verbal Icon: Studies in the Meaning of Poetry* (1970). The view that the author's intentions are 'neither available nor desirable' (*id.*, p. 3) has its obvious counterpart in the debate as to the admissibility in courtrooms of the official record of the parliamentary passage of the legislation now being interpreted; see the Law Commissions, *op. cit.*, para. 53: 'In considering the admissibility of Parliamentary proceedings, it is necessary to consider how far the material admitted might be *relevant* to the interpretative task of the courts, how far it would afford them *reliable* guidance, and how far it would be sufficiently *available* to those to whom the statute is addressed' (original emphasis). The current judicial practice, that recourse cannot be made to *Hansard*, is based on the unavailability and undesirability of this text as a record of the author's intentions; see *Davis* v. *Johnson* and *Hadmor Productions* v. *Hamilton, op. cit.*, and Miers, 'Citing Hansard as an Aid to Interpretation' [1983] *Statute Law Rev.* 98.

31 See, e.g., *dicta* on interpretation in such cases as *Duport Steel* v. *Sirs* [1980] 1 All ER 529; *Black-Clawson International* v. *Papierwerke Waldhof-Aschaffenburg* [1975] AC 591; *James Buchanan* v. *Babco Forwarding and Shipping* [1977] 3 WLR 907; *Carter* v. *Bradbeer, Maunsell* v. *Olins* and *Shah* v. *Barnet LBC, op. cit.*

32 Belsey, *op. cit.*, p. 7.

33 *Id.*, p. 13.

34 *Id.*, p. 14 (original emphasis). On the issue of judicial recourse to parliamentary texts as evidence of the intention of the legislature see Radin, 'Statutory Interpretation' (1929-30) 43 *Harvard Law Rev.* 863; Landis, 'A Note on Statutory Interpretation',

id., p. 886; H. Laski, *Report of the Committee on Ministers' Powers* (1932; Cmd 4060) Annex V; Jones, 'Statutory Doubts and Legislative Intention' (1940) 40 *Columbia Law Rev.* 957; Barwick, 'Divining the Legislative Intent' (1961) 35 *Australian Law J* 197; R. Dickerson, 'Statutory Interpretation: A Peek into the Mind and Will of a Legislature' (1975) 50 *Indiana Law J* 206; R. Dworkin, 'How to Read the Civil Rights Act' *New York Review of Books*, 20 December 1979; and Twining and Miers, *op. cit.*, pp. 192-200.

35 See generally Fish, *op. cit.* The thesis developed by Fish is based on a theory of linguistics associated initially with Saussure that language antedates phenomena, not the other way around; see F. de Saussure, *Course in General Linguistics* (1974); Belsey, *op. cit.*, ch. 2; and Goodrich, *op. cit.*

36 Fish, *op. cit.*, p. 171.

37 *Id.*, p. 11.

38 Abrahams, *op. cit.*, p. 686.

39 Fish, *op. cit.*, p. 356.

40 *Id.*, p. 14.

41 Reprinted in R. Dworkin, *Taking Rights Seriously* (1977); especially pp. 107-10. See also 'Political Judges and the Rule of Law' (1978) 64 *Proc. Brit. Academy* 259.

42 'Law as Interpretation' (1982) 60 *Texas Law Rev.* 527. Reprinted in R. Dworkin, *A Matter of Principle* (1985) pp. 146-66. See also 'On Interpretation and Objectivity', *id.*, pp. 167-77.

43 In *Law, Morality and Society* (1977); ed. P. Hacker and J. Raz) pp. 58 and 78ff.

44 *Royal College of Nursing* v. *DHSS* [1981] 2 WLR 292.

45 *Op. cit.*

46 *Id.*, p. 543. Dworkin's argument is not confined to statutory interpretation, but is applicable also to such other interpretive activities as reading cases and formulating propositions of law for which the cases can be claimed to be authorities.

47 Fish does, however, accept the point behind Dworkin's argument: 'Dworkin is right, I think, to link his argument about legal practice to an argument about the practice of literary criticism, not only because in both disciplines the central question is, "What is the source of interpretative authority?" but also because in both disciplines answers to that question typically take the form of the two positions Dworkin rejects. Just as there are those in the legal community who have insisted on construing statutes and decisions "strictly" (that is, by attending only to the words themselves), so there are those in the literary community who have insisted that interpretation is, or should be, constrained by what is "in the text"; and just as the opposing doctrine of legal realism holds that judges' "readings" are always rationalizations of their political or personal desires, so do proponents of critical subjectivity hold that what a reader sees is merely a reflection of his predispositions and biases. The field is divided, in short, between those who believe that interpretation is grounded in objectivity and those who believe that interpreters are, for all intents and purposes, free.' 'Working on the Chain Gang: Interpretation in Law and Literature' (1982) 60 *Texas Law Rev.* 551. See Schelley, 'Interpretation in Law: the Dworkin-Fish debate' (1985) 73 *California Law Rev.* 158-80.

48 Fish, *op. cit.*, n. 47, pp. 556-7.

49 *Id.*, p. 562.

50 *Id.*, p. 551. Fish also takes issue with Dworkin's assumption that the author/draftsman is 'free' to choose the direction the novel/statute will take in a way that is qualitatively different from the way in which successive interpreters make that choice. Leaving aside the obvious constraints imposed on the draftsman by his instructions, Fish argues that while the author is free to choose the subject-matter of his novel, to initiate an enterprise such as a novel is by that very act to initiate a set of constraints about *what it is* to write a novel. This point applies with equal force to the drafting of statutes. Both statutes

and novels are conventional categories and can only proceed on the basis of those conventions.

51 These descriptive accounts may of course be open to criticism on the grounds, *inter alia*, of inaccuracy; see, e.g., MacCormick, *op. cit.*; J. Bell, *Policy Arguments in Judicial Decisions* (1983); Woodman, 'Dworkin's "Right Answer" Thesis and the Frustration of Legislative Intent-A Case-Study on the Leasehold Reform Act' (1982) 45 *Modern Law Rev.* 121; and Hart, 'American Jurisprudence through English Eyes' (1977) 11 *Georgia Law Rev.* 969.

52 Twining and Miers, *op. cit.*, pp. 276-91.

53 It is doubtful whether any judge faced with a difficult point of statutory interpretation would be much helped by being told that he should interpret the word(s) 'in the way that a fine musician interprets a musical score'; Payne, *op. cit.*, p. 109.

54 *Newbury DC* v. *Secretary of State for the Environment*, in which a unanimous Court of Appeal held that 'no one conversant with the English language would dream of calling these hangars a "repository" when filled with fire-pumps or synthetic rubber' ([1979] 1 All ER 243 at p. 250, *per* Lord Denning) and an equally unanimous House of Lords held, reversing that decision, 'that to describe the use of the hangars when so filled as use for a repository is a perfectly accurate and correct use of the English language' ([1980] 1 All ER 731 at p. 737, *per* Viscount Dilhorne).

55 *R* v. *Chard* [1984] AC 279.

56 Fish, *op. cit.*, n. 8, pp. 370-1.

57 *Op. cit.*, p. 177.

58 Miers and Page, *op. cit.*, p. 211. Coercion can of course be achieved by means of private legal documents; *id.*, pp. 11-12.

59 B. Jackson, 'Hart and Dworkin on Discretion: Some Semiotic Perspectives' in *Semiotics, Law and Social Science* (1985; ed. D. Carzo and B. Jackson) pp. 145 and 155-6.

60 There are of course other points of similarity and dissimilarity. Literary texts, like statutory texts, contain propositions in fixed verbal form, but unlike statutory texts, there may be more than one authoritative version. Literary texts are written to achieve a number of effects (descriptive, inspirational, metaphorical, spiritual and so on) whereas the prime and standard objective of a statutory text is legal effect. The interpretation of statutes is freighted with complex and controversial issues of constitutional significance which in turn have implications for the kinds of extrinsic evidence of the author's 'intent' that may properly be relied upon; although interpreters of *Hamlet* may argue whether Shakespeare's laundry list is a reliable or relevant source of such evidence, the matter hardly bears the same normative significance.

61 Belsey, *op. cit.*, pp. 32ff; and Dworkin, 'Law as Interpretation', *op. cit.*, pp. 529-30.

62 See, e.g., Bennion, 'The Literal rule of Interpretation' (1980) 130 *New Law J* 1156; and Griffith, *op. cit.*, p. 179.

63 Twining and Miers, *op. cit.*

64 MacCormick, *op. cit.*, p. 250. For his treatment of statutory interpretation, see pp. 203-13. See also Summers, 'Two Types of Substantive Reasons: The Core of a Theory of Common-Law Justification' (1978) 63 *Cornell Law Rev.* 707.

65 F. Bennion has proposed a useful procedure for formulating issues of statutory interpretation and for marshalling arguments in support of competing interpretations; see 'Propositions of Law in Conviction Appeals' [1984] *Criminal Law Rev.* 282; 'Scientific Statutory Interpretation and the Franco Scheme' [1983] *British Tax Rev.* 74; and *Statutory Interpretation* (1984) part 3. See Twining and Miers, *op. cit.*, pp. 320-8.

66 See, e.g., Goodrich, 'Law and Language' (1984) 11 *J Law and Society* 173, which briefly illustrates, by reference to *Bromley LBC* v. *GLC* [1982] 1 All ER 129, how linguistic analysis can apply to judicial decisions. Of greater particularity is the kind of linguistic

analysis exemplified by M. Halliday and R. Hasan, *Cohesion in English* (1976). Cohesion is a semantic concept: 'it refers to relations of meaning that exist within the text, and that define it as a text' and 'occurs where the interpretation of some element in the discourse is dependent on that of another', para. 1.1.4. The specific techniques for achieving cohesion – reference, substitution, ellipsis, conjunction and lexical cohesion – have an immediately obvious relevance to both the interpretation and the drafting of statutes.For a refreshing approach to the deconstruction of statutory provisions, see Benson, 'Up a Statute with Gun and Camera: Isolating linguistic and logical structures in the analysis of legal language' (1984-5) 8 *Seton Hall Legislative J* pp. 279–305.

67 See the introduction to R. Summers (ed.), *Essays in Legal Philosophy* (1968); MacCallum, 'Legislative Intent (1966) 75 *Yale Law J* 754 (reprinted *id.*, p. 237) and the references above n. 34.

68 *Statutory Interpretation, op. cit.*

69 Twining and Miers, *op. cit.*, pp. 235–41 and 262–5.

8
Contract and Legal Theory

HUGH COLLINS

Teachers of the law of contract ponder an intriguing dilemma. When organizing an exposition of the subject, we can draw upon a vigorous intellectual tradition which established a unified law of contract based upon a remarkably small set of interlocking principles. This classical law of contract, as it is often called, represents one of the acmes of legal formalist scholarship by virtue of its clear rules and their clusters of logical derivatives. Like any closed system of classification and rule-bound rationality, the classical law suffers from omissions, contradictions and absurdities, but these problems have been masterfully overcome by generations of scholarly hair-splitting and judicial creativity. Yet the time has come when many doubt whether it remains sensible to persevere in recycling the classical law in order to incorporate all the new challenges to its doctrinal system. Though few proceed so far as Grant Gilmore[1] in awarding a death certificate to the classical law of contract, as exceptions to the rules multiply, most writers at least acknowledge that novel principles destroy the crispness and generality of such doctrines as consideration and privity.[2] The Critical Legal Studies Movement even perceives a counter-vision of the law of contract emerging from the exceptions and novel principles, so that, in effect, the movement welds together a new doctrinal synthesis.[3] Given this degree of disenchantment with the classical system, teachers of the law of contract must recognize that the organizing principles are shifting.

Yet we hesitate to take this step – and here is the source of the dilemma – for the modern law of contract appears so uncertain in its scope and mysterious in its moral vision. In sharp contrast, inside the tidy framework of the classical law, we sense intuitively the liberal principles which inspire the legal rules and determine the province of contractual obligations. Plainly the prevailing legal principle of freedom of contract mirrors the liberal's adherence to the ideal of liberty of the individual. More specifically, the classical requirement of consent or agreement for the creation of contractual obligations provides a justification for the obligation, which appears compatible with respect for individual liberty, and, at the same time, the need for consent preserves that liberty from unwanted imposed obligations. In contrast to this robust concern for liberal ideals in the classical rules, modern developments in the law of contracts rest upon uncertain and doubtful moral and political principles. What is the purpose, for example, of awarding compensation to a person who has acted to his detriment in reliance upon another's words or conduct when the parties have not reached an agreement?[4] Does this incursion upon individual liberty without consent serve a worthwhile purpose or rest upon some important principle? Similarly, why do courts discuss the inequality of bargaining power of the parties and the unreasonableness or unfairness of the terms of the contract and then sometimes refuse to enforce agreements on those grounds?[5] On what basis does the modern law deprive the parties of their freedom to choose the terms of their bargain? Finally, as the division between contract and tort loses its significance in modern decisions such as *Junior Books Ltd* v. *Veitchi Co. Ltd*,[6] we begin to wonder whether any of those pillars of classical doctrine will escape destruction by the acid rain of modern legal values. Such questions as these receive quite disparate answers, ranging from claims that all these legal practices can be explained by a new principle, such as the protection of reliance, through to denials that anything significant has happened.

Until we have resolved our uncertainty about what values these modern legal developments represent, our hesitation in embarking upon a radical break with established legal doctrine is surely justified. In order to comprehend the direction and scope of the modern law of contract, it is therefore helpful to return to some first principles of political and moral philosophy. Normally, like planets circling a star, political philosophy and the law of contracts affect each other's path without their orbits ever coinciding. In the face of the current crisis in contract doctrine, however, recent studies have partially overcome this disciplinary isolation. Lawyers and philosophers have reappraised the moral significance of promises, each interpretation of the modern law discovering confirmation in alleged moral practices.[7] Similarly, the objectives of judicial controls over the terms of contracts in the name of fairness and reasonableness have received illuminating philosophical examination.[8] Much work remains to be done, however, building upon these important first steps towards an understanding of the values and direction of modern contract law.

As a contribution to this agenda for legal scholarship, this essay endeavours to identify the principles which determine the substance of modern contract law. In brief, I suggest that we can best understand the form of modern doctrines by situating them in a broader dialogue within liberal political philosophy concerning the relation between the citizen and the state. The background of liberal philosophy shapes the opposing interpretations of the modern law of contract presented in recent books and articles. Yet I shall argue that, behind this dialogue within liberalism, there lurks a deeper controversy between rival schemes of moral virtue and distributive justice which seek to define a legitimate market order. This deeper controversy sustains the debate between liberal interpretations of the modern law of contract, but paradoxically at the same time demonstrates its pointlessness.

I LIBERALISM AND CONTRACTS

The gravitational force of liberal values exerts its influence at the core of contract doctrine, namely the justifications for the enforcement of contracts. In response to the related questions of why do we enforce contracts and what contracts should we enforce, liberal philosophy points towards two kinds of answer. Both interpretations of liberalism take as their starting-point a commitment to the value of individual liberty. They diverge in their justifications for the subjection of individuals to the exercise of state power during the enforcement of contractual obligations. In order to grasp the principal attributes of these two interpretations of liberalism, we must examine the nature of the problem which they address.

Indubitably liberalism parades under many guises and has spawned a multitude of distinctive political theories.[9] Yet two threads run through all these diverse patterns of liberal thought: the commitment to respect both the equality of citizens and the autonomy of individuals. In the name of equality, liberals reject all claims of an inherent right to govern or possess superior wealth based upon caste or status. For the sake of individual autonomy, liberals attempt to establish a political system which defers to each person's chosen way of life rather than one which imposes a conception of the virtuous life upon everyone. The constitution should guarantee respect for equality and autonomy, yet leave individuals to pursue their own interests as they wish. As Rawls remarks,[10] liberalism insists upon the priority of 'the right' over 'the good', that is, it upholds the right to choose whilst remaining agnostic on the question of the best path to follow.

The priority accorded to 'the right' by liberalism is reflected in the considerable freedom of contract permitted by Western legal systems. In general, under the classical law, a person may choose whether or not to enter a contract and may select the terms which constitute the substantive obligations of the transaction. By respecting these freedoms, the law upholds the right to choose a particular way of life. But once we progress beyond the formation of a contract to its enforcement, a difficulty in reconciling liberalism with the law of contracts emerges. Given that individual autonomy comprises a fundamental tenet for liberalism, legal enforcement of contracts demands a careful justification, for legal sanctions inevitably place fetters upon a person's freedom of action. As soon as a contract becomes legally binding, performance ceases to be optional, thereby curtailing individual autonomy. Since this restriction arises from an exercise of state power, liberal theory requires a justification to explain what permits the state, which is created to protect individual autonomy, to become an instrument of constraint.

At first sight the paradox that liberalism requires not only freedom of contract but also freedom to breach any contract is quickly resolved. It is alleged that, far from contradicting the value of respect for individual liberty, the justification for the enforcement of contracts derives logically from that value. Fried states this claim most clearly:

> In order to be as free as possible, that my will have the greatest possible range consistent with the similar will of others, it is necessary that there be a way in which I may commit myself. . . . The restrictions involved in promising are restrictions undertaken just in order to increase one's options in the long run, and thus are perfectly consistent with the principle of autonomy and the autonomy of others.[11]

But this purported resolution of the paradox, as Fried concedes, only demonstrates the compatibility of uninhibited freedom to enter contracts with respect for autonomy; it 'does not show that I am morally obligated to perform my promise at a later time if to do so proves inconvenient or costly'.[12] The duty to perform a contract cannot be derived from the principle of respect for autonomy.

Another, more complex, attempted resolution of the above paradox, which suggests, similarly, that the justification for enforcement can be derived from the principle of respect for individual autonomy, returns to liberalism's definition of 'the right' or the constitution of society. In order to express their concern for equality and individual autonomy, liberals often insist that certain rights should be fundamental to the framework of society. These fundamental terms of the 'social contract' ensure the freedom to choose a way of life by providing such constitutional guarantees as freedom of the person, freedom of speech and the right to privacy. Can the right to enforce a contract, with its correlative duty to perform it, be regarded as one of these constitutional guarantees?[13] If so, the paradox is resolved. But this proposal must also be rejected. Each of the other fundamental rights reveals an aspect of the value of private autonomy, whereas, in contrast, a right to enforce a contract involves an assertion of the justice of commandeering state power to curtail economic liberty and restrict autonomy. In a more formal way we can state that fundamental rights which protect individual autonomy comprise immunities against state interference whereas the right to enforce a contract asserts a claim to harness state power to control the actions of another. Again, therefore, we conclude that the right to enforce a contract cannot be derived from the liberal principle of respect for individual autonomy.

This failure to explain the enforceability of contracts as a logical derivation from liberal principles foreshadows the emergence of the two interpretations which dominate current discussions of the substance of the modern law of contract. These rival proposals for reconciling the legal enforcement of contracts with a fidelity to liberal principles do not purport to derive a justification for enforcement from the value of individual autonomy, but rather they assert a justification which minimizes the conflict with individual autonomy. It is a central thesis of this essay that the attempt to reconcile the enforcement of contracts with liberal principles has led to the formation of two dominant views of the content of the law of contract. I shall outline these two interpretations of the law in the context of their formal justifications for the exercise of state power to enforce contracts before examining each one critically.

The more traditional analysis of contracts, which figures widely in classical law as well as in modern texts, explains and justifies the imposition of contractual obligations on the ground of a special exercise of choice. Where a person has voluntarily chosen to undertake an economic transaction, he is legally bound to complete it. The requirement of choice ensures respect for the freedom of individuals to select their market opportunities. But the exercise of choice must be a special one, for it must alert the parties to the fact that they are about to enter a binding commitment from which they cannot simply opt out. At this point within this traditional interpretation of the principles of liberalism, any number of definitions of the special exercise of choice thrive. Some say that any serious promise should count,[14] whilst others insist that there should be an intention to enter legal relations;[15] meanwhile other theorists prefer the language of agreement and consent to that of promises and intention.[16] Although these differences of terminology amount to more than semantic predilections, for they support – perhaps even generate – rival conceptions of the limits of contractual obligations, the generic idea remains a special exercise of choice by an individual, through which he deliberately incurs a binding legal responsibility.

A popular modern interpretation of liberal ideas argues that private autonomy should be lost not through a special exercise of choice but rather through causing harm, or the risk of causing harm, to others. Under this modern view, contractual obligations may only be justified in order to deter or compensate some harm to the interests of another person.[17] The argument runs that individuals should enjoy the liberty to pursue their own interests and preferences, provided that in so doing they avoid harm to the interests of others. Where a person's actions either cause direct physical and economic harm to another, or cause another to incur wasted expenditure, then a legal duty arises to compensate the other for the harm done. By an extension of the argument, the duty is imposed in advance to deter acts which will potentially cause harm to the interests of others. Again this generic theory of legal obligations is expressed in a variety of forms such as a duty of care, rules about fair competition, and the protection of the reliance interest. In the last resort, the key to these interpretations of liberalism lies in the requirement of harm to the interests of others, for individual autonomy may only be curtailed in order to preserve the liberty of others.

Considerable practical implications derive from a selection between these rival explanations of the enforceability of contracts. Whilst choice theories firmly limit the range of legal obligations to the parties to an agreement, the 'harm to interests' theory envisages a broader range of obligations owed not only to persons who have chosen to enter an agreement together but also to anyone whose interests are subjected to the risk of harm. In other words, the 'harm to interests' theory suppresses rules about privity of contract and the distinction between contractual and tortious liability.[18] In other respects as well, choice theories confine the scope of legal liability more narrowly than do the 'harm to interests' theories. During negotiations leading up to an economic transaction, choice theories insist that no legal obligations should arise since the parties have not yet reached an agreement. In contrast, the 'harm to interests' theories decline to make any sharp break between contractual and pre-contractual liability; consequently, many duties of care and other forms of liability such as promissory estoppel arise as soon as negotiations commence.[19] On the other hand, in some respects choice theories imply a more rigorous attitude towards legal obligations. Choice theories frequently insist that a person's duty under a contract is to perform his obligation[20] and that accordingly the courts should use every available means to secure compliance with that duty, including threats of fines, penal damages[21] and imprisonment for contempt of court. Against this vision of debtors' prisons, 'harm to interests' theories merely require a person in default to pay monetary compensation for any harm which he has caused to protected interests.[22] We can glimpse from these brief illustrations that the rival interpretations of liberalism constitute more than idle philosophical speculations about the rationale for the existing law of contract. Using these frames of reference, lawyers advocate particular legal doctrines and mould the fundamental principles of the law of obligations.

Of course, these two theories of contractual obligations mirror a broader concern among liberals about the relation of the citizen to the state. Given the initial insistence upon the autonomy of the individual, each exercise of state power which places limits upon freedom of action requires a justification. Choice theories correspond to a libertarian strand in liberal political theory under which state power may only be legitimated by consent of the individual.[23] Hence libertarians normally justify state power by reference to a 'social contract' or a series of contracts. The 'harm to interests' theory reflects the analysis of J. S. Mill concerning the relation between the citizen and the state.[24] In his famous discussion of the legitimate province of state power, Mill argued that power could only be rightfully exercised in order to prevent one individual from harming another. Although philosophers have seldom tried to generate an entire political philosophy from that elementary principle, in the law of contract the 'harm to interests' theory dominates modern legal thought.

In summary, I suggest that the debates about the prognosis for contract law can be conveniently reduced to two liberal perspectives on the fundamental question of the enforceability of contracts, which parallel broader debates about the relation between the citizen and the state. The choice theory picks up the libertarian strand, which insists that all state power must be legitimated by consent, whereas the 'harm to interests' theory taps the slender source of Millian liberalism to defend a broadening of the scope of contractual obligations. In both theories, however, the guiding vision and uniting theme remains a fidelity to the liberal ideal of individual autonomy.

II RESPONSIBILITY AND OBLIGATION

Before we examine these two interpretations of liberalism which prevail in modern contract theory, we must draw one further distinction because it will assist us in assessing the merits and implications of the two theories. This distinction is more familiar in connection with the criminal law. In developing a celebrated liberal position, H. L. A. Hart argues that criminal laws can only be justified where they deter harm or offensive behaviour to others, or, in limited instances of 'legal paternalism', where the laws discourage serious harm to oneself.[25] He also insists that a breach of legal duty occurs only when a person chooses to violate a criminal law, this requirement of choice being signified legally by the doctrine of *mens rea*.[26] Notice that Hart's liberal theory of the criminal law adopts both of the theories of legal liability put forward to justify contractual obligations. He selects a version of the 'harm to interests' principle to set the scope of the obligations of criminal law, and then adopts a choice theory in order to determine the issue of personal responsibility.

This combination of theories in relation to the criminal law suggests that much of the debate between the rival liberal justifications of contractual obligations may be misplaced. Hart's analysis of the criminal law separates two questions: the first considers what kinds of obligations the state should impose upon citizens; and the second examines when a person is responsible for a breach of an established duty. He answers the first question by reference to the 'harm to interests' theory, and the second by requiring a choice to incur the legal duty. Once we have separated the question of obligation from that of responsibility, we naturally begin to wonder whether the debate about the scope of contractual obligations has been confused by an inappropriate amalgamation of the issues. Our surmise is plainly correct, at least in many cases. Advocates of each conception of contracts have failed to recognize that they may not be so much disagreeing as attempting to answer different questions. For example, Fuller and Perdue, who argue that the generic principle of the law of private obligations should be compensation for harm to the reliance interest, pay scant attention to the issue of personal responsibility. They recognize that not every instance of misplaced reliance deserves compensation,[27] but fail to devise an adequate theory of personal responsibility which distinguishes between compensable and unprotected invasions of the reliance interest. Yet, as this example illustrates, few expositions of the rival conceptions of contract entirely miss the division of questions which we have identified. Their errors stem instead from exaggeration of one dimension of the problem of justifying the enforcement of contractual obligations.

In the following two sections we will redress the balance of the choice and 'harm to interests' theories of the basis of contractual obligations. In effect, we will complete each theory by articulating both their criterion of responsibility and their test for the limits of obligations, so that they may face each other as fully prepared contestants for the honour of being liberal theories of contract law. Our refinement of these theories will reveal, however, certain defects in their interpretations of the liberal ideal of private autonomy. It is the unwillingness of theorists of contract to recognize and come to terms with these defects which suggests that in fact the rival interpretations of liberalism rest upon concealed visions of the legitimate market order.

III CHOICE THEORY

Choice theories of contract primarily direct their attention to the issue of personal responsibility. The core of these theories maintains that contractual obligations may only be incurred by voluntary consent. Instead of defining the state of mind which represents the required concept of voluntary consent, choice theories follow the normal pattern of common law reasoning and resort to an 'extrovert' approach.[28] This method of reasoning identifies the conditions or circumstances which negative voluntariness or vitiate consent. The law compiles doctrines such as fraud, mistake, duress, undue influence and incapacity, which share the task of specifying the occasions when the normal presumption that a person acts voluntarily may be rebutted. Provided that none of these tests are satisfied, personal responsibility arises by virtue of a voluntary choice to undertake the obligation. Although I shall cricitize this theory of responsibility below, we should next complete this outline of choice theories by examining how they deal with the question of what kinds of obligation should the state enforce.

In answer to that question, choice theories find it hard to resist the temptation to jump to the conclusion that all voluntary undertakings should be binding. Of course, choice theories acknowledge some limits upon this principle in order to avoid the enforcement of illegal or immoral acts. Leaving aside these qualifications, however, many choice theories introduce a further general limitation upon legal enforceability. Theorists feel compelled to do so for two reasons. In the first place, as we noted earlier, in order to justify binding legal obligations, choice theories must isolate those cases of a special exercise of choice where a binding legal commitment is consistent with respect for private autonomy. In the second place, some choice theorists, working within the traditions of the common law, feel compelled to acknowledge the existence of a limitation upon the enforcement of promises and agreements in order to account for the common law's doctrine of consideration. We will briefly consider how choice theorists have tackled the latter problem before examining the defects of the main thrust of this liberal interpretation of contractual obligations.

The doctrine of consideration provides that a promise will bind the promisor only if it is given as the price for another's promise or as the price for an action which involves a detriment to the promisee. On its face, the doctrine of consideration limits the types of voluntary undertakings which are legally enforceable by excluding donative promises. Some choice theorists attempt a reconciliation with this legal doctrine by purporting to show that consideration provides a test of the deliberateness of a choice rather than an imposition of a paternalistic or economically motivated control over the scope of enforceable voluntary obligations. The two main variants of this approach are, first, that the requirement of consideration restricts voluntary obligations to those created by an agreement establishing an exchange relation because such agreements are in all probability moments of careful deliberation;[29] and secondly, consideration functions like a formality, such as notorization or a seal, in order to ensure the seriousness of the promise.[30] Neither interpretation of consideration provides a convincing account of the doctrine, for an inevitable distortion arises if one attempts to reduce this substantive requirement of an economic exchange to a test of the deliberateness of an exercise of choice. In particular, the first theory fails to encompass examples of consideration in unilateral contracts, where there is no agreement but simply an offer which is contingent upon the performance of an action involving detriment to the promisee.[31] The second variant fails both because the requirement of consideration may be satisfied casually by an informal exchange of promises and because the courts invoke another doctrine, the requirement of an intention to enter legal relations, when they wish to claw back certain informal promises made in social and domestic contexts from the realm of contractual obligations.[32] In short, consideration does not ensure the seriousness of a promise, and if this were the aim of the doctrine, it would surely be more straightforward to devise an explicit test of seriousness.

Not every choice theory defers to the practice of the common law courts. Pound[33] and Fried[34] criticize the doctrine of consideration as an unjustifiable impediment to economic freedom. They urge that the law should enforce every promise. Yet, once the doctrine of consideration has been abandoned, the central dilemma of choice theories becomes even more obvious. They cannot reconcile the liberal precept that private autonomy should be respected as far as possible with the practice of legally enforcing all promises. On the contrary, economic liberty requires the ability to withdraw from undertakings, as for example in an employee's right to strike. Choice theories verge upon a serious contradiction with liberal philosophy to the extent that reliance is placed upon the principle that promises ought to be kept. For liberalism prides itself on its rejection of moral paternalism, that is the imposition of a particular scheme of the virtuous life upon all citizens. Liberalism insists that merely because a moral belief is generally held, that fact provides an insufficient reason to enforce that moral belief through law.[35] Each person should be permitted the maximum liberty consistent with the enjoyment of a similar degree of liberty by others. Unless the principle that promises ought to be kept can be shown to be compatible with the appropriate respect for liberty, it offends liberalism by imposing a kind of moral paternalism. We have good reason to doubt the compatibility of these moral aspirations, for an absolute restriction on the power to withdraw promises imposes a constraint upon liberty without necessarily promoting the liberty of others or oneself.

We find on close examination that those choice theorists who invoke the principle that promises ought to be kept in order to complete their account of contractual obligations ultimately concede that they are engaging in a form of moral paternalism. They allege that the advantages of a society in which promises are kept outweigh the proper concern for liberty. They present these advantages either in terms of utility[36] or in the intrinsic moral worth of a community in which individuals may place trust and confidence in others.[37] Whichever way the argument is presented, however, it violates the priority accorded to private autonomy by liberalism.

In summary, though choice theories appear to take as their point of departure the priority of individual autonomy, when we step beyond their criterion of personal responsibility, as defined by the concept of voluntary consent, to the question of the kinds of obligation which the state will enforce, we find that choice theorists admit that they introduce a style of moral paternalism at odds with liberal values. The exercise of choice turns out to be sufficiently special to justify the imposition of contractual obligations because it meets the criterion of a moral principle that promises ought to be kept.

IV INTERESTS THEORY

The alternative candidate for the honour of being the liberal theory of contracts insists that obligations should only arise in order to discourage and compensate harm to the interests of others. At first sight, by following the route charted by J. S. Mill, this theory appears to avoid the temptations of moral paternalism by restricting legal intervention to calculable harms which violate the autonomy of others. Under the interests theory, obligations arise in order to protect economic liberty, not curtail it. Obligations figure as side constraints upon economic activity which respect the inviolability of other persons.[38] Yet, when we dig a little deeper, we find simply another style of moral paternalism lies buried beneath the surface.

We should first note, however, that the 'harm to interests' theory, as we have stated it, remains radically incomplete, for it lacks a theory of personal responsibility. The question is when should a person be under a duty to compensate others for harm to their interests.[39] This question is as important for interests theories as it is rarely discussed, for harm to interests may be caused by remote actors. Unless everyone who participates in a lengthy causal chain is to be held responsible, the interests theory needs a criterion of personal responsibility. Consider the following case: I miss my dental appointment, because the bus is late, because the driver was late for work, because his alarm clock failed to ring, because of a manufacturing defect. Who should pay for the wasted time of the dentist? – I? the bus driver? the bus company? or the clock manufacturer? In order to break these lengthy causal chains and thus put a cap on liability by devising a test of personal responsibility, interests theories invoke such criteria as a voluntary act, consent, acquiescence, a duty of care and foreseen or foreseeable consequences. These criteria represent answers to the question of personal responsibility, but, in another sense, they provide no answer at all, for they conflict with each other by drawing the boundaries of responsibility in a series of concentric circles. Interests theories lack any uniformity in their criteria of responsibility.

At best, we can discern a pattern in the cases and views expressed about them. The scope of personal responsibility expands and contracts in inverse proportion to the extent of the protected interests. Thus where the protected interest is only physical harm, the criterion of personal responsibility will be drawn as loosely as all foreseeable consequences. In contrast, where we expand the protected interests to include loss of profits, as in the example of the dentist's wasted time, the test of personal responsibility is likely to require consent or knowledge of the probability of loss.[40]

This pattern of criteria for personal responsibility adopted by interests theories reveals that, under this explanation of the basis of contracts, liberty is a relative concept: one is less free to cause physical harm to others than to reduce their profits. Similar reasoning occurs in the criminal law; for example, liability for death is much stricter than liability for theft.[41] In the theory of criminal responsibility, however, this variety of tests of responsibility is challenged on the ground that the stricter tests of responsibility deviate from the principle of individual liberty which the doctrine of *mens rea* is designed to respect.[42] Similarly, in the context of economic transactions, we should doubt the compatibility of such a variety of tests of responsibility with a liberal respect for personal autonomy.

Indeed, we must suspect that under the interests theory the criterion of personal responsibility is no more than a function of social policy: the more highly the interest is regarded, the closer we are drawn towards unlimited personal responsibility. This relative concept of liberty undermines the claim of interests theory to don the mantle of a liberal theory of contract. Even if this flaw can be explained away, however, a further examination of the concept of protected interests should deprive interests theory of the title of a contender for the proper articulation of a liberal theory of contract.

For when we ask which interests should be protected, we immediately become engaged in a debate about distributive justice rather than an examination of the concept of personal autonomy. This debate surrounds the reliance theory of contracts, for example. Here advocates suggest that the principal fact generating legal liability should be an invasion of the reliance interest. This interest comprises the out-of-pocket expenses resulting from misplaced reliance upon another, including wasted expenditure in preparing for the performance of a transaction, or partly performing it, losses arising from damage to property, and missed opportunities.[43] A sharp contrast is drawn between the reliance interest and the expectation interest, for the latter includes profits expected from the undertaking and any quantifiable pleasure anticipated from completed performance. Advocates of the reliance theory insist that the proper scope of legal obligations should be confined to invasions of the reliance interest rather than the expectation interest. The reason why reliance is more deserving of protection than expectations is that the former involves merely a restoration to the position once held, whereas the latter entails a transfer of wealth or the enrichment of one party at the expense of the other. Advocates of the reliance theory approve Aristotle's view that the purpose of justice is the maintenance of an equilibrium of goods among members of society. They argue that the protection of reliance fits into this corrective model of justice, whereas to award damages for harm to the expectation interest involves an inappropriate redistribution of wealth.[44]

Leaving aside for a moment the question of the cogency of this argument, on its surface it reveals a decisive break from liberal principles. Instead of the definition of interest to be protected depending upon a balance between the economic liberty of individuals insofar as they conflict, the justification for protection of the reliance interest comprises appeals to the conservative distributive consequences of selecting an interest for legal protection. Whilst it is not inconsistent for liberals to hold a theory of distributive justice, for in a sense any advocacy of the free market implies certain distributive consequences, the 'harm to interests' theorists cannot deny that their theory of obligation rests entirely upon a cryptic theory of distributive justice rather than an extrapolation of fundamental precepts of liberalism.[45]

Further investigation would demonstrate that all interests theories depend, in the last resort, upon principles of distributive justice which identify those interests that deserve protection. Indeed, to speak of interests at all provokes confusion, for it suggests that these interests pre-exist the determination of the question where liabilities ought to be created according to distributive principles. In fact, the term 'interest' is applied to a claim in order to distinguish it from other claims, usually with the implication that the claim labelled an interest deserves a remedy. The adoption of this form of reification in legal reasoning tends to conceal the distributive aim behind a rhetoric which is superficially compatible with liberalism.[46]

In summary, our examination of interests theories demonstrates their fundamental inconsistency with liberal ideals. Their criteria of personal responsibility enjoy the fluidity necessary to achieve social policies rather than the rigour demanded by respect for individual autonomy. The 'harm to interests' test for the kinds of enforceable obligation conceals rival conceptions of distributive justice rather than a balancing of economic liberties.

V CONTRACT AND MARKET

The preceding discussion reaches the conclusion that neither of the dominant theories of contract achieves its aims of being an exposition of liberal philosophy. Choice theory rests its justification for the enforceability of contracts upon moral paternalism, which seriously detracts from the principle of respect for personal autonomy. Interests theories degenerate into the pursuit of patterns of distributive justice instead of circumscribing the scope of protected autonomous action by reference to the need to respect the liberty of others. Yet despite these fundamental flaws, both theories continue to attract supporters who regard them as 'a fair implication of liberal individualism'.[47] I will suggest in this section of the essay that the reason why the antithesis between liberal principles and contract theory is so frequently overlooked lies in a second level of debate which the discussion of liberalism masks. On this second level of debate, the dispute between choice and 'harm to interests' theories concerns rival conceptions of the market and the patterns of distributive justice determined by it. The importance attached to these distributive ideals both explains the heat of the argument and the willingness to qualify the principles of liberalism.

The clue to the identity of the conception of the market and the corresponding theory of distributive justice implicit in choice theories lies in their concept of voluntariness. We have seen how law and theory unite to provide a list of excuses which rebut the normal presumption of voluntariness. The ensuing doctrines of fraud, mistake, duress, undue influence and capacity reflect in their details a particular view of the appropriate operation of the market.

This vision of the market comprises individuals who trade with each other, but they lack many of their normal characteristics. These traders are presented in a form in which they are disembodied and unsituated.[48] This amounts to a view of the person which ignores basic needs such as food, housing, security and work, and also suppresses differences in knowledge, skill and wealth. The hypothetical trader who lacks these needs and characteristics is used as the benchmark for normal market trading. If this person would have agreed to the contract, then there was a voluntary act which qualifies for the imposition of contractual responsibility. In other words, none of the recognized legal excuses will permit the individual to avoid the contract.

In addition, choice theories complete their concept of voluntariness by positing a concept of the ordinary market.[49] If the transaction takes place in the context of market conditions normal for such commodities or services, then the transaction is presumptively voluntary, even though competition is absent. If, on the other hand, there is a violent distortion of the market in a particular case, as for example when only one tug-boat is available to save a ship from foundering on a reef, then the element of voluntariness is missing.[50]

This two-pronged analysis of voluntary acts, composed of the disembodied, unsituated self and the distinction between the ordinary and aberrational market explains the range of excuses acknowledged by the classical law of contract. This definition of voluntariness exhibits a particular ideal of distributive justice. Relations of power and wealth established between disembodied, unsituated traders within an ordinary market appear perfectly legitimate, for they are bound to satisfy the standard of Pareto optimality. By excluding from view the potentialities provided by wealth and knowledge for securing power through contracts, the choice theory ignores precisely those matters which might render organizations of power established by contracts suspect. By restricting the realm of contractual liability to the ordinary interplay of market forces, it is the invisible hand of the market which judges the fairness of the resulting distribution of wealth, and the law purports to remain neutral.

The values which the choice theory represents are the values of a strong *laissez-faire* conception of the market. Indubitably this vision of distributive justice satisfies the demands of liberal philosophy, because it respects both formal equality and individual autonomy. Yet the importance attached to this scheme of distributive justice by advocates of choice theory encourages them to ignore the contradiction which we noticed above between the liberal ideal of individual autonomy and the moral paternalism of the principle that promises ought to be kept which lies at the heart of their theory of contract. We can compare this concept of distributive justice found in choice theories with an equivalent pattern found in interests theories.

We noted above how advocates of the reliance theory, a leading example of interests theory, proclaim the conservative implications of their distributive scheme. In fact, a similar vaunting of a purely restorative aim occurs within all interests theories, since the purported objective is to compensate a person for an invasion of his interests in order to make him whole. Yet when we examine this restorative process in operation, we observe considerable redistributive exercises taking place. Whenever the courts enforce a promise on the ground that another has relied upon it, a transfer of wealth occurs. Whenever damages are paid for harm to property in breach of a duty of care, a transfer of wealth takes place. Sometimes the plaintiff will be better off than before, but the defendant is always worse off. Interests theories justify a redistribution of wealth and, like choice theories, they are premised upon a particular conception of the market order.

The key to an understanding of the distributive scheme of interests theories is to notice the tension between a fostering of the economic interdependence in an advanced division of labour and the aim of economic efficiency. In order to appreciate how this tension determines the pattern of interests theories, we must first examine the web of economic relations in an advanced capitalist society. Whereas choice theories imagine a market full of independent traders, who make isolated purposive exchanges, interests theories recognize that in the twentieth century the division of labour has become much more fragmented. Modern economic transactions assume forms of complex association between a number of parties, not all of which can be described as agreements or exchanges.

Look, for example, at the web of relations surrounding the sale of an automobile.[51] In addition to the consumer who plans to buy the car, there is a dealer who runs a franchised retail outlet, a property owner from whom he leases the premises, a finance company which provides the consumer purchasers with credit, and a manufacturing company which supplies the dealer with automobiles under a requirements contract and probably a credit arrangement as well. The manufacturer may provide the consumer with a warranty of quality either directly or through a third party. Finally, insurance companies may bear the risks of some or all of the parties. Because the interdependence of these parties forms a complex pattern which cannot be reduced to exchange relations alone, breakdowns of trust and reliance can jeopardize the existence of the entire retail operation.

Such a breakdown occurred in *Lusk-Harbison-Jones Inc.* v. *Universal Credit Co.*,[52] where the retailer failed to insure automobiles which had been repossessed after the consumer had missed payments on the credit arrangements provided by a finance company. The dealer omitted to insure the automobiles in reliance on a pamphlet distributed by the finance company which said that the finance company would arrange insurance protection for the dealer's interest, which would continue in force until the loan was liquidated. Unfortunately, when the cars were destroyed by fire, the dealer discovered that no insurance coverage had been arranged by the finance company. Notice that the relation between the dealer and finance company was not based upon agreement or exchange, even though they co-operated in securing sales. Nevertheless, the Supreme Court of Mississippi found that the finance company was liable to the dealer for compensation for damage to the automobiles, because his failure to insure was caused by reasonable reliance upon the promise of the finance company. This case provides a commonplace illustration of how the division of labour in an advanced capitalist society cannot be grasped in terms of agreements and exchanges between autonomous traders, and so the security craved by such relations of interdependence must be satisfied by the wider conception of contractual obligations envisaged by the interests theory.

In this context of an advanced division of labour, interests theories specify the legitimate range of economic interdependence. But each version of interests theory moves cautiously towards the protection of such economic relations for fear of dampening the growth of these relations by imposing too heavy a burden of liabilities. The courts certainly wish to avoid a reduction in the market for automobiles which would happen if finance companies were forced out of business as a result of imposing liabilities upon them to all and sundry. At one time courts hesitated to render manufacturers liable for all losses arising from defective products. Now that such liability is firmly established, the question becomes whether persons who give advice or perform services should be liable to all persons who may foreseeably rely upon their work being properly performed with all due care.[53] It has even been speculated that a community which has grown up around a manufacturing plant may have a claim for compensation against the owners, if the latter decide to close the plant, in order to compensate for the diminution of land values and the destruction of the local economy.[54] In response to each of these challenges, interests theories try to support the growth of an advanced division of labour by protecting persons within relations of interdependence without at the same time destroying those relations by imposing unbearable liabilities in the event of mishap.

At bottom, interests theories define the scope of loss redistribution which the law imposes as a tax upon economic relations. Like any progressive tax, liability increases where the pocket is deeper. Businesses and government agencies are more vulnerable than private individuals to liability because they can afford it.

Similarly, configurations of insurance against liability enlarge the ability to pay this tax and tend to attract legal obligations. It must be admitted that the common law courts lack any discernible scheme for this redistributive pattern. Judges present decisions behind the veil of abstract principle which often conceals the naked face of consequentialist considerations of loss distribution. But we glimpse from time to time those considerations at work when courts examine the insurance position of the parties and reflect upon the implications of unlimited liability to an indeterminate number of plaintiffs.

In summary, behind the rival interpretations of contract law provided by the choice and interests theories, we find two distributive schemes and conceptions of the legitimate market order. On the one hand, the choice theory advocates the distributive consequences of a free market under which obligations can only be incurred through exchange relations between independent traders. These exchanges must be fair because the traders presumptively enjoy equal bargaining power. On the other hand, the 'harm to interests' theory redistributes losses arising within complex relations of economic interdependence, whilst avoiding destruction of this advanced division of labour by excessive liabilities. In order to legitimate this conception of the market, this legal process is misleadingly described as purely corrective justice. Neither scheme rests upon a simple extrapolation from liberal precepts, but should be judged on its merits as a theory of distributive justice.

Viewed from this perspective, we must observe that choice theory signally fails to respond to the hardship suffered by unsuccessful participants in the market. Furthermore, by refusing to generate obligations outside exchange relations, it favours uninhibited development of the forces of production without regard to the social costs imposed by injuries to third parties, pollution, health care and unemployment. Interests theory comprises a response to these social costs. It generates either a law of tort alongside a law of contract confined by choice theory, or, more dramatically, forces a reconstruction of the law of obligations which eliminates these traditional categories. Whatever the legal concepts employed, interests theory promotes communitarian values in its theory of distributive justice. It constitutes an economic order which encourages trust and responsibility for the interests of others – a form of solidarity.[55]

Yet these virtues of trust and solidarity remain imperfectly realized by current understandings of interests theory. Even on the most expansive views of what interests should receive compensation, serious omissions stand out. In particular, both the interest in receiving information about an economic transaction and the interest in receiving a fair exchange of values are generally discounted. Only a more thorough duty of disclosure (perhaps achieved indirectly through a doctrine of unilateral mistake) could satisfy the former interest, for the common law generally limits its protection – in line with a narrow conception of the reliance interest – to reliance upon false statements. Similarly, a fair exchange of values can only be realized by either a broad doctrine of unconscionability or a reversal of the rule that a court will not assess the adequacy of consideration. Without the protection of these interests, the market order legitimated by interests theory countenances too many opportunities to trick and exploit others to live up to the virtues of trust and solidarity.

VI CONCLUSION

I hope that these reflections upon the justifications for the enforcement of contracts place the difficulties experienced by teachers of contract law in a clearer perspective than before. We have vindicated the suspicion that modern legal developments cannot be encompassed by the classical scheme of contract doctrine. That scheme rests upon an interpretation of liberal ideals and the justice of the market order for the distribution of wealth and power which has been overshadowed by a rival interpretation of liberalism and a redefinition of legitimate market relations. The modern legal doctrine embraces a conception of the market which emphasizes the heavy interdependence of economic actors in an advanced capitalist society. In order to sustain this market, the law encourages trust and responsibility for the interests of others. Accordingly, contractual obligations are not limited to agreements, but extend to cases of mutual reliance and financial dependence. In order to regulate this market to prevent domination and exploitation, the terms of contractual obligations cannot be freely chosen by the parties but are shaped by a concern for trust, solidarity and fairness.

Nevertheless, the modern law of contracts tenaciously clings to the liberal ideal of individual autonomy. For example, the law still insists that before responsibility is incurred, an individual should signify, if not his consent, at least his acquiescence in the creation of the obligation. Even so, the grip of liberal ideas upon the law of contract is weakening, because, as I have tried to show, the legal doctrine is ultimately shaped not by fidelity to liberal precepts but by a particular scheme of distributive justice and a vision of the legitimate market order. That is not to say that the element of voluntariness will cease to provide the distinguishing mark of contractual obligations. Voluntariness will be understood, however, not as the decisive act by which an individual surrenders private autonomy, but rather as a deliberate entry into market relations under which certain obligations will arise in order to sustain and regulate an advanced division of labour.

These reflections upon the character of the new vision of contracts may assist teachers in organizing their teaching of the modern doctrine. Yet it must be confessed that obscurities persist at the centre of this vision of the law. The balance between efficiency and social cost requires a more exacting standard of measurement before legal doctrine can be reformulated in a coherent pattern. Similarly, the details of laws encouraging disclosure of information and requiring fairness in an exchange depend upon a more rigorous development of the communitarian political philosophy which values trust and solidarity. These are tasks which confront legal theory and political philosophy together. We may even suggest that the theory of contracts presents an ideal terrain for an examination of these fundamental issues of political philosophy, for the law of contract lies at the intersection of the market and the state, using the coercive power of the latter to reinforce the discipline of the former.

NOTES

I am grateful to J. Beatson, M. R. Freedland, M. E. Stokes, and D. Sugarman for helpful criticisms.

1 G. Gilmore, *The Death of Contract* (1974).
2 E.g. E. Allan Farnsworth, *Contracts* (1982) pp. 88–9: 'To the extent that [the doctrine of consideration] may enforce too few promises, it has been supplemented by reliance as an alternative ground for enforcement'; and P. S. Atiyah, *An Introduction to the Law of Contract* (3rd edn; 1981) p. 267: 'Although the general principle of privity of contract still stands, a very considerable number of exceptions has gradually nibbled away at the principle itself. Indeed, it must be confessed that there are few circumstances of practical importance today where the principle is liable to be applicable and to work serious injustice or inconvenience.'
3 Unger, 'The Critical Legal Studies Movement' (1983) 96 *Harvard Law Rev.* 563; Kennedy, 'Form and Substance in Private Law Adjudication' (1976) 89 *Harvard Law Rev.* 1685; Macneil, 'The Many Futures of Contracts' (1974) 47 *Southern California Law Rev.* 691; P. Gabel and J. M. Feinman, 'Contract Law as Ideology' in *The Politics of Law* (1982; ed. D. Kairys) ch. 8. Feinman, 'Critical Approaches to Contract Law' (1983) 30 *U.C.L.A. Law Rev.* 829.
4 This effect is achieved by promissory estoppel and more generally by the impositon of duties of care through the law of tort. See Fuller and Perdue, 'The Reliance Interest in Contract Damages' (1936) 46 *Yale Law J* 52 and 373; P. S. Atiyah, *The Rise and Fall of Freedom of Contract* (1979) pp. 1–7 and 771–8; Metzger and Phillips, 'The Emergence of Promissory Estoppel as an Independent Theory of Recovery' (1983) 35 *Rutgers Law Rev.* 472; and Gilmore, *op. cit.*
5 Answers to this question are offered by Gordley, 'Equality in Exchange' (1981) 69 *California Law Rev.* 1587; Kronman, 'Contract Law and Distributive Justice' (1980) 89 *Yale Law J* 472; Eisenberg, 'The Bargain Principle and Its Limits' (1982) 95 *Harvard Law Rev.* 741.
6 [1982] 3 WLR 477.
7 C. Fried, *Contract as Promise* (1981); P. S. Atiyah, *Promises, Morals and Law* (1981); Raz, 'Promises in Morality and Law' (1982) 95 *Harvard Law Rev.* 916.
8 See Gordley *op. cit.*, and Kronman, *op. cit.*
9 For the purposes of this analysis the important differences between liberal and more libertarian positions appear not to matter. Therefore the ensuing discussion of liberalism draws upon such works as: R. Dworkin, 'Liberalism' in *Public and Private Morality* (1978: ed. S. Hampshire); M. Sandel (ed.) *Liberalism and Its Critics* (1984); J. Rawls, *A Theory of Justice* (1971); R. Nozick, *Anarchy, State and Utopia* (1974).
10 Rawls, *op. cit.*, p. 31.
11 Fried, *op. cit.*, pp. 13–14.
12 *Id.*
13 Both David Hume (T. H. Green and T. H. Grose eds, London, 1890), *A Treatise of Human Nature*, book III, part II, ss.V and VI, and Nozick, *op. cit.*, p. ix, place the right to enforce a contract in the list of fundamental rights, but neither explicitly derives the right from the principle of individual autonomy.
14 E.g. Fried, *op. cit.*; Pound, 'Promise or Bargain?' (1959) *Tulane Law Rev.* 455; *Restatement of Contracts, Second, s.1;* Farnsworth, *op. cit.*, ch. 1.
15 F. Pollock, *Principles of Contract* (3rd edn; 1881) p. 2; cp. Friedrich Carl von Savigny, *System des heutigen römischen Rechts* (Berlin, 1840) Book II, ch. III, s.140; and P. Heck,

Grundriss des Schuldrechts (1929) pp. 121-2, quoted in A. T. von Mehren and J. R. Gordley, *The Civil Law System* (2nd edn; 1977) p. 830.

16 G. H. Treitel, *The Law of Contract* (6th edn; 1983) p. 1; cp. French Civil Code, art. 1108.

17 Fuller and Perdue, *op. cit.*; Atiyah, 'Contracts, Promises and the Law of Obligations' (1978) 94 *Law Quarterly Rev.* 193.

18 Fuller and Perdue, *op. cit.*; Atiyah, *op. cit.*; and Gilmore, *op. cit.*

19 Kessler and Fine, 'Culpa in Contrahendo, Bargaining in Good Faith, and Freedom of Contract: A Comparative Study' (1964) 77 *Harvard Law Rev.* 401; and Unger, *op. cit.*, p. 620.

20 See the discussion of 'will theory' in Atiyah, *op. cit.*, n. 4, pp. 405-31; cp. French Civil Code, arts 1183 and 1184; German Civil Code (B.G.B.), s.241.

21 This is the French method: Dawson, 'Specific Performance in France and Germany' (1959) 57 *Michigan Law Rev.* 495, 510-25; and Loi No. 72-626 of 5 July 1972. Some American states use the law of tort to the same effect: see Farnsworth, *op. cit.*, pp. 842-4.

22 Fuller and Perdue, *op. cit.* This emphasis upon monetary compensation as the natural remedy so dominates American legal thought that even in traditional expositions of choice theory such as Fried, *op. cit.*, specific relief is not considered. Similarly, arguments in favour of the use of specific performance are put forward in economic terms rather than as a natural corollary of the duty to perform one's promise: e.g. Kronman, 'Specific Performance' (1978) 45 *University of Chicago Law Rev.* 351; Swartz, 'The Case for Specific Performance' (1979) 89 *Yale Law J* 271.

23 E.g. Nozick, *op. cit.*; F. A. Hayek, *The Constitution of Liberty* (1960) ch. 16.

24 J. S. Mill, *On Liberty and Considerations on Representative Government* (1946; ed. R. B. McCallum); H. L. A. Hart, *Law, Liberty and Morality* (1963); R. M. Dworkin, *Taking Rights Seriously* (1977) ch. 11; N. MacCormick, *Legal Right and Social Democracy* (1982) ch. 2.

25 Hart, *op. cit.*

26 H. L. A. Hart, *Punishment and Responsibility* (1968).

27 Fuller and Perdue, *op. cit.*, p. 420.

28 A. Kenny, *Will, Freedom and Power* (1975) ch. 2.

29 A. G. Guest, *Anson's Law of Contract* (26th edn; 1984).

30 Fuller, 'Consideration and Form' (1941) 41 *Columbia Law Rev.* 799; O. W. Holmes, *The Common Law* (1963; ed. M. Howe) p. 215.

31 Farnsworth, *op. cit.*, p. 43; Treitel, *op. cit.*, p. 115.

32 Farnsworth, *op. cit.*, pp. 116-19; Treitel, *op. cit.*, ch. 4; Unger, *op. cit.*, pp. 621-5.

33 Pound, *op. cit.*

34 Fried, *op. cit.*

35 *Supra*, n. 24.

36 In this form the position becomes indistinguishable from interests theory: e.g. MacCormick, *op. cit.*, ch. 10. For an account of the utilitarian position and criticisms levelled against it, see Atiyah, *op. cit.*, n. 7, ch. 3.

37 Fried, *op. cit.*, pp. 14-17.

38 This terminology is adapted from Nozick, *op. cit.*

39 Logically we should distinguish between the two questions of who is placed under an obligation and to whom is the obligation owed. But since this distinction rarely surfaces in discussions of 'harm to interests' theory, it will be ignored here as well.

40 See the brilliant analysis put forward by Lord Denning MR in *H. Parsons (Livestock) Ltd.* v. *Uttley Ingham & Co. Ltd* [1978] QB 791.

41 Theft Act 1968, s.1, requires intent and dishonesty, understood in part subjectively: *Ghosh* [1982] QB 1053; manslaughter only requires recklessness or gross negligence: *Andrews* v. *DPP* [1937] AC 576, *Stone and Dobinson* [1977] QB 354.

42 Criminal Law Revision Committee, *Report on Offences against the Person* (1980) (Fourteenth Report, Cmnd 7844) paras 11 and 88-94; G. Williams, *Textbook of Criminal Law* (2nd edn; 1983) ch. 5; Hart, *op. cit.*, n. 26, ch. 3.

43 This follows the definition provided by Fuller and Perdue, *op. cit.*

44 This argument is presented by *id.*, pp. 56-7; Atiyah, *op. cit.*, n. 4, p. 4; and Atiyah, *op. cit.*, n. 17, p. 202.

45 For many liberals, especially libertarians, a free market is both necessary and sufficient as a theory of distributive justice: e.g. Hayek, *op. cit.* Other Liberals acknowledge that marginal adjustments to the distributive consequences of an unbridled market are essential in order to compensate for disadvantages arising from differences in resources and talents and from handicaps: e.g. Rawls, *op. cit.*, and Dworkin, *op. cit.*, n. 9. The best justification for intervention in these cases of hardship rests ultimately upon the belief that without the ability to satisfy basic wants through the market, these persons cannot achieve the state of well-being envisaged by liberalism, that is the ability to lead their own way of life. But those liberals who support redistributive measures bear a heavy burden of proof to demonstrate that an interference with the economic liberty of others is justified.

46 M. Magdalena Schoch (ed.) *The Jurisprudence of Interests* (1948), and Pound, 'Survey of Social Interests' (1943) 57 *Harvard Law Rev.* 1, and Burrows, 'Contract, Tort and Restitution – A Satisfactory Division or Not?' (1983) 99 *Law Quarterly Rev.* 217, exhibit this concealment.

47 This phrase is used by Fried, *op. cit.*, p. 2, to describe 'will theories' of contracts.

48 This discussion reflects a general criticism of liberalism contained in Sandel, *op. cit.*, pp. 5-7; see also A. MacIntyre, *After Virtue* (1981) ch. 15 and Unger, *op. cit.*, pp. 656-60.

49 This discussion draws on Unger, *op. cit.*, pp. 625-33.

50 *The Port Caledonia* [1903] P 184; cp. *Lebret* c. *Fleischer*, Cas. req. 27.4.1887, D.1888.i.263; S.1887.i.372.

51 See Gabel and Feinman, *op. cit.*, p. 179; S. Macaulay, 'The Standardised Contracts of United States Automobile Manufacturers' in *International Encyclopaedia of Comparative Law* (1974), vol. VII, ch. 3.

52 164 Miss. 693, 145 So. 623 (1933).

53 *Ross* v. *Caunters* [1980] ch. 297; *J. E. B. Fasteners Ltd* v. *Marks Bloom & Co.* [1983] 1 All ER 583; *Junior Books Ltd* v. *Veitchi Co. Ltd* [1982] 3 WLR 477; *Leigh and Sullivan* v. *Aliakmon Shipping* [1985] 2 WLR 289; *Lucas* v. *Hamm* 56 Cal. 2d 583, 364 P 2d 685, 15 Cal. Reptr 821 (1961), *cert. denied* 368 US 987 (1962).

54 *United Steelworkers of America, Local No. 1330* v. *United States Steel Corporation* 492 F Supp. 1 (1980) aff'd 631 F 2d 1264 (1980 6th Circ.).

55 See Unger, *op. cit.*

9
Company Law
and Legal Theory

MARY STOKES

Students of company law very often complain that the subject is technical, difficult and dull. This is not without some justification. The reason can perhaps be found in the fact that company law as an academic discipline boasts no long and distinguished pedigree. The result is that company lawyers lack an intellectual tradition which places the particular rules and doctrines of their discipline within a broader theoretical framework which gives meaning and coherence to them.

One object of this essay will be to suggest such a theoretical framework. The framework aims to provide a tool for analysing and explaining many of the fundamental rules of company law. It will be argued that one of the central features of the business company is the way in which it centralizes the authority to manage the capital which it aggregates from its investors in the hands of corporate managers. Clearly the nature and extent of the power thus vested in the management of a company vary according to the type and size of the company. But whatever its extent the power of corporate managers poses a problem of legitimacy. This essay will seek to explain the nature of that problem. It will also endeavour to illustrate how much of company law can be understood as a response to the problem of the legitimacy of corporate managerial power. Thus the theoretical framework takes the legitimation of corporate managerial power to be one of the underlying and unifying themes of company law.[1] More concretely, those areas of company law which are best viewed as a response to the problem of the legitimacy of corporate managerial power will be examined. Thus it will be shown how the changing popularity of a number of theoretical models of the company can be linked to the need to offer an explanation for the power which the company vests in corporate managers. Similarly, the rules allocating power between shareholders and directors and those imposing fiduciary duties on directors will be analysed in terms of the need to confer legitimacy upon the power of corporate management.

A second object of this essay will be to show how the law's attempt to justify the power vested in corporate managers has failed.[2] This in turn will lead us to an examination of how corporate law scholars have sought to offer new ways of legitimating corporate managerial power and how these too prove to be unequal to the task. Finally, some fresh methods by which managerial power might be justified will be explored.

Mary Stokes

THE PROBLEM OF THE LEGITIMACY OF
CORPORATE MANAGERIAL POWER

The reason why company law should have been so concerned to legitimate the power of corporate managers is that this power potentially threatens the political-economic organization we associate with a liberal democracy.

We make a distinction between public and private power. This distinction reflects the separation of the state from the individual in a liberal society. Liberal democracy has been concerned most explicitly with legitimating the power of the state, or public power. This is because the assumption is made that all important power in society is concentrated in the hands of the state. The arguments used to justify public power are very familiar. They are that the system of representative democracy gives authority to the legislature to make law, and that the power conferred upon all administrative or public bodies is legitimate as it is derived from the legislature. However, in a liberal society a democratic system of government is not considered sufficient by itself to legitimate public power. Liberalism is hostile to the existence of centres of unbridled power, believing that power unless limited and controlled may threaten the liberty and the equality of the individual which are the two fundamental tenets of liberalism itself. Thus it is sought to subject public power to the Rule of Law. At its broadest the Rule of Law aims to impose limits, controls and checks on the exercise of power. Power must be prevented from being used arbitrarily. Arbitrariness is a difficult concept to define. It will be used to mean the exercise of power for purposes alien to those for which it was conferred.

Notice the structure of the argument legitimating public power. It breaks down into two parts. We are concerned, firstly, to provide a justification for power being vested in the state; and then, secondly, we seek to demonstrate that there are constraints upon the exercise of that power which prevent it from being used to infringe the liberty or equality of individuals. As we have seen, the power vested in the state is justified by a system of democratic government; and the assurance that the state's power is subject to constraints which prevent it from being used arbitrarily is found in the adherence to the ideal of the Rule of Law. The structure of this argument is important because we find it repeated when we look at the traditional ways in which it is sought to legitimate private power.

Although the theory is that all important power is concentrated in the hands of the state, this has not meant that the individual has been regarded as powerless. It has always been acknowledged that a system of private property ownership confers upon the owners of property private economic (and perhaps political and social) power.

Indeed, one of the justifications of private property takes as its premise the idea that property ownership confers power. This provides a necessary bulwark against the danger of an all-powerful state invading the individual's liberty. In other words private property serves to protect the individual's freedom. Private ownership is also justified because by permitting individual property owners to pursue their own self-interest in a competitive market it is argued that we achieve an optimal allocation of society's resources.

It is not enough simply to suggest justifications for the existence of private ownership. If private property is to be legitimate within the framework of a liberal society it is also necessary to show that there are constraints which prevent it from becoming a source of power which threatens the liberty of the individual or rivals the power of the state. Two arguments are used for this purpose.

Firstly, it is claimed that the economic power associated with the ownership of property does not threaten liberty because it is not concentrated in the hands of an individual or small group of individuals. Everyone is entitled to own property. It is true that the actual distribution of property in society is far from equal; but it is not so skewed as to give any individual a monopoly of economic power. The power of each property owner is checked by the corresponding power of each other property owner. Thus the distribution of property is not so unequal that it can threaten the liberty of the individual. Private economic power differs in this respect from the public power of the state. The state has a monopoly over the use of coercion which is perceived to be legitimate only because those exercising such power have been democratically elected or derive their authority from a democratic legislature.

A second argument has traditionally been used to reassure us that the economic power derived from the ownership of property is subject to constraints. It is claimed that economic power is constrained by the competitive market.[3] In a competitive market the bargaining power of the owner of a particular commodity is limited. Because many others own identical commodities or commodities which are close substitutes which they are willing to sell, the owner will not be free to charge any price he chooses for his commodity. Rather the price will be determined by the demand for and the supply of that commodity. In addition, if a property owner is manufacturing and selling goods in a competitive market he will be obliged to produce any given level of output of those goods at the lowest cost possible. And the quantity of goods which he produces will be such that the marginal cost of production is the same as the price of the product. If he fails to follow these simple rules the consequence will be economic failure. This flows from the assumptions made by the model of perfect competition that the individual entrepreneur maximizes his profits, that there is a price taker and that there is freedom of entry and exit from the industry in which he is producing goods. It is true that this model does not purport to describe accurately the way in which the market economy actually functions. Nevertheless, the model of economic theory is often taken to embody in an ideal form many of the characteristics of the actual market economy. Because this market controls and disciplines the economic power associated with property ownership it serves to legitimate that power within the framework of liberalism.

An analogy can here be made between the market and the Rule of Law.[4] The market is the mechanism which has traditionally been invoked to limit, control and thereby legitimate private power, whereas the mechanism by which it has been sought to control and justify the exercise of public power has traditionally been the ideal of the Rule of Law. Both mechanisms can be viewed as part of the liberal response to the threat to freedom which it is believed is posed by the existence of untrammelled power, be it public or private.

The economic power of the company was not thought to pose any particular difficulty within this framework of legitimation. Although the corporate form together with limited liability enabled large sums of capital to be aggregated for a common purpose, this was not perceived as problematic. Economic theory assumed that the company, like the individual entrepreneur, behaved as a profit-maximizing unit. It was obliged to do so if it was to operate within a competitive market where there were a sufficient number of firms producing the same or a substitutable commodity so that each firm was incapable of influencing the price of the commodity by adjusting its output. Thus the firm in economic theory behaved identically and was subject to the same constraints whether it took the form of an individual proprietorship, a partnership or a company.

Theory was, however, divorced from reality. The reality was that the growth of corporate enterprise shattered three of the assumptions which underlay the belief that economic power of the company was regulated and thereby legitimated by the competitive market. Firstly, the growth of corporate enterprise falsified the theory that in any given industry there were numerous small firms so that each firm had no market power but was obliged to accept the market price for its products. The company facilitated the aggregation of vast sums of capital from numerous small investors and this together with changes in technology and organizational techniques led to a vast expansion in the size of the firm and a reduction in the number of firms operating in any particular industry. As a result the market structure very often ceased to be purely competitive, becoming monopolistic or oligopolistic. The consequence was that the company no longer had to accept the market price for its products but could affect that price by varying the output of the product.

Secondly, the assumption that the company behaved as a profit-maximizing unit of production just like an individual entrepreneur or a partnership was manifestly open to doubt. One of the central features of the company is that it separates out the functions of ownership and management. Those who manage the company do not own the company. If the managers of the company display the characteristics which economic theory credits to all other individuals they will be concerned to maximize their own utility rather than the profits of the company. Adam Smith himself understood this problem. He was hostile to the joint-stock company as a medium through which to carry on business enterprise.

> The directors of such companies being the managers rather of other people's money than of their own, it cannot well be expected that they should watch over it with the same anxious vigilance with which the partners in a private copartnery frequently watch over their own. . . . Negligence and profusion, therefore, must always prevail, more or less, in the management of the affairs of such a company.[5]

Of course, it was the oligopolistic character of product markets which gave those who ran the company discretion to pursue goals other than profit-maximization. In a world of perfect competition it would not be possible for managers to deviate from the profit-maximization norm for any length of time even if they were tempted to pursue their own rather than the shareholders' interests. The failure of the market due to imperfect competition to regulate the company as an economic unit is thus indissolubly linked with the increased and potentially unconstrained power of corporate managers. It is for this reason that we can treat both imperfect competition and the separation of ownership and management as creating a problem for the legitimacy of corporate managerial power.[6]

Thirdly, one of the cardinal features of the market model of legitimation was that economic power was exercised through exchange transactions in the market. Yet as the company grew in size it was plain that much economic activity was being withdrawn from the sphere of the market and being replaced by a hierarchical, bureaucratic organization within the company. The invisible hand was being replaced by the visible hand.[7]

The effect of these three changes brought about by the growth of corporate enterprise was that the market could no longer be viewed as regulating and thereby legitimating the exercise of corporate power. The power conferred upon corporate managers by the business company was potentially unchecked and hence illegitimate within the framework of liberal democracy.

At a deeper level the concentration of economic power brought about by the growth in the size of companies and the oligopolistic nature of product markets undermined some of the traditional justifications for private ownership itself. The concentration of power in the hands of the managers of the largest companies could not be seen as a necessary bulwark against the power of the state. Nor could it be argued that private property ensured an efficient allocation of resources since the market no longer resembled the model of perfect competition.

THE RESPONSE OF THE LAW
TO THE PROBLEM OF THE LEGITIMACY OF
CORPORATE MANAGERIAL POWER

How did the law respond to this crisis of legitimacy of the business company?

The first reason why the market could no longer be perceived as limiting economic power was that the structure of the market ceased to correspond even loosely with the model of perfect competition which required numerous firms operating in the same industry so that no firm was capable of affecting the price of its product by varying the level of the output of that product. Ultimately the law has responded to this problem by intervening to try to ensure that the market resembles as closely as possible the paradigm of perfect competition, outlawing monopoly and trade practices that deviate from that paradigm. Although it can be argued that the *ultra vires* doctrine in company law was originally used to try to prevent concentration in industry this task has fallen primarily to competition law.

Company law has instead focused its attention on the problems created by the second characteristic of corporate enterprise which undercut the ability of the market to regulate the exercise of economic power: the separation of ownership and management. This feature of the company together with the increasing substitution of the organization of economic activity within the company rather than through the market[8] suggested that there had been an enormous growth in the power of corporate management. Both characteristics also suggested that

that power was relatively uncontrolled by the market. There are two ways in which company law set about tackling the problem of legitimacy of corporate managerial power which was thus posed. Firstly, company law sought to explain and justify why broad discretionary authority was conferred upon corporate managers. And, secondly, company law set about the task of demonstrating that the power of corporate managers was not unlimited but was subject to checks and controls which ensured that it could not be used for the manager's own purposes or for any other arbitrary end. The discussion of the methods by which company law has sought to legitimate the power conferred upon corporate managers and an assessment of their efficacy will be broken into parts to reflect these two strategies. The two strategies echo the structure of the argument which we have already seen used to legitimate public power and private power associated with the ordinary ownership of property. This suggests that there has always been an underlying awareness that company law doctrine was engaged in a discourse about the legitimation of power.

I will also seek to show how many parallels can be drawn between the arguments used to legitimate corporate managerial power and the arguments used in administrative law to explain, control and legitimate the power conferred upon administrative bodies.[9] Given that the market has ceased to be an effective mode of regulating the exercise of the economic power of the company it is hardly surprising that arguments employed to regulate the exercise of public power should have been drawn upon to regulate the private economic power of corporate managers.

Before proceeding with an elaboration of the two strategies invoked by company law to legitimate the power of corporate managers, I will give an overview of the traditional model of the company with the object of showing how its development is characterized both by an increasing centralization of the authority to manage the company in the hands of the directors of the company and by a concern to justify this vesting of broad discretionary power in corporate management.

THE TRADITIONAL LEGAL MODEL OF THE COMPANY

The traditional legal model of the company originally treated the directors of the company as agents of the company.[10] This meant that their authority was rather limited since it could at any moment be revoked by the shareholders. Furthermore, the shareholders as the principal were entitled to issue specific instructions to the directors which as agents they were obliged to implement.

The beginning of the twentieth century saw the abandonment of this theory of the relationship between the shareholders and the directors. Instead of being perceived simply as agents of the shareholders the board of directors came to be viewed as an organ of the company which for many purposes could be treated as the company. Directors were given the exclusive right to manage the day-to-day business of the company. Shareholders were precluded from intervening in the ordinary business of the company, no longer being entitled to issue instructions to the directors as to how to exercise their powers. The courts justified this vesting of managerial autonomy over the everyday business of the company in the hands of the directors by arguing that it flowed from the construction of a company's articles of association which formed a contract between the members of the company.[11]

Although the shareholders no longer exercised the direct control of principals over the directors as their agents, the model nevertheless asserts that any danger that the directors might use their considerable discretionary powers to manage the business in their own interest is precluded. It is precluded because the model gives power to the shareholders to appoint and dismiss the directors[12] and power to supervise them once they are in office. A system of indirect control and accountability is thereby established over the directors as those responsible for the management of the company. This system of indirect control through the internal division of power between shareholders and directors is strengthened by providing that the assistance of the courts can be called upon to enforce it.

The legal model has one further method by which it attempts to balance the desirability of giving to the managers of the company substantial discretionary power so that they have sufficient flexibility to act effectively, whilst at the same time minimizing the danger that the existence of such discretion creates, which is that it will be used arbitrarily. This further method is found in the imposition upon directors of fiduciary duties. Directors are treated as being in a position analogous to that of trustees, so powers conferred upon them are given to them in a fiduciary capacity. This means that directors are under a duty to act in the best interests of the shareholders. They cannot place their own interests above those of the shareholders. The fiduciary duties of directors are not merely abstract injunctions to act only in the interests of the shareholders for they are once again enforceable in the courts.[13]

In the following two sections the two strategies employed by this model to legitimate corporate managerial power will be examined more closely. Firstly, the justification given by the model for vesting substantial managerial power in the hands of the directors will be investigated. Secondly, the nature of the controls imposed on management so as to assure us that their power cannot be used arbitrarily will be analysed and criticized.

THE LEGAL MODEL'S LEGITIMATION OF THE VESTING OF BROAD DISCRETIONARY POWER TO MANAGE THE COMPANY IN THE HANDS OF THE DIRECTORS

In trying to analyse the reasons for conferring upon the management of the company substantial power to run the company the law has relied heavily on a variety of conceptions of the company. There is a tendency among corporate law scholars to dismiss the debate about the nature of the company and corporate personality as too rarefied and speculative an enquiry better left to properly qualified jurisprudential writers. This is a mistake. For the different theoretical conceptions of the company have been intimately embroiled in the effort of company law to justify the vesting of substantial power in corporate management.

Before trying to link the legal model of corporate managerial power to a particular conception of the company a sketch of three conceptions of the company

which have vied at different periods for dominance in corporate law doctrine
and scholarship will be given. The first and traditional conception of the company
might be labelled the fiction/concession theory.[14] This theory treats the company
as an artificial entity whose separate legal personality is granted as a privilege
by the state. It was a privilege which the state guarded jealously and which was
made available to business enterprises whose purposes aimed to benefit the public
in general as well as enrich the corporators. Thus many of the early joint-stock
enterprises which were granted the privilege of corporate identity were concerned
with building and operating canals and railways. What gave legitimacy to these
companies was the theory that as creatures of the state they were supervised and
regulated by the state. In the eighteenth and early nineteenth centuries the theory
found its doctrinal expression in the *ultra vires* rule. The *ultra vires* doctrine was
used by the courts to keep corporate bodies within the narrowly defined powers
granted to them by the statute or charter of incorporation conferring corporate
identity upon them. Clearly there is a very strong resemblance between this
method of legitimating corporate power and that which still prevails today in
respect of administrative bodies. Their powers are granted to them by the state
and the courts ensure through the *ultra vires* or jurisdictional principle that they
do not act outside their powers. However, the fiction/concession theory came
under tension once incorporation became freely available on compliance with
some simple formalities, for it no longer made sense then to treat the incorporation
as a special privilege or concession from the state.[15] We have seen that the more
modern legitimation of corporate power, which has prevailed since the demise
of the fiction/concession theory, is based upon the discipline which the competitive
market exerts over the economic power of the company.

The second theory of the nature of the company is the contractual one.[16] The
company is a form created by the free agreement amongst the shareholders, much
like an extended partnership. This view has long been linked with those who
have argued that the company should not be specially regulated by the state since
it owed its existence to nothing more than a contract between individual property
owners. It is unsurprising that the lawyers in the nineteenth and early twentieth
centuries should have been attracted by a contractual analysis of the company.
Contract was once the greediest of legal categories intent on devouring as many
areas of the law as possible (e.g. quasi-contract) and indeed was even invoked
to explain the nature of the state itself.[17] This contractual vision of the company
focuses on the internal relation of the members within the company. It does not
say anything explicit about the legitimacy of corporate power in relation to society
generally. This is because the more modern justification for corporate power is
assumed. That justification is, as we have seen, that the competitive market
disciplines the economic power of the company. So the company is regulated
both internally and externally by contract.

The third view of the company is one which has prevailed in the academic
literature rather more forcefully than in company law doctrine itself. It is that
the company is a natural or real entity which exists separately and distinctly from
the shareholders. In Dicey's words it meant that 'whenever men act in concert
for a common purpose they tend to create a body, which from no fiction of law
but from the very nature of things, differs from the individuals of whom it is

constituted.'[18] Sometimes the natural entity theory has been called a 'group person' theory. This posits that the company or any group of individuals acting together for a common purpose creates a living organism, or a real person, capable of willing and acting through the people who are its organs just as a natural person wills and acts through their brain, mouth and hands.[19] It was a theory originally popularized by the German realists who were not slow to make the connection between a natural-entity theory of the corporation and a theory of the state. It was enthusiastically adopted by academic writers in this country at the beginning of this century.[20]

Quite clearly the conception of the company explicitly adopted by the legal model is the contractual one. The company is simply treated as an organization constituted by the contract between its members. That contract confers power on the directors of the company to manage the company. This contractual analysis formed the basis of the early theory that the relationship between the shareholders and the directors was that of principal and agent. It also forms the key to the courts' justification of managerial autonomy in the model which superseded the agency theory at the beginning of this century. For the conclusion that the powers vested in directors are to be exercised exclusively by the directors is arrived at by a careful analysis of the wording of the article giving to the directors of the company general managerial powers which is found in the constitution of most companies.[21]

By adopting a contractual conception of the company the legal model gives as the reason for the vesting of centralized authority to manage the company in the board of directors the contractual agreement of the owners of the company. Thus by invoking the idea of the freedom of a property owner to make any contract with respect to his property the power accorded to corporate managers appears legitimate, being the outcome of ordinary principles of freedom of contract. It reassures us that the hierarchy created within the company does not threaten individual liberty because it is the outcome of a voluntary consensual arrangement. This model of the company is one which has proved very attractive to some commentators. Some of the features of the legal model which we have depicted such as the power of the shareholders to dismiss the directors and the fiduciary duties imposed upon the directors are provided for by the law rather than by the articles of association. Nevertheless, commentators have argued that the function of these legal rules is to provide a standard set of terms to govern the relationship between the shareholders and the directors, the object being to reduce the transaction costs involved in the parties negotiating a private bargain. In other words these legal rules simply reflect the agreement the parties would have reached if bargaining on these questions had taken place at arm's length.[22]

The use of the contractual conception of the company to give legitimacy to the vesting of managerial power in the directors of the company encountered two difficulties. The first was that this contractual conception of the company conflicted with the theory prevailing in the case-law that treated the company as an artificial entity, separate and distinct from its shareholders.[23] This traditional fiction/concession theory had been embraced by legal doctrine in order to make the limited liability of the company seem a natural and inevitable incident of corporate personality. Clearly this would only be the case if the company was perceived as an entity distinct from its shareholders so that it followed that the company and not the shareholders would be liable for any debts. If, by contrast, the company was viewed as no more than a contractual association between the members much like a partnership, it was difficult to explain why each shareholder should not be liable for the full extent of any debts, as was the case in a partnership.[24] In other words what had happened is that legal doctrine had drawn upon conflicting conceptions of the company to legitimate limited liability and to endorse the power conferred upon directors to manage the company. Legal doctrine was in danger of appearing incoherent unless some reconciliation could be found between these two visions of the company.

The second difficulty which arose as a result of the legal model's reliance on the contractual conception of the company was the increasing artificiality of this analysis as the size of companies grew and the shareholders became increasingly passive investors. Any notion that the internal division of power within a company was the result of a consensual arrangement between the shareholders seemed purely fictional.

The difficulties associated with the contractual model of the company led academics in the early decades of this century to adopt instead in their writing the natural-entity conception of the company.

The natural-entity theory had several advantages compared with the contractual and the fiction/concession models of the company. Firstly, it viewed the company as distinct from its shareholders and therefore, unlike the contractual model, it could be seen to support the theory that it was the company which was liable for any debts. The limited liability of the shareholders then appeared as a sort of concession to the creditors of the company rather than an arbitrary limitation on the normal liability imposed on partners in a business association. Secondly, the fiction/concession theory could have supplied an image of the company as separate and distinct from its shareholders which would also have supported the institution of limited liability, but there were strong reasons for preferring the natural-entity model of the company. The fiction/concession theory saw the company as entirely the creature of the state and therefore potentially accorded to the state the power to regulate and control the company as it saw fit. These implications of the fiction/concession theory were neither compatible with the reality of free incorporation on compliance with some simple formalities nor congenial to academics who did not favour state intervention in corporate enterprise. By contrast the natural-entity theory fitted perfectly a world where there was free incorporation and where the general belief was that there was no particular need to regulate the business company. Thirdly, and most importantly for our purposes, the natural-entity theory overcame the problems of the artificiality in the case of large companies of analysing the directors' managerial power as being derived from the contractual agreement of the shareholders. Its conception of the company as a real person or living organism suggested that the corporate managers could be treated as the brain of the organism formulating the policy of the company and directing its implementation by corporate executives. The fact that the shareholders within the large company were increasingly becoming passive investors, irrelevant within the company except for their function in supplying the capital of the company, was entirely consonant with this image of the company. They could be viewed as the organ within the living organism whose task it was to supply the basic necessity of capital without any need to accord them a fuller role within the enterprise. The natural-entity theory thus legitimated the fact that in the large public company, as we shall see, the shareholders no longer controlled corporate management, so that control as well as management came to be separated from ownership.

The enthusiasm for the natural-entity model of the company can be linked with a new justification given for the vesting of very extensive discretionary power in corporate management which is independent of the contractual justification which appears so clearly in English case-law. This justification is that the managers of the company have the time, information, organizational skills and other expertise to manage the business, which the shareholders themselves lack. It is this expertise of the managers which justifies their being treated as the brain of the company, formulating corporate policy to further the ends of the enterprise. This modern justification of the discretionary power of corporate managers has a parallel in administrative law where we find that one of the arguments used to legitimate conferring discretionary power on administrative agencies has been their expertise and special competence in a particular field.[25]

THE LEGAL MODEL'S ATTEMPT TO LEGITIMATE CORPORATE MANAGERIAL POWER THROUGH SUBJECTING IT TO CHECKS PREVENTING IT FROM BEING EXERCISED ARBITRARILY

The discussion thus far has focused on the reasons given in legal doctrine to support the legal model's centralization of the power to manage the company in the hands of the directors of the company. I have argued that company law in its attempt to establish the legitimacy of corporate managerial power has been concerned also to show that the power conferred on managers is subject to controls which prevent it from being used arbitrarily. These controls are necessary if the business company is not to threaten the traditional liberal distrust of unconstrained power normally encapsulated in the adherence to the Rule of Law.

As we have seen the legal model adopts two mechanisms for ensuring that the directors of the company are subject to the control of the shareholders. The directors are, firstly, made accountable to the shareholders by structuring the internal division of power within the company so that the shareholders have the power to appoint and dismiss directors and to supervise them whilst in office. Secondly, directors are treated as fiduciaries required to act in the best interests of the shareholders. These mechanisms share in common the following features. Both mechanisms accept and endorse the separation of the management of the company from its ownership. They accept that it is no longer plausible to assume that those operating the business have their freedom of action constrained by the competitive market or their own self-interest. It is more probable that the managers will seek to pursue their own goals rather than subject their decisions to the norm of profit-maximization. Thus the common aim of both legal mechanisms is to force managers to maximize profits for their company and prevent them from maximizing their own utility.[26] If this can be done successfully the company will once again correspond to the profit-maximizing firm of economic theory. Corporate managers' discretion will be legitimated since their power will be severely limited by the requirement that all their decisions must aim simply at profit-maximization.

The efficacy of each of the mechanisms will be examined in turn.

The Internal Division of Power within the Company as a Means of Controlling Managerial Power

The traditional legal model divides power within the company between the directors and the shareholders. The object is to organize the internal structure of the company so that, whilst the directors as the managers of the company are given ample discretionary power to operate the company effectively, they are nevertheless obliged to exercise that power in the interests of the owners of the company.

The legal model of the company is often treated as establishing a basic constitution for the company, defining the powers of the different organs of the company and regulating the relationship between them.[27] An analogy is drawn between the company and the state. The argument is that just as direct democracy is ruled out by the size of the modern state, so too once companies grow beyond a certain size it is no longer possible to involve all their members directly in the decisions concerning the running of the company. In both cases therefore a system of representative democracy is adopted. This system relies upon the ability of the electorate to elect and dismiss leaders at periodic intervals. It is this which establishes the control of the people over their political leaders or of the shareholders over their directors. Thus the shareholders in the company are treated as the electorate, and the directors are regarded as the legislature. The legal model envisages the board of directors as actually carrying on the day-to-day business of the company so that there is no separate executive organ within the legal model. But once the size of companies expanded further it was very easy to accommodate the fact that whilst directors remained responsible for the formulation of the overall policy of the company the ordinary management was entrusted to executives. For the corporate executives could be viewed (as their name suggests) as executives implementing the broad objectives set by the directors as the legislature.

The comparison drawn between the company and the state in no way detracts from the contractual conception of the company, which we have seen was originally adopted to legitimate the vesting of broad discretion to manage the company in the hands of the directors. The two are entirely compatible if it is remembered that one of the popular theories of the nature of the state itself has always been that it was founded on a contract between the individual members of a society.

The powers conferred by the legal model on the shareholders can be analysed neatly in terms of the analogy between the constitution of a company and the constitution of a nation-state. Shareholders as the electorate are given the power to elect and dismiss their leaders, the directors. They are also given power to vote on fundamental structural changes to the company, such as altering the memorandum[28] and articles of association[29] or merging with another company[30] or dissolving the enterprise[31] which are thought to resemble constitutional issues. In addition the received legal model of the company gives powers to the shareholders to ensure that the directors once in office do not use their powers for their own self-interest. Thus the law insists that a director who wishes to enter into a transaction where there is any possibility of a conflict between his own interest and his duty to act in the best interests of the company must disclose the transaction to the shareholders in general meeting and obtain their consent to it.[32] The shareholders are thereby given the power to judge for themselves whether the directors are using their managerial powers for their own benefit at the expense of the company and if this is so to veto the transaction or at least hold the director liable for any profits thereby made.

How effective is this constitutional structure of the company in ensuring that directors do not use their powers arbitrarily? The constitutional framework makes the shareholders responsible for monitoring and supervising the directors of the company. Its efficacy in providing adequate controls over the directors therefore depends on the shareholders performing this task. Yet the reality is that it is only in companies where each shareholder has a sufficiently substantial stake in the company to make it worth his or her while performing the tasks of monitoring and supervising the behaviour of the directors that this constitutional framework can hope to provide an adequate control on the behaviour of directors. In the large public company it is now accepted as part of conventional wisdom that the shareholding is so widely dispersed that each shareholder does not own a significant enough proportion of the company to perform any of the functions of monitoring and supervising the directors that the legal model casts upon him. The consequence in the terminology of Berle and Means[33] is that there is a separation between ownership and control. The managers become a self-selecting body and cease to be effectively monitored by the shareholders once in office. Control is vested in their hands rather than the shareholders'.

The legal model of the company which separates ownership and management but still asserts that ultimate control resides with the owners of the company no longer corresponds to the realities of the modern large public company. Yet company law doctrine has failed to acknowledge this. Indeed the obstinacy with which company law has clung to the traditional legal model of the division of power in the company between the managers and the shareholders has sometimes had the effect of concealing from us the fact that company law regulates a variety of different sorts of companies. It is only by looking outside legal doctrine itself that we are made aware that neither the small closely held company (where there is no separation of ownership and management) nor the large public company (where there is a separation of ownership and control) conform to the legal model. Because company law fails to differentiate in any consistent fashion between these different sorts of companies all are treated as regulated by the traditional legal framework which we have been examining. The result is that there is a tendency to assume that corporate management are adequately controlled by the shareholders in all companies, including the large public company. The problem of legitimacy posed for liberalism by the fact that in reality the managers of a large public company wield power which is unconstrained by the shareholders is quietly ignored by legal doctrine itself.

This point can perhaps also be illustrated by some of the recent legislative reforms of company law. The Companies Act 1980 (now consolidated in the Companies Act 1985) has extended the occasions when the consent of the shareholders to a transaction is required, so that, for example, before directors enter into long-term service agreements with their company,[34] or substantial property transactions with their company,[35] they must disclose the details of these transactions and obtain the consent of the shareholders. What these legislative reforms seem to be suggesting is that all is basically well with the traditional model where the directors of the company manage the company but are supervised in that task by the share-holders who, if given the requisite powers, can be relied upon to ensure that directors do not use their powers for their own purposes. All that is needed is to specify clearly those occasions when there is a strong danger that directors may be tempted to act in their own self-interest and then to make the shareholders' consent necessary in those circumstances. But the attempt to assure us that directors are controlled by their shareholders must fail, for no matter how far the law goes in strengthening the powers conferred upon shareholders to monitor the managers of their company the reality is that where each shareholder only holds a tiny proportion of the share capital of the company none of the shareholders will avail themselves of the powers given to them to monitor the management. The attempt to revitalize shareholder democracy in this fashion is doomed to failure in the large public company. Efforts to do so are misplaced and can positively mislead us into believing in the efficacy of the internal organization of the structure of the company as a means of legitimating corporate managerial power.

Outside legal doctrine itself there has been a greater willingness to accept that in the large public company the shareholders may not perform the task of monitoring and controlling the management of the company, so that the managers are potentially left in a position of unchecked power. Several attempts have been made, however, to breathe new life into the traditional model which relies on structuring the internal organization of the company appropriately to ensure that controls are exercised over corporate managers.

It is sometimes argued that the rise of institutional investment and the decline of individual direct investment in large public companies means that the traditional model of the shareholder controlling the directors of the company is once again a realistic one. Although each institutional investor may still only own a very small percentage of the issued share capital of the company, nevertheless, they have the requisite skills to monitor management effectively, and can act collectively to exert pressure on the managers of the company, thereby overcoming the problem that there is little incentive for the individual shareholder to spend the necessary time and money to inform himself of and perhaps challenge the actions of the directors as the managers of the company. The empirical evidence suggests, however, that the supervision which institutional investors exercise over the management of a company is minimal and cannot be regarded as a sufficient control over the managers of large public companies.[36]

Others have argued that the traditional legal model overlooks a significant development which has taken place in the large public company. The legal model assumes that the board of directors manages the ordinary business of the company. Yet the truth is that the board of directors will only very rarely be involved in the day-to-day running of the company which is instead usually entrusted to the officers and executives of the company. Even the policy-making functions will generally be carried out by the executives rather than the board itself. The role of the board within the company needs to be re-examined. Since it is not involved in the management of the company it is in a position to monitor and check the performance of the executives actually managing the company, to ensure that they act only in the interests of the shareholders. This role can best be fulfilled by the board if the majority of directors are independent of the executive over whom they exercise a supervisory, checking function.[37] This model of the internal structure of the company acknowledges that the shareholders do not control those who manage the company and instead entrusts this task to a reconstituted board. As a means of assuring us that the management of large public companies do not wield arbitrary power it is unsatisfactory. Firstly, it represents no more than a proposal for reform of the internal structure of the public company and not an accurate description of how the board at present functions in such a company. Secondly, even if implemented, the question would arise as to whether adequate checks existed to prevent the reconstituted board from exercising its powers in an arbitrary fashion. Without such checks the old problem arises of who is to be responsible for monitoring and supervising the supervisors.

The conclusion that must be drawn is that corporate management in the large public company are not controlled by the shareholders exercising the powers accorded to them by law to appoint, dismiss and monitor the directors of the company. Unless there are other effective ways in which the managers of the public company are constrained, it would seem that the power of corporate management threatens liberalism's ideal that all power should be limited or subjected to checks.

Fiduciary Duties as a Mechanism for Controlling Managerial Power

The second mechanism for controlling managerial power which was singled out in the legal model was the fiduciary duties imposed upon the directors and officers of the company. These duties can be formulated as three distinct rules. Directors owe a duty of care and skill; a duty of loyalty; and a duty to act *bona fide* in the best interests of the company and not for any improper purpose.

One analysis of the function of these duties is that they ensure that the directors of the *company* have sufficient discretion and flexibility to be able to manage the company efficiently, whilst precluding them from exercising this discretion contrary to the interests of the shareholders. Much the same problem has arisen in administrative law. Here the problem is one of balancing an administrative body's need for substantial discretion to make choices between different courses of action and the desirability of giving the courts power to intervene to prevent the discretion being exercised contrary to the intention of the legislature. Judicial review of the exercise of discretionary powers by administrative bodies has been self-consciously based on the need to ensure that the intention of the legislature is implemented and that discretionary power is subjected to some sort of control in the name of the Rule of Law. The review of directors' managerial decisions can be viewed as being motivated by a similar desire to ensure that directors exercise their powers only in accordance with the will of their constituents (the shareholders) and that they are subjected to the controls often associated with the Rule of Law to prevent them from using their power arbitrarily.

The idea that there is a strong parallel to be drawn between judicial review in administrative law and company law is further strengthened by the similarities between the standards of review used in these two fields. Where broad discretionary powers have been conferred upon public authorities the courts take it upon themselves to review the exercise of those powers to ensure that the body does not make decisions which are so unreasonable that no reasonable body could have come to such a decision; to ensure that the decision-makers are not biased and that decisions are not made *mala fide* or for any improper purpose. It can be suggested that the fiduciary duties imposed on directors subject them to similar standards of review by the courts. Thus the duty of care prevents directors from acting wholly unreasonably; the duty of loyalty ensures that their decisions are not biased; and the duty to act *bona fide* in the interests of the company and not for any improper purpose is almost identical in its formulation as a standard of review to the administrative law test striking down decisions which are taken for an improper purpose.[38]

In administrative law the theory is that the courts are simply implementing the will of the legislature by subjecting the exercise of discretionary power to these standards of review. In company law it can equally be argued that by casting trustee-like duties on directors so that they are required to act only in the interests of the shareholders the law aims to ensure that the will of the shareholders is implemented. If this is the object of imposing fiduciary duties on directors it fails. This is because in considering what are the interests of the shareholders the directors are not obliged actually to consider what the subjective desires of the shareholders might be. The interests of the shareholders become an objective standard to govern the actions of the directors. Yet it is an objective standard which the directors themselves define, and not one that is imposed upon them by the courts, who regard it as illegitimate to substitute their own view of what constitutes the best interests of the company or the shareholders for that of the directors of the company. So the injunction to directors is that they must act *bona fide* in what they, and not the court, thinks are the best interests of the company.

In conclusion, the argument that the duty of directors to act only in the interests of the shareholders operates to ensure that the will of the shareholders is implemented by the management of the company is fundamentally flawed because the directors have considerable discretion in defining exactly what the interests of the shareholders are. Sometimes it is argued that the interests of the shareholders can provide the directors of the company with a purely objective standard on which to base their decisions if the interests of the shareholders are equated with profit-maximization. Apart from the fact that this ignores the possibility that shareholders may have other objectives in investing (such as opposing investment in countries practising apartheid, or opposing the manufacture of armaments or cigarettes, etc.) the profit-maximization norm does not provide a hard guideline as to how directors should exercise their discretion. They still have discretion to determine whether it is long-term or short-term profitability that they should be striving to achieve and discretion as to how to go about realizing that goal. Thus even if we accept that the duty of directors to act in the best interests of shareholders can be equated with a duty to maximize profits this does not provide us with any real assurance that the wishes of the shareholders are being executed by the directors or that we have a satisfactory way of controlling the discretion accorded to directors in the name of the Rule of Law.[39]

Another analysis of the function of imposing fiduciary duties on directors is that these duties are designed to ensure that directors act only within the ambit of their special expertise.[40] It has been seen that the modern justification for conferring broad discretionary power upon both corporate managers and administrative agencies is their special expertise. Not only is expertise the justification for giving broad discretionary power to both corporate managers and administrative bodies, it also supposedly limits and controls the exercise of their power. The theory is that the range of decisions open to managers and administrative agencies is limited because a set of criteria derived from their expert background and training governs their decisions. The function of fiduciary duties is to provide the courts with standards of review that enable them to guarantee that corporate managers do not act outside the limits of their special competence. Once again a similar argument exists in administrative law – namely that the function of judicial review is to ensure that public bodies only take decisions which are within the scope of their expertise. Thus it can be argued that although the courts proclaim that in reviewing the decisions of an administrative body they are merely attempting to keep the body within the jurisdiction conferred upon it by Parliament, in fact they do sometimes explicitly justify their decisions by reference to the expertise or lack of expertise of the body whose decision it is sought to review.[41]

There is an ambivalence in the expertise theory. There are two views of the purposes for which corporate managers will use their expertise. One view is that the expertise of the managers will ensure that they use their broad discretionary power to maximize the profits of the company in the interests of the shareholders. By preventing management from straying outside their competence fiduciary duties act as an alternative mechanism to the internal organization of power within the company for forcing managers to maximize profits. The common aim is to bring the company back in line with the profit-maximizing firm of the model of perfect competition. An alternative to this view is that corporate managers use their expertise to help define and implement the broad purpose of the organization, which is assumed to be that of furthering the public interest. This view is part of the corporatist vision of the company which will be examined more fully later. The contrast I wish to draw here is between an image of the corporate manager as an expert profit-maximizer and an image of him as a trained public servant. It is the former image which the courts have tended to have before them when reviewing the decisions of corporate managers.

Both these versions of the expertise theory assure us that the special expertise of directors at once justifies conferring upon them the discretion to run the business and imposes a restraint on how they exercise that discretion. Directors will only act according to professional standards of behaviour and the range of decisions available to them will be indicated by their own expertise. In theory it would be possible to rely simply on the professional background and training of corporate managers to act as a self-imposed limit on their discretion. Instead, however, we rely on the courts to review managerial decisions as a means of double checking that the directors are acting professionally (that is impersonally and for ends related to that of their organization). The courts' own role in reviewing managerial decisions is in turn defined by their own expertise. They are not competent to make business judgments but they have a special skill in detecting and thwarting management self-dealing. Hence they will not substitute their views as to the proper management of a company but they are prepared to articulate standards of review which are designed to catch self-dealing on the part of managers. The duty of loyalty has generally been invoked to prevent directors from having a personal financial interest in a decision, whilst the duty to act not for any improper purpose has sometimes been invoked to rule out decisions where directors have some other sort of personal but not directly financial interest in the decision.

The difficulty encountered by the expertise theory in trying to demonstrate the legitimacy of corporate managerial power by showing that there are restraints on the discretion of the managers stems from its attempt to combine a deference to the judgments of business managers with an insistence that corporate managers are subject to fiduciary duties that prevent them from exercising their power for their own purposes or for other non-corporate ends. The problem is that there is no satisfactory way of drawing a line between decisions of corporate managers which ought to be respected because they are based solely on the expertise of the directors and those which should be challenged as based on personal considerations or other non-corporate purposes. This is well illustrated by the controversy in the case-law about the legitimacy of a company's board of directors taking defensive action against a threatened take-over bid by issuing shares to someone who can be relied upon to support the incumbent management. The Canadian position is that the board of directors, provided it is acting in what it considers to be the best interests of the company, must have the discretion to take defensive measures against an imminent take-over.[42] The assessment of the bidder's capacity to run the target company is, in other words, something which lies within the range of the directors' expertise. By contrast, the position ultimately reached in the English cases is that if the primary reason for issuing new shares is to fend off a potential bidder for the company then the decision of the directors will be one that the courts can overturn even if the directors are acting *bona fide* in the best interests of the company.[43] It can be argued that the English courts have concluded that the danger that the judgment of the directors might be swayed by their own personal interest in retaining control of the company takes the decision outside the province where we should defer to their skill and judgment. Thus there is enormous difficulty both in defining precisely what we mean by expertise and in marking out what decisions will be considered to be taken for personal or other non-organizational ends. This difficulty in drawing a line between those decisions that are based on expertise and those that are influenced by personal or other non-corporate considerations means that we become suspicious of legal argument. Arguments based on deference to the judgment of corporate managers or those based on the finding of a personal interest or a non-corporate purpose on the part of the directors have the appearance of mere slogans to justify either judicial restraint or intervention. This in turn can lead us to query the legitimacy of judicial review, since it appears to be an *ad hoc* affair rather than a process governed by any firm and coherent standards.[44]

There is one further practical consideration which suggests that fiduciary duties are ineffective in constraining the discretion of directors. Fiduciary duties depend for their enforcement on the shareholders taking action against the wrongdoing corporate managers. Yet we have seen that due to the dispersion of shareholding in the large public company they have no incentive to inform themselves of the actions of their managers or to seek a remedy against them.

We can conclude that so far the law's quest to subject the power conferred on corporate managers to controls to prevent it from being exercised arbitrarily has not been successful. The internal organization of the company does not provide an adequate safeguard against the power of the managers being used for their own ends; and the imposition of fiduciary duties does not ensure that the discretion of the managers is only exercised either in accordance with the wishes of the shareholders or in accordance only with the expertise of the managers, since both these concepts prove impossibly difficult to define. Added to this is the doubt whether, because of the wide dispersion of shareholding in the large public company, shareholders can be relied upon to invoke the legal remedies at their disposal.

The legal model's attempt to equate corporate managers with ordinary entrepreneurs acting so as to maximize the profits of the company should be recognized for what it is – a failure.

IMPLICATIONS FOR THE STUDY OF COMPANY LAW

There are two types of response which can be made to the failure of company law to legitimate corporate managerial power.

Firstly, renewed efforts can be made to constrain the power of those who manage the large public company. Two basic strategies are employed for this purpose. Either attempts can be made to ensure that corporate managers behave as profit-maximizers by making them responsive once again to the market; or, alternatively, new life can be breathed into the legal model of the company so that managers are once again forced to act in the interests of the shareholders.

The market which is envisaged as capable of disciplining managers may be the product market;[45] the market for corporate control;[46] or the market for managerial talent.[47] Or it may be that the internal organization of the firm is such that it replicates a capital market so that middle managers are obliged to profit-maximize.[48] In recent years much energy and ingenuity has been poured into the task of showing that such markets do in fact exist and can be made to force managers to profit-maximize.

It is suggested that the aim of constraining the managers of the large public company by organizing the internal division of power in the company appropriately can be achieved in a variety of ways. Faith is very often placed either in institutional investors[49] or in redefining the role of the board of directors as that of monitoring executive management.[50]

Both the hunt for new forms of market constraints on corporate managers and the search for appropriate ways of revitalizing the internal structure of the company to limit the ability of managers to pursue goals other than those of profit-maximization clearly accept that the traditional method of legitimating corporate managerial power has failed. That method depended, as we have seen, on managerial power being limited in two ways. It was limited because the company and hence the managers running the company were seen to exercise no greater power than any other ordinary individual participant in the product market in which the company operated. This had the effect of limiting the power of corporate managers both *vis-à-vis* their shareholders within the company and externally *vis-à-vis* society in general. If the market could not always be relied upon, due to its increasingly imperfect character, to constrain the powers of corporate managers there was a second way in which corporate managerial power was limited. The legal model which allocated powers to manage to the directors but vested ultimate control in the shareholders ensured that managers were adequately constrained. The failure of the product market and the legal model of the company to impose any real limits on managerial power has been the point of departure of the two avenues of corporate law scholarship already outlined. Nevertheless, both avenues of research do not seek to break out of the basic structure adopted by the traditional method of legitimating the authority of corporate managers. Instead they prefer simply to tinker with the particular mechanisms advocated for controlling corporate managerial power. Thus alternative external market constraints on managerial behaviour are isolated; or proposals are made reasserting the potency of the internal structure of the company as a means of preventing abuse of the discretion exercised by corporate managers.

A second approach to the problem of the legitimacy of corporate managerial power might begin by showing that the response outlined so far is fundamentally misguided. It is misguided in believing that a solution to the problem of the legitimacy of corporate managerial power can ever be found by looking to either the market or the ordering of power within the company. The search for such solutions fails to draw out the full implications of the criticisms of the traditional method of legitimating corporate managerial power. I will illustrate this by looking, firstly, at the claim that some form of market can legitimate the power of corporate managers, and, secondly, at the argument that the internal structure of the company can be so designed and used as to legitimate corporate managerial power.

The idea that some form of market will act so as to restrain corporate managers from abusing their discretion by failing to serve the interests of the shareholders is flawed in two ways. Firstly, if the argument is that any of the suggested markets – be they for products, corporate control or managerial talent – at present actually operates to constrain corporate managers, this is not something which is empirically demonstrated, and given the present nature of these markets it seems an implausible claim. Take, for instance, the market for corporate control. It is said to function through the mechanism of the take-over bid so as to allocate the assets of companies to those managers who can put them to their best use, thereby disciplining managers to maximize profits or face the threat of a take-over bid ousting them from their jobs. However, the rules which regulate take-over bids are so riddled with occasions when the managers of a target company can affect the outcome of the bid that the take-over bid ceases to act as the potent threat to self-serving or inefficient corporate managers which it is supposed to be.[51]

Secondly, if, instead of being treated as a claim about the actual functioning of the suggested markets, the argument is taken to mean that it is possible to design a set of rules such that the proposed markets do operate to restrain corporate managerial power, it encounters an overwhelming obstacle. It overlooks the fact that the very notion that the market is capable of legitimating power is widely acknowledged as being open to serious doubt today. There is no one institutional set of arrangements which implements the abstract ideal of the market. That ideal of a multiplicity of individuals bargaining freely is translated into social practice through the rules of property, contract, tort and criminal law. But those rules can take an almost infinite variety of forms. The market cannot be seen to be a neutral, fair process whose structure simply permits participants to exercise free choice in negotiating and concluding exchange transactions. Rather the rules which constitute the market structure people's available range of choices and consequently themselves help to define the distribution of wealth and power in society, for which an independent justification is required. Thus, for example, the way in which it is proposed to structure the rules regulating take-over bids simply reflects a judgment about how far acquiring companies should, through the mechanism of the take-over bid, be given the opportunity of dislodging the managers of the target company – a judgment which cannot be justified simply by appealing to the ideal of a free market. This is not to deny that it is possible for the market (of whatever kind) to impose some form of restraint on corporate managers. The difficulty is that it is impossible to draw the line, by appealing to any abstract ideal of the market, between the degree of constraint and the degree of discretion which will be accorded to corporate managers through, for example, the device of the take-over bid.[52]

Equally flawed is the idea that it is possible to legitimate the power of corporate managers by structuring the internal division of power in the company so that the managers are prevented from deviating from the narrow path of profit-maximization. It has already been shown above that the argument cannot be taken to mean that either institutional investors or the board of directors do in reality constrain corporate managers to profit-maximize. This, as we have seen, is simply not borne out by the facts. Even if institutional investors could be persuaded to exercise the responsibilities of ownership by playing an alert and activist part in monitoring corporate managers, difficulties would remain. Who would monitor the management of financial institutions? Equally, if the board of directors could be restructured so that it effectively monitored the executive managers of the company, who would monitor the board itself?

The second response to the problem of the legitimacy of corporate managerial power thus rejects the traditional strategies of company law for legitimating corporate managerial power. Neither the market nor the internal structuring of power within the company is accepted as a viable means of constraining managerial power. As a consequence this response breaks with the traditional obsession of the mainstream of corporate law scholarship. It abandons any attempt to design market or internal controls over managers to ensure that their discretion is only exercised in the interests of shareholders.

The problem of how to legitimate managerial power must be tackled from an entirely new perspective. This perspective takes as its point of departure the discrepancy between the law's assertion that shareholders control corporate managers and the reality of their more or less total failure to exercise any of the responsibilities of ownership. Instead of viewing this development with hostility it celebrates the way in which the modern public company has reduced the shareholders to passive property owners, thus freeing the managers from having to act purely in the interests of shareholders. Equally the way in which economic activity has increasingly come to be organized within the company rather than through the market is something to be celebrated instead of feared. At the level of legal reasoning these developments cannot be accommodated within the traditional contractual conception of the company. Instead a means of legitimating the power of corporate managers can be found by drawing upon and transforming the deviations within current legal thought.[55] The rejection of the ruling mode of dealing with the problem of the legitimacy of corporate managerial power (through market constraints or the internal structure of the company) does not necessarily lead one into an inconclusive political debate about the merits of the capitalist system. This style of deviationist doctrine seeks to 'integrate into the standard doctrinal arguments the explicit controversies over the right and feasible structure of society'.[54]

The seeds of such an approach are already present within corporate law scholarship. They are found in the corporatist model of the company. It provides a countervision to the traditional contractual model, dominant within legal theory. Three important characteristics of this model need to be singled out. Firstly, it is accepted that the modern public company has become an organization whose significance almost rivals that of the state. It is the primary institution for organizing and employing much of our capital and labour resources and the primary supplier of goods and services in our community.[55] The rise of the corporate economy is said to lead to a 'gradual approximation of the state and society, of the public and private sphere'.[56] Society comes to resemble 'a constellation of governments, rather than an association of individuals held together by a single government'.[57] The second characteristic of the corporatist vision of the company takes up the theme of the obliteration of the distinction between state and society and between public and private to supply a normative vision of the role of corporate management. The more or less complete independence of corporate managers from their shareholders enables managers to pursue goals other than those of profit-maximization in the interests of the shareholders. Released from the constraints of both shareholders and any market, managers are free to become public servants, 'a purely neutral technocracy, balancing a variety of claims by various groups in the community and assigning to each a portion of the income stream on the basis of public policy rather than private cupidity'.[58] Thus the power of corporate managers *vis-à-vis* society is legitimated because they are perceived as experts wielding power for the benefit of society generally. The third characteristic of the corporatist vision is that it views the company as an organic body which unifies the interests of the participants into a harmonious and common purpose under the direction of its leaders. Within the company the power of the managers is legitimated because they are seen simply to help formulate, articulate and execute the common purpose of shareholders, creditors, employees and the community.

Traces of this countervision of the company can be found embedded in the legal materials. At the level of legal theory the natural-entity model of the company attempts to encapsulate many of the features of the corporatist countervision. The company is viewed as an organic body, bound together by a common purpose under the direction of its expert managers. At the more concrete level of legal rules, we find that many of the difficulties which the law has faced in defining the duties of directors to act in the best interests of the company stem from a conflict between the traditional contractual model of the company and the corporatist countervision. The traditional view was that the interests of the company meant the interests of the shareholders. But increasingly the view is that the interests of the company include not only the interests of the shareholders but the interests of the company's creditors[59] and employees.[60] And if these groups' interests must be considered, why not also require the directors to consider the interests of the local community, the environment and consumers? Insofar as English law requires the directors to take into account the interests of groups other than the shareholders it adopts the position that these interests do not fundamentally conflict with those of the shareholders and that it is therefore possible to arrive at a decision that balances all the relevant interests, subsuming them under or subordinating them to the vaguely defined collective goal of the organization. Thus s.309 of the Companies Act 1985 does not regard the interests of the employees and the shareholders of the company as irreconcilably opposed, expecting the directors to be able to take the interests of the employees into account whilst performing their duties to the company, including the shareholders. To this extent the law can be considered to have endorsed the corporatist perspective.

The tendency of legal doctrine to permit and even require the directors of a company to weigh the interests of groups other than those of the shareholders is closely allied with the claims that a revolution is occurring in the goals which corporate enterprise sets itself and that corporate managers are assuming for their companies' social responsibilities. Their sole concern is no longer the maximization of the company's profits. This goal is tempered by the pursuit of other social goals, such as donating corporate funds to charity, supporting community projects, promoting the welfare of employees and taking steps to prevent pollution beyond those required by straightforward compliance with the law. It is because the shareholders no longer control the management of a large public company and the product market is no longer perfectly competitive that the management are free to use their discretion for these socially worthwhile ends. The argument is that provided they do use their power for the benefit of the public rather than for their own personal gain that power is legitimate. This vision of the company as socially responsible can be interpreted as being very closely linked if not identical to the corporatist vision.

The corporatist countervision argues that corporate managers are obliged to weigh the interests of a whole range of different constituents. In so doing it rejects the classical vision of the company which defines the interests of the company as those of the shareholders, who are the only members of the company. The reason why the corporatist vision takes a different stance on the question of whose interests corporate managers ought to further is because it pursues to its logical conclusion the implication for the classical view of the company of the separation of ownership and control in the large public company. The classical view of the company is that shareholders as the property owners are entitled to all the profits of the enterprise and hence that the company should be run in their interests alone. That view rested, however, on the assumption that the shareholders exercised ultimate control and responsibility over their property, even if the function of managing the property had been delegated to corporate managers. Since shareholders controlled the company they should be entitled to the profits and the managers obliged to act in their interests, for this ensured that the shareholders had the incentive to exploit wealth-maximizing opportunities. In other words one of the traditional defences of private property which states that an optimal allocation of resources results from owners (who it is assumed control their property) pursuing their own self-interest could be invoked to justify insisting that the company was run in the interests of the shareholders alone. Clearly that justification collapsed once it became clear that shareholders in large public companies no longer exercised any real control or responsibility over their property. Once the link between property ownership and control is severed there no longer seems to be any compelling reason why the shareholders should receive all the profits of the company or why corporate managers should run the company in their interest alone.[61] Indeed if the aim is to provide those who control corporate assets with an incentive for putting those assets to their best use it should be the managers who receive the profits of the company and in whose interests it should be run, a conclusion which no one has as yet advocated seriously.

Once it has been demonstrated how the logic behind the traditional fidelity to the interests of the shareholders is flawed in the context of the large public company, we are free to examine exactly the nature of the stake which shareholders and others have in the company. Clearly the shareholders' interest tends to be a purely financial one; employees have an interest in the security of their jobs and the type of life they lead within the workplace; consumers have an interest in the type and quality of the goods and services produced; and the local community has an interest in the company as a supplier of jobs and livelihoods and as a potential threat to the local environment. Having freed ourselves of the shackles of the classical conception of the company and its assertion that it is only the interest of the shareholders as property owners that the law should seek to protect, it becomes evident that a whole web of relationships of interdependence exist around and within the company. Although some of the relations between the company and these other groups are contractual it is clear that the formal contractual relationship does not always define and protect all facets of the relationship. The issue for company law is whether the law should recognize and how far it should protect these non-contractual expectations and relationships of trust and dependence. The corporatist view suggests that the interests of all these groups must be balanced against each other by the managers. They are placed in a position analogous to that of a government agency and must ultimately reach a decision on the basis of the public good.

It has been suggested that we have contradictory ideals of human association informing three areas of our lives which are kept separate and distinct from each other. The relationship of the citizen to the state is informed by the democratic ideal; contract and impersonal technical hierarchy are the principles which govern our work and exchange relationships; and the ideal of community informs and structures relations between friends and within the family.[62] The corporatist view, by perceiving the company as a unit which welds together the interests of its participants into a harmonious common purpose defined as the public good, seems to draw on the ideal of community and seeks to inject it into an area which the dominant legal ideology regulates through contract and hierarchy.

The ideal is attractive. Nevertheless, powerful objections can be made to it. The ideal of community can become warped in its actual implementation in the context of the family. The family becomes a structure of 'power ennobled by sentiment'.[63] Undoubtedly a similar danger exists if we seek to implement the corporatist goal of community in the corporation. We may find that the corporatist vision of the company is legitimating a structure of hierarchical managerial power by appealing to the purposes for which that power is exercised. The purposes are assumed to be the public good. Yet there is great difficulty in defining what we mean by the public benefit. In a liberal society we assume that it cannot be objectively defined. Permitting management to use their discretion to run a company for the public benefit may be tantamount to encouraging them to run it according to their own moral and political views about what constitutes the public benefit. That this can be dangerous is illustrated by the facts of *Medical Committee for Human Rights* v. *SEC.*[64] The management of Dow Chemical Company resolved during the Vietnam war to continue to manufacture napalm in order to support the US government's involvement in Vietnam. They believed that this course of action was morally and politically desirable despite the fact that the manufacture of napalm did not generate much profit, that the company's manufacturing facilities could have been more profitably employed in the manufacture of some other chemical, and that the company's public image and recruitment activities were being damaged by the continued manufacture of napalm. Is it really self-evident that the manufacture of napalm to be used in war is something for the benefit of the public? Even if we believed that the public interest could perhaps be equated with goals supported by a broad social consensus so that the spectre of management indulging its own personal moral and political preferences under the guise of pursuing socially worthwhile goals no longer haunted us difficulties would still remain. It is unlikely that corporate management has the information available to it to determine what social goals are supported by a broad consensus or what their order of priority might be. For example, how is management to determine whether the object of minimizing pollution to the environment or supporting scientific research establishments are objectives supported by a general social consensus and if so which of these should take priority?

By ignoring these sorts of objections it is clear that the corporatist vision of
the company is attempting to break with some of the basic assumptions of
liberalism. If it is to be successful in this objective it needs to articulate much
more clearly the rival communitarian philosophy which one senses underpins
its practical proposals.

If we are troubled by the fact that the corporatist countervision we find hinted
at in the legal materials might become simply a mask behind which corporate
managers exercise unconstrained economic and social power, an alternative
avenue for research is available to us. We have seen how the corporatist vision
of the company draws upon the ideal of community which within our present
legal system and our everyday thinking is generally allowed to operate only
within the realm of family and friendship. A different vision of the company
might draw upon the democratic ideal which inspires the relation of the citizen
to the state. The democratic ideal asserts that those who are substantially affected
by the decisions made by political and social institutions in our society should
be involved in the making of those decisions. If we take that ideal seriously there
seems no good reason why it should be excluded from an important area of our
lives, our relations within and to the workplace. Within company law doctrine
this idea has no real impact. But it often provides the guiding principle for a
series of proposals for putting representatives of employees,[65] consumers,
environmentalists and the neighbouring community on the boards of companies.
These proposals can also be seen as a response to the weakening of the claims
of the shareholders as property owners due to the separation of ownership and
control in the large public company. The framework for legitimating corporate
managerial power is a novel one. It justifies managerial power by showing that
those who are affected by it are involved in making managerial decisions. A
framework for justifying such transformations in the power structure of the
company could be developed from the available set of legal ideas. In distributing
power between the shareholders and the directors it will be remembered that
the legal model invoked a powerful comparison between the company and the
state. That comparison is made even more potent given that the large company
tends to collapse the distinction between private and public power. The company
can thus plausibly be viewed as a miniature state. All those affected by its decisions
are citizens of that state and should therefore be involved in making those
decisions. Whether this view should lead us to endorse a fully participatory style
of democracy or to rest content with some form of interest-group pluralism
should be one of the key issues on the agenda for corporate law research.

CONCLUSION

In teaching and thinking about company law one of the themes which we cannot
afford to ignore is the way in which legal doctrine and scholarship provide a
mode of legitimating corporate managerial power which draws on a set of
background assumptions of political theory. The inadequacy of the current
strategies of legitimation needs to be acknowledged so that company law scholars
can focus their efforts on rethinking the legitimation of managerial power. Two

potential avenues for this enterprise have been suggested: the corporatist and the democratic ideal of the company. It is suggested that these are not merely speculative lines of enquiry but can be developed from within the current body of legal materials. At the same time these avenues depend for their inspiration on a more abstract set of values of community and democracy which can be found in political theory.

NOTES

I am grateful to Hugh Collins, Dan Prentice and David Sugarman for their helpful comments on an earlier draft of this article.

1 Frug, 'The Ideology of Bureaucracy in American Law' (1984) 97 *Harvard Law Rev.* 1277. Frug believes that much of company law is concerned to justify large-scale bureaucratic power. I would argue that company law has been concerned to explain and legitimate all corporate managerial power.

2 *Id.*

3 E.g. A. Chayes, 'The Modern Corporation and the Rule of Law' in *The Corporation in Modern Society* (1959; ed. E. Mason) p. 36.

4 *Id.*

5 A. Smith, *The Wealth of Nations* (1776; Everyman's Library Edn), vol. II, p. 229, quoted by A. Berle and G. Means, *The Modern Corporation and Private Property* (rev. edn; 1967) p. 304.

6 This is not to deny that imperfect competition could be said to undermine the legitimacy of all corporate power, whether it is exercised by owners or managers. The reason is that imperfect competition undermines one of the traditional justifications for private property. In an imperfectly competitive market we can no longer assume that there is an optimal allocation of society's resources. Furthermore, imperfect competition undermines the constraints on the exercise of economic power, be it wielded by managers or owners. Nevertheless, the primary focus of company law has been on corporate managerial power. The theory is that, if corporate managers can be made to operate the company as a profit-maximizing unit of production, market forces will control the power of the company in society. Hence if company law is successful in its objective not only will the power of corporate managers be legitimate but so will be the power of the company in society. This warrants focusing on the strategies adopted by company law to legitimate corporate managerial power.

7 This observation has been amongst others by P. Baran and P. Sweezy, *Monopoly Capital* (1966) p. 337. It is the focus of the economic literature on the theory of the firm, including the seminal article of R. Coase, 'The Nature of the Firm', 4 *Economica* (Ns) (1937) 386, and forms the point of departure of an examination of the growth of and changes in the organization of the firm by A. Chandler in *The Visible Hand, The Managerial Revolution in American Business* (1977).

8 Company law does not directly address the problem of the increasing organization of economic activity within a hierarchically structured firm rather than through the market. Competition law is concerned with the associated problem of vertical integration. Labour law might be said to address rather half-heartedly the problem created by the power of the head office of a multi-divisional company to determine the fate of the company's divisions. It imposes on the managers a duty to consult a recognized trade union before making employees of a division redundant or before selling one of the divisions.

9 Frug, *op. cit.*

10 E.g. *Isle of Wight Rly* v. *Tahourdin* [1883] 25 Ch.D 320.

11 *Automatic Self-Cleansing Filter Syndicate Co.* v. *Cuninghame* [1906] 2 Ch. 34

12 See L. Gower, *The Principles of Modern Company Law* (4th edn; 1979) p. 141, and Companies Act 1985, s. 303.

13 Gower, *op. cit.*, pp. 571–613.

14 See, e.g., Maitland's introduction to O. Gierke, *Political Theories of the Middle Ages* (1900); and the numerous jurisprudence treatises of the nineteenth century: e.g. W. Markby, *Elements of Law* (1871); T. E. Holland, *The Elements of Jurisprudence* (1880). The discussion of the conceptions of the corporation owes much to a seminar on the history of the business corporation given by Professor M. J. Horwitz at Harvard Law School in 1982.

15 Maitland's introduction to Gierke, *op. cit.*, p. xxxviii.

16 This conception of the company is best articulated in the case-law itself. See, e.g., *Riche* v. *Ashbury Rly Co. Ltd* [1874] LR 9 Ex. 224.

17 'Contract, that greediest of legal categories, which once wanted to devour the State, resents being told that it cannot painlessly digest even a joint-stock company.' Maitland's introduction to Gierke, *op. cit.*, pp. xxiv–xxv.

18 A. V. Dicey, *Law and Public Opinion* (1st edn; 1905) p. 165.

19 Maitland's introduction to Gierke, *op. cit.*, p. xxvi.

20 E.g. Pollock (1911) 27 *Law Quarterly Rev.* 219. The natural or organic theory of the nature of corporate personality also had some influence on company law doctrine. It was first adopted in *Lennard's Carrying Co.* v. *Asiatic Petroleum Co. Ltd* [1915] AC 705. For further examples of its use in the case-law see Gower, *op. cit.*, pp. 205–12.

21 E.g. *Automatic Self-Cleansing Filter Syndicate* v. *Cuninghame*, *op. cit.*

22 E.g. Winter, 'State Law, Shareholder Protection, and the Theory of the Corporation' (1977) 6 *J Legal Studies* 251.

23 E.g. *Ashbury Rly Carriage & Iron Co.* v. *Riche* [1875] LR 7 HL 653; *Salomon* v. *Salomon & Co.* [1897] AC 22.

24 See M. Stokes, 'Frankenstein's Monster, A History of the Ultra Vires Rule in Nineteenth Century English Company Law', unpublished LL.M paper on file at Harvard Law School.

25 See e.g. P. Craig, *Administrative Law* (1983) pp. 5–6.

26 Fiduciary duties are often seen to be the mechanism whereby the law seeks to catch blatant forms of self-dealing and cheating. They are seen as a negative restraint on directors rather than as requiring them positively to maximize profits. I would argue that an understanding of the problem which the separation of ownership and management creates for the traditional mode of legitimating private economic power suggests that the overall purpose of imposing fiduciary duties on corporate managers is the more positive one of requiring them to maximize profits. The fact that their function is often explained in terms of controlling the worst cases of managerial cheating is simply a reflection of their failure to achieve their objective.

27 See, e.g., M. Eisenberg, *The Structure of the Corporation* (1976) p. 1; Chayes, *op. cit.*, pp. 39; Gower, *op. cit.*, pp. 17–21.

28 Companies Act 1985, s. 4.

29 *Id.*, s. 9.

30 *Id.*, ss. 425–427.

31 *Id.*, s. 278.

32 E.g. *Regal (Hastings) Ltd* v. *Gulliver* [1967] 2 AC 134n.; Companies Act 1985, ss. 80, 312–316, 319, 320–322.

33 Berle and Means, *op. cit.*

34 Companies Act 1985, s. 80.

35 *Id.*, s. 319.

36 *The Committee to Review the Functioning of Financial Institutions* (The Wilson Committee) (1980; Cmnd 7937) pp. 249-53.
37 E.g. Eisenberg, *op. cit.*, ch. 11.
38 Frug, *op. cit.*, pp. 1307-11 and 1322-7.
39 *Id.*, pp. 1307-11.
40 *Id.*, pp. 1318-33.
41 E.g. *Anisminic Ltd* v. *Foreign Compensation Commission* [1968] 2 QB 862, Diplock LJ; [1969] 2 AC 147, in particular Lord Wilberforce.
42 *Teck Corp. Ltd* v. *Millar* [1972] 33 DLR (3d) 288.
43 *Howard Smith Ltd* v. *Ampol Petroleum Ltd* [1974] AC 821.
44 A similar argument has been made in the context of the very open-ended standards used by the courts to review administrative action. See Galligan, 'Judicial Review and the Textbook Writers' (1982) 2 *Oxford J Legal Studies* 257.
45 E.g. Hart, 'The Market Mechanism as an Incentive Scheme' *Cambridge University Discussion Paper*, no. 53 (1982).
46 The literature is vast. The theory was first articulated by Manne, 'Mergers and the Market for Corporate Control' (1965) 73 *J Pol. Economy* 110.
47 E.g. Fama, 'Agency Problems and the Theory of the Firm' (1980) 88 *J. Pol. Economy 288*; Jensen and Meckling, 'Theory of the Firm: Managerial Behaviour, Agency Costs and Ownership Structure' (1976) 3 *J Fin. Economics* 305.
48 O. Williamson, *Markets and Hierarchies* (1975) pp. 132-54.
49 *Supra*, n. 36.
50 *Supra*, n. 37.
51 E.g. rule 5 of *The City Code on Take-overs and Mergers* (April 1985) permits the board of a target company to favour one bidder over another.
52 Frug, *op. cit.*, pp. 1361-8.
53 Unger, 'The Critical Legal Studies Movement' (1983) 96 *Harvard Law Rev.* 563.
54 *Id.*, p. 578.
55 E.g. *Teck Corp.* v. *Millar, op. cit.*
56 R. M. Unger, *Law in Modern Society* (1976) p. 193.
57 *Id.*
58 Berle and Means, *op. cit.*, p. 312.
59 *Lonrho Ltd* v. *Shell Petroleum Co. Ltd* [1980] 1 WLR 627.
60 Companies Act 1985, s. 309.
61 Berle and Means, *op. cit.*, book 4, ch. 2.
62 Unger, *op. cit.*, n. 53.
63 *Id.*, p. 624.
64 139 US App. DC 226.
65 E.g. *The Committee of Inquiry on Industrial Democracy* (1977; Cmnd 6706).

10
Family Law and Legal Theory

KATHERINE O'DONOVAN

I INTRODUCTION

The view that family law is not really law seems to be gaining credence. This is not a new version of the Austinian denial that international law is law properly so called. Rather this view asserts that law cannot deal with family disputes and behaviour, and that law's instrumental functions of conflict-resolution and behaviour-guidance are not applicable to personal and family life. Law's inability is explained by reference to unenforceability or to unsuitability; attempts to deal with family problems are said to bring law into disrepute. In another version of this theme family law stands accused of having so far departed from principle and precedent as to be arbitrary, thereby losing its claim to guide conduct. This, it is alleged, undermines the rule of law. These criticisms of family law express beliefs about law which are tacitly underpinned by legal theory. Through examination of the denial of the title 'real law' to family law this paper seeks to explore the theoretical positions which inform such criticisms.

It would be possible to set about this exercise with the assumption that legal regulation of family and personal behaviour is law insofar as its pedigree passes the appropriate test. Or one might look to the content of specific rules and judicial pronouncements to see whether they conform to certain moral standards for family behaviour laid down by community or authority. The outcome would probably be that much, or even most, of what we call family law would pass these tests. The question pursued here is different. It asks the following: what is it about family law that gives rise to challenges to its authenticity as law? Does that tell us anything about theories of law? Beliefs about law, whether they are held by lawmakers or legal subjects are different from law itself. Yet the two are connected, for if law's authority is held to depend on its reputation and predictability then this presents a challenge to what Simpson calls the 'school-rules concept' of law. And if certain areas of life and behaviour are deemed suitable for morality, but not law, this suggests a view that law has internal limitations which do not relate to its pedigree.[1]

II LAW'S DEFECTS IN THE FAMILY ARENA

The assertion that law is unsuitable or unable to deal with family and personal behaviour has a long history. Expressions of this belief can be found in legislative debates, judicial opinions and academic writings of many periods. Lurking behind this are views about law and about the family. Questions about what law can or cannot do raise wider issues about people, behaviour and social theory. Empirical investigation may provide some answers. But the pervasiveness of the belief that personal matters are 'not the law's business' suggests that we are up against something deep-rooted in social consciousness. It is clear that if this point is to be elaborated the notion of personal matters must be defined. For present purposes family behaviour is identified as personal; however the conception of the personal is broader than, and does not necessarily involve, the family. Legal withdrawal in the recent past from regulation of personal matters such as sexuality and birth control suggests that the uneasiness about law's role in relation to the family may be explained in part by looking at the history of the debate on law and private morality.

Arguments advanced to show law's defects in dealing with the family fall into three groups. The first set posits inability. Law cannot tell people how to behave in their own homes; they will not obey; such rules are unenforceable because the necessary information is unobtainable, unless you put 'a spy under the bed'. What is being expressed here is a statement about the limits of law's hortatory function. It goes something like this: 'It is all very well to exhort people to behave properly in their personal relationships but law on such matters is unenforceable. Therefore it is better not to legislate.'

The second set of arguments propose unsuitability. Law is the 'wrong' mechanism for dealing with personal behaviour, emotions, feelings; it is cold, antagonistic, adversarial and alienating. Families are about love and trust; law is the guarantor of distrust. What is being expressed here is a statement about the limits of law in the resolution of disputes. Against this version of criticism of law is set a vision of another mechanism of dispute resolution which is cosy and friendly, in which there are no winners and losers.

The third set of arguments points to the bad effects of using law on the family. Law is only a negative force which destroys what it intends to help. Its entrance into the family arena escalates existing disputes. This viewpoint has been expressed as follows: 'the mere hint by anyone concerned that the law may come in is the surest sign that things are or will soon be going wrong.'[2] Again, this suggests a theory of the limits of law as a method of dealing with conflict.

Behind these three sets of arguments about the limits to law's powers in dealing with family matters may lie a fourth argument about law itself. Is it too pure to be sullied by the messiness of domestic life? Certainly the argument that law will be brought into disrepute if it enters areas where it is unenforceable is motivated by a concern to protect law's reputation.

Arguments about law's limits in its exhortatory and dispute-resolution functions present a strong case and are widely advanced.[3] What is less widely recognized is that, whatever their claims to empirical evidence in support, these arguments reflect a particular intellectual tradition, that of liberal political philosophy. This is where the recent history of law's withdrawal from the regulation of private morality provides a useful perspective. John Stuart Mill's definition of the limits of law to curtail individual freedom laid down a simple principle: 'that the sole end for which mankind are warranted, individually or collectively, in interfering with the liberty of action of any of their number, is self-protection. That the only purpose for which power can be rightfully exercised over any member of a civilised community, against his will, is to prevent harm to others.'[4] The application of this principle in the Sexual Offences Act 1967 following upon the publication of the Wolfenden Report in 1957 is well known. So too is the debate between Hart and Devlin on law and morality.[5] Whatever the merits of Devlin's position, of the crimes in private between consenting adults which he wished to retain, homosexuality, abortion, incest, pornography and prostitution have either been partially decriminalized or some proposals therefor have been put forward.[6] This suggests that the privatization of personal morality is well on its way.

In relation to family behaviour one could argue that since this matter has been little regulated no privatization can take place. The point is, however, precisely that. This is an area of personal relationships which is private, into which law does not venture, whether for the instrumental reasons suggested above, or out of concern for its reputation for purity.

III LAW'S DEPARTURE FROM PRINCIPLE

The philosophical case against law's intervention in the family stems from the liberal tradition. From academic and practising lawyers has come an argument bewailing what is identified as family law's departure from true legal character. This arises from the conferral on the judiciary, and on administrators, by Parliament of discretion in deciding matters of custody, childcare, divorce, maintenance, matrimonial property and inheritance. Discretion permits the individualization of justice according to the particular facts of each case. Criticism of this laments the loss of law's hortatory function in laying down rules for the future, lack of predictability, universality or generality of the law, the undermining of the moral authority of the judiciary, and the expansion of litigation as each case seeks its individual adjudication.

As expressed by Atiyah the 'weakening belief in the importance of the hortatory effect of the judicial process has been accompanied by, and has surely been part cause of, a change in the sense of justice itself'.[7] Individualized justice is a response both to a twentieth-century tendency to view consequences in the short term, and to greater diversity of moral beliefs. Discretion enables the concealment of the values which inform the judicial decision. Atiyah recognizes that there is no longer a consensus on the moral, religious or aesthetic ideals which supported the legal rules and principles of the nineteenth century. Discretionary standards and the redefinition of certain concerns as private mask both the values which are still implicit in legislation and in judicial decisions, and the lack of consensus on matters identified as personal.

Open-ended standards in legislation confer discretion permitting a wide variety of factors to be taken into account in adjudication. Atiyah's doubts about this trend in late-twentieth-century family law relate to his own model of law as serving conflict-adjustment and hortatory functions, and to his concern for 'the generality and universality which the very nature of law seems to require'.[8] His ideal rule of law is characterized by generality, neutrality, uniformity, predictability and autonomy. It is his hope that with a return to what he calls principles[9] law may yet recover its hortatory function. But correct as the analysis may be it is limited to pragmatic instrumentalist legal theory, and the prescription fails to take account of social theories which may help to explain the changes in the rule of law over time.

What does this mean for family law? The response to the recognition of law's instrumental limitations, and to the growth of discretion, has been contradictory. There has been a strong movement in favour of delegalization and privatization of family and personal matters; but when moral panic breaks out law continues to be invoked as 'binding on everyone in society, whatever their beliefs . . . the embodiment of a common moral position', despite the recognition that 'in our pluralistic society it is not to be expected that any one set of principles can be enunciated to be completely accepted by everyone.'[10] Thus the tension persists between the liberal position, which advocates non-regulation or delegalization of matters identified as personal or private, and the absolutist position which advocates regulation on the outbreak of moral panic.

IV DELEGALIZATION

Arguments in favour of delegalization of family law stem from dissatisfaction with law as an instrument for dealing with family relationships; law is seen as the 'wrong' mechanism. And there is also concern expressed by lawyers of various kinds about what family law is doing to the ideal of the rule of law. So the removal of family behaviour and disputes to some other arena is regarded as advantageous for instrumental purposes and for the preservation of law's purity.

Delegalization takes various forms. It ranges from conciliation of divorcing spouses in the settlement of custody and property matters, mediation, the family court, informal negotiation and bargaining, to contractual agreements for personal relations. The common thread linking arguments favouring these methods is the claim that they are new, and are alternatives to legal regulation. Whether either of these claims can be sustained is doubtful.

In an earlier part of this paper the arguments criticizing law's effectiveness in dealing with the family were summarized. It is time to investigate further. It has already been postulated that the intellectual origin of these criticisms lies in liberal political philosophy; however, confirmation has come from empirical research. In the expansion of academic legal scholarship that has taken place in the past 20 years family law was one of the first of the traditional areas of study to be 'broadened'.[11] Empirical research on custody and divorce, on the personal experiences of divorcees both as solicitors' clients and as consumers of the judicial process, and on the experiences and attitudes of registrars and lawyers added up to proposals for legal reform from an instrumental perspective.[12] The outcome was a search for a 'nicer', informal, that is non-legal, way of handling these trouble-cases.

Arguments based on a combination of liberalism and empiricism are cogent. With the addition of a third element of expediency it is not surprising that informalism or delegalization is the fashion in family law today. The expediency argument arises partly from the development of individualized justice. Since each matrimonial property or custody dispute is to be decided according to judicial discretion the result is that litigation abounds. This has proved expensive in terms of court costs and judicial time. Delegalization offers the promise of financial savings, even if the divorce rate remains high.

Because family law has remained stuck in its empiricist mode the limitations of this approach have not been appreciated by academic family lawyers. If the answers to problems are sought only in empirical research the 'broader perspective' remains unrealized. The categories used pre-determine empirical investigation as the 'facts' produced are within the structure of concepts used. Researchers may be unaware of their uncritical acceptance of categories and consequent results. In order to provide coherent explanations for developments in family law general and abstract perspectives must be introduced. These can be labelled 'theory'. Much of the writing on family law lacks any stated theoretical position, although it is generally underpinned by a welfare approach. But theory is implicit in the academic activities of research and writing and in the political acts of legislating and judging. Our understanding of the world around us is based on theory. We can choose between accepting the categories already defined, in which case theory remains implicit; or we can 'commit ourselves to working out critical and explicit theory'.[13] Welfare as a discretionary standard contains contradictions and thus provides little guidance to the disposition of trouble cases.[14] It needs to be informed by explicit theory.

The espousal of informalism as the answer to critiques of the effectiveness of judicial methods of handling family disputes is likely to give rise to disappointment. In order to understand the limitations of law as an instrument in the family arena, and the rise of discretion, one must have theoretical or abstract perspectives not only on law but also on the family in its present social context. For this we can turn to social theories. An example is available from Unger's study of modern law. With a broad sweep of his brush Unger has painted an explanation for the replacement of rule with discretion. His thesis is that in Western societies today state involvement in redistribution of the benefits and burdens of citizenship, and state planning and regulation in public law, has led to an abandonment of concern with formal justice and a turning to procedural and substantive justice. This gives rise to discretionary decisions by adjudicators and administrators, undermining generality and discrediting the ideal of the rule of law. But, as the realists had earlier pointed out, the ideals of the generality, neutrality, uniformity, predictability and autonomy of law have never been a reality. So, Unger argues, the quest for substantive justice in what he terms 'post-liberal society' openly corrupts legal generality and leads to the dissolution of the rule of law. A return to formalism is highly unlikely given popular expectations of individualized justice.[15] Unger's view is confirmed by the transformation of divorce from a judicial to an administrative process. The divorce stage no longer requires a court appearance, except for the children's appointment in chambers, at which the petitioner attends.[16] Financial and child custody disputes are dealt with informally by the Registrar. Yet the trend towards bureaucratization has not been uniform. Contests over children's entrance into and exit from the care of the state are moving from administrative to judicial control.

Explanations for these apparently contradictory tendencies will not be found by taking an instrumental approach to family law. Although delegalization in one area is justified by the search for a 'nicer' way out, judicialization of child-care hearings, with separate representation of the interests of the child, is the result of disillusionment with a process which does not provide traditional legal procedural safeguards. This relates to conceptions of justice embodied in the rule of law in a procedural sense, as exemplified in the work of Lon Fuller.[17] Administrative decision-making on deprivation of parental rights and the coming and going of children into and out of the care of the state is perceived by many as an abuse of legal process. As Neil MacCormick has observed: 'It remains a contested issue whether an aspiration to justice is to be treated as essential to or definitive of the legal enterprise in all its manifestations, or is to be distinguished as a specially urgent demand issued in the name of critical morality.' MacCormick suggests that it matters little, when faced with 'possible unjust exercises of the power of modern states organised under and in the name of "law" . . . whether or not these represent a corruption of law in its ideal essence or simply an abuse of public power.'[18] Yet it is clear in references to natural justice that our conception of law is bound up with ideas of notice, fair hearing, representation and open judgment, aspects of which have been denied in the admission of children to the care of the state, and particularly in parental rights resolutions by local authorities.[19]

The choice then appears to be between informalism, in which individualized solutions to disputes are worked out and accepted by the parties, and the formal judicial process. In instrumental terms there is much to be said for the informal approach. It induces parties to submit their disputes voluntarily to conciliation or administrative decision and, in some areas such as divorce and custody, it involves them in working out a private solution, thus enhancing their acceptance of the outcome. Formal justice as an alternative offers openness, ostensible neutrality, and rules. One response to this choice might be to suggest that it depends on the type of dispute in question. Formal justice and procedural safeguards are best for child-care cases, whereas informal methods suit divorce and custody disputes. This can be raised to a higher level by suggesting that personal disputes be settled informally and those between state and citizen formally. But fundamentally the instrumental approach fails to reconcile and explain contradictory tendencies. Furthermore, the evidence is of the proliferation of informal administrative agencies in the modern welfare state with discretion to determine the claims of citizens. For instance, in other areas of law concerning children, such as fostering, adoption and parental access to children in care, social workers as agents of the state have developed informal rules for decision-making. There is no appeal against these to the courts. These rules cannot be placed in the category of formal law; but neither do they fit into my previous description of informal justice. There is no voluntary acceptance of the decision, rather it is imposed, often without discussion, and with no possibility of judicial review. So informalism pervades bureaucratic law.

It has already been suggested that informal methods of dispute-resolution in the family arena are not new, nor are they alternatives to legal regulation. The assumption that they are reveals a very limited conception of law. This relates to the limitations of instrumentalist legal theory. Informal methods are merely other forms of social control allied to law in a corporate state. To understand this point one has to ask how the family has been internally regulated, given that law has claimed no hortatory function over family behaviour and has limited itself to dispute-resolution when things go wrong. I suggest that the answer to this can be found by looking to theories of the family and to legal structures.

V A THEORETICAL FRAMEWORK FOR FAMILY LAW?

Hitherto the instrumental approach to law has been criticized as inadequate to provide a coherent explanation for contradictory tendencies in legal developments. This criticism is not that instrumentalism is untheoretical, but rather that its hidden assumptions when made explicit are revealed as limited. Before proceeding to an analysis of the inadequacies of instrumentalist legal theory it is important to clarify the point that statements about law, whether in instrumental, therapeutic or welfare terms, are based on beliefs about law. These beliefs in turn are informed by theory, that is, by general and abstract perspectives. In the case of family law, views about people, their relationships to each other and to the world are contained in legal statements. Theories that inform these beliefs must be exposed and examined. The purpose is to clarify and test and, ultimately, to understand and explain.[20]

My position therefore is that even seemingly untheoretical statements about family law of a common-sensical and pragmatic mode are based on theory. One strategy in theorizing family law is to uncover hidden assumptions concerning both family and law. Bringing these out in the open and subjecting them to scrutiny and analysis will yield fruitful results. To some extent this work is under cultivation. I suggest that, important as such analysis is, there are more fundamental issues which have to be tackled first. This can be illustrated by a deepened critique of instrumental legal theory.

Instrumentalists believe that law in essence is a means to serve certain goals. This is sometimes described in terms of social engineering, and the resources that law brings as machinery are distinguished from its social goals. Robert Summers has identified five different forms of legal techniques for implementing these goals. These range from private arrangements to penalty.[21] Allied to this are views about the limited efficacy of law. One believer in the limits of law puts it like this: 'laws are often ineffective, doomed to stultification almost at birth, doomed by the over-ambitions of the legislator and the under-provision of the necessary requirements for an effective law, such as adequate preliminary survey, communication, acceptance, and enforcement machinery.'[22] This judgment of law according to its perceived limits is based on a misconception of the nature of law. In posing law as an external force to those it purports to control the judgment fails to recognize law's part in constructing experience of the world; how knowledge is possible only through categories and symbols of language; how meaning is produced out of legal ordering of supposed differences.

An early question relates to ways of thinking about claims that people make on each other within families and the expression of these in law. I have already pointed out that law has imposed on itself a self-denying ordinance in its relation to the personal. In the ritual legal opera only certain kinds of song can be performed; only certain persons can sing.[23] Less powerful characters may not be allowed on stage. This point goes to the formulation of ideas, their presentation in language and their legitimacy in law. Elsewhere this has been described in terms of semiology.[24] Law is a powerful mechanism for recognizing or hiding the desires and perspectives of those whose lives it governs. In its legal forms it legitimates or ignores the voices under its control. But it goes further than that. Its structure and language may prevent not just the voice from being heard, but feelings from moving to ideas and into speech. Thus some may remain forever the audience without the power to express their point of view.

Points of view could be said to be central to the formal legal enterprise. This is certainly the belief of liberals for whom the heart of the law is 'the open hearing in which one point of view, one construction of language and reality is tested against another. The multiplicity of readings that the law permits is not its weakness but its strength, for it is this that makes room for different voices. . . .'[25] This presupposes that all voices have an equal possibility of speech and hearing. Bernard Williams defines the respect that is owed to all persons as an effort of understanding, 'to see the world from his point of view'.[26] For him this is an essential component of the idea of equality. As an ideal of law this is attractive, and in going deeper than instrumentalism it raises a number of issues. If equality before the law is to be an equality of voices then there are issues about formal procedures and the extent to which these are accessible to all. There are further issues about the availability of language and concepts to the silent.

Where lies the power to identify and define points of view? In legal procedures personal and family relations have been deemed to be beyond law's limits. The location of certain family members, in particular women and children, in the private domain in which 'the King's writ does not seek to run, and to which its officers do not seek to be admitted'[27] ensures their silence. This is taken as natural but is a cultural definition of law's limits produced by those with the power of speech. And, more evidently, formal equality before the law is limited. As Anatole France explained: 'equality of the laws . . . forbids rich and poor alike to sleep under the bridges, to beg in the streets, and to steal . . . bread.'[28]

Power in the family is not just concerned with the formulation and definition of points of view and the claims family members make on one another; it also affects internal regulation. Instrumentalists should ask themselves the following: in the absence of law who controls the family? Answering this question is a complex matter but I suggest that empirical and theoretical investigation is long overdue. Traditional family law sees no problem of the legitimate exercise of power between spouses because of beliefs in the formal equality of the sexes. Yet it is precisely because this ideology is not lived up to in private, and because the state is involved both in its promulgation and its violation, that feminist theory can take a highly critical moral stance. Looking to internal power and control within the family is one consequent strategy. A second is based on the constitution of the family by structures external to it.

Social theory of the family has a long history of debate on structural explanations, that is on whether family types adapt as appropriate to the social and economic world. What has been less recognized is that legal structures constitute the family and roles within it. If we look to laws external to the family we can begin to develop a body of substantive analyses guided by theory. The economic world in which the family has its being is not just the market, for it is also affected by state allocation of the benefits and burdens of citizenship according to its own criteria. Investigations of public law on taxation and social security reveal how internally the family is constituted by legal structures external to it. The roles of wife and husband are defined in legislation in which the state is concerned with economic redistribution.[29] Legal forms not only constitute gender relations but represent ways of seeing roles and relations.

Discussions about structures must not be limited to rather arid chicken-and-egg problems. Much more fundamental issues are raised. Recent work on the history of the family uses structural explanations for family form as an expression of a particular culture and as a mechanism for creating personality types consonant with that culture. This, Lawrence Stone argues, is done through the structuring of relationships, and through methods of children-rearing.[30] We should be asking ourselves about the character of individuals which are being produced by the family forms that we have today and about law's part in creating the domestic group. Thus questions about structure can raise deeper issues of phenomenology, whose contribution has been 'to show the ways in which ways of living a life work themselves into complex ways of thinking'.[31]

The preceding discussion of law's self-imposed limits and the consequent silence of those whose lives are largely lived in private is intended to criticize instrumentalism for failing to take account of ideology, 'the sum of the ways in which people both live and represent to themselves their relationship to the conditions of their existence'.[32] More difficult is the point made earlier about the lack of language and concepts to enable the silent to speak. The contribution of Saussure's theory of language has been to point out how personal identity and subjectivity are constructed through differentiation.[33] Experience of the world is mediated and made intelligible through discourse. But language and interpretation assume a structure of values of which they form a part. Thus the available language is imposed. How can other viewpoints be expressed? If we are to go beyond nihilism we shall have to devise a strategy to examine this.

My conclusions are that work which looks to family law as instrument is inadequate; the 'school-rules concept' of law overlooks law's part in representing and naturalizing 'the way things are'; law's self-denying ordinance in relation to the personal and the private is a cultural construct and not an inevitable element of ideas of law or justice. The alternative approaches which have been outlined above will lead to a deepened analysis. No doubt there are other ways to criticize the legal opera; these I leave to other critics.

NOTES

1 The view that certain matters are unsuitable for legal regulation and should therefore be left to morality is an instrumental view of law's limits. It is quite different from

Fuller's 'internal morality of law', in which Fuller advanced the thesis that eight procedural requirements such as generality, clarity and prospectivity, must be satisfied before a legal system can be said to exist. See L. Fuller, *The Morality of Law*, (1969) ch. 2.

2 O. Kahn-Freund and K. W. Wedderburn, 'Editorial Foreword' to J. Eekelaar, *Family Security and Family Breakdown* (1971) p. 7.

3 E.g. M. A. Glendon, *The New Family and the New Property* (1981); J. Goldstein, A. Freud and A. Solnit, *Beyond the Best Interests of the Child* (1973).

4 J. S. Mill, *On Liberty* (1910) p. 73.

5 H. L. A. Hart, *Law, Liberty and Morality* (1963); P. Devlin, *The Enforcement of Morals* (1968).

6 *The Criminal Law Revision Committee, Fifteenth and Sixteenth Reports on Sexual Offences* (1984; Cmnd 9213 and 9326) have dealt with most of these crimes.

7 P. S. Atiyah, *From Principles to Pragmatism* (1978).

8 *Id.*, p. 29.

9 Julius Stone has criticized Atiyah's use of the word 'principles'. See 'From Principles to Principles' (1981) 97 *Law Quarterly Rev.* 224.

10 *Report of the Committee of Inquiry into Human Fertilisation and Embryology* (Warnock Report) (1984; Cmnd 9314) para. 6.

11 See Twining, 'Goodbye to Lewis Eliot. The Academic Lawyer as Scholar' (1980) 15 *J.S.P.T.L.* (NS) 2.

12 E.g. W. Barrington Baker *et al.*, *The Matrimonial Jurisdiction of Registrars* (1977); Davis *et al.*, 'Undefended Divorce: Should S.41 Be Repealed?' (1983) 46 *Modern Law Rev.* 121.

13 N. Hartsock, 'Feminist Theory and Revolutionary Strategy' in Z. Eisenstein (ed.), *Capitalist Patriarchy and the Case for Socialist Feminism* (1979) p. 57.

14 I wish to call personal experience in aid. Some years ago I attended a conference on family law in which a speaker posed a number of cases to the participants for resolution. The first case revealed the dangers of state intervention; the second the dangers of state inaction; the third the desirability of a maternal-preference rule in child-custody cases; the fourth the disadvantages of such a rule. I looked around the room. The participants were reeling. Given their *ad hoc* approach to family issues there was no way they could reconcile the decisions they had made.

15 R. M. Unger, *Law in Modern Society* (1976), pp. 166–200.

16 Special procedure or 'divorce by post' was introduced in 1973. By 1977 it had been extended to all undefended divorce cases. It is now the ordinary and administrative procedure for dealing with divorce.

17 L. L. Fuller, *The Morality of Law* (rev. edn; 1969).

18 MacCormick, 'Contemporary Legal Philosophy: The Rediscovery of Practical Reason' (1983) 10 *J Law and Society* 1 at p. 11.

19 Under the Child Care Act 1980, s.3, a child who comes into care on a voluntary basis can, after six months, be the subject of a 'parental rights resolution' whereby the local authority assumes parental powers. No court hearing is necessary for such a resolution.

20 W. L. Twining, 'Evidence and Legal Theory' (chapter 4 above) pp. 62–4.

21 Summers, 'The Technique Element in Law' (1971) 59 *California Law Rev.* 733.

22 A. Allott, *The Limits of Law* (1980) p. 287. See also R. S. Summers, *Instrumentalism and American Legal Theory* (1982) ch. 12.

23 Nancy Fulton, a participant in my family law course in 1984–5, first made this point to me.

24 Tushnet, 'Post-Realist Legal Scholarship' (1980) *J.S.P.T.L.* (NS) 20 at p. 31.

25 J. Boyd White, *When Words Lose Their Meaning: Constitutions and Reconstitutions of Language, Character, and Community* (1984) p. 273.

26 B. Williams, 'The Idea of Equality' in *Philosophy, Politics and Society* (2nd series) (1962; ed. P. Laslett and W. G. Runciman) p. 117.
27 *Balfour* v. *Balfour* [1919] 2 KB 571 at p. 579, *per* Atkin LJ.
28 Quoted by Hutchinson, 'From Cultural Construction to Historical Deconstruction' (1984) 94 *Yale Law J* 209 at p. 227.
29 K. O'Donovan, *Sexual Divisions in Law* (1985) ch. 6.
30 L. Stone, *Family, Sex and Marriage in England, 1500–1800* (1977). See the discussion in C. C. Harris, *The Family and Industrial Society* (1983) ch. 8.
31 Tushnet, *op. cit.*, p. 31.
32 C. Belsey, *Critical Practice* (1980) p. 42.
33 F. de Saussure, *Course in General Linguistics* (1960).

11
Criminal Law and Legal Theory

RICHARD TUR

I CRIMINAL LAW AS GRIST FOR THE JURISPRUDENT'S MILL

Criminal law appears to be regarded in legal education as something of a Cinderella subject, being widely regarded as suitable for beginners in the study of law to cut their teeth on before tackling the real business of legal study, viz. contract, tort, trusts and land law. It is, however, difficult, for a number of reasons, to accept the 'introductory' status of criminal law and its isolation from the mainstream of law teaching.

First, criminal law relates closely to other branches of law both substantively and theoretically. Thus criminal law seeks to determine the illegitimate modes of the acquisition of property and therefore is, in part, an integral part of the law of property. Again, the law of the supermarket reveals that the rules of criminal law and of contract interrelate very closely. Theoretically, it is taken as axiomatic in criminal law that intention is 'subjective' whereas contract lawyers by and large accept that intention is 'objective'. It is, at the very least, remarkable that the common law should be so schizophrenic concerning so central a concept. Crime and tort relate closely as well, not only obviously by virtue of the same facts giving rise to different legal consequences but also, more interestingly, since the coming into effect of s. 35 of the Powers of the Criminal Courts Act 1973, by virtue of the criminal courts pre-empting the civil courts in the matter of compensation, perhaps even in circumstances where no private right of action otherwise obtains.

Secondly, criminal law involves complex institutional arrangements, for example, magistrates, Crown Courts, juries, the Court of Appeal, Criminal Division (which remarkably retains a power to overrule its own decisions, see *R* v. *Gould*),[1] and the House of Lords (of which it has been asked whether we can continue to afford it as a court of ultimate resort in criminal law, a question prompted less by economics than by an expositor's desire for consistency).[2] Unique lawmaking devices such as 'applying the proviso' or the 'Attorney-General's reference' complicate the operation of the criminal law. One has also to contend with the contribution of the Criminal Law Revision Committee, about which much could be said not least on the remarkable sortie into the defences of intoxication and mistake in its 14th Report.[3] The Law Commission, too, is heavily involved in a long-term codification project with which it now has the assistance of a powerful Society of Public Teachers of Law group.[4] The right of private prosecution (now under threat), the role of the police in prosecution as against the comparative advantages of public prosecutors, the function of the DPP, the involvement of the Attorney-General in the question of injunctions against criminal activity, and the prerogative of mercy all add to the institutional complexity. Beyond all these institutional complexities lies the prison, the probation service and mechanisms for dealing with the convicted offender. Fully to appreciate the operation of the substantive rules of criminal law requires some appreciation of this complex institutional framework.

Thirdly, criminal law is conceptually demanding. The major area of academic industry has been analysis of central mental concepts such as intention or recklessness. This necessitates a philosophy of mind and action. Given that we have no privileged access to the minds of others we must proceed on some hypothesis about mental events or mental states. In this regard criminal law shares a problem with contract law, which adopts the ambivalent posture of holding both that the devil himself cannot know the mind of man and that the state of a man's mind is as much a question of fact as is the state of his digestion.[5] The problem is dealt with mainly by presumptions about normal people. Both criminal law and contract exhibit a tendency to convert such presumptions into irrebuttable rules of law. Herein lies the crux of the debate between the honest subjectivist and the reasonable objectivist. Lord Diplock was right in *Caldwell*[6] about one thing, namely the obsessive interest of academics in solving all legal questions by the exhaustive application of one or other of these principles.[7] In practice, given the institutional necessity for the tribunal of fact to reach decisions on past states of mind, a synthesist approach is called for. This is best brought out by Gordon's analysis of the reasonable man as a test and the reasonable man as a standard.[8]

Conceptual analysis may, of course, focus on issues other than the central concepts of *mens rea*. Defences such as duress or provocation may be analysed in the expectation of laying bare the rules which apply. However, there is a danger here of what I call the definitional fallacy, that is a tendency to seek to present the law as if everything was completely cut and dried, whereas such 'defences' may be better understood as 'excuses' the primary function of which, from a (negative) ultilitarian point of view, is simply to minimize the amount of punishment actually imposed without jeopardizing the credibility of the general system of threat through which, arguably, criminal law realizes its prescriptive function. I believe it possible to analyse the role of equity in contract as functionally analogous to the role of excuses in crime. In both areas of law there is a collective system of general prospective rules concerned with the guidance of conduct and it is necessary that the credibility of such rules be preserved if the system is to perform its central social function. Thus, as Kelsen observes, 'the legal norm obliges the debtor not only, and, perhaps, not so much in order to protect the creditor, but in order to maintain a certain economic system.'[10]

However, the other side of the coin is the application of the rules to particular cases. Here there is a tendency in contract to do justice and in crime to be merciful. These tendencies would ultimately subvert the collective system unless no one could rely upon his case falling under equity in contract or excuse in criminal law. The nature of excuses in crime and of equity in contract is, however, so particularistic and so dependent upon the facts of the case that it strains credulity to imagine someone seeking in advance to bring his case under such categories. Excuses and equity function retrospectively in particular cases rather than as general prospective rules seeking to guide conduct. If these intuitions are justified it follows that some exhaustive analyses of the concepts of excuse misconceive the social function and thereby distort the nature and operation of the criminal law.

Another concept which sometimes falls to be analysed in such all or nothing fashion is 'dishonesty' as it impinges upon the definition of theft and a cluster of deception offences under the Theft Acts. Some argue for an exhaustive definition of what is in effect a moral excuse.[10] Such, if established, would narrow down the range of circumstances under which a court (and as things stand that means, in principle, a jury) could acquit. Whether a particular accused should be acquitted because his conduct was not dishonest appears to me to be a moral question. Therefore, by closing down the range of possible moral excuse, the definitionalist is imposing his morality upon the law and breaking the vital nexus between the current standards of ordinary decent people and the content of the criminal law. No one, suggested a judge in a leading case, should be held to be guilty of theft by reason of conduct to which no moral obloquy could reasonably attach.[11] These considerations suggest that conceptual analysis in criminal law is complex, turning upon philosophies of mind and action, theories of the social function of law or upon moral philosophy.

Fourthly, criminal law, in common with all branches of substantive law, presupposes a complex body of procedural rules and the law of evidence. As to the impact of procedural rules upon substantive law, I turn to the doctrine, now partly exploded by *Caldwell*,[12] of specific and basic intent. The academic establishment refused to entertain the possibility that this doctrine was of any wider significance to criminal law beyond the local issue of what is to be done with the drunken offender and, within that narrow compass, that the doctrine was coherent or justifiable. I believe that a formidable case can be made out in support of Lord Simon's conviction that 'the concept of "crime of basic intent" is a useful tool of analysis'.[13] The arguments in support of my belief cannot be detailed here but the point of departure in common with Lord Simon in *Morgan* is that the distinction between crimes of basic and crimes of specific intent can only be appreciated against the backdrop of the probative–evidential dialogue which characterizes the criminal trial.[14]

Only by ignoring the procedural context can the expositor present criminal law in a way that makes nonsense of the sophisticated doctrine of crimes of specific intent. Again, the academic establishment in criminal law has pursued subjectivism with evangelical zeal.[15] Consequently, decisions of the House of Lords have been hailed as great subjectivist triumphs, e.g. *Morgan*[16] and *Camplin*[17] or as subjectivist disasters, e.g. *Caldwell*.[18] This I refer to as the 'Nottingham Forest Approach to law'. Mistake, which has been the central football in this tournament, may however be analysed in a way which is neither exclusively subjectivist nor exclusively objectivist by adopting the synthesist approach immanent in Gordon's 'reasonable man as a test'. On such a view the reasonableness of a belief is not a substantive necessity but an evidential requirement. This requires appreciation, again, of our lack of privileged access to the minds of others and the necessity of assumptions as to evidence of states of mind. *(Gladstone) Williams,*[19] which is hailed as a goal for Nottingham Forest, may in reality simply be an affirmation of the synthesist line visible in *Mark*[20] and in *Kenlin* v. *Gardiner,*[21] where the judge was careful to speak in terms of justification rather than insist that a belief be both honest and reasonable.

Fifthly, it is evident that criminal law is in some sense of the term a subject which calls for interdisciplinary study. There is a need not only for some 'sociological' appreciation of the institutional framework and the social function of law and punishment but also for some philosophy of mind and action and a moral philosophy. Beyond this, especially as one proceeds into issues of criminology and penology, account must be taken of psychology and arguably of medical science. Consequently the complete criminal lawyer is no narrow expositor of black-letter legal rules and exhaustive conceptual analyses. Although a full, detailed and accurate exposition of the law is an essential prerequisite to jurisprudential activity in the field of criminal law as in others, it is not and cannot be the limit of the concerns of those who teach and study criminal law. Nonetheless there is a tendency within the academic establishment to regard the exposition of the black-letter law and the exhaustive analyses of concepts as the totality of the concerns of the academic criminal lawyer; indeed one may speak of an attempt, conscious or otherwise, to distort the data to fit the expositor's ideal. Nowhere is this more obvious than in the ideological distinction between real crimes and regulatory crimes, whereby law-school curricula can be restricted to a limited number of crimes calling for proof of a mental element as a condition of conviction. The large number of strict-liability offences, at least 3,750 of 7,200 separate and distinct criminal offences listed on the basis of the 1975 edition of *Stone's Justices' Manual* (that is, more than half), are then dismissed from serious study.[22] Such eclecticism fosters a false picture of criminal law and more seriously deflects criticism of the circumstance that for most individuals contact with the criminal law is contact with an objectivist regime of strictly liability. If the *mens rea* principle and the principle of proof are objectives worthy of a rational and humane system of criminal law they ought to be used critically to assess the achievement of the total system rather than circularly to select an acceptable portion of the criminal law.

Given these observations upon the complexity of criminal law as a social and moral phenomenon it follows that it can exist as an 'introductory' subject only through its radical distortion, simplification, amputation and eclecticism. This is condemnation indeed, but more crucial is the circumstance that in its diminished state, criminal law remains for some students the first impression of serious legal study. Consequently the attitude of students to legal study is predetermined by their exposure to a substantive body of law designed more to develop their memories than to expand their minds. The remedy may not be to delay criminal law teaching to a later stage in curricula, because the observations already made might well apply to whatever introductory course in substantive law one selects. Rather one must teach criminal law jurisprudentially and the circumstance that criminal law throws up so much grist for the jurisprudential mill fits it rather well for the role of an introductory course. However, constraints of time and the intellectual range of those who have the teaching of criminal law in charge counsel pessimism, and unless and until the four-year degree is established legal education in general will suffer through the narrowing effect of criminal law as it is now taught.

II CRIMINAL LAW AND LEGAL THEORY

'Legal theory' is sometimes taken as being synonymous with 'jurisprudence' and is sometimes regarded as concerning itself with a narrower range of questions – in particular, What is the nature of law? Juxtaposing criminal law and legal theory offers a number of intellectual enquiries. First, rather in the style of Simpson's 'The Common Law and Legal Theory' (chapter 2 above), one might take criminal law as a test of some version of legal theory, thereby confirming or refuting the theory in question.[23] *That* should not be too difficult an exercise. Thus, for example, all versions of positivism which rely upon an exhaustive sources thesis might be refuted by the undoubted circumstance that criminal law incorporates and generates moral standards. Consequently the separation of law and morals is rendered suspect, as is the notion that the content of the law can be read off exhaustively given the sources identified by the rule of recognition. Of course the game can be played the other way round and even crude Austinian positivism might be treated as vindicated by the English criminal statute. There appears to me to be little intellectual stimulus in such an approach, because it is wholly circular. One can only use criminal *law* to test theories of law on the assumption that independently of the theory in question one has in criminal law a genuine instance of law. That is not an unreasonable assumption, but it is, no matter how tacitly, informed by some other legal theory. Simpson assumes that the common law is law. Therefore any theory which denies that it is must be rejected as unacceptable. Bentham was willing, however, on the basis of his version of the command theory of law to take the heroic step of denying that the common law was law.[24] Austin took the equally heroic step of denying that constitutional law and international law were law properly so called.[25] Since most versions of legal theory are at least partial visions of law it is unsurprising that the criminal law will throw up both confirmations and refutations of most legal theories.

Secondly, one might ask just what legal theory can contribute to criminal law. At once we encounter a problem, namely which legal theory do we contemplate? If legal theories do not speak with one voice the contribution of legal theory will very much depend upon which legal theory is chosen. However, it is notoriously difficult to capture and exhibit any legal theorist who unequivocally espouses formalism, that is who insists that the application of the general principles and rules of law to particular cases is a matter of deductive reasoning and nothing else. Here theorists such as Austin,[26] Hart,[27] Kelsen,[28] Unger,[29] Holmes[30] and even Aquinas, as interpreted by Finnis,[31] speak with one voice in proclaiming that the relationship between rule and decision is more complex than mere deduction. We should therefore be suspicious of any expository textbook which presents the criminal law as if it could be stated in a finite number of propositions from which all solutions could ultimately be derived without further choices at the point of application. We should also be very suspicious of any codification project which attempts to pre-empt or disguise the irreducibly dispositive element in decision-making. If 'all criminal laws admit of cases of just excuse'[32] then it is simply impossible exhaustively to describe the existing content of criminal law beyond a certain level of generality. Equally it is impossible to prescribe in advance for all factual contingencies. Consequently, one lesson to criminal law from legal theory is that it should not aim at a comprehensiveness inconsistent with its subject-matter. One of Kelsen's most puzzling doctrines, namely the alternative character of the norm, is vindicated by the criminal law once it is appreciated that every criminal law allows of cases of just excuse.[33] Precisely what these cases are cannot be defined in advance but must await the decision of the appropriate organ. This also vindicates the Kelsenian thesis of the primacy of the principle of delegation over the principle of subsumption. Consequently, we should not attempt to frame our legal rules with the precision of a logician's statement of the conditions necessary and sufficient for a determination.[34] The rules of criminal law always end with an undefined and indefinable 'unless . . .' clause.

Another issue within legal theory that has consequences for criminal law is the extent to which, if at all, it is possible to present a value-neutral description of law. Some, of course, deny that such purity of method is possible but few would argue with the proposition that where a description of law is coloured by the expositor's own values it is a virtue for these values explicitly to be registered. Thus it is one thing to adopt a radically subjectivist posture towards law reform and another thing entirely to purport merely to be describing the law as it is and then to conclude that it is wholly or even primarily subjectivist. The latter approach inevitably leads to distortion. Consider the doctrine of mistake. Nowhere in one leading textbook is it treated of as a defence.[35] Rather it is presented as simply a mirror image of the subjectivist principle of *mens rea*. However, it is clear that a mistake can relate to two quite different types of circumstance, namely circumstances qualified by *mens rea* and circumstances not qualified by *mens rea*. *Morgan*[36] illustrates the first type of case and *Tolson*[37] the other; *(David Raymond) Smith*[38] shows one type of approach in play, *Phekoo*[39] the other. It is significant that in *(David Raymond) Smith* the Court of Appeal had first to perform some surgery on the relationship of *mens rea* to the *actus reus* of criminal damage to reach the desired conclusion and it is therefore unsurprising that adverse comment was expressed by some of their Lordships in *Morgan*.[40] In *Phekoo* by contrast the Court of Appeal went directly to the general principle, asking themselves Brett's question, 'What would the position of the accused have been if the facts had been as he believed them to be?'[41] This is the approach adopted by the House of Lords in *Albert* v. *Lavin*[42] and, on my understanding, by the Court of Appeal in *(Gladstone) Williams*.[43]

It is clear that in cases where the mistake relates to a circumstance qualified by *mens rea* the outcome will be the same whether one adopts the definitional or the defence doctrine of mistake, that is 'the prosecution will wither on the bough'.[44] It is by no means clear, however, that the outcome will be the same where the mistake relates to a circumstance not qualified by *mens rea*. In order to secure an acquittal, the definitionalist will first have to argue that *mens rea* runs to the circumstance in question. That argument succeeded in *(David Raymond) Smith* but counsel wisely declined the House of Lords' invitation to attempt it in *Albert* v. *Lavin*, it being unarguable on the present state of the law that the policemanliness of the victim is a circumstance to which *mens rea* runs. It is by no means certain that the courts would always be willing to redefine the *mens rea* requirement in order to secure an acquittal. Consequently, the defence account of mistake is of general applicability whereas the definitional account can apply only to a limited range of cases.[45] Indeed the Court of Appeal in *Phekoo* expressed the opinion that it only applied to rape but I hope that one might interpret that to mean 'rape-like offences', that is all offences where the mistake in question relates to a circumstance qualified by *mens rea*.

The definitionalist might seek to save his position by arguing for a general principle of law to the effect that to intend an act is to intend it under a full description and that therefore in all crimes where the *actus reus* contains not only a conduct element but also circumstances and consequences, *mens rea* is to be taken as being 'coextensive with the *actus reus*.'[46] If such were genuinely a principle of English criminal law then definitionalism concerning mistake would be vindicated. However, the alleged principle appears to go a long way beyond authority. It was circumvented by the Divisional Court in *Jaggard* v. *Dickinson*[47] and the only clear authority, *(David Raymond) Smith*,[48] has been called into question in the House of Lords.[49] Further, there are so many instances of what I call 'partial *mens rea* offences', that is crimes in which *mens rea* runs to some but not all of the elements in the *actus reus*, that the alleged principle simply does not square with the data. Such crimes include those treated of in *Prince*,[50] *Tolson*,[51] *Phekoo*[52] and *Albert* v. *Lavin*[53] and that created by s. 47 of the Offences Against the Person Act, 1861.

The point of this brief account of mistake is to show that at least one leading textbook of criminal law has distorted its presentation of the data because of a prior commitment to subjectivism. Such distortion of the data leads on to a misperception of problems. The current debate between the honest subjectivist and the reasonable objectivist is more illusory than real and has its roots in ideological commitment rather than thoroughgoing analysis. The criminal law may depend less upon one monolithic principle and more upon a synthesis of conflicting principles. In the defence of mistake (as in dishonesty, duress, provocation and unwarranted demands) one can see just how the criminal law rests upon a mixture of subjectivism and objectivism. In particular, the subjectivist's charge that the defence doctrine leads to the harsh objectivism of the reasonable man as a standard can be refuted by treating the reasonableness requirement as not being a second and subsequent question which must be answered in the affirmative in order to secure an acquittal, but as an integral part of the first question: Did the accused hold the belief he claims to have held? As an evidential rather than a substantive doctrine 'reasonable' cashes out as 'credible'. Once it is accepted that the reasonableness of a belief is merely evidence of its actually being held and if it is allowed that other cogent evidence may be admitted to prove the existence of the belief, there seems to be no difference at all between the honest subjectivist and the reasonable objectivist. On either account, of course, a judicial tendency will remain to pre-empt jury decision on the question whether the accused actually held the belief claimed. This is well illustrated by *Pappajohn*,[54] wherein the Canadian Supreme Court, purporting to apply *Morgan*,[55] held that the direction on mistake need only be put where there was some evidence beyond the mere *ipse dixit* of the accused to support it, as indeed there was in *Morgan*. The issue of judicial control over juries with a view to pre-empting decisions of fact, however, is neutral as between objectivist and subjectivist approaches to mistake.

Thirdly, one might ask what criminal law can contribute to legal theory. Here I raise three issues: (1) judicial lawmaking; (2) normative positivism; (3) moral luck. As to judicial lawmaking, the practice of prospective overruling has attracted my attention as a hard case for those theories of judicial process which involve a strong commitment to coherence, consistency and institutional fit.[56] I have, elsewhere, identified a functional equivalent to prospective overruling in the English legal system which I have christened 'gross obiter dicta'.[57] I relied heavily upon *Hedley Byrne*[58] as illustrative. Since then both *Woodar* v. *Wimpey*[59] and *National Carriers* v. *Panalpina*[60] have been handed down by the House of Lords. Such cases illustrate the capacity of English judges prospectively to make law and reveal a sharp bifurcation between the decision in a particular case and the rule of law which it supports. Criminal law illustrates just such bifurcated prospective lawmaking. I have already referred to the Attorney-General's reference, a type of public-interest action on behalf of the criminal classes, which is one example of the technique which I have in mind. A recent illustration of the technique occurs in *R* v. *Tan*.[61]

Miss Tan had advertised in 'contact magazines' as follows:

> Humiliation enthusiast, my favourite pastime is humiliating and disciplining mature male submissives, in strict bondage, lovely tan coloured mistress invites humble applicants, T.V., C.P., B., D. and rubber wear. 12 noon to 7 p.m., Mon. to Fri. Basement Flat, 89 Warwick Way, Victoria SW1.

The law report records:

> The services provided at . . . [the] premises were of a particularly revolting and perverted kind. Straightforward sexual intercourse was not provided at all. With the aid of a mass of equipment, some manual (such as whips and chains), some mechanical and some electrical, clients were subjected, at their own wish and with their full consent, to a variety of forms of humiliation, flagellation, bondage and torture, accompanied often by masturbation.

Miss Tan could not be charged with running a brothel because she worked alone in her basement flat. She was charged with and convicted of running a disorderly house, sentenced to 18 months' imprisonment and subjected to a property confiscation order in respect of the apparatus. In order to secure this conviction the trial court itself had to massage the current legal definition of a 'disorderly house' which hitherto has always involved some element of concurrent multiplicity of parties. The jury were directed:

> a single prostitute who provides services in private premises to one client at a time without spectators is guilty of the common law offence of keeping a disorderly house if it is proved that the services provided are of such a character and are

conducted in such a manner . . . that their provision amounts to an outrage of public decency or is otherwise calculated to harm the public interest to such an extent as to call for condemnation and punishment.[62]

On appeal, the Court of Appeal upheld the new definition of a disorderly house, upheld the direction to the jury, upheld the property confiscation order but reduced the custodial sentence to six months which is, as it happens, the statutory maximum for running a brothel, a consideration which influenced the same court in *R* v. *Payne*.[63] Then, in open recognition of the novelty of the charge and the conviction, and the circumstance that Tan genuinely believed herself to be operating within current criminal law, the Court of Appeal suspended the custodial sentence for two years with, however, a stern warning that others offending in like manner would receive immediate and substantial custodial sentences.

Legal theory has long been bedevilled by a sterile debate between positivists and natural lawyers. The debate has been sterile because each side has begged the question by assuming itself to be correct. But of course natural law is false judged by positivist assumptions just as positivism is false judged by natural law assumptions. Since no further theory is available whereby the competitors might be assessed, legal theory appears to have reached an impasse. Here I can merely indicate how an alternative theory might be constructed. I shall attempt to demonstrate that a synthesis of positivism and natural law is possible and that what I shall call 'normative positivism' is consistent with the account of criminal law which I favour. That conceives of law in general and criminal law in particular as a socially valid positive moral order. Ideal-typically, positivism may be characterized by such notions as 'fact', 'will', 'power', 'instrumentalism', 'discretion', '*mala prohibita*', etc. The dialectical contraries to these notions are 'value', 'reason', 'authority', 'legitimacy', 'deduction', '*mala in se*', etc. These characterize natural law thinking. If positivism and natural law, ideally conceived, represent the end points on a spectrum, 'normative positivism' might occupy a middle position. Various authors can be placed notionally at different points on the spectrum depending on how closely their accounts of law approach the ideal models of positivism or natural law. The idea can be illustrated diagramatically:

← — — — — — — — — — — — — — — — — →

POSITIVISM	'NORMATIVE POSITIVISM'	NATURAL LAW
no ought	formal ought	material ought
fact		value
will		reason
power		authority
instrumentalism		legitimacy
discretion		deduction
mala prohibita		*mala in se*

Bentham	Hart	Kelsen		Blackstone
Austin			Aquinas(Finnis)	Fuller
Hagerström				← Dworkin →
Olivecrona				
(early) Ross	(mature) Ross			
Cook	Moore	Llewellyn		

Richard Tur

Of course actual authors are dialectically difficult to classify and my examples
are fairly arbitrarily drawn, the diagram being illustrative rather than an exercise
in exegesis. For present purposes it suffices to concentrate on two important
aspects of the diagram, the discretion–deduction spectrum and the nature of the
'ought'. Natural law thinking is characterized by two major problems. First, the
identification of its fundamental principle or principles and, secondly, the correct
application of such principles to fact situations. I shall allow my hypothetical
ideal natural lawyer his fundamental principle or principles and enter no objections
as to the difficulties of conflicts between and priorities amongst fundamental
principles where more than one is in question. All such principles are general
and abstract and even if there was complete agreement as to *the* principle the
problem of application to particular and concrete facts would remain.

John Finnis criticizes positivists for attributing to natural law thinking a wholly
deductive methodology such that given the fundamental principle as major premise
and a statement of fact as minor premise the one right answer pops out auto-
matically. Finnis remarks that the relationship between principles and decisions
is too complex to be characterized as pure deduction and nothing else.[64] This
is no new thought and many theorists, although moving from quite different
assumptions, could readily give assent. Holmes, for example, held that 'General
propositions do not decide particular cases'.[65] Hart exhorts us that 'we should
not cherish even as an ideal a rule so detailed that no new choices arise at the
point of application'.[66] Unger remarks that 'language is no longer credited with
the fixidity of categories and the transparent representation of the world that
would make formalism plausible in legal reasoning or in ideas about justice'.[67]
Kelsen insists that 'every law applying act is only partly determined by law' and
presents actual legal systems as a synthesis of formal, static deduction and informal,
dynamic determination.[68] It is, therefore, difficult to find a pure deductivist.

Finnis explains that Aquinas regarded law as consisting in part of rules which
are 'derived from natural law like conclusions deduced from principles' and for
the rest of 'rules which are derived from natural laws like implementations
[*determinationes*] of general directives'.[69] Finnis observes in a footnote that
there is no happy English equivalent of *determinatio* but suggests that
'implementation' is more elegant than Kelsen's 'concretization'.[70] What Finnis
does not comment upon is the remarkable similarity between this doctrine and
the Kelsenian account of the legal norm or rule as a 'frame' within which a range
of determinations is possible.[71] Thus it would appear that Kelsen and Aquinas
agree that law sometimes involves applications of general rules by way of
subsumption of the particular under the general, that is a deductive process, and
sometimes concretization by way of delegation. Kelsen distinguishes, as ideal-
types, 'static' and 'dynamic' systems. A static system is one in which the content
of all individual applications of the rules is at least tacitly contained within the
general rules and principles and is discoverable therefore by a purely intellectual
process. By contrast, a dynamic system involves delegation to the lawmaker of
the determination of the content of the decision. For Kelsen, the dynamic principle
is characteristic of legal positivism which understands law to be in some sense
a product of human acts and decisions rather than a deduction from timeless
and immutable principles. However, he also acknowledges that any actual legal

system synthesizes the static and the dynamic principles. Kelsen further holds, in one of his most mysterious doctrines, that the primacy of the principle of delegation means that even a determination *outside* the frame is valid and binding unless and until set aside by a higher decision. Thus for Kelsen, as for legal positivism in general, law can have any content.[72]

Clearly these Kelsenian doctrines go well beyond what Finnis would concede on behalf of Aquinas. However it is difficult to see how, having once admitted determinations into his system, Aquinas can hold the line against such Kelsenian conclusions. Finnis illustrates the notion of a determination by the example of an architect's instructions to an artificer to put a 'doorway' in a wall of a building.[73] Clearly there are minimum and maximum dimensions outwith which no opening in a human habitation can count as a 'doorway'. Equally clearly once the doorway is installed it must have precise dimensions. Since these dimensions cannot be read off intellectually from the concept of doorway, the artificer, by decision, determines the general and abstract instruction in its particular and concrete application. The important thing to note about this example is just how favourable it is to the general natural law case which Finnis, I take it, is at pains to defend. All that has been conceded so far is that law, consistent with natural law methodology, can have, within limits, a variable content. It does not follow that law can have *any* content. However, 'doorway' is a concept exhibiting what I shall call 'middle-order generality', that is a concept the descriptive content of which is relatively clearly defined. Clearly not all determinations of the artificer could reasonably be regarded as doorways and even more clearly should he step outside the 'frame' and install a window no one could reasonably regard that as a determination of the architect's concept.

However, another example given by Finnis is somewhat more problematical. He observes that 'if material goods are to be used efficiently for human well-being there must be a regime of private property'.[74] He acknowledges that precisely what rules of property there should be is undetermined by this 'general requirement of justice' and he also concedes that the choice of rules will be to some extent arbitrary. Even so, Finnis remains committed to the proposition that in determining the concept of property the legislator's choice cannot be regarded as wholly unfettered or arbitrary. With respect, this is altogether less plausible with 'property' than with 'doorway'. Even allowing Finnis his large claim that *private* property is a general requirement of justice, it must be evident that a remarkably wide range of possible determinations present themselves to the legislator. Once the legislator's choice is admitted as a source of content it is entirely possible that two positive legislators will not only determine a concept differently but will determine a concept in a contradictory fashion. It is one thing to concede, as Finnis does, that the determination of the general requirements of justice leaves open a variable content but it is quite another should that concession logically entail that, given determination, *any* content is possible. Indeed, if it could be shown that any content is possible consistent with the general requirements of justice, then 'justice' or 'natural law' would be stripped of their critical function whereby that which does not exhibit conformity of content with 'justice' or with 'natural law' is disqualified as law or, at least, is in some way a law less compelling upon conscience.

It seems to me possible to demonstrate that some of the general requirements of justice are compatible with any determinations including contradictory determinations. The quintessential formulation of justice is 'live honestly, harm no one and render to each his due'.[75] This is not the doctrine adopted by Finnis and I would have to show that the arguments applied here could be applied equally effectively to the very much more sophisticated account presented in *Natural Law and Natural Rights*. However, the classical formulation serves as an initial and simplified target. Presumably, the lawmaker must determine the content of these general requirements of justice. Suppose that the lawmakers in England and Victoria have determined the concept of 'honesty' not only differently but in such a manner that on identical facts an individual would be 'dishonest' and therefore liable to conviction for theft in Victoria but 'honest' and therefore fall to be acquitted in England. I believe something like this to be very much the case.[76] Can one accept that both decisions are determinations of the concept of 'honesty'? If so, the whole edifice so carefully reconstructed by Finnis is in danger of collapse. Once a logical contradiction is admitted to a system of propositions any other proposition and its negation can be proved to be true by virtue of the rules of formal logic.[77] Consequently, Finnis must either deny that one or other of the contradictory determinations is a genuine determination or accept that his account of natural law is, ultimately, consistent with any positive law whatever. If he admits that his account of natural law is consistent with any positive law whatever he has, in my submission, conceded that natural law, like positive law, can have any content. Then, of course, any critical function which natural law might be supposed to have in constraining the content of positive law is dissolved and Finnis's natural law with a variable and changing content is revealed as serving the purely ideological function of justification and not an epistemological function in respect of what ought to be.

Similar considerations present themselves as regards 'rendering to each his due'. Suppose the lawmakers in England and in Scotland have determined differently the question whether a man is entitled to whatever another has gratuitously promised. Again, I believe something like this to be very much the case.[78] Are both genuine determinations of a man's due? If so, natural law is again exposed as consistent with any possible content of positive law and it thereby loses its critical function. If not, as with 'honesty', the onus remains on Finnis to explain what, consistent with his methodology, distinguishes genuine or legitimate determinations from false or illegitimate determinations. If this burden is not discharged one may conclude that there is very little difference indeed between some versions of positivism and Finnis's account of natural law. This suspicion is reinforced by another concession whereby Finnis allows that an unjust law may be a *law* for all that.[79] Of course if determination is as open-ended as I have argued it is, absent any criterion to distinguish the genuine from the false determination, then no positive law could be unjust because every positive law, whatever its content, being a determination of the natural law, will necessarily be consistent with the natural law and therefore valid. It follows that it is at least possible in principle to regard some versions of positivism and some versions of natural law as tending towards a middle position on my spectrum. Both Kelsen and Aquinas acknowledge the role of determination and subsumption and both regard positive law as normative in the sense that it consists of precepts intimating how men ought to behave under particular circumstances. Finnis, on behalf of Aquinas, would doubtless be disposed to argue that Kelsen admits and he excludes *any* content whatever but if the general requirements of justice are indeed so indeterminate as to allow of even contradictory determinations then this objection falls. Further, the quaint Kelsenian point that the lawmaker can even determine outside the frame cannot offer Finnis much of a target because, if the frame is as indeterminate as to admit of contradictory determinations, then the distinction between a determination within and a determination outwith the frame is meaningless.

As to 'harming no one', I have presented arguments elsewhere to the effect that 'harm', being a rule-dependent concept, is indeterminate unless and until moral principles or legal rules are brought into play to define with greater or lesser precision the legitimate interests and the general good.[80] Even death need not necessarily constitute a 'harm'. Whether the physical fact of death is a 'harm' depends upon circumstances. Thus to those who favour euthanasia death is not a 'harm'. There is therefore no direct inference ticket from physical harm to harm normatively defined. Thus the general requirement of justice, 'harm no one', is utterly indeterminate and can accommodate the content of any positive law whatever insofar as 'harm' is not a precondition of a legal rule or moral principle but a consequence of the definitions of legitimate interests and the common good established by such rules and principles.

So far, I have attempted in limited compass to render plausible the claim that an account of law which synthesizes salient features of natural law and positivism is possible. A detailed exposition and defence would require considerably more ingenuity and effort. The argument thus far can be fortified by a consideration of the nature of the 'ought'. The schematic account suggested that legal positivism first presented itself as a matter of fact whereby theorists sought to reduce law to one or other favoured fact. Austin thus reduced law to the psychological fact of command and some American Realists are associated with the predictive account of law. Hart's most significant criticism of both is that they leave no or little room for a normative conception of law. One cannot, he says, arrive at the normative concept of a rule from the factual elements of commands and habits of obedience. Thus crude or naive positivism might well be characterized as including no 'ought' whatever. Natural law thinking, however, is overtly normative and therefore includes an 'ought'. The 'ought' of natural law thinking is, in my view, irreducibly a material ought, that is to say that somehow the 'ought' of natural law predetermines to some extent what can be the content of an ought statement.

Consider the related concept of 'good' as an illustration. The notion of a 'good thumbscrew' is troublesome if the meaning of 'good' is not exhausted by 'efficient' and if, but only if, 'good' necessarily imports some generalized conception of human welfare. If one operates with such a material concept of 'good' then the idea of a 'good thumbscrew' is a contradiction in terms. A formal concept of 'good' would be wholly indeterminate as to content such that anything, irrespective of its impact upon human welfare, could be characterized as 'good'. 'Good' on such a formal account is wholly undefinable *a priori* because, to adopt Moore's reasoning, moral propositions would otherwise be tautologies or self-contradictions.[81] The argument as to 'ought' is similar. Natural law thinking adopts an ought which somehow incorporates some material content such that, for example, the statement 'You ought to kill' is not merely immoral but incoherent. I seek to contrast that material ought with a formal ought which is a necessary element in the theory of law that I refer to as 'normative positivism'. Such an utterly formal, undefinable and wholly unanalysable concept of 'ought' is necessary if law is to be regarded as normative and if the positivist proposition that law may have any content is to be sustained.

One could then regard law conceptually as a wholly empty series of ought statements to which content is added not by any logical deductions from some fundamental principles or from any material content lurking within the 'ought' itself but from the acts and decisions of the lawmakers in a society. What content the law has would then be entirely a contingent and empirical matter dependent upon the values, beliefs, intuitions, ideals, interests and emotions of whosoever has the lawmaking function in hand. But even the most detailed body of laws will still themselves require concretization in particular applications, and the final stage of law creation is the actual human conduct that occurs. In a sense, therefore, one may adopt Hare's significant point that what people *do* is a matter of some importance.[82] Not only may law influence human conduct but human conduct may influence the content of the law. It follows, too, for anyone who refuses to believe that universalizability is a necessary element in the meaning of 'ought' as opposed to the meaning of 'all', that such a normative system, replete with content flowing from the 'millenary labour' of many heads, hearts and hands, constantly in flux, but also sufficiently determinate to guide conduct, may be regarded as a socially valid positive system of morality.[83] If so, 'normative positivism' legitimates the view that law is *necessarily* in the business of upholding moral values. With a formal ought it seems possible to move from the anormativity of crude, fact-based positivism to a position short of the material ought of natural law. Thus, as we saw in regard to determination so with the ought, a theory occupying a middle position between classical positivism and classical natural law appears possible.

The formal ought may look rather too like an artificial construct brought in to make the theory work and some might well wonder how the special functional legal ought could simultaneously be regarded, as I purport to regard it, as a *moral* ought. On this point I pray Kelsen in aid: 'in this relative sense, every law is moral; every law constitutes a - relative - moral value. And this means; the question about the relationship between law and morals is not a question about the content of the law but one about its form.'[84] Hart's account of law may be interpreted in similar fashion. Others have observed that, for a 'positivist', he makes significant concessions to natural law thought.[85] But it is not merely the minimum content of natural law which supports such a view. Consider Hart's account of what it is for a social rule to exist and his distinction between the internal and the external points of view.[86] The crucial point about rules, as opposed to habits, is the critical reflective attitude which *justifies* hostile reactions and, ultimately, sanctions. In a 'healthy' legal system the citizens and the officials alike exhibit such an internal attitude. Even in a healthy society it is enough that the officials accept the secondary rules of recognition, adjudication and change and that the citizens acquiesce.[87] Since 'acceptance', for Hart, involves a critical, hostile attitude, his concept of law comes very close to being the morality of the legal officials of the society or even the morality of the 'ruling class'.

Normative positivism asserts what legal positivists deny, namely that there is a *necessary* connection between law and positive morality. At the same time, by refusing to adopt a material ought, normative positivism radically separates itself from any suggestion that there is a necessary connection between law and any critical morality. On pain of committing the naturalistic fallacy, all critical moralities, utilitarianism just as much as natural law, rest upon an unproved and unprovable axiom.[88] Mill's famous 'proof' is unpersuasive, as all such proofs must be, given either the infinite regress of supposed justifications higher than the ultimate justification or the viciously circular proposition that the ultimate justification is, illogically, its own justification.

Insofar as the criminal law reflects and generates a common positive morality, criminal law invites the legal theorist to reconsider the established types of legal theory and to think again about the nature of law. One objection, however, is so obvious that I cannot leave the matter there. The criminal law of England (it might well be argued) is shot through with inconsistencies and irrationalities, and, however a subjectivist may present it, exhibits a considerable amount of objective liability. This last may be a source of considerable disquiet and one might not at first see how such obviously 'immoral' content could be defended as part of a system of morality. However, one could invoke the concept of 'moral luck', discussed by both Nagel[89] and Williams.[90]

Academic criminal lawyers seem divisible almost without remainder into pure subjectivists or pure objectivists. Both groups purport to find their principle validated within the criminal law but both tend to assume that they have found the master principle and seek to defend it at every turn. Ultimately, therefore, such academics abandon the rigorous analysis of the current content of criminal law and substitute criticism for legal exposition. Subjectivists look primarily to the state of mind of the accused and deny the appropriateness of a conviction in the absence of *mens rea*. They oppose with greater or lesser emphasis any 'objective' substitutes for *mens rea*, especially the reasonable man, though intoxication is treated as an exception. Objectivists, though not necessarily denying the importance of subjective mental states in the attribution of responsibility, refuse to give the *mens rea* principle exhaustive sway and look also to 'harmful consequences liability'[91] as a basis for conviction. There are plenty of examples in English criminal law of crimes which appear to include harmful consequences as a definitional element irrespective of any actual state of mind referable thereto: s. 47, Offences Against the Person Act 1861; s. 51 (1), Police Act 1964; s. 1 (2), Criminal Damage Act 1971 (since *Caldwell*),[92] etc. Subjectivists regard such instances as anomalous, contrary to principle and therefore as objects of reform. However, if 'moral luck' is a feature of conventional morality, no less than the 'emphatic sexual taboos' taken by Hart to justify the exclusion of 'rationality' from the criteria of the 'moral',[93] then there is a moral basis for objective, harmful consequence liability in the criminal law. What, then, is 'moral luck'?

Nagel observes that 'it is intuitively plausible that people cannot be morally assessed for what is not their fault, or for what is due to factors beyond their control'.[94] Of course this makes sense in the case of insanity, automatism or involuntary movement but the range of factors over which one has no control is obviously wider than such clear instances of total lack of control. Nagel identifies four classes of situation in which the agent might plausibly be regarded as lacking control. These are constitutive luck – the kind of person one is; contemporary circumstantial luck – the kind of circumstances in which one is placed; antecedent circumstantial luck – the kind of circumstances which led up to the situation one faces; and consequential luck – the way things turn out. These categories of luck threaten the very notion of moral responsibility in that if the precondition of control is consistently applied we would be disbarred from making the wide range of moral judgments that we find it entirely natural to make. Nagel offers several examples:

> whether we succeed or fail in what we try to do nearly always depends to some extent on factors beyond our control. This is true of murder, altruism, revolution, the sacrifice of certain interests for the sake of others – almost any morally important act. What has been done, and what is morally judged, is partly determined by external factors. However jewel-like the good will may be in its own right, there is a morally significant difference between rescuing someone from a burning building and dropping him from a twelfth storey window while trying to rescue him. Similarly there is a morally significant difference between reckless driving and manslaughter. But whether a reckless driver hits a pedestrian depends upon the presence of the pedestrian at the point where he recklessly passes a red light.[95]

Such examples lead on to Nagel's definition of moral luck: 'Where a significant aspect of what someone does depends upon factors beyond his control, yet we continue to treat him in that respect as an object of moral judgment, it can be called moral luck.'[96] In such circumstances actual results influence judgments of responsibility and culpability even though the agent did not contemplate the result which occurred. The traditional response of moral philosophy has been to narrow down each act to its pure and innermost core, an act of pure will that, alone, is susceptible of moral assessment. This is how Kant, for example, dealt with morality.[97] Nagel's profound point is that even where the agent is at the mercy of fate, and though it seems irrational upon reflection, our ordinary moral attitudes would be unrecognizable without attributing to the agent responsibility and culpability in a wide range of cases of moral luck. Nagel refers to Adam Smith whom he takes to be advocating, as a matter of reason, the restriction of moral judgment only to that which the agent has done in a narrow sense because to attribute responsibility for that beyond the agent's control seems irrational and is akin to strict liability. However, Nagel is well aware that Smith himself had doubts as to the social validity of the subjective principle and he cites a passage from *The Theory of Moral Sentiments*:

> But how well soever we may seem to be persuaded of the truth of this equitable maxim, when we consider it after this manner, in abstract, yet when we come to particular cases, the actual consequences which happen to proceed from any action,

have a very great effect upon our sentiments concerning its merit or demerit, and almost always either enhance or diminish our sense of both. Scarce in any one instance, perhaps, will our sentiments be found, after examination, to be entirely regulated by this rule, which we acknowledge ought entirely to regulate them.[98]

In this paper I have argued that criminal law is an extremely sophisticated, demanding and complex subject which can be presented as an 'introductory' course in legal education only by serious amputation and therefore distortion. Further, the current mode and role of criminal law teaching has consequences for legal education in general. I have not, however, argued that criminal law should *not* be one of the first subjects studied. Rather I have argued that, properly taught, it is a highly suitable place to begin serious legal study. Turning, then, to the relationship of criminal law and legal theory, I asked what legal theory might contribute to criminal law and I dealt with two central issues; first, the limits of exposition imposed by the nature of legal rules which, I argue, are essentially incomplete and therefore incapable of a final, exhaustive statement; and, secondly, the nature of methodological purity, where I argue against a tendency to distort data to fit a favoured critical principle. Finally I asked what criminal law might contribute to legal theory. Here I directed attention to three issues. First, the circumstance that criminal law exhibits some particularly interesting judicial techniques of lawmaking which must be relevant in any account of judicial process which purports at least in part to be descriptive, rather than purely normative. Secondly, I assumed, partly on the basis of other work,[99] that the criminal law can be understood as a socially valid positive moral order and that, if so, some revision of legal theory might be called for. I therefore proposed an account of law, 'normative positivism', which I take to synthesize salient features of positivism and natural law thinking and which seems to me wholly to fit the nature of criminal law. Thirdly, and consequentially, I argued that the elements of harmful consequences liability which are exhibited by the criminal law do not disqualify it from the status of positive moral order, because conventional morality (as opposed to the critical morality of Kant or Smith, for example) incorporates a notion of moral luck and indeed our ordinary moral attitudes would be unrecognizable without some such idea. Consequently such apparently irrational attribution of responsibility exhibited by criminal law strengthens rather than weakens the claim that criminal law may be understood as positive morality.

NOTES

1 [1968] 2 QB 65, cf *R* v. Spencer [1985] 1 All ER 673.
2 [1981] *Crim. Law Rev.* 393.
3 Criminal Law Revision Committee, 14th Report, *Offences Against the Person* (1980; Cmnd 7844) part VI.
4 [1981] *Crim. Law Rev.* 281; Law Commission, *Codification of the Criminal Law* (1985).
5 *Anon.* (1478) YB 17 Ed. IV, Pasch. Fo. 1, pl. 2, *per* Brian CJ; *Edgington* v. *Fitzmaurice* (1885) 29 Ch. D 459 at p. 483, *per* Bowen, LJ.
6 [1981] 1 All ER 961.
7 [1981] 1 All ER 961 at p. 965.

8 G. H. Gordon, *The Criminal Law of Scotland* (2nd edn.; 1978), paras 7-53 and 7-54.
9 H. Kelsen, *Pure Theory of Law* (1967) p. 349.
10 Elliott, 'Dishonesty in Theft: A Dispensable Concept' [1982] *Crim. Law Rev.* 395-410.
11 *Feely* [1973] QB 530 at p. 541, *per* Lawton LJ; and see R. Tur, 'Dishonesty and the Jury' in *Philosophy and Practice* (1985; ed. A. Phillips Griffiths) pp. 75-96.
12 [1981] 1 All ER 961; and see now *Hardie* [1984] 3 All ER 848.
13 *Majewski* [1977] AC 443 at p. 478, *per* Lord Simon.
14 *Morgan* [1976] AC 182 at pp. 217-18.
15 See Wells, 'Swatting the Subjectivist Bug' [1982] *Crim. Law Rev.* 209 at p. 210.
16 [1976] AC 182.
17 [1978] AC 705.
18 [1981] 1 All ER 961.
19 (1984) 78 Cr. App. R 276; [1984] *Crim. Law Rev.* 163.
20 [1961] *Crim. Law Rev.* 173.
21 [1967] 2 QB 510.
22 See Justice Report (P. Sieghart, chairman), *Breaking the Rules* (1980) pp. 15-16.
23 A. W. B. Simpson, 'The Common Law and Legal Theory' (chapter 2 above).
24 J. Bentham, *Collected Works* (1838; ed. J. Bowring) IV, p. 483.
25 J. Austin, *The Province of Jurisprudence Determined* (1965; ed. H. L. A. Hart) pp. 258-9 and 142.
26 Austin, *op. cit.*, p. 191.
27 H. L. A. Hart, *The Concept of Law* (1961) p. 189.
28 Kelsen, *op. cit.*, 349.
29 R. M. Unger, *Law in Modern Society* (1976) p. 196.
30 *Lockner* v. *New York* (1905) 198 US 76.
31 J. Finnis, *Natural Law and Natural Rights* (1980) ch. X.7.
32 *Moore* v. *Hussey* 1609 Hob. 93 at p. 96.
33 H. Kelsen, *General Theory of Law and State* (1945) pp. 154-6 and 161.
34 N. MacCormick (1974) 90 *Law Quarterly Rev.* 102 at p. 125.
35 J. C. Smith and B. Hogan, *Criminal Law* (5th edn; 1983); cf. R. Cross and P. A. Jones, *Introduction to Criminal Law* (10th edn; 1984) pp. 65-7.
36 [1976] AC 182.
37 (1889) 23 QBD 168.
38 [1974] QB 354.
39 [1981] 1 WLR 1117.
40 [1976] AC 182 at p. 215, *per* Lord Hailsham; at p. 234, *per* Lord Edmund-Davies.
41 *R* v. *Prince* [1874-80] All ER 881 at p. 887; 'what would have been the legal position of the prisoner if the facts had been as he believed them to be . . . ?', *per* Brett J.
42 [1981] 3 All ER 878.
43 (1984) 78 Cr. App. R 276; [1984] *Crim. Law Rev.* 163.
44 [1976] AC 182 at p. 214, *per* Lord Hailsham.
45 Though the development of the practice of treating 'unlawful' as an element of the *actus reus* to which *mens rea* is thought to run, as illustrated in *Kimber* [1983] 3 All ER 316, widens the range considerably, albeit arbitrarily.
46 *(David Raymond) Smith* [1974] 1 All ER 632 at p. 636.
47 [1980] 3 All ER 716.
48 [1974] 1 All ER 632.
49 [1976] AC 182 at p. 215, *per* Lord Hailsham; at p. 234, *per* Lord Edmund-Davies.
50 [1874-80] All ER 881.
51 (1889) 23 QBD 168.
52 [1981] 1 WLR 1117.

53 [1981] 1 All ER 623; [1981] 3 All ER 878.
54 (1980) 111 DLR 1; and see Tur, 'Rape, Reasonableness and Time' (1981) 1 *Oxford J Legal Studies* 432; *Taylor* (1985) 80 Cr. App. Rep. 327.
55 [1976] AC 182.
56 See R. Dworkin, *Taking Rights Seriously* (1977) ch. 4, and N. MacCormick, *Legal Reasoning and Legal Theory* (1978) chs 7 and 8.
57 Tur, 'Varieties of Overruling and Judicial Law-Making; Prospective Overruling in a Comparative Perspective' [1978] *Juridical Rev.* 33.
58 [1964] AC 465.
59 [1980] 1 All ER 571.
60 [1981] 1 All ER 161.
61 [1983] 2 All ER 12.
62 [1983] 2 All ER 12 at p. 18.
63 (1980) 2 Cr. App. R (S) 161; [1980] *Crim. Law Rev.* 595.
64 Finnis, *op. cit.*, ch. X.7.
65 *Lochner* v. *New York* (1905) 198 US 76.
66 Hart, *op. cit.*, p. 125.
67 Unger, *op. cit.*, p. 196.
68 Kelsen, *op. cit.*, n. 9, p. 349.
69 Finnis, *op. cit.*, p. 284.
70 *Id.*, p. 284, n. 16.
71 Kelsen, *op. cit.*, n. 9, p. 245.
72 *Id.*, p. 198.
73 Finnis, *op. cit.*, pp. 284-5.
74 *Id.*, p. 285.
75 Justinian, *Institutes*, I.I.3.
76 *Salvo* [1980] VR 401.
77 K. Popper, *Conjectures and Refutations* (5th edn; 1974) p. 317.
78 D. M. Walker *The Law of Contracts and Related Obligations in Scotland* (1979) p. 34: 'valuable consideration . . . is not a requisite of a Scottish contract.' G. H. Treitel, *The Law of Contract* (6th edn; 1983) p. 51; 'In English law, a promise is not, as a general rule, binding as a contract unless . . . supported by some "consideration".' It follows that the content of a gratuitous promise is a man's due in Scotland but not in England and that the two legal systems have determined the concept in different, indeed mutually contradictory, fashion.
79 Finnis, *op. cit.*, p. 351.
80 See Tur, 'Paternalism and the Criminal Law' (1985) 2 *J Applied Philosophy* pp. 173-89.
81 G. E. Moore, *Principia Ethica* (1903) p. 15: 'whatever definition be offered, it may be always asked, with significance, of the complex so defined, whether it is itself good.'
82 R. M. Hare, *The Language of Morals* (1952) p. 1.
83 Cf. R. M. Hare, *Freedom and Reason* (1963) p. 35: 'the word "ought" cannot be used in making legal judgments; if a person has a certain legal obligation, we cannot express this by saying that he *ought* to do such and such a thing, for the reason that "ought" - judgments have to be universalizable, which in a strict sense, legal judgments are not. The reason why they are not is that a statement of law always contains an implicit reference to a particular jurisdiction.'
84 Kelsen, *op. cit.*, n. 9, 65.
85 A. P. D'Entreves, *Natural Law; An Introduction to Legal Philosophy* (1951) p. 185: 'represents a remarkable effort on the part of an avowed positivist to recognise the

merits of that ancient and venerable notion'; pp. 185-6: 'to recognise a core of good sense . . . is to show an understanding that goes beyond tolerance.'
86 Hart, *op. cit.*, pp. 54-9.
87 *Id.*, p. 113.
88 See J. Glover, *Causing Death and Saving Lives* (1977) pp. 23-6.
89 T. Nagel, 'Moral Luck' in *Mortal Questions* (1979) pp. 24-38.
90 B. Williams, 'Moral Luck' in *Moral Luck: Philosophical Papers 1973-1980* (1981) pp. 20-39.
91 G. P. Fletcher, *Rethinking Criminal Law* (1978) pp. 115ff.
92 [1981] 1 All ER 961.
93 Hart, *op. cit.*, pp. 176-80.
94 Nagel, *op. cit.*, p. 25.
95 *Id.*
96 *Id.*, p. 26.
97 I. Kant, *Foundations of the Metaphysics of Morals* (1785) First Section: 'Nothing can possibly be conceived in the world, or even out of it, which can be called good without qualification, except a good will.'
98 Nagel, *op. cit.*, p. 32; A. Smith, *The Theory of Moral Sentiments* (1759) part II, section 3, Introduction, para. 5.
99 See Tur, *op. cit.*, n. 11, and *op. cit.*, n. 80.

12
Legal Theory, Economic Analysis and the Law of Torts

CENTO VELJANOVSKI

Another . . . problem . . . is that the article must deal in theory – often, unfortunately, in the most dismal of theories, economics. Hopefully, it will do so in terms which are intelligible to law teachers, if not lawyers, and without that suicidal desire of the economist to make his theories so pervasive and detailed that it is rendered utterly useless to the lawyer who lives in the world of men, and even to the law teacher, wherever he lives.[1]

Guido Calabresi[1]

At the broadest level . . . the practice of economic debate often takes the form of legal reasoning. . . . Economists would do well to study jurisprudence, then, with some other aim than subordinating it to economic theory.

Donald McCloskey[2]

Economics can claim to have had an influential impact on the way many lawyers talk and think about tort law. It has contributed to a deeper analysis of public policy in the area of accident compensation and safety regulation and also somewhat surprisingly it has been used to interpret legal doctrine.[3] However, while many tort scholars are ready to admit the relevance of economic factors they are less willing to concede the value of economic theorizing. This is particularly so in England where lawyers tend to have a narrower training than their American counterparts and where legal scholarship is still in the 'black-letter' mould.[4]

In this chapter I want to consider the way economics has been used in legal theory, to explain the nature of the enterprise and to identify the differences and similarities between legal reasoning and economic reasoning with particular reference to the law of torts. The discussion will focus mainly on one comparatively new and innovative use of economics. This is the so-called new law-and-economics which attempts to use economic concepts to define and interpret legal doctrine. It is a positive theory of law in the sense that it seeks to explain legal institutions in ethically neutral and ultimately empirical terms.

It is also a problematic and controversial use of economics because its explanations of law are economic rather than legal, thus denying the possibility of confirmation through examination of the way judges express themselves and the reasoning they use to justify their decisions.[5] Moreover, since the theory does not deal with easily measured or quantitative data the ability to undertake a rigorous test of the theory is extremely difficult, if not impossible.

I THE ECONOMIC CONCEPTION OF POSITIVE THEORY

Nature and Types of Economic Theory

The first question which must be addressed is what is an economic theory of tort. At its most general level the answer is a belief that the law can be modelled using the economic theory of rational choice under conditions of scarcity and that such a theory is capable of generating insights into the operation of the legal system. The theory has as its central reference point the rigorous analysis of purposeful behaviour directed at the attainment of any pre-specified goals or objectives. Thus the economic analysis of the law is not confined to those aspects of the legal system where economic factors are important or where the law has an impact on costs, money and material welfare. Rather, it is an instrumental approach to legal reasoning which is compatible with the law pursuing non-economic objectives. The engine of economic analysis is the theory of rational choice and its subject-matter is coextensive with that of the legal system itself.

Economics stands out among the social sciences as having the most formally elegant theoretical structure and one which is accepted by the overwhelming majority of economists. Economic reasoning attempts to mimic that of the physical sciences. Formal models are developed, assumptions made and results produced. It is usual to divide economic theory into positive (what is) and normative theory (what ought to be). If the model is positive, the conclusions are usually subjected to empirical testing. Regardless of whether economics is used as a method of doctrinal interpretation, criticism or empirical prediction, a similar method is used. All positive theories must generate testable propositions which in principle can be resolved by an appeal to fact.

Economics has a wide variety of uses in the theory and practice of the law. In the practice of law it has been used both to frame laws and as part of the process of marshalling evidence in litigation, particularly in US antitrust, employment discrimination and personal injury cases. Economics has also been used extensively as a vehicle for law reform and evaluation of the costs and benefits of legal institutions and practices. In the public law area a vast transition is taking place in the nature and form of government intervention in the economy based on economic precepts and arguments about efficiency, free trade and competition.[6]

In the area of legal theory economics also has a wide variety of positive and normative applications.[7] It is most commonly associated with the strong claim of Judge Richard Posner that the common law can be understood 'as if' judges seek to minimize the social costs of accidents.[8] Posner's theory is typically regarded as a descriptive claim that the common law doctrines and remedies are the most efficient ones in the sense that in practice they minimize social costs or maximize net economic benefits.[9] Alternatively, Posner's efficiency hypothesis may be regarded as an attempt to use economics to interpret legal doctrine through the redefinition of legal concepts in economic terms.[10] A more common use of economics is as a normative tool for critical analysis. Calabresi's work on tort provides the best-known example of this approach. He begins with the assumption that the objective of accident law is to minimize the sum of accident and accident-prevention costs and evaluates tort law and its alternatives critically in terms of this objective.[11] Another branch of positive economics is the use of models to generate testable predictions about the consequences of change on the law or of changes in the law on non-legal variables.[12] This is sometimes called legal impact studies. Finally, the most controversial use of economics is to make normative statements about the law. Normative law-and-economics proffers a desirable ethical norm, such as wealth-maximization, that the legal system should follow.[13]

Rationality and Simplicity

There are two central premises of economic theory which have been the subject of endless criticisms: the behavioural claim that people are rational and the idea that models should be as simple as possible.

All economic models assume that the actors in the legal system are rational and maximize some end goal whether it be wealth, utility or some other objective. The term rational or utility-maximization is a technical term which for economists has a very specific meaning. A rational person makes consistent choices in pursuit of some objective and prefers more to less. The assumption therefore means little more than that people act purposively in pursuit of their own chosen goals and that they are doing the best given the circumstances. The meaning of rational action therefore depends on the assumptions one makes about the individual's objectives and the constraints which he or she faces. In any formal model both these must be explicitly stated if the axiom is to have any operational meaning.

The rationality assumption has been the subject of two perennial attacks. One is that it is a sterile truism: people maximize utility and what they do is utility-maximizing.[14] The criticism is correct of a certain segment of the literature which uses the rationality assumption descriptively and fails to identify from the beginning what the individual is assumed to maximize and/or the constraints he or she faces. When the axiom is used to predict the response of individuals to changes in the costs and benefits of alternative courses of action, then the axiom does generate refutable propositions which are not truistic. The economists' laws of supply and demand are an example of such refutable propositions.[15]

The second criticism is the claim that people are not rational. In part this results from a semantic confusion between rational as it is used as a term of art by the economist (and indeed the philosopher and logician) and its common usage as defining behaviour which is in the best interests of a person. In positive economics rational action has no such interpretation. Economists assume that the individual is the best judge of his or her own welfare in order to determine how he or she will respond to changes in their environment and not to evaluate the desirability of human action. Thus if a group of lunatics (predictably) respond to sunlight by dousing themselves with water because they believe they will otherwise burn, then this is an economically rational action although not a desirable or sane response. To repeat, the term as used in economics means only that an individual does the best he can given the circumstances and not that he acted wisely or sensibly or maximized some socially or ethically desirable state of affairs.

The postulate of rational behaviour is not a descriptive claim about the psychology or motivation of an identifiable individual which is to be directly tested. There are a number of grounds for saying this apart from the definitional one already stated. First, economic models purport to explain not individual behaviour but group behaviour in order to identify the predictable component. That is, the purpose of the assumption is to determine the consequences of rational behaviour in specified settings and to see whether those consequences have occurred. Economic man is therefore an average of the group of individuals under study. It follows that it is never sufficient to attack a positive economic model by arguing that not all people calculate costs and benefits, or maximize utility or wealth or any other direct test of the axiom itself. The claim of the positive economist is that a model based on this assumption yields explanations or predictions which can be tested. It is 'as if' theorizing; the law can be explained 'as if' individuals and institutions pursued the stated goal.

The use of a model of man that is objective and artificial also lies at the heart of tort law. The reasonable man is an artefact, a legal norm by which the conduct of real people is to be judged. It sweeps away the idiosyncracies of human personality and replaces them with a standard of the average person in the circumstances.[16] Thus the reasonable man shares the salient characteristics of the rational man: objective, descriptively inaccurate and used as a tool to 'predict' and determine liability.

Economic models are also often criticized for being far too simple and unrealistic. There are two problems or misconceptions underlying this type of criticism.

The first is that it presupposes that the test of a good theory is the realism of its assumptions. This has caused considerable debate in economics. One school of thought most identified with Milton Friedman totally rejects this view and claims that the only test of a positive theory is its ability to predict.[17] Friedman has gone further to argue that unrealistic assumptions are a necessary component of a good theory.[18]

It is not necessary, however, to rehearse this debate because underlying much of this type of criticism is the erroneous belief that theory is description, that it should reflect reality as closely as possible. Theories are not mirrors. The goal of a theory, whether it be predictive or explanatory, is not to provide a photographic reproduction of reality but to isolate those factors which explain outcomes. A theory should be internally consistent, elegant (in the sense of employing the minimum number of assumptions, symbols and the clearest and neatest derivation of results) and simple. It is for this reason that when two theories are equally capable of explaining the same phenomenon, the simpler is to be preferred. This is because theory and science seek generality. The more assumptions we employ and the more specific we make the theory, the less general it will become and the less it can explain. Thus the plea for greater realism in theory often leads to an untenable situation where concepts and categories abound, where the theory has so many degrees of freedom that it is capable of explaining everything and hence tells us nothing.

Even if one does not agree with the details of the above defence of simple modelling, the point still remains that a theory is not necessarily deficient merely because its assumptions are unrealistic. In the application of economics to tort doctrine this is not hard to accept. Most economic theories of tort assume either that individuals are risk-neutral or that insurance markets are perfect and focus exclusively on the impact of the rules on accident costs. Since people are generally risk-averse this assumption is false. Nonetheless, it is an assumption built into the law of torts: liability generally fixes on conduct not insurance policies.[19]

II ECONOMIC DOCTRINALISM

The Nature of the Common Law

Much of the recent economic theorizing about tort has set for itself the task of explaining the content and nature of legal doctrine. This is for the economist an unusual use of economics and more so given that the data with which to test the theory are not facts and figures but interpretations of legal doctrines. This has occurred because most of the practitioners of the application of economics to law have been lawyers – a rare example where those colonized have been the imperialists. The burning question for legal scholars is to discover whether the common law has a rational basis and consistency. It is the idea of unification of the law through some overarching principle that lies behind the current wave of theorizing. This branch of economic analysis, like the majority of legal theories about tort, treats the law as a logically self-contained system to be explained and the theory is 'tested' by its ability to interpret legal doctrine. It is a new type of doctrinal analysis which seeks to provide answers to the question: What is the basis of the law? Or perhaps: What is the law?[20] – rather than the question it is frequently viewed as examining, the effects of the tort system on accidents, costs and compensation.

The need for this enquiry arises, as no lawyer needs to be told, because of the nature of the common law. The development of the common law is an intensely practical activity. Judges resolve disputes and the law arises as a by-product of this dispute-resolution process. The doctrines of the common law are therefore rarely stated in precise or even explicit terms and English judges are as a rule extremely reluctant to state general principles of law in the abstract. Simpson's essay captures the essence of common law adjudication when he describes it as a system of law which places a 'particular value on dissension, obscurity and the tentative character of judicial utterances' so 'that uniquely authentic statements of the [legal] rule . . . cannot be made'.[21] The common law is, according to Simpson, 'chaotic' and 'shadowy'; 'more a muddle than a system',[22] and this is nowhere more evident than in the law of torts.

The vagueness inherent in the common law is amply illustrated by the classic definitions of negligence. In *Blyth* v. *Birmingham Waterworks* Alderson B stated:

Negligence is the omission to do something which a reasonable man, guided upon
those considerations which ordinarily regulate the conduct of human affairs, would
do, or do something which a prudent and reasonable man would not do.[23]

Atkin's neighbour test in *Donoghue* v. *Stevenson* has the same 'featureless
generality':

> you must not injure your neighbour, and the lawyer's question, Who is my
> neighbour? receives a restricted reply. You must take reasonable care to avoid acts
> or omissions which you can reasonably foresee would be likely to injure your
> neighbour. Who, then, in law is my neighbour? The answer seems to be – persons
> who are so closely and directly affected by my act that I ought reasonably to have
> them in contemplation as being so affected when I am directing my mind to the
> acts or omissions.[24]

Alderson's statement read in isolation appears to make the test an objective
one determined by custom and community practice, whereas Atkin's conveys
the impression that it is subjective and to be sought from the introspection of
the defendant. Neither of these interpretations is correct since it is for the court
to decide what the prudent man would have done and what is reasonable in the
circumstances. The constituent parts of the neighbour principle – reasonable care,
reasonable foreseeability and proximity – are supplied by the decision of judges
in specific cases. It is here where the problems of consistent terminology and
interpretation arise. The linguistic formulations used by judges, such as duty,
reasonable foreseeability, proximity and reasonable care, have a chameleon-like
quality and are frequently used interchangeably. An illustration of this is provided
by Lord Reid's dicta in *Wagon Mound (No. 2)* reviewing the cases on whether
foreseeability has any place in the determination of liability in nuisance:

> the most striking feature . . . [is] the variety of words used. . . . The word 'natural'
> is found very often, and it is peculiarly ambiguous. It can often and does mean
> a result which one would naturally expect, i.e., which would not be surprising:
> or it can mean the result at the end of a chain of causation unbroken by any conscious
> act, the result produced by so-called natural laws however surprising or even
> unforeseeable in the particular case. Another word frequently used is 'probable'.
> It is used with various shades of meaning. Sometimes it appears to mean more
> probable than not, sometimes it appears to include events likely but not very likely
> to occur, sometimes it has a still wider meaning and refers to events the chance
> of which is anything more than a bare possibility, and sometimes, when used in
> conjunction with other adjectives, it appears to serve no purpose beyond rounding
> off a phrase.[25]

The result is that general principles are open-ended and the cases applying
the standard supply a patchwork of decisions where the logic is not evident. This
lack of precision, apparent lack of purpose and the elasticity of legal terms are
both virtues and vices of the common law. They are virtues because they give
the court flexibility to adapt and to accommodate to the infinite variety of fact
situations. They are vices because it makes it difficult to construct some systematic

representation of the law. They are also vices because the law should be clear, prospective and accessible to the ordinary citizen who is subject to it (or at least accessible to his legal adviser). If these are not the inherent characteristics of the law then it implies that positive injustice is a basic feature of the common law. We thus have as our data a system of law and adjudication where general principles are given question-begging formulations, where legal terms are used with considerable imprecision and where there is considerable confusion about the exact state of the law in substantial areas.

Orthodox Doctrinal Analysis

Orthodox doctrinal analysis relies heavily on logic and the skilful interpretation of the reasoning in decided cases. The formalist model discussed by Sugarman (chapter 3 above) illustrates that the principal objective of doctrinal analysis, or what he terms the 'formalist model', is the exposition and classification of the law. Since the medium of the law is the written word, although it is perhaps truer to say that in England it is more the spoken word, it comes as no surprise that legal analysis places great importance on the form and interpretation of words. This emphasis on exposition and linguistic techniques creates, in my view, a severe paradox for law as an academic subject. If it is correct that the common law is chaotic and that its approach and terminology is a source of confusion and lack of clarity; and if it is further argued that what judges say is an unreliable and sometimes misleading guide to the true grounds for their decisions, then one is compelled to conclude that the logic of the law will not be found by linguistic analysis or the traditional tools of legal analysis. Academic lawyers who use the same language as judges, their categories and distinctions and their conceptional framework, both confuse their role with that of the practitioners of law and must end up just as confused as the common law, concluding, as Simpson does, that the common law is 'more like a muddle than a system'.

Analytical Method and Legal Rhetoric

The solution to this problem is to employ a conceptual system that is exterior to the legal system. Hence the attraction of economics: if one is looking for a rational basis for the common law then the conceptual framework of economics provides the obvious tools for this task.

As an interpretive device the economic approach declines to use the same categories, reasoning and linguistic formulations as judges and legal scholars. The central tenet of the economic approach is that it is only by employing a conceptual structure which is exterior to the way cases are decided that one can generate new insights. Economic analysis does not seek to replicate the judicial reasoning in individual cases but to identify the regularities and tendencies in the pattern of decisions taken over a period of time. These theories are very much 'black boxes' since they are concerned with the configuration of rules and procedures, not with the reasoning that led to them. To take Hart's characterization, economic analysis in this guise takes an 'extreme external point of view' of the law 'purely in terms of observable regularities of conduct, predictions, probabilities and signs'.[26]

The above argument is an extreme one because as will be shown later legal reasoning and language do contain a large 'economic' component and economics can be used to improve judicial decisions and the law generally. However, even if one discounted this, the case for a theory which does not claim either to improve judicial decision-making or to use language and concepts which can be readily applied to practical problems can still be made out, and strongly. The following quotations (by lawyers) capture the type of criticisms made of the economic theory of tort on this score:

> the lack of realism does not invalidate an economic theory of law, but it certainly renders it a barren tool in solving actual disputes. It may well explain the effects and tendencies of actual decisions, but cannot substitute for them.[27]

and:

> it would be a major argument against . . . economic analysis of law . . . to show . . . that judges did not talk in cost-effective terms.[28]

An economist offers a similar criticism:

> There are . . . weaknesses in the economic approach which limit its value. One of the dangers is not unique to economics, but shared with all theories of law which attempt to deduce judicial outcomes from general propositions not stated in the courts' opinions. If judicial decisions can be explained without reproducing the opinions, then the reasons given in the opinions are not the real reasons for the decisions. If the real reasons are latent . . . then the opinions are diminished in dignity and stature. To be taken seriously by courts, a theory of law must take the opinions of judges seriously. In so far as judges are regarded as moved by principles which they do not utter, and unmoved by principles which they do utter, the theory will be worthless in arguing a case.[29]

Lack of sophistication on this point leads to the simplistic criticism that because judges do not use economic language and reasoning, an economic theory of the law is irrelevant. I would dispute the contention that common law reasoning is not economic in character. But even if it were correct it would not in the absence of other evidence damage the attempt to explain the law in terms other than those used by judges. The economic theory of tort doctrine does not rely on explicit economic theorizing by courts nor is it confined to occasions when the courts decide in terms of policy rather than principle. The fact that judges do not appear to use economics explicitly is no more a rebuttal of the theory than are the instances where judges express themselves in economic terms a confirmation of the theory. For example, judges may not refer to deterrence in their speeches and they may not attach weight to this factor. Yet I think few would deny that a theory which assumed that the objective of the law was deterrence would be a useful theory if it predicted how judges decided future cases or showed that the cases fitted a consistent pattern. It would not follow that a theory which achieved this would also be one that we would want judges to use in order to make better decisions. All the theory is trying to do is to explain the behaviour of a part of the legal system. It does not seek to influence the way the system operates or to change the way those in the system think or act. It is in the nature of a 'social' theory in much the same way as the idea that the development of the common law can be explained by the class bias of judges[30] or the desire by judges to subsidize the industrial revolution in its formative stages.[31]

Invisible-Hand Explanations

The sceptical reader may question whether a theory which so wholeheartedly rejects judicial techniques of analysis can really explain the 'law'. The proposition that the behaviour of a social system or organization can be quite different from the psychology or motivations of the individuals making it up is not novel. Invisible-hand theories, which have a venerable pedigree going back to Adam Smith's *Wealth of Nations*, claim precisely this.[32]

Invisible-hand theories are based on two propositions. First, that one cannot understand a social system simply by looking at individual behaviour or bilateral transactions between individuals. One must focus on the environment and processes at play. Secondly, that the motivations and aspirations of individuals, whether articulated or not, do not explain the driving force of the system and therefore are not the key to understanding. Individuals may be forced to act in a way they neither plan nor intend and which produces a collective rationality because of the constraints which operate upon them. It was Adam Smith's key insight that greed and selfishness constrained by competitive forces in the marketplace would bring about the attainment of a coherent collective goal even though this goal was not the intended or desired result of those individual actions. The goal is wealth-maximization and its constituent parts are consumer sovereignty and productive and allocative efficiency. A model which assumes that individuals act as if they are rational may enable us to understand how our social and legal systems work even though the assumption at the individual level is counter-factual.

Similar theories have been advanced for the common law, most notably by Hayek.[33] Out of the case-by-case decisions of the judges springs up, according to Hayek, a 'spontaneous order'. In the same spirit economists have developed formal models to explain why the common law might evolve efficient laws over time even when the judiciary are not interested in economics or are even hostile to economics. These theories argue that the cases coming to court are not totally random and generate pressures for the evolution of more efficient law over time.[34] Although the details (and results) of these models differ among their various proponents, they essentially turn on the proposition that inefficient law creates large losses to one or the other party which will encourage him to litigate the case in order to get the law changed. Thus inefficient laws tend to be relitigated more often than efficient laws, and hence the probability that the law will be overturned is higher for those rules which are inefficient. Thus over time the body of law grows more efficient despite the wishes or predilections of the judges deciding these cases.

The idea that one can construct a unitary theory of the common law has been attacked from many quarters. It is to be found in Simpson's denial that the common law can be reduced to a system of rules and more recently by Epstein who has argued[35] that the individualized anarchic nature of common law litigation makes it an extremely uncertain vehicle for affecting social goals. Indeed, Epstein makes a rather 'odd' proposition for a libertarian, which I take him to be, namely that 'A single vision of an efficient system cannot emerge from such a haphazard and decentralised process.'[36] Simpson puts the point more forcefully:

> the common law is more like a muddle than a system. . . . The systematization of the common law – its reduction to a code of rules which satisfy accepted tests provided by other rules – is . . . an ideal . . . not a description of the *status quo*. It is the ideal of an expositor of the law, grappling with the untidy shambles of the law reports, the product of the common law mind which is repelled by brevity, lucidity and system. . . . But to portray the common law as actually conforming to this ideal is to confuse the aspirations of those who are attempting to arrest the collapse of a degenerate system of customary law with the reality.[37]

The same argument lies at the heart of critical legal studies which brings 'nihilism to center stage' and contends 'that there are no rational, objective criteria that can govern how we describe . . . [the legal] system'.[38]

These criticisms seem to miss their mark in a rather perverse way. For what they are saying is that a social or legal system that is individualistic and has no explicit set of objectives defies rational explanation and cannot be subject to theoretical analysis. The above discussion of invisible-hand theories shows this idea to be wrong and it is precisely because of the apparent purposelessness of the common law that a theory is required. This type of criticism takes a very literal interpretation of the law and theory that virtually amounts to the proposition that if a statement or theory is not obviously evident it is wrong.

What Counts as an Explanation

The major difficulty with the attempt to use economics as an interpretive device is not so much its premises as what will count as an adequate explanation – or more accurately, how does one rigorously test the theory? This is an issue that plagues all theories of law and one to which I see no easy resolution if the parameters of the debate are confined to the doctrinal analysis of the law as a closed system.

Consider Posner's strong hypothesis that the common law can be explained as if judges seek to maximize wealth. What does this mean? How is the theory to be tested? Invariably the theory is interpreted as a descriptive empirical claim which can be tested by collecting data on costs and benefits to determine whether a particular legal rule is efficient. If this is the theory then it is easily refuted and, perhaps what is more to the point, there is negligible evidence to support it some 12 years after it was originally advanced. It follows that if the theory is to remain viable it must not make an empirical claim that the law reduces costs. Also from what has been said above, it is not an adequate 'test' of the theory to search for instances where the courts have used efficiency-like statements or reasoning.

The methodological underpinnings of the economic interpretation of tort are hard to reconcile with positivism. According to Friedman, positive theories seek to make predictions about the consequences of change and to test those predictions by a procedure known as falsification. That is, it must be possible to design a test of a positive theory which is capable of falsifying it. Foremost in the mind of a positive economist is not the question whether the theory is 'right' but how to subject the theory to numerous tests with the object of refuting it.[39] This is well-nigh impossible when applied to the interpretation of legal doctrine. Law is not quantitative but a subtle qualitative data-base which must be interpreted, and this is very much a subjective exercise. The uncertain and subjective nature of the data makes any positivistic analysis fruitless according to Kelvin's dictum (as inscribed on the front of the Social Science Research Building at the University of Chicago: 'When you cannot express it in numbers, your knowledge is of a meagre and unsatisfactory kind'). This ambiguity about what is to be tested, how it is to be tested and the unusual nature of the data calls into question attempts to retreat into the strictures of positive economics, particularly the irrelevance of realistic assumptions.

The negative nature of falsificationism ensures that it will not be followed. And this is in fact the situation with much of the new law-and-economics. Posner's model is 'tested' not by rigorous empirical analysis but by what is sometimes referred to as 'crude verificationism'.[40] That is, selected cases are discussed which 'illustrate' a coincidence between the economics of a particular problem and the way the judges have reasoned or decided. In fact much of the application of economics to politics, sociology and law takes this form. The power of the models is demonstrated by application to new areas previously thought impervious to economics and this alone is taken as evidence of the strength and utility of the approach.[41] This is not a problem confined to economics, nor does economics fare badly when the procedures used to support non-economic theories of tort are used. The general criticism of all this work is that simply to show that something can be explained in terms of the theory is not enough. What must be demonstrated is that the economic explanation and redefinition of legal concepts generates new insights and hitherto unrecognized relationships between what were previously thought to be disparate, inconsistent areas of law.

The evolutionary nature of the common law also points to another difficulty inherent in any theory of tort law. Such theories can never provide comprehensive explanations of the law or 'explain' the details of every case. If the law is in a state of flux and development then there will always be cases and doctrines that cannot be explained by the theory.[42] This problem is compounded by the nature of the data. Thus even the best theory will not be able to explain everything, if only because it is a simplification. It must, therefore, always be true that there is a significant subset of cases that are not explained by the theory. What is required is, to borrow some terms from statistics, an idea of the strength of correlation between the law and the economic explanation and what confidence we can have in the 'predicted' relationship.

There are no simple answers to the data and testing problems raised by positive theories of law which rely exclusively on the interpretation of legal doctrine as the data and sole test of their validity. If the theory does in fact make a quantitative empirical claim - tort deters accidents or reduces costs - then we have, in principle at least, a clear idea of the type of data and test needed to refute the theory.

I have come to the conclusion that attempts to retreat into the strictures of positivism are misguided and that to the extent that economics does make a contribution to our understanding of the law it is due not to the scientific status of the enterprise but more modestly to the rigour of its logic, the economic way of thinking and the new language and concepts that it offers the lawyer. It is simply a different approach to the same material.

III   ECONOMIC VERSUS LEGAL REASONING

It is often claimed that lawyers and economists think and argue in radically different ways. Anyone familiar with both camps will find this easy to accept. In one sense law as an academic discipline is parasitic on the social sciences, philosophy and other disciplines such as psychology precisely because it does not have a well-developed theoretical framework. Yet many of the alleged differences between lawyers and economists are more apparent than real and the subject of a great deal of misunderstanding. For example, it is folklore amongst economists that lawyers (and the law) are concerned with justice defined in some abstract sense such as truth or just deserts, and that lawyers think in terms of absolutes and on/off solutions instead of the marginal analysis that is the basic gruel of the economist. It is therefore worthwhile to explore some of the major differences and similarities between legal reasoning and economic reasoning.

Economic analysis provides lawyers with a totally new set of terms, concepts and analytical techniques. Concepts such as choice, the costs and benefits of alternative courses of action, trade-offs, incentive effects, marginal analysis, externalities, optimal care and the cheapest cost avoider become the basis for each discussion of tort law.[43] Areas of tort law tend to be treated in terms of functional categories such as distinctions between care and activity levels,[44] alternative and joint care,[45] accidents between strangers and those occurring in situations where the parties have a pre-existing 'exchange' relationship.[46] The legal theorist is thus offered a different vocabulary and categories which can be used to redefine and critically appraise legal terms. For example, the way courts determine whether the defendant has breached his standard of care in negligence will be recast in terms of the costs and benefits of accident prevention, and the judicial test given an apparently quantitative precision.[47] This redefinition of fault can then be applied to interpret the case-law and to see whether other legal concepts can be rationalized in similar terms.

The (literary) devices used to extend the application of economics to law and other subjects are ones common in legal reasoning: analogy and metaphor. An 'important metaphor in economics', states McCloskey, 'has the quality admired in a successful scientific theory, a capacity to astonish us with important implications yet unseen.'[48] For example, consider the way economists have applied standard price theory to the analysis of crime. An individual's participation in crime is treated in the same way as the choice of one's job. A rational individual will engage in crime if the net returns (pecuniary and other) are greater than legitimate uses of his labour. Criminal sanctions act as a 'tax' on crime which, all other things being equal, decreases the attractiveness of a criminal career and/or the level of participation in criminal activity.[49] In short, there is an implicit market in crime where the criminals are seen to 'supply' crime and victims to 'demand' crime prevention. Metaphors like this recast the law in a new light and enable the theorist to model an area of law by simple application of standard price theory.

The treatment of crime and tort in these terms appears strained because it is unusual and perhaps even offensive to some. But the metaphors of the marketplace are deeply embedded in the (moral) language used to describe crime and punishment: 'pay the price for his misdeeds', 'reap your rewards', 'the wages of sin', 'pay his debt to society' and so on. Moreover, the predominant sanction of the common law is financial damages and the fine is the cornerstone of the Anglo-American penal system. These legal sanctions can be viewed as a penalty or, alternatively, as a price for the right to engage in the activity, just as the price of a loaf of bread can be viewed as measuring its value, giving producers a reward and incentive to produce bread, penalizing the consumer who buys bread for making a call on society's scarce resources and/or deterring those from consuming bread who do not value it very highly or cannot afford it. Just because something is called a price, penalty or civil or criminal sanction should not seduce us into thinking that the mere label necessarily carries with it analytical and behavioural differences.

Treating the law as another aspect of the pricing system forces a broad analysis of the law, revealing the formal rules of law as only one complementary component of a system in which the impact and nature of law depends crucially on legal procedures and non-legal factors. In the private law area the parties have the option of not using the courts, and quantitatively most of those with meritorious cases settle their disputes without the assistance of a judge. The common law system operates by discouraging people from litigating and it surely must be one of the oddities of English legal education that undergraduates are rarely taught legal procedure and that so much of their formal training is devoted to doctrinal analysis and appellate disputations which comprise a minor part of the output and activity of the legal system.

Economic analysis obviously collapses fundamental legal distinctions by employing functional categories and this carries with it the danger of gross simplification and distortion of the law. The economist will treat a tort and a crime as specific examples of the same analytical category of an externality – that is, an act which imposes an uncompensated loss on an individual. Externalities imply inefficiency because the party causing the harm is not taking into account the full costs of his actions. Law is little more than a rule which allocates costs and benefits between individuals. While it cannot be disputed that this is the effect of the law, many will deny that the legal system can be properly understood by taking such a primitive view of law. Nonetheless, this altered perspective does suggest explanations for certain features of the common law. For example, consider the following. Why are criminals incarcerated and tortfeasors not? The answer some economists have given is that pure compensatory penalties are an insufficient deterrent because criminals, especially those committing serious crimes, may be judgment-proof.[50] Why is the criminal law publicly enforced? One economic explanation is because it is cheaper due to economies of scale in the detection and apprehension of criminals and that private enforcement through a system of bounties would lead to over-enforcement of the law.[51] Why are defendants often open to both criminal and civil actions in cases of assault and battery? Again, because purely compensatory damages would only make the tortfeasor indifferent between intentionally inflicting harm and the substitute voluntary transaction. To provide an adequate deterrent damages must exceed the harm to the victim.[52]

Many have regarded and will regard economic analysis as claiming that the common law has no moral basis and does not serve to express society's moral precepts. In one respect this is correct. Economists do not have a comparative advantage in dealing with moral issues, although moral principles are amenable to economic analysis. For the most part the economist assumes that preferences are given and do not change over time. The law therefore serves no educative role in creating good citizens by providing a ready-made moral code.[53] Put in an extreme form, in the economic framework the only effect of law is to alter the distribution of costs and benefits, and individuals only comply with the law when it 'pays' in terms of the avoidance of the penalties inflicted on wrongdoers. This, however, does not deny that, say, a tort and a crime are morally very different acts. Only that economics is concerned not with the law's morality but with its effects. Notwithstanding this, any normative discussion of the law must consider the costs of enforcing legal rights and the wider economic effects of those legal rights. The magnitude and distribution of costs and benefits among individuals is equal in importance to the question of how rights should be assigned. For the man in the street the most scandalous injustices are those surrounding the costs and uncertainties of litigation, which deny all but the wealthy access to the common law. Justice and morality are not matters of pure legal form or philosophical theory; they are also empirical concepts.

Another difference between doctrinal analysis and economic reasoning is that the latter is instrumental, consequential reasoning; choices are evaluated in terms of tradeoffs between desired or practical goals.[54] The economist is usually interested only in the pattern of end-states. This follows from the rationality postulate. Tort lawyers, on the other hand, do not think in terms of objectives nor do judges openly state what objective they or the law is seeking to achieve.[55] As a consequence when lawyers venture outside the realm of doctrine their utterances are frequently *ad hoc*, unsystematic and swamped by vague claims about injustice, inconsistency and undesirable trends which are as question-begging as the judicial formulations they criticize. The instrumental nature of economic reasoning produces a more systematic and sophisticated treatment of the relationships between ends and means, and prevents the theorist from making *ad hoc* claims without showing how they relate to other propositions and other aspects of the problem.

Something has already been said about the role of assumptions in economic model-building. Economists not only make assumptions but are very good at identifying the necessary and sufficient assumptions required for the validity of an argument or proposition. A considerable amount of legal analysis, and indeed the law, proceeds on the basis of assumptions that are never stated or are merely asserted to be true. The most notorious judicial example of this is the 'floodgates' of litigation argument which has been used until recently to deny recovery for pure economic loss and emotional shock. This justification for denying recovery is an empirical proposition which the judges have made no attempt empirically to verify or to examine the logical consistency of the various arguments underpinning their analysis. Economics forces one to state explicitly one's assumptions and premises.

Another major difference between economic and legal reasoning has to do with time frames. For the most part the common law is a reactive method of law. It reacts to situations and its primary function is to resolve disputes, which usually means that the harm complained of has already occurred. Lawyers naturally take an *ex post* view of the law. They see the law as a system of rules, a method of dispute-resolution and a set of rights dictated by fundamental notions of justice. Adjudication tends to be treated in legal discussions as an on/off affair and legal disputes as having a zero-sum quality, i.e. what is at issue is the distribution of a known loss between two parties.

The economist takes a longer view. Law is seen principally as an incentive system which affects the behavior of individuals. The law imposes costs, constrains behaviour and provides a framework for the protection and reward of individuals who have recognized legal rights. The emphasis is on the incentive effects of the law. This focuses attention on the adaptive responses of individuals to the law. Lawyers too often talk about the law as if the mere distillation of a legal principle from the cases leads to full compliance by those to whom the law is addressed. Economic analysis is not given to such formalism, although there is a tendency to reduce the law to a system of rules. The approach emphasizes the intimate connection between legal rules and the way they are enforced and the remedies available to the parties. A rule or doctrine of law cannot be understood or even defined unless the remedies and level of enforcement are known. The whole nature of a legal rule is determined by the form and intensity of its enforcement. A law which is uncertain and imperfectly enforced is a different law in terms of consequences from one that is concise, clear and vigorously enforced. If this approach is taken it enables the theorists to see equivalences between laws which are radically different. For example, if on the one hand outlawing prostitution and, on the other, introducing a system that allows it, but places a 30 per cent sales tax on each 'transaction', leads to the same level of prostitution then these laws are substitutes for one another.[56] Economics prevents the legal theorist from concentrating exclusively on the formal law, thereby ignoring the fact that in practice the effects and nature of the law may be quite different.

Legal doctrines can also only be understood in relation to the ability of individuals to reorder their activities in the light of the law. This is obvious in contract law where legal restrictions on the ability of parties to incorporate certain terms, such as exclusion clauses, will lead to adjustments in other contractual terms, such as price, that preserve the bargaining advantages of the seller, albeit in a more roundabout and possibly more expensive way. This rejection of formalism also leads to a clearer appreciation of the role of legal remedies. For example, the critical literature on the law of nuisance has often claimed that the injunction is a blunt instrument because it freezes land use, and that the doctrinal framework does not take sufficient account of the benefits of the defendants' activities.[57] The most extreme case of this kind is *Bellew* v. *Cement Co. Ltd*,[58] where the court awarded the plaintiff an injunction that would have halted the operations of the only cement-producer in the Irish Republic at a time when building was an urgent public necessity. The courts seem in these rights-based torts often not to 'balance the equities' in a way that would be implied by economic consideration. This, however, overlooks the fact that in many of these situations the parties are in a position to bargain both before and after litigation. The judges determine, not a final solution which imposes on the parties some immutable set of consequences, but the starting-points for negotiations between the disputing parties. A great deal of the law of nuisance can be viewed as a framework for bargaining, either preventively if the law is clear, or after the injunction has been granted.[59] It is naive to assume, as does much legal discussion, that when the stakes at hand are so disproportionate and the defendant stands to lose so much, as in *Bellew*, he would not be driven to bargain with the plaintiff.

The systematic considerations of the private reordering of relationships between individuals in the shadow of the law pervades the whole of the economic approach. The most sophisticated formulation is the so-called Coase theorem.[60] Cast in terms of nuisance law, the Coase theorem states that land will be put to the same uses regardless of whether a nuisance is actionable or not, provided the parties can bargain at negligible costs (the 'zero transaction costs' assumption). The assumption of zero transaction costs dramatically alters the legal theorist's perception of the relevant facts. When transaction costs are zero all problems in tort law become an aspect of contract. Tort arises from the inability of the parties to bargain. Thus the analyst is required to explain why and how bargaining is distorted in the real world. The Coase theorem leads, as Ackerman brilliantly describes, to a 'reconstruction of the facts'.[61] Instead of restricting attention to the conduct and activities of the parties at the time of the accident or harm, economic analysis forces the lawyer to go back much further in time to a point before the dispute when the parties had an opportunity to reorganize their activities. It considers the question: Was there a reorganization which could have taken place that would either have avoided the dispute or minimized the resultant losses? This way of looking at cases – a natural concomitant to the behavioural nature of economics – jars with traditional tort scholarship, which is backward-looking but, I would argue, no more than superficially.

The Coase theorem also indicates that causation is not helpful in assigning liability in tort. The information that A injured B carries with it no natural attribution of who caused the loss, because harm is inherently reciprocal in character.[62] Accident losses and the expenses of the tort system are the result of the interaction of two conflicting or interfering activities and therefore are the joint cost of both activities. This suggests that all victims are partly the authors of their own misfortune. But the issue here is to recognize, as tort law does, that what is primarily at issue is a conflict of interests, a clash between the right (desire?) of the defendant to carry on his activities and that of the plaintiff to be free of interference from the defendant's activities. As long as both activities are regarded as socially desirable the loss needs to be allocated in a way that does not unduly reduce the joint benefits. In terms of the legal choice that has to be made, the 'harm' is reciprocal in character: to permit the defendant to continue is to harm the plaintiff; to decide in favour of the plaintiff inflicts harm on the defendant. This is recognized to varying degrees in the law of torts, most notably in the fault concept, which is the linchpin of liability in tort.

IV THE ECONOMIC CHARACTER OF COMMON LAW ADJUDICATION

The principal reason for the plausibility of the economic interpretation of tort law is that in an important sense common law adjudication has an economic character. Judges reason in an 'economic' way even if they do not speak in the language of economics. They must decide between the competing interests of the plaintiff and the defendant, they must balance their claims and in the end, by deciding in favour of one of the parties, they trade off the relative merits of the litigants' respective claims. This judgmental process is 'economic' in the following sense: a choice has been made after balancing the parties' interests. This may seem a sleight of hand since a consistency between the two has been achieved by regarding economics as synonymous with choice, in which case, it will be asserted, of course the law is 'economic' but this claim is neither a startling nor a novel finding.

However, the claim is a substantial one and not a semantic ploy. The adversarial style of common law adjudication forces the lawyer and judge to think in terms not of absolutes but of incrementalism or of what economists would call marginal analysis. The judge determines whether or not the defendant has acted unreasonably and makes a binary choice: guilty or not. But this emphasis on the rule disguises the way the courts determine fault and how counsel presents his client's case. To establish fault the plaintiff has to convince the judge that on the balance of probabilities the defendant did not act with reasonable care. In much of the law of negligence and nuisance interests are balanced and the merits of the disputants' claims are evaluated to determine who has the right to prevail. The courts in effect engage in a 'cost-benefit' analysis and they make choices. As Posner has recently emphasized, cost-benefit analysis 'at least describes the judgmental process' of the courts in tort cases.[63] Even though a judge's decision is binary and is expressed in terms of rights and legal duties, the basis on which he decides and the process by which he arrives at this decision is very similar to the way an economist would *approach* the problem. Thus the ability to apply economic reasoning to tort inheres in the nature of the law itself. There should therefore be nothing extraordinary in the idea that economics can contribute to a deeper understanding of the judgmental process of the common law.

This is most clearly seen in the determination of the legal standard of care in negligence. Much has been made of the Learned Hand test which reduces the defendants' culpability to a quantitative test that balances the burden of adequate precautions against the likelihood of an accident multiplied by the gravity of the harm should the accident occur.[64] This test encapsulates the main considerations used by the courts in England and other Commonwealth countries, and most casebooks and texts use the three factors (risks, precautions and gravity) to organize their discussion of the cases.[65] The Hand formula can be regarded as a convenient summary of some of the factors relevant to determining whether the defendant has breached his duty.

The principal value of the economic version of the Hand formula is that it enables one to think systematically about the interplay between the three components of the Hand test and points to a greater consistency and subtlety in the law's recognition of costs and tradeoffs. The cases of *Haley* v. *London Electricity Board*,[66] *Paris* v. *Stepney Borough Council*[67] and *Latimer* v. *AEC*[68] are English cases that can be cited. The last is of particular interest since it illustrates the incremental nature of judicial reasoning. The respondent's factory was flooded by an unusually heavy rainstorm causing the floor to become slippery. There was insufficient sawdust to cover the entire floor and as a result the appellant slipped, injuring his ankle. The issue before the court was whether the respondent should have closed the factory rather than let his employees run the risk of slipping. It was held that the risks were so low as not to impose on a reasonable employer the additional obligation to shut down the factory for the night. Here the court was, in effect, comparing the costs of an additional precaution against the reduction in the risk of injury that it would bring about. Also, the Hand formula stresses that the courts are more likely to find the defendant liable if the risk is high, the costs of precaution low and/or the gravity of the harm high and the way it would trade off these factors. For example, an action which was relatively cheap to undertake would tend to attract liability even if the risk was low, provided that the gravity of harm was high. In the *Wagon Mound (No. 2)*[69] Lord Reid (implicitly) examined the question of the foreseeability of harm in terms of the Hand formula. He related the risk to the difficulty of precautions, stating that a 'real risk' which is 'remote' is not for that reason alone 'not reasonably foreseeable' 'when it is easy to prevent'.

The economists' functional distinction between care and activity levels is also recognized in the law of torts. This is illustrated by *Daborn* v. *Bath Tramways*.[70] The plaintiff was driving a lefthand-drive ambulance during a time of emergency and was hit from behind by a bus whilst attempting to execute a right-hand turn. Here the court made two economic calculations. Given the existence of lefthand-drive ambulances, did the plaintiff exercise sufficient care (Hand test)? The second was: do the benefits of lefthand ambulances outweigh their social costs? The court stated that a sufficiently important purpose 'justifies the assumption of abnormal risk'. The distinction between care and activity levels can be employed in other areas. In nuisance law the care/activity distinction is evident. The locality test stated in *St Helens* v. *Tipping*,[71] that what is a nuisance in one area need not be so in another and that it is for the courts to decide, effectively compares the total social benefits and costs of conflicting activities. Negligence or malice or the fact that the defendant's activity has no social utility may be weighed by the courts, but the fact that the defendant has taken reasonable care to abate the nuisance is not an adequate defence. Economic theory indicates that this is correct because the question has to be considered at two levels: do we want activity A and B together and what care should each party exercise? It is not economically sensible to have a munitions factory operating with the highest safety standards next to the Houses of Parliament. If reasonable care were an adequate defence we would get this solution even though the best solution is to locate the munitions factory in an area where it can do the least damage.

There are other features of tort law which fit in neatly with economics. The assignment of liability in much of the law of tort is conduct based. That is, the courts look at the conduct of the defendant and the plaintiff relative to the norm of the reasonable man to determine whether the defendant should bear the loss. The loss-allocation process fixes on the behaviour of the parties, as does the economic approach. This is treated differently by lawyer and economist. The lawyer looks at conduct to allocate the loss according to the common law rules. The economist looks at the problem the other way around: how does the allocation of losses affect conduct. It is a forward-looking approach; an incentive analysis. In one respect the law in practice recognizes this. The defendant's actions are evaluated not on the assumption that he had perfect knowledge and must guard against all risks but in terms of what is reasonably foreseeable. Negligence depends on foreseeability: the foresight the reasonable man in the circumstances of the defendant has exercised to take account of and avoid harm. Thus the judicial enquiry is backward only superficially, as indicated by the fact that in negligence the risk or likelihood of injury is an important factor.

The argument can be pushed further. In substantial areas of the law incentive analysis has been used by the courts and has been the critical factor. The doctrine of common employment and the pre-1880 common law of employers' liability were heavily influenced by incentive arguments concerning the effects of the rules on wage rates and accident-prevention. Denial and limitations of recovery for economic loss and emotional shock can only be explained by the endorsement by judges of the 'floodgates of litigation' fear that to allow recovery would lead to a mass of claims. My own interpretation is that incentive analysis is pervasive in the common law reasoning, especially in areas where the common law is currently expanding.

NOTES

I would like to thank John Boal and William Twining for comments on an earlier draft of this chapter. This chapter develops some themes found in two of my earlier articles: 'The Role of Economics in the Common Law' [1985] *Research Law and Economics* 41; 'Economic Theorising About Tort' [1985] *Current Legal Problems*, p. 71.

1 Calabresi, 'Some Thoughts on Risk Distribution and the Law of Torts' (1961) 70 *Yale Law J* 499 at p. 500.
2 McCloskey, 'The Rhetoric of Economics' (1983) 21 *J Econ. Literature* 481 at p. 501.
3 R. Rabin (ed.), *Perspectives on Tort law* (2nd edn; 1983); R. A. Posner, *Tort: Cases and Economic Analysis* (1982); M. Kuperberg and C. Beitz (eds), *Law, Economics, and Philosophy: A Critical Introduction with Applications to the Law of Torts* (1983); A. I. Ogus and C. G. Veljanovski (eds), *Readings in the Economics of Law and Regulation* (1984). Also references cited in C. G. Veljanovski, *Economics of the Common Law: A Bibliography* (1984).
4 Professor Atiyah observes: 'English judges are emphatically neither intellectuals nor theorists . . . most are deeply sceptical of the value of theory.' P. S. Atiyah, 'The Legacy of Holmes Through English Eyes' (1983) 63 *Boston University Law Rev.* 341 at p. 380.

234 Cento Veljanovski

This is confirmed by Lord Denning's view of jurisprudence: 'Jurisprudence was too abstract a subject for my liking. All about ideologies, legal norms, basic norms, 'ought' and 'is', realism and behaviourism, and goodness knows what else. The jargon of philosophers of law has always been beyond me.' Denning, *The Family Story* (1981) p. 38. Also A. Paterson, *The Law Lords* (1982) ch. 2. Cf. Professor (now Judge) Easterbrook's conclusion: 'The Justices [of the US Supreme Court] are more sophisticated in economic reasoning, and they apply it in a more thoroughgoing way, than at any time in our history.' Easterbrook, 'Foreword: The Court and the Economic System' (1984) 98 *Harvard Law Rev.* 4 at p. 45. cf Aronson, 'Judicial Control of the Political Branches: Public Purpose and Public Law' (1985) 4 *Cato Journal* 719.

5 See symposium issues 'Change in the Common Law: Legal and Economic Perspectives' (1980) 9 *J Legal Studies* 189; 'Efficiency as a Legal Concern' (1980) 8 *Hofstra Law Rev.* 485–972.
6 Baldwin and Veljanovski, 'Regulation by Cost-Benefit Analysis' (1984) 62 *Public Administration*, p. 51.
7 Discussions of different uses of economics in legal analysis can be found in Komesar, 'In Search of a General Approach to Legal Analysis: A Comparative Institutional Alternative' (1981) 79 *Michigan Law Rev.* 1350; Kornhauser, 'The Great Image of Authority' (1984) 36 *Stanford Law Rev.* 349.
8 Posner, 'A Theory of Negligence' (1972) 1 *J Legal Studies* 29; R. A. Posner, *Economic Analysis of Law* (2nd edn; 1977); Landes and Posner, The Positive Economic Theory of Tort Law' (1981) 15 *Georgia Law Rev.* 851.
9 R. S. Markovits, 'Legal Analysis and the Economic Analysis of Allocative Efficiency' (1980) 8 *Hofstra Law Rev.* 811.
10 Posner, 'The Present Situation in Legal Scholarship' (1981) 90 Yale *Law J* 1113.
11 G. Calabresi, *The Costs of Accidents: A Legal and Economic Analysis* (1970).
12 Chelius, 'Liability for Industrial Accidents: A Comparison of Negligence and Strict Liability' (1976) 5 *J Legal Studies* 293 Higgins, 'Producers' Liability and Product-Related Accidents' (1978) 7 *J Legal Studies* 299; Landes, 'Insurance, Liability and Accidents: A Theoretical and Empirical Investigation of the Effect of No-Fault on Accidents' (1982) 25 *J Legal Studies* 49.
13 Posner, 'Utilitarianism, Economics and Legal Theory' (1979) 8 *J Legal Studies* 103; R. A. Posner, *The Economics of Justice* (1981).
14 Leff, 'Economic Analysis of Law: Some Realism About Nominalism' (1974) 60 *Virginia Law Rev.* 451. The view is shared by Coase: 'Economics and Contiguous Disciplines' (1978) 7 *J Legal Studies* 201.
15 The law of demand holds that there is an inverse relationship between the quantity of a good demanded and the price. The law of supply holds that there is a positive relationship between the willingness of producers to produce and supply a commodity and the price.
16 'The foresight of the reasonable man is in one sense an impersonal test. It eliminates the personal equation and is independent of the idiosyncrasies of the particular person whose conduct is in question.' *Glasgow Corporation* v. *Muir* [1943] AC 448 at p. 457, *per* Lord Macmillan.
17 M. Friedman, 'The Methodology of Positive Economics' in his *Essays in Positive Economics* (1953).
18 'Truly important and significant hypothesis', states Friedman, 'will be found to have "assumptions" that are wildly inaccurate descriptions of reality, and, in general, the more significant the theory, the more unrealistic the assumptions (in this sense).' *Id.*, p. 14.
19 'As a general proposition it has not, I think, been questioned for nearly two hundred years that in determining the rights *inter se* A and B, the fact that one of them is insured

is to be disregarded.' *Lister* v. *Romford Ice & Cold Storage Co. Ltd* [1957] 1 All ER 125 at p. 133, *per* Viscount Simonds. This compares with Denning's dictum in *Nettleship* v. *Weston* [1971] 3 All ER 125 at p. 133, that a high standard of care is imposed on motorists today because of compulsory insurance and that 'this branch of the law [is] moving away from the concept: "no liability without fault". We are beginning to apply the test: "on whom should the risk fall?".'

20 'Few questions', states Hart, 'concerning human society have been asked with such persistence and answered by serious thinkers in so many diverse, strange, and even paradoxical ways as the question "What is law?"' H. L. A. Hart, *The Concept of Law* (rev. edn; 1972) p. 1.

21 A. W. B. Simpson, 'The Common Law and Legal Theory' (chapter 2 above) p. 17.

22 *Id.*, p. 24. 'The conceptual structure of tort law', states Atiyah, 'is a disorganised and ramshackle affair.' P. S. Atiyah, *Accidents, Compensation and the Law* (3rd edn; 1980) pp. 35–6.

23 *Blyth* v. *Birmingham Waterworks* (1856) 156 ER 1047 at p. 1049.

24 *Donoghue* v. *Stevenson* [1932] AC 562 at p. 580.

25 *Overseas Tankship (United Kingdom) Ltd* v. *Miller Steamship Co. Pty Ltd (The Wagon Mound No. 2)* [1967] 1 AC 617 at p. 642.

26 Hart, *op. cit.*, p. 87.

27 England, 'The System Builders – A Critical Appraisal of Modern American Tort Theory' (1980) 9 *J Legal Studies* 27 at p. 52.

28 Guest, 'The Economic Analysis of Law' [1984] *Current Legal Problems* 233 at p. 244.

29 Cooter, 'Law and the Imperialism of Economics: An Introduction to the Economic Analysis of Law and a Review of the Major Books' (1982) 29 *U.C.L.A. Law Rev.* 1260 at p. 1266.

30 Abel, 'A Critique of American Tort Theory' (1981) 8 *Brit. J Law and Society* 199. Cf. Pound, 'The Economic Interpretation of the Law of torts' (1940) 53 *Harvard Law Rev.* 365.

31 Schwartz, 'Tort Law and the Economy in Nineteenth-Century America: A Reinterpretation' (1981) 90 *Yale Law J* 1717; Rabin, 'The Historical Development of the Fault Principle: A Reinterpretation' (1980) 15 *Georgia Law Rev.* 925.

32 The classic use of the invisible-hand mechanism to support positive economic theorizing is A. A. Alchian, 'Uncertainty, Evolution, and Economic Theory' in *Economic Forces at Work* (1977) ch. 1.

33 F. von Hayek, *Law, Legislation and Liberty*, 3 vols (1973–9).

34 Rubin, 'Why is the Common Law Efficient? (1977) 6 *J Legal Studies* 51; Priest 'The Common Law Process and the Selection of Efficient Rules' (1977) 6 *J Legal Studies* 65; Elliot, 'The Evolutionary Tradition in Jurisprudence' (1985) 85 *Columbia Law Rev.* 35.

35 Epstein, 'The Social Consequences of Common Law Rules' (1982) 95 *Harvard Law Rev.* 1717.

36 *Id.*, p. 1743.

37 Simpson, *op. cit.*, p. 24.

38 Singer, 'The Player and the Cards: Nihilism and Legal Theory' (1984) 94 *Yale Law J* 1 at p. 5.

39 M. Blaug, *The Methodology of Economics* (1980). Also Jackson, 'The Economic Explanation of Legal Phenomena' (1984) 4 *International Rev. Law and Economics* 163.

40 Blaug, *op. cit.*, ch. 3.

41 *Id.*, ch. 14.

42 An apposite analogy to the common law is offered by Hoebel when he likens it to 'channels' which 'shift and bend like the course of a meandering river across the bed

of a flat flood plain, though flowing ever in a given direction.' E. A. Hoebel, *The Law of Primitive Man* (1967) p. 283.

43 See 'Symposium: The Place of Economics in Legal Education' (1983) 33 *J Legal Education* 183, *passim*.

44 See, for example, S. Shavell, 'Strict Liability and Negligence' (1980) 9 *J Legal Studies* 1.

45 Landes and Posner, *op. cit.*, pp. 865–85.

46 E.g. D. Harris and C. G. Veljanovski, 'Liability for Economic Loss in Tort' in *The Law of Torts: Policies and Trends* (1985, ed. H. Beale and M. Furmston).

47 *United States* v. *Carroll Towing Co.*, 159 F. 2d 169, 173 (2d Cir. 1947).

48 McCloskey, *op. cit.*, p. 503.

49 Becker, 'Crime and Punishment: An Economic Approach' (1968) 76 *J Pol. Economy*, 169.

50 *Id.*

51 Landes and Posner, 'The Private Enforcement of Law' (1975) 4 *J Legal Studies* 1.

52 Calabresi and Melamed, 'Property Rules, Liability Rules and Inalienability: One View of the Cathedral' (1972) 85 *Harvard Law Rev.* 1089.

53 Reder, 'Chicago Economics: Permanence and Change' (1982) 20 *J Econ. Literature* 2.

54 Murphy and Coleman argue: 'the economic analysis of law is apparently committed to legal realism as a jurisprudential thesis. For it is essential to the enterprise that judges decide cases according to the dictates of efficiency, rather than in accordance with any set of pre-existing claims that one litigant may have against another. In addition, economic analysis is an instrumental theory of law, since it views litigation in terms of the opportunities claimants give the courts to promote global or collective interests.' J. Murphy and J. Coleman, *The Philosophy of Law: An Introduction to Jurisprudence* (1984) p. 237.

55 Williams, 'The Aims of the Law of Tort' [1951] *Current Legal Problems* 137.

56 The example is borrowed from Friedman's provocative article: 'Two Faces of Law' [1984] *Wisconsin Law Rev.* 13.

57 Eg. Ogus and Richardson, 'Economics and the Environment: A Study of Private Nuisance' (1977) 36 *Cambridge Law J* 284.

58 *Bellew* v. *Cement Co. Ltd.* [1948] IR 62.

59 Thompson, 'Injunction Negotiations: An Economic, Moral and Legal Analysis' (1975) 27 *Stanford Law Rev.* 1563; Polinsky, 'Resolving Nuisance Disputes: The Simple Economics of Injunctive and Damage Remedies' (1980) 32 *Stanford Law Rev.* 1075.

60 Coase, 'The Problem of Social Cost' (1960) 3 *J Law and Economics* 1. Also Calabresi, 'Concerning Cause and the Law of Tort'. (1975/6) 43 *University of Chicago Law Rev.* 69.

61 B. Ackerman, *Reconstructing American Law* (1983) ch. 4.

62 For criticism of the economic approach to causation see: Epstein, 'Nuisance Law: Corrective Justice and Its Utilitarian Constraints' (1979) 8 *J Legal Studies* 49; H. L. A. Hart and A. Honoré, *Causation in the Law* (2nd edn; 1985) pp. lxvii–lxxxi.

63 Posner, 'Wealth Maximization and Judicial Decision-making' (1984) 4 *International Rev. Law and Economics* 131 at p. 134.

64 *Supra*, n. 47.

65 Hand-like statements of the 'breach of duty' test can be found in *Mackintosh* v. *Mackintosh* 2 M 1357 (1864); *Ryan* v. *Fisher* (1976) 51 ALJR 125; *Morris* v. *West Hartlepool Steam Navig. Co.* [1956] HL 574/5. A number of casebooks and texts covering the principal common law jurisdictions are organized around the Hand formula: B. Hepple and M. Matthews, *Tort – Cases and Materials* (2nd edn; 1980) ch. 4; R. A. Posner, *Tort Law – Cases and Economic Analysis* (1983); A. Linden, *Canadian Tort Law* (1977) pp. 80–90; H. Luntz *et al.*, *Torts: Cases and Commentary* (1980) ch. 3.

66 [1965] AC 778.
67 [1951] AC 367.
68 *Latimer* v. *AEC Ltd* [1952] 2 QB 701.
69 *Supra* n. 25.
70 *Daborn* v. *Bath Tramways Motor Co. Ltd* [1946] 2 All ER 333 (CA).
71 *St Helens* v. *Tipping* (1865) 11 HLC 642.

13
Theory in the Law Curriculum

NEIL MACCORMICK
AND WILLIAM TWINING

To be sure, there are lawyers, judges and even law professors who tell us
that they have no legal philosophy. In law, as in other things, we shall
find that the only difference between a person 'without a philosophy' and
someone with a philosophy is that the latter knows what his philosophy is.

Filmer Northrop[1]

Once upon a time the School of Law in Xanadu celebrated its fifth anniversary
by holding a curriculum discussion. Having decided not to take facts seriously,[2]
they had salved their consciences with a compulsory final year course in jurisprudence, while making most other courses optional. On this occasion, uncertain
where to start, they decided to open the proceedings by debating whether jurisprudence should remain compulsory. Opinion was divided almost equally, as
appears from the following passage from the debate:

Why should intending lawyers be coerced into studying philosophy?
Do we really want our graduates to leave us unreflective, uncritical and unaware?
Students should have complete freedom of choice.
Students are not the best judges of what is good for them.
What relevance has Kelsen to drafting a conveyance?
Can someone who has not done Kelsen claim to be a member of a learned profession?
How embarrassing for learned counsel or a learned judge to have to ask: 'Who is
Ronald Dworkin?'
Legal theory is too hard for undergraduates.
Jurisprudence is a soft option, too vague and woolly to compete with hard law.
Our aim should be to train our students to think like lawyers, not philosophers.
How can anyone learn to think like a lawyer without studying legal reasoning?
There is no need for a specialized course in jurisprudence; we teach theory in every
course already.
There is no need for a specialized course in jurisprudence; law is a practical
art.
Jurisprudence is the most practical course in the whole curriculum.

Eventually the Oldest Member spoke up: 'All of your arguments are fallacious.
It is important that we should not do the right deed for the wrong reason.

Therefore let us consult some experts.' His colleagues disliked his premise, but liked his conclusion. So they decided to invite two teachers of jurisprudence of seemingly divergent views to justify their way of life. To the surprise of all, including the authors, they produced an almost unanimous report, from which the following extracts are taken:

INTRODUCTION

'. . . The question put to us was: 'Should we continue to have a compulsory course on jurisprudence in our curriculum?' We suggest that it is appropriate to restate the issue as follows: 'What learning objectives might be served by making the direct study of legal theory an integral part of an undergraduate degree programme in law?' There are two different kinds of reasons for this reformulation. First, the issue is posed in general terms, because any specific decisions on a particular curriculum inevitably involve local factors such as the interests (vested and intellectual), expertise, personalities and prejudices of the existing faculty and the educational background, attitudes and predominant motives of its students. Specific decisions about whether, when, how much and how legal theory should be directly studied have to be made in a particular context. Our task is to intellectualize the issue; it is for the locals to contextualize it.

Secondly, this kind of educational question deserves to be framed with a reasonable degree of precision. Our formulation is preferred for the following reasons: An educational question of this kind is better expressed in terms of learning objectives rather than courses and teaching; similarly 'programme' is preferred to 'curriculum' because the latter too often tends to be conceived largely in terms of coverage of particular subject-matters by teachers rather than in terms of a programme of study directed to a range of learning objectives. 'Direct study' is contrasted with incidental or pervasive or pick-it-up approaches in which the objectives or subject-matters in question are not the primary focus of attention: for example, when 'legal method' is left to be picked up or mastered while studying courses on torts or contracts or revenue law. Our phrasing also leaves open for consideration the question whether the relevant learning objectives should be pursued mainly or exclusively in a single course.

The phrase 'integral part' is less emotive than 'compulsory'. Both of us favour educational programmes that give wide scope to students to choose to pursue a range of objectives by diverse means in respect of a variety of subject-matters; but we also believe that, in first degrees in law, such choices are usually best made within a coherent structure with sufficient common ground as to objectives, subject-matter and methods to allow for integration of different parts of the programme, for sequencing of study and for a reasonably coherent and balanced educational experience for each student. A law school, especially one that seeks to develop a distinctive educational ethos, should aspire to be more like a restaurant than a cafeteria.

Thus as educators we tend to favour structured choice. In order to present a coherent argument about the educational values of studying legal theory we also have to make some further general assumptions about undergraduate legal education in this country as an educational enterprise, but at a more general level than that of a particular law school or programme. The issue cannot be totally decontextualized. However, before considering possible rationales for theory courses here, we propose to explore in general terms the nature of legal theory and some general claims that are sometimes made for theoretical studies.

THEORY WHAT?

Invite a dozen specialists in particular areas of law to discuss the relationship between legal theory and their area of expertise and they are likely to interpret the task in a number of different ways. This is rather clearly illustrated by the essays in _Legal Theory and Common Law_. Some contributors have treated it as an invitation to explore critically assumptions underlying orthodox or traditional modes of discourse in the relevant field; Veljanovski conceives the task of theory as giving a general empirical explanation of particular phenomena (in this case judicial decisions); Twining emphasizes the value of constructing coherent frames of reference; Simpson explores the relationship between the common law and a selection from the existing stock of theories of law; Cotterrell asks what kind of theory can provide a means of identifying and interpreting legal doctrine in the property field and general contemporary problems underlying analysis of such doctrine. Stokes attempts to show that a great deal of company law 'can be understood as a response to the problem of the legitimacy of corporate managerial power'.[3] Collins critically examines the claim that 'liberalism' provides a coherent basis for the law of contract. O'Donovan casts doubt on all attempts to explain family law solely in instrumental terms.

This diversity is perhaps not as great as it seems. All the contributors to this symposium have been selective; but they have all interpreted the invitation to look at their subject in general terms; some have explored underlying assumptions; some have related specialized discourses, such as contract or property talk, to standard bodies of inherited theory; they have chosen somewhat varied levels of generality, although all have been concerned with what Austin called 'particular Jurisprudence'.[4] But, we suggest, these seemingly different views of theory and theorizing are all intimately related.

Let us briefly consider four different perspectives on legal theorizing and legal theory. First, theorizing can be viewed as an activity directed to reflecting on, reasoning about and trying to answer general questions about laws, legal practices, legal institutions and processes and about the nature of law as a social phenomenon and as a subject of study.[5] Secondly, theorizing can be a matter of articulating, refining and critically examining important underlying assumptions and presuppositions of legal discourse. Thirdly, there is a received heritage or tradition of ideas about and approaches to the first two sets of topics, and theorizing involves critical appraisal, selection and exploitation of these ideas and approaches independently of their historical provenance. But, fourthly, the propounding and development of these ideas and approaches has a history of its own. Legal theory can be perceived as a vast body of literature, a heritage of texts and texts about texts, emanating from individuals and groups of thinkers who lived and worked and debated in particular contexts. Accordingly, theorizing may involve reading, interpreting and criticizing at least some of those texts in their historical settings. All of these perspectives are intimately related, but each merits special consideration.

Theorizing as Abstraction

Talk of theory is sometimes associated with mystery or pretentiousness. One can avoid this by looking on theorizing as nothing more than the business of asking and tackling general or abstract questions. Typically such questions have somehow or other come to be matters of interest or concern at a more or less particular or concrete level. Theorizing involves trying to get a better understanding of particulars by seeing them in a more abstract and general way. In this, the movement of our thought is nearly always towards the establishment of links or connections of things such that we in some measure see the reasons of things or the reasons for things. Sometimes the connections found are causal, sometimes statistical or probabilistic. Sometimes they are conceptual, and sometimes they are normative, evaluative or justificatory. So our theorizing may lead us towards causal or probabilistic generalizations, or to analytical understandings or to critical or justificatory accounts of things. As many as are the illuminating kinds of general connections we can make between things-in-particular, so many are the kinds of theorizing there are.

Not all theorizing involves constructing or proposing full-blown theories, in the sense of a relatively articulated, coherent and complete set of answers to one or more general questions.[6] Indeed, it would not be a sign of a discipline's being in good health if everybody theoretically interested in it were always proposing their own new theoretical account of it. Much theoretical work goes forward within or in the shadow of some already proposed theory. One's focus may be on *improving* or refining a going theory, whether in general or for some particular range of topics, as Mill tried to do for Bentham's principle of utility, or many of his followers have done for Marx and, more recently, MacCormick has attempted to do for Hart.[7] Or one may be *applying* a theory with a view to explaining, accounting for or justifying some position, as Richard Posner purports to do for much of the common law; or one can use a theory as the basis of a *critique* of some received understanding in a field, as several contributors to *Legal Theory and Common Law* have set out to do. Or one's application of a theory to a topic may have the special purpose of *testing* the theory, or testing a whole range of theories sharing some common hypothesis. An excellent example of this is Brian Simpson's essay of 1973, here reprinted, which tests against a historical view of the common law the theoretical proposition that legal systems are 'systems of rules'.[8] The thesis that one cannot account for the common law in those terms deals a devastating blow to any theory of law which depends on that proposition. Such a theory will have to be refined or abandoned – or Simpson's evidence reconsidered – in order to defend a 'rules' theory of law.

Among the most general and abstract questions that we can pursue in our theorizing are included a range of questions which Neil MacCormick has recently suggested to be foundational for any philosophical approach to law.[9] The suggested list ran to six:

(1) He begins with ontological questions, questions about what there is, in the sense of demanding an account of the kinds of things that there are and that go to making up our world – questions which at a fairly concrete level keep cropping up, as Roger Cotterrell's essay shows, in a law of property. We can make a 'law of things' intelligible only through some reflections on the quality of 'a thing'.

(2) Then there are questions of structure – how do different modes and levels of existence interrelate? How, for example, do we connect together law and legal relations with economic relations, socio-political power with ideology? The problem of these interrelationships in various ways preoccupies many of the contributors to *Legal Theory and Common Law*. They are by no means in agreement as to the answers – but none doubts the importance of trying to address the question with critical reference to other possible answers.

(3) There are also epistemological questions, questions about how we know and about how knowledge is possible as to some or any subject-matter. Local and particular variants crop up in William Twining's discussion of evidence and proof, i.e. of the lawyer's modes of apprehending 'facts' and also in Richard Tur's invocation of the Kelsenian approach to an epistemology of law.

(4) Closely related are methodological questions, in the book perhaps best represented by David Miers's reflections on methods of interpretation of statutory materials and David Sugarman's critique of traditional approaches to legal exposition.

(5) Then there are questions about the relationships of humans as rational agents to each other and to whatever else there is, and for present purposes this encompasses all the sociological aspects and elements of theoretical studies of law.

(6) Finally there are the questions of how people ought to live and conduct themselves; here belong all aspects of practical reason and critical or justificatory theory, such as one finds, for example, in Katherine O'Donovan's discussion of the part which law can and should (not) play in domestic and familial relations or Ronald Dworkin's accounts of what constitute valid and cogent legal arguments.

The conception of 'legal philosophy' which this range of questions defines is plainly a broad one, and (as indicated) one which does not exclude the pursuit of enquiries at a quite low level of abstraction as well as at the high level represented by the 'six questions' in their more general statement. Such a conception of philosophical theorizing about law is thus probably safe from Twining's *caveat* against equating all legal theory with philosophy and thus opening up a gap between the middle-range theorizing of some jurists and 'high' or 'grand' theory.[10] Whether or not that is so, it remains quite obvious that, even given so broad and generous a conception of the sphere of the philosophical, there would remain areas of theoretical enquiry about law which lie beyond its scope, for example, the kind of positive economic theorizing discussed by Veljanovski. The activity of theorizing as a search for general and abstract explanations or connections includes philosophical enquiry at its most fundamental level, but goes beyond it too. It is primarily an activity, not an end-product; though when it goes well it may yield more or less satisfying and relatively comprehensive theory or theories.

Presuppositions and Assumptions

A particular kind of theoretical investigation is that which tries to dig out and expose underlying presuppositions and assumptions of taken-for-granted ways of explaining things and deeming them intelligible. Here, as it were, there is implicit theory in the way we account for things. But not until it is articulated and made explicit are we able to check it and criticize it. All exposition and explanation presupposes some explanatory framework, some abstract connectedness of things which makes particular connections meaningful. In this sense all expository or explanatory or justificatory discourse has theoretical assumptions which are usually, but not always, implicit. Thus, underlying any expository textbook, however modest its intellectual pretensions, lurks a series of assumptions, which may be more or less coherent and consistent, about the nature of the enterprise of legal exposition and methods appropriate to it.[11] Similarly any argument about a disputed question of law by a barrister or a judge or a legal commentator involves assumptions about what constitute valid and cogent justifications in the kind of context in which the argument is advanced. More generally, assumptions and presuppositions involving MacCormick's six questions abound in all our thought and talk about law and other things. We all have – perhaps have to have – implicit assumptions about what there is, about how we know and how we should explain, and on what basis we recommend or criticize or make evaluations. The six questions represent an attempt to flesh out the idea, adopted from Northrop, that all lawyers have some philosophy, but only some have a developed awareness of what that philosophy is.[12] Only in making ontological, epistemological, methodological and evaluative assumptions explicit can we begin to check, refine and test them, by 'theorizing' them, rather than assuming them unreflectively. Analytical work can often have this character, as when we try to explain or elucidate the implicit ideas about possession or ownership which lie behind, for example, parts of the law of property; or when we try to work out the values which must be presupposed in order to make justificatory sense of contract or company law.

Exploiting the Inheritance

All that has been said so far might conjure up a picture of us going forward with theorizings and with digging out theoretical assumptions as though we had to do so completely from scratch. But of course this is not the case. It is not a theoretical vacuum but an embarrassment of theoretical riches that we actually face in the field of law. Others have been at the explanatory, justificatory and analytical tasks long before us, and a broad sweep of ideas about and approaches to the understandings, analysis and justification (or critique) of law exists, often at the most ambitious and comprehensive levels of generalization. As foolish as reinventing the wheel generation by generation would it be to ignore this inheritance of ideas and approaches. Our theorizing is not to be tackled *ab initio*, but standing on the shoulders of our predecessors, as likely as not working within some particular intellectual and ideological tradition. There one is not merely advancing one's own explanations and justifications and testing one's own assumptions. Just as likely one is testing and repruning or rejecting some body of theoretical ideas or some leading idea which is already given in the voluminous literature of jurisprudence. For example, many contributions to jurisprudence have centred around the idea of law as in some way or sense a system of rules of a relatively coherent and ordered kind. Again, as Brian Simpson's 'Common Law and Legal Theory' shows, even so cherished an idea is challengeable.[13] Tested against the common law, it seems inadequate to explain it historically or at the present. Faced with the anomaly, what becomes of this idea? Do we abandon it, or do we refine it and adjust it, perhaps in some wider theoretical framework, in order to develop a more coherent and intelligible account of the common law? Or do we challenge the evidence on methodological or other grounds so as to reject the claim that common law is more muddle than system, hence perhaps saving the idea of law as a system of rules? A latter-day Benthamite, a Kelsenian, a disciple of Llewellyn or Dworkin, or an economic analyst could all be expected to adopt different strategies in tackling these questions. Each would be drawing on part of the existing stock of ideas and approaches that are already available to us in tackling almost any theoretical question.

Dialogues With Past Thinkers

Ideas, theories, methods, arguments, even questions are human constructs, stimulated, articulated, promulgated, disseminated, debated, revised, refined and distorted by actual people in particular situations. To describe the heritage of legal theory as a body of literature, as a collection of texts, is no more than a convenient simplification. Our subject conspicuously lacks any counterpart to the encyclopaedic guides that exist for English literature or music or political thought. Jurisprudence has no Grove or Kobbé or even a Quentin Skinner or a Margaret Drabble. If such a work were to exist its subject-matter would resemble not so much the tip of an iceberg, as a motley collection of flotsam and treasures fished out of a turbulent and murky ocean of discourse and debate.

Why should undergraduates devote time to studying the works of leading thinkers? A jurist may be significant because of his place in intellectual history, because he originated, developed or promulgated ideas that became widely adopted or otherwise important; or a jurist may be thought to have been more or less directly influential on historical events – as historians debate how far certain nineteenth-century reforms are attributable to the 'influence' of Jeremy Bentham. Or a jurist's work may be worth reading because it addresses in a worthwhile way issues that are of contemporary significance. Both of us welcome recent developments in the history of ideas[14] and are emphatic that juristic texts should be read in context.[15] But, in our view, the main intellectual value of studying juristic texts is as an aid to addressing important contemporary issues in legal theory. Any worthwhile text raises and attempts to answer one or more questions. Studying a text involves a form of dialogue between the author and the reader about such questions. Thus it is the study of issues-via-texts, not intellectual history or the study of texts for their own sake, that provides the main educational justification for paying attention to our intellectual heritage. Because we are fortunate to live in a period of great liveliness in jurisprudence a remarkably high proportion of the texts that are currently studied are by modern authors, many of whom are still alive and battling. Reading jurisprudence need not be a form of ritual obeisance to dead ancestors.

LEGAL THEORY - WHY?

Three general types of justification are commonly advanced for compulsory courses on legal theory or jurisprudence. Firstly, such courses are sometimes claimed to have a symbolic function. In its crudest version this is little more than a cynical kind of window-dressing: a law degree needs to be seen to include one or two 'cultural' subjects in order to be accepted as belonging in a university. To argue thus is no more respectable nor plausible than maintaining that lawyers need to be able to drop the names of at least ten famous jurists in order to be able to pass themselves off as members of a learned profession.

A more interesting symbolic argument is that unless a law degree contains a required course on jurisprudence students will not believe any claims made for it as a serious intellectual or academic enterprise.[16] At first sight this argument is appealing; for it is difficult to take seriously the intellectual claims of a degree programme that does not contain a substantial theoretical element. However, direct study of theory does not take place only in courses labelled 'Jurisprudence'; and to require any course merely or mainly for symbolic or window-dressing reasons hardly counts as a justification either for such courses or for the programme as a whole.

A second kind of argument stresses the vocational relevance of theory courses. Concentration on analytical jurisprudence, for example, has sometimes been justified as a kind of gymnastic exercise in clear thinking - a particularly demanding assault course in the enterprise of teaching people 'to think like lawyers'[17]. Similar utilitarian or instrumental justifications are made for particular topics. Such arguments need to be treated with caution, not because they are fallacious, but because typically they are not the main or the strongest reasons for studying theory. Furthermore instrumental justifications may have a distorting effect on what is studied. And jurisprudence courses may not be the only or the best means of achieving such ends. It would be as absurd to claim that all theoretical study is of direct practical value as it would be to claim that all theorizing is useless. Working at a high level of abstraction may be of great utility for some particular purpose, for example, because it is more economical or opens up possibilities or makes illuminating connections or helps to destroy the arguments of an opponent. But the purposes for which theory may be of immediate practical value are many and varied and do not provide a general or a coherent rationale for whole courses on jurisprudence. Practical training can undoubtedly benefit from injections of theory;[18] but the most urgent reasons for theoretical study are independent of its immediate utility.

The vocational relevance of some kinds of jurisprudence course is sometimes advanced in general terms. Perhaps the most eloquent exponent of this view is Karl Llewellyn.[19] His argument can be restated as follows: a liberal education in law is the best practical training that a university law school can offer to intending lawyers. A compulsory course on jurisprudence can play a central role in such a liberal education by helping students to integrate their study of law with their knowledge of other subjects, with their own first-hand experiences and with their beliefs concerning religion, morals, politics and life. Llewellyn's fullest statement of this is set out in a paper, written in 1940, which has not previously been published *in toto*.[20] It is an eloquent plea for a particular kind of course directed to the objective of helping each student, in Northrop's words, 'to know what his legal philosophy is'. We have appended it here, as the best statement we know of the vocational relevance of our subject.

We agree with Llewellyn's emphasis on understanding law, on the integrative role of legal theory and on the value of clarifying connections between one's 'life work' and one's general beliefs – of integrating one's legal philosophy and one's general philosophy, in Northrop's sense. We are personally quite sympathetic with the notion of 'the good lawyer' that underlies his argument and with the claim that the kind of jurisprudence course that he advocated could have immediate practical utility as well as helping to serve this noble aspiration. However, not everyone accepts his notion of 'the good lawyer' and, more important, our case for direct study of legal theory has to be made in a rather different educational context: Xanadu and British law students tend to be younger and less extensively educated than their American counterparts; many law graduates either do not seek, or fail to obtain, professional qualifications; many who qualify do not practise law for a substantial period, if at all; many undergraduate law students have not yet decided whether to qualify or to practise and many who think they have decided one way or the other are destined to change their minds. Within our structure of preparation for practice the law degree represents only the first, explicitly 'academic' stage of a process that continues for a substantial period after graduation.

Because law degrees are multifunctional and have been explicitly given the role of satisfying the 'academic' stage in the four-stage structure of preparation for legal practice (academic, professional, apprenticeship, continuing legal education), the task of making the case for courses on jurisprudence within law degrees is easier; on the other hand, because our students tend to be less mature and less broadly educated than their American counterparts, our expectations of what can realistically be achieved by a single course may have to be lower. We propose to argue that in this context the 'why?' of studying jurisprudence is essentially the same as Llewellyn put forward, but the which?, when? and how? have to take account of the characteristics of our system of legal education and of particular degree programmes.

In the present context the general case for direct study of theory can be summarized as follows: A serious understanding of law is an intellectual objective of plain and obvious intrinsic value. In the context of the United Kingdom, and anywhere else that similar conditions apply, if law degrees are to have a coherent rationale, the primary objective of an education in law is to promote such understanding. Successful pursuit of legal education through some kind of academic course of study is nowadays properly demanded as a precondition of entry into the professional practice of law. So whether a student takes a law degree with a view to legal practice or takes one as a general educational qualification, perhaps before he or she has decided on a career, it seems safe to say that the course for a law degree ought to be geared, so far as it can be, to the aim of generating a serious understanding of law, and that the condition for award of a law degree should be proof that the student has pursued such an understanding with a tolerable or hopefully even a substantial measure of success. It is accordingly neither necessary nor desirable to construct the rationale for law degrees, and for theory courses, in narrowly vocational terms, that is to say in terms of direct relevance to particular practical or professional goals. The strongest vocational justification for the study of legal theory is that it promotes understanding of law.

That understanding law requires a real and considerable element of theory in the curriculum is a point which the other contributors to *Legal Theory and Common Law* have saved us the trouble of having to argue at any length. Each of the chapters of this book which is dedicated to a particular 'branch' of legal study demonstrates the integral involvement of theoretical considerations in any valid understanding of the subject in view. Each of the authors interprets the special relevance of theory to his or her part of the discipline of law in an individual way; there is no single theory-monolith upon which each inscribes or from which each transcribes the unitary wisdom for the legal enterprise. For theorizing is not the kind of activity which postulates or generates a single all-encompassing body of doctrine upon the authority of which laws are expounded subject by subject and branch by branch. It is much more exciting and challenging because it is a much more pluralistic and dialectical business than that.

Thus the task of explicating the role of theory in the law curriculum has its job half done for it already. Asked whether there is a place for theory in an undergraduate law degree, we are able to say in the light of our colleagues' papers that theory has to be omnipresent in the law curriculum. In all the various ways that they describe and argue for, and doubtless in many others besides, theory must penetrate and infuse all that is taught and studied in legal education. There could be some kind of rote learning otherwise; but no serious understanding. This is not mere dogma – it is a claim needing proof. But the proof is already given. We rest this part of the case on our colleagues' arguments.

Theory is necessary to understanding law. But are separate courses of study on 'Jurisprudence' or 'Legal Philosophy' or 'Sociology of Law' necessary for this purpose or at least sufficiently important to justify giving them space in an already crowded programme? The very success of arguments for injection of theoretical elements with all else that is taught as law may ostensibly weaken the case for independent treatment; and, indeed, some law teachers argue that separate theory courses are unnecessary precisely because 'we all do it already'. We are sceptical that this last claim is true of the actual practice of most law teachers; but assuming, for the sake of argument, that this were the case, it suggests a number of questions: If other courses contain a proper measure of theoretical study, what is left for a special course on 'theory'? If they do not, of what help will a discrete 'theory course' be? And following on from there: Is there not even a risk that specialized theory classes will impoverish the curriculum by encouraging teachers and students in the other courses to suppose that all the theory they need is covered there?

Let us start from this last question. For we do think that there is such a risk. We are aware that theory can be thought of as something special and apart.

So theoretical elements may tend to drop out of the contract class or the constitutional or family law class, while on the other hand the theorizing that goes on in the theory class does, or seems to, say little or nothing which connects up with the content of contract, constitutional or family law or indeed anything much else in the law syllabus. As William Twining warns in 'Evidence and Legal Theory',[21] a jurisprudence course can become too much a matter of high theory, a purely philosophical (or sociological, for that matter, adds MacCormick) discoursing about some rather vague and undifferentiated 'law' in its relations to the political, the social, the moral or the economic or in its character as a special topic for analytical reflection. An always present, and in itself laudable, ambition to draw from and contribute to philosophy and sociology can nevertheless lure the theorist away from the ordinary discourse of the discipline or disciplines of law; and the jurist in the 'straight law' class loses touch with 'theorists' theory' and may even lose sight of the essential theoretical element in his or her own branch of legal study. So there is always some risk of a gap opening between law and theory, or, rather, between law courses and theory courses. A large part of the point of this book as a collaborative work has been to do a bit of gap-closing. But the movement must be a two-way one; if law must keep open to theory so must theory keep open to law and, in teaching jurisprudence, one of the most pressing problems is to prevent it from becoming, or from being perceived to be, remote or redundant. Jurisprudence should not be a subject apart.

What special role is left for separate theory courses in a curriculum that is generally informed by theory? In our view the answer is quite simple. Of course, much depends on context – on what is adequately dealt with in other courses and what are the main learning objectives that are proposed for the specific theory course or courses in question. Nevertheless, it seems likely that none of Twining's five functions of legal theory can be done as economically or as efficiently by means of a 'pervasive approach'.[22] It is difficult to see how intellectual history or central questions of legal philosophy can be dealt with systematically or in depth other than by direct study. Certain kinds of middle-order theorizing can no doubt be accommodated in other courses; for example, it may be possible to accommodate theories of adjudication or legislation, or even some aspects of the sociology of the legal profession, within courses on legal institutions or legal process or legal method. But, insofar as such courses deal adequately with those topics they become in effect 'theory courses'. Furthermore, it is not easy to get to grips with, for example, Ronald Dworkin's theory of adjudication or the nature of legal reasoning if one is divorced from the context of broader theoretical debates. Similarly, while a broad approach to family law or criminal law or constitutional law inevitably involves drawing on material from other disciplines, a more systematic exploration of the relationships between law and these other disciplines requires attention to be focused directly on such relationships at a higher level of generality than would be appropriate for most standard law courses. Most important of all is the integrative function. One role of 'theory' within a course on contract or torts or constitutional law is to provide a coherent view of the subject as a whole. But it is difficult to see how a coherent view of law as a whole or, more mundanely, of all the subjects studied by an individual student within his or her degree course can be achieved other than by direct study. Whatever other educational objectives are served by separate theory courses, perhaps their most important function is to provide an opportunity to students to stand back from the detailed study of particular topics and to look at their subject as a whole at a higher level of generality and from a variety of perspectives. Such a course, whatever it is called, which draws on and feeds into all other courses in the curriculum and thereby helps to provide the basis for an integrated educational experience, is performing one of the main jobs of jurisprudence.

WHICH THEORY?

The picture that we have painted of the nature and scope of legal theory is rather daunting. It includes many basic issues of philosophy and much else besides. The heritage of juristic texts, if not quite as extensive as English literature, is vast, rich and amorphous. As anyone who has been involved in curriculum planning should know, many of the sharpest disagreements in legal education relate to priorities. It is not enough just to make a general case for the desirability of a particular subject. Reasons have to be advanced for giving it priority over other desirable subjects; when it is claimed that the subject should be a required or integral part of a degree programme the reasons have to be even more cogent. In the case of vast subjects like international law or legal history, selection and ordering of priorities *within* the subject are also required. One must then take care to ensure that the rationale for including the subject within the curriculum fits the aspects of the subject that have been selected for inclusion.

This is especially important in the case of jurisprudence. It is hardly plausible to claim that studying jurisprudence provides an excellent form of training in analytical skills or helps to integrate all the other subjects in the curriculum, if what is in fact involved is a superficial and inaccurate Cook's tour of so-called 'schools'. Similarly rigorous in-depth study of one or two major texts may serve some valuable educational objectives, but is less likely to sustain claims that the jurisprudence course provides a map of our intellectual heritage. Accordingly general justifications for the study of legal theory need to be treated with caution; what learning objectives are likely to be served in fact depends on which from a range of possible objectives have been selected. However, this caution can easily be exaggerated for two reasons: first, the most cogent justifications for giving direct study of theoretical issues a high priority all relate to MacCormick's six basic questions of legal philosophy. These, we would suggest, can reasonably be treated as the core of the subject, provided it is recognized that each of them is open to consideration in a variety of contexts at a number of levels of generality. Secondly, the heritage of attempted answers is much more extensive than the range of questions. The corpus of juristic texts can be seen as a series of more or less ambitious attempts to provide answers to one or more of a less extensive number of interrelated questions. Juristic debate is notoriously repetitive, often involving false polemics and the ritual exaggeration of minute differences. If the main purpose of direct study of legal theory is for students to reflect critically about important issues, it is of secondary importance which theories or theorists they use to assist this enterprise. In order to confront questions about justice, it is not necessary for an undergraduate to consider more than two or three from the vast stock of attempted answers to such questions. If, as we shall argue, students should be exposed to a reasonably wide range of important *issues* in legal theory, the problem of selection becomes less acute. One should not be too selective about fundamental questions, but one can be ruthless about coverage of texts, theorists and theories, for these are mainly to be treated as aids to confronting the questions.

THEORY – WHEN?

If the primary objective of a law degree is to promote understanding of law, and if wrestling with abstract questions, answers and concepts is a necessary part of that enterprise, then theorizing should not only be an integral part of the programme, it should also pervade it. At the very outset of their studies, and at every stage, students will be helped by maps which establish connections both within and between particular areas of study. From the start they need to be persuaded that understanding law involves continuous movement through different levels of abstraction; they need to be acclimatized to the atmosphere of abstract discourse and to the problems of moving from the general to the particular and *vice versa*. Most will almost certainly benefit from direct instruction in some of the specific techniques of theoretical analysis, such as elucidating abstract concepts, digging out hidden assumptions, constructing logical arguments and spotting common kinds of fallacy. Much of this is as much a matter of confidence as competence, for in our experience student resistance to theorizing is grounded as much in unfamiliarity, fear and indolence as in anti-intellectualism. Generally speaking law teachers are more likely to differ about the means of achieving these ends than about the ends themselves.

A more controversial question is *when* space should be made for direct study of theoretical questions. In particular, in law degrees in which one or more theory courses are an integral part of the programme, what is the best place for such courses? In most, but by no means all, undergraduate degrees in the United Kingdom jurisprudence courses have traditionally been postponed until the final year. Similarly Llewellyn argued that a required course on jurisprudence in an American law school should come at the end, building on all that has gone before and bringing it together into a coherent whole.[23] Without claiming that there is a single right answer to this question, we would venture a different opinion. The thrust of the foregoing analysis, backed by our practical experience as teachers, is that jurisprudence courses work best towards the middle of the programme. They should feed into other courses as well as feed off them. The implications of general ideas and approaches for particular fields of study can be more readily perceived and understood after these ideas have been assimilated and when the opportunity is given to apply them in an academic context. It is our impression that student resistance to theory tends to be less entrenched in the second year (of a three- or four-year degree) than it is later, partly because by their third year many students have been socialized into habits and attitudes that are inimical to theoretical study. This is due not only to crude anti-intellectualism, but also to the particularizing tendency of much legal education. Moreover, the tendency to perceive theory courses as separate and irrelevant to other courses is fortified by postponing them until last, by which time most students are beginning to think about the next stage of their career, whatever that may be. Finally, one practical reason for favouring placing jurisprudence in the second year is that it can serve as a building-block for more advanced theory courses. There are obvious limits to what can be achieved by a single course and teachers of jurisprudence are no less imperialistic about their subject than their colleagues, though (if our argument is valid) with better justification.

JURISPRUDENCE - HOW?

There are, of course, almost as many different jurisprudence courses as there are jurisprudence teachers. And given the conception presented here as to the why, the which and the when of such courses it is plain that there are many possible ways of dealing with the range of subject-matters which a theory class should address. We are certainly opposed to the idea that there could or should be any single prescription for every self-respecting course in jurisprudence. Indeed, it has been part of the point of this paper to exhibit the multiplicity of valuable possibilities in the way of jurisprudence teaching.

To one style of approach to this multiplicity of possibilities we are firmly opposed – viz. that of the comprehensive survey of all the possibilities. Any attempt at total comprehensiveness in a single course can lead only to a kind of second- or third-hand rehashing through lectures or textbooks of bundles of ideas ascribed – with almost inevitable distortions – to given authors or to 'schools' of thought. Such an approach replicates some of the more problematic and indeed undesirable features of teaching and learning in a certain style of 'black-letter' approach to substantive law subjects. Even if (which we doubt) such concern for 'coverage' is necessary in the study of most branches of substantive law, it is totally stultifying if applied to legal theory, the chief point of which is to help students to think out and articulate their own philosophy of law (in the wide sense of 'philosophy' favoured by Northrop and MacCormick) or some aspects of it.

What is perhaps most damaging about the potted-theories approach is that it actually obscures to students both the difficulties and the fascinations of working out a careful theoretical position on law or on anything else. For students to experience that it is as important for them to study primary sources as 'in case-law subjects' it is important that they actually read cases. That is they must read some text or texts of legal theory or philosophy at least in very substantial extract and preferably *in toto*. They should confront some theorizing in the raw, and develop their own critique of it.

Certainly, whatever texts are prescribed in a course – and the range of reasonable possibilities to be read is enormous – it is necessary for course teachers to help with filling in context and background. And for context and background a good general text can be helpful. But even at the risk of some selectivity in concentration both as to topics and as to approaches, the encouragement of students to engage seriously with serious texts is of the first importance in jurisprudence. It is also of value as an input into a law-degree course as an educational experience. For law students in other courses are unlikely ever to find themselves reading and assessing whole books as wholes. Most legal texts are hardly written to be read in that way.

Against that background of inevitable selectivity, fairness of mind does require some breadth of coverage, if only to keep students fully aware of the controversial quality of the subject and the range of positions among which they can reasonably seek to find their own point of view. MacCormick, at least, would be unhappy with any general legal-theory course which did not expose students to some version of legal positivism, some statement of the natural law view, and some variant on liberal and on socialist thought in the sociology of law or applied political theory. He also believes that some work or works on the nature of reasoning about law and about facts has to be included in any serious course; and this should involve confrontation with legal realist or sociological versions of scepticism about legal processes, as well as some statement, for example Ronald Dworkin's, of a more rationalistic view on these matters.[24]

These are only barebones suggestions anyway; to go further would compromise our stated view that there are many reasonable possibilities. What line is taken depends on many variables – on the relationship of the theory class to other classes in a degree curriculum, and, in particular, on the extent to which a general course on jurisprudence may be followed up by more specialized courses in special aspects of philosophy and sociology of law and in studies of legal processes, as is common in at least the Scottish universities and in Northern Ireland. At this point in the discussion, we therefore return to the proposition that while it is for locals (that is, for each of us as a local of some locality) to contextualize the teaching of legal theory, the task of the present authors is to intellectualize it.'

Here ended the report to the Law Faculty of Xanadu. History does not record the reception it was given by the faculty. However, one of us heard a rumour (or was it a dream?) that over-expenditure on prestige building led to such pressure on public funds in Xanadu that the university was closed down and training for the professions reverted to a system of pure apprenticeship. It is not thought that this had enhanced the quality of either legal practice or legal understanding in Xanadu.

NOTES

1 F. Northrop, *The Complexity of Legal and Ethical Experience* (1959) p. 6.
2 On the first curriculum discussion in Xanadu see W. Twining 'Taking Facts Seriously' in *Essays on Legal Education* (1982; ed. N. Gold), reprinted in (1984) 34 *J Legal Education* 22.
3 See above p. 155.
4 J. Austin, 'The Uses of the Study of Jurisprudence' in *the Province of Jurisprudence Determined* (1954; ed. H. L. A. Hart) p. 366.

5 To look on theorizing as an activity enables us to locate examples of that activity in specific historical contexts; for actual people theorize in particular times and places. From the perspective of what might be called the ethnography of knowledge it is possible to make meaningful statements about the nature and state of this kind of activity, and trends relating to it, in a given legal culture. Twining was adopting this kind of perspective when he suggested that one way of looking at legal theorizing is as an activity directed to a variety of tasks within the discipline of law, itself an intellectual enterprise involving a variety of activities (see above p. 64). In his paper (chapter 5) Roger Cotterrell suggests that Twining contradicts himself by asserting that there is a distinct discipline of law, but giving only a very limited place to the notion of 'law as an autonomous discipline'. To view legal research, legal education and legal theorizing as activities that are carried out in the context of a distinctive legal culture ('the culture' of law schools in England, for example, is markedly different from the culture of medical schools or history departments) involves no commitment to any particular view on the autonomy of disciplines. Ethnographic statements about intellectual cultures belong to a different sphere of discourse from epistemological claims about the 'autonomy' of particular kinds of knowledge. It is not possible to pursue this complex issue here, but it seems that Twining and Cotterrell differ rather than disagree on this matter, as they have adopted different perspectives in pursuit of rather different concerns.

6 See above p. 78.

7 D. N. MacCormick, *H. L. A. Hart* (1981).

8 See above chapter 2.

9 MacCormick, 'The Democratic Intellect and the Law', Presidential Address, Society of Public Teachers of Law (1985) 5 *Legal Studies* 172.

10 In the past we, the two authors, have expressed somewhat different opinions about the relationship between legal philosophy and jurisprudence and we are still inclined to express our conclusions differently. But what divides us is more a difference of terminology and expression than a disagreement of substance. William Twining treats 'jurisprudence' and 'legal theory' as synonymous; he has suggested that jurisprudence is much wider than legal philosophy and that the term 'philosophy' should in this context be confined to the most general or abstract questions of legal theory (High Theory). Behind this point lie several interrelated concerns: first, that there has been a tendency to treat jurisprudence and legal philosophy as coextensive, with the result that many other theoretical questions have tended to be neglected; secondly, that if there is to be a continuing and fruitful interaction between the general and the particular in legal discourse, it is important to explore and to make explicit the relations between different levels of generality. A third concern is that there is a tendency to treat all legal theories as rival answers to the same questions and to interpret and criticize all jurists at the level of philosophy. By no means all questions in legal theory are in first instance philosophical questions and not all jurists are philosophers. Finally, there has been a tendency in English analytical philosophy to emphasize analysis and to be suspicious of grand synthesizing theories or even of more modest attempts to construct coherent frames of reference. Yet one of the primary jobs of jurisprudence is to perform this synthesizing function for law as a whole and for particular branches, fields or topics. Whether this activity is considered 'philosophical' is a secondary matter.

Neil MacCormick, on the other hand, following the broad usages of the enlightenment writers of the eighteenth century, is more disposed to use the term 'philosophy' to include any abstract or general thought or talk about law. This usage serves to make the point that professionals and specialists in departments of philosophy have no monopoly rights in the concept of 'philosophy'. More important, it sets up no artificial barriers between the multiple levels of generality at which nearly all theorizing takes place. In this view, the absence of discontinuity between different levels of theorizing could justify treating the whole range of theoretical work as 'philosophical' in the broad sense of the term. But this broad sense is one in which lawyers are as fully entitled to have 'philosophies' as any others; indeed, according to Northrop, all who engage in legal discourse are committed to having 'legal philosophies' in this sense.

11 See above pp. 26-7, 48-54 (Sugarman), and Twining, 'Treatises and Textbooks' (1973) 12 *J Society of Public Teachers of Law* (NS) 267.

12 *Op. cit.*

13 See above chapter 2.

14 E.g. Q. Skinner, *The Foundations of Modern Political Thought* (1978); S. Collini, D. Winch and J. Burrow *The Noble Science of Politics* (1983).

15 This theme is developed in Twining, 'Talk about Realism' (1985) *New York University Law Rev.* (forthcoming).

16 This argument was put eloquently and persuasively to one of us recently by student representatives in an Australian university. In the context the argument was cogent, as it was in essence a plea for a coherent educational philosophy for a law degree of the kind advocated in this paper. This does not vitiate the point, made in the text, that required courses need to be justified in terms of their educational rather than their symbolic value.

17 E.g. Hart, 'Analytical Jurisprudence in Mid-Twentieth Century: A Reply to Professor Bodenheimer' (1957) 105 *University of Pennsylvania Law Rev.* 953.

18 It is beyond the scope of this paper to consider the role of theory in formal training in professional legal skills and in continuing legal education. One implication of our argument is that specific theoretical inputs can be valuable, sometimes necessary, in such courses. In recent years there has been a strong trend, especially in the United States, in this direction in the teaching of negotiation, advocacy, analysis of evidence and professional responsibility. See, for example, Twining, *op. cit.*, n. 2.

19 K. Llewellyn, 'The Study of Law as a Liberal Art' in *Jurisprudence: Realism in Theory and Practice* (1962) ch. 17, and 'A Required Course in Jurisprudence' (chapter 14 below).

20 See below p. 258 n.

21 See above p. 65.

22 See above p. 64.

23 See below p. 255.

24 Twining would be rather more cautious about making general prescriptions here; cf. Llewellyn, below pp. 256-7.

14
A Required Course in Jurisprudence

KARL LLEWELLYN

I stand for a third year course, because whatever the values of Jurisprudence may be as an introduction or as an accompaniment to the study of law, the greatest and most necessary value of Jurisprudence lies in leading the student to understanding his work; to putting it together as a whole whose parts have relation to one another; to getting clear for himself what meaning the materials and techniques he has been studying have, and are to have, for his life-work and for his life. And those values cannot be had until he has already been over most of his study, until he has something in hand and in head, to *be* put together, and to *be* understood.

I stand for a special course, devoted to Jurisprudence and nothing else, because however much of jurisprudential thinking one may add to or gain from other courses, one can never escape the need of a course to focus centrally upon what that course is about. The only way to focus on the Whole, and the meaning of the Whole, is to devote a course *To* the Whole.

I stand for a compulsory course, because we have in my opinion a duty, an inescapable duty, to do our best to awaken in every student without exception some appreciation of the law as a whole in its relation to society, on the one hand, and, on the other, to the follower of the law. First year Procedure, and Contracts, no one of us thinks properly made optional. The relation of a man's life-work to his society and to himself is a duty-job for himself to wrestle with, and a duty-job for us to see that he wrestles with.

Neither do I have any fear that the impending bar exams and the pressure to get bread-and-butter stuff under the belt will block off student interest. I do not mean to make light of student resistance. I am aware of the degree to which they wish their time well-spent upon the practical, and the immediately practical, and indeed upon what *they* happen to believe practical. I am aware also that they come into the third year with ideas pretty well set about how law ought to be taught, pretty obstinate about having any new wrinkles tried out on them, and with a lawyer-like difficulty in dealing with any modes of thought or manner of material to which they have not been accustomed. Which means four weeks, or maybe six, of pulling back on the leash, and grumbling.

But what we have tended to pay altogether too little attention to, covers two matters that deserve attention. The first is that our students, though most of them do not know it, have a real hunger in them to find out what it is all about. They have a real hunger to see it all fit into a whole, with meaning. A good part of the third year restlessness goes back to that hunger being there, and being undiagnosed, and being unsatisfied. Once a course in Jurisprudence begins to get its teeth into them, they get their teeth into it; and that holds of any third year student, from anywhere, [with] whom one gets into conversation for an evening.

The second thing we tend to pay too little attention to, is that Jurisprudence is an exceedingly practical subject, and that students come to see that fact. If you pick up, for example, the leeway which the rules allow the court, and get from there into the relatively steady course of decision despite that leeway, you come up against the judge's search for that decision which will *satisfy*, as seeming to do justice and fit sense. And from there you come inevitably to the advocate's problem of handling his statement of his facts, of setting and maintaining the 'atmosphere' of his case, which makes *his* version of the rules and their application appeal as the right and just and sensible version. And the student not only studies the problem of 'certainty' and 'justice', but knows that he has better equipment for his work. The illustration is not unique, but typical. Good Jurisprudence, in addition to its other values, has that of illumining the lawyer's working skills.

I stand thus for a compulsory third year special course in Jurisprudence, in every school that trains lawyers for their great profession. It is feasible to give. It is a joy to teach. And, after the first floundering, the students take it with enthusiasm as well as profit.

But when it comes to what is to go into such a course, let me speak in warning. You have two-semester hours, maybe three. To have three semester-hours for Jurisprudence is like having three semester-hours for the LL.B. course in Law. Make no mistake about that. Jurisprudence is as big as Law, and bigger. And as a teaching matter, it is twice as big, because a student *gets* not what you tell him, but what he *goes* and *gets* out of the telling, and makes his own. He has to think it through, test it out, make it his own; and to get him to do that is slow going. In three semester-hours you can scratch a bit in one corner or two corners. Jurisprudence as a subject you will never even get to looking at.

That makes very little difference. It makes very little difference, because the job does not call for 'covering' Jurisprudence. The job calls for putting together what a student knows of law, and for getting some meaning out of the putting; and there is not one corner of Jurisprudence in which two or three semester-hours of work will not give you a very satisfying result on that main job.

But I am much concerned to make clear that it is utterly impossible to 'cover' the whole of Jurisprudence, because that makes clear in turn two other things. The first is, that seven courses which have no single common topic can be, each and all, superb courses for the job and for the student. The second is, that anybody planning a course can afford no time of lamentation on omissions. He can begin by knowing that he will have to omit seventy-four semester-hours' work. The important thing is to get whatever he does choose into such shape as to make his man *think* about it, and put what they know together around it.

Indeed it is almost startling to run over even a few of the angles of approach and areas of inquiry which open in Jurisprudence – any one of them capable of filling six semester-hours as full of good meat as any egg; any one of them capable of profitable less extended treatment, if only the treatment of some such as is chosen for treatment be intensive, and go deep, and get into concrete material from all over the prior or contemporaneous courses. Here is the philosophical foundation of law – which you might think of as the beginning of Jurisprudence – and which can be handled either from a comparative angle or from that of a chosen philosophy. Do that beginning right, and you will never get much beyond the beginning, in any two or three unit course; at Columbia, we have wanted to get into other matters, and so have just been forced to begin without the beginning. But it is a rousing and worthwhile field of study. Another is the nature of law, and its definition, and the values to be had from one or another definition; or the nature of justice, either ideal justice or what men feel to be justice, and the bearing of the quest for justice on the content of law and the ways of judges and lawyers with law. I suppose those would be questions in the philosophy of law as distinct from the philosophical and metaphysical foundations of law. Then there is the discipline which Wigmore calls legal method, and which Kantorowicz called dogmatics, and which I should call casuistry: study of how one goes about getting a right answer to problems, out of the authoritative given materials, and within the framework of the accepted techniques. It is a very different thing to just get the hang of doing this in a dozen courses, from what it is to look the process and the art over as a special job, and to figure out how the job is best done. And if there be one thing which can wake a law-class up to the depth and color there is in cases, it is to start reading cases for a while not for the rule laid down, but for how the judge went to work to find, test, and phrase the rule laid down.

All of such things, or any of them, occur to anyone as possible subject matter for a course in Jurisprudence. But there is a wholly different slant available. There is a theory of legal institutions to be inquired into, quite as illuminating as any theory of law: What is a court? Why is a court? How much of what we know as 'court' is accidental, historically conditioned – how much is essential to the job? The problem of administrative tribunal[s] can become very interesting, in that light. The lawyer is another legal institution, and so is contract, and so is trust. And *res judicata* and day in court have a good deal more to them than the doctrines on the subject. Again, I should suppose that study of the relation between law and what law accomplishes is Jurisprudence, quite as solidly as is the inquiry into how law comes into being, or changes. I should suppose that the relation between our discipline and the social sciences is Jurisprudence, and a kind that rewards study, too. I should think an amazingly fine course in Jurisprudence could be built around the life-work of a Holmes, watching his ideas ripen, watching influences at work on him, watching the interaction of the doctrine of the time, the time itself, and the man. Or again, history read for its meaning is Jurisprudence: say, over a hundred years, the relative roles played by the courts, the legislatures, the writers, political leaders, and the movement of the times, in the shaping and working of our law.

No, by the time one comes thus to the end of a first page of angles into Jurisprudence, one finds the wherewithal to fill one solid year and more of work. Choice must be made, ruthless choice. Only two things seem to me vital, as to subject matter: there ought to be *some* study of some part of our legal techniques, viewed just as such, because such study cross-illumines all the cases any boy has read. And there ought to be *some* study of the quest for justice, for that is one of the more hidden things in law, and yet the finest of them.

But it is very clear that there is no royal road to choosing subject-matter. And a faculty ought to remember that. For if there is consultation on the point, faculty members can get exceedingly unreasonable with one another. It seems to me often that no conviction of rightness about a point of law can be a third as self-assured, obstinate, immutable, and unarguable as a conviction of rightness about a point of Jurisprudence. My brother Patterson and I have lived in amity for years, until this matter of a course in Jurisprudence came up. Then we became as two prowling tom-cats in the spring. Jurisprudence is Philosophy of Law! said Patterson, and his mouth got grim. Jurisprudence is Philosophy of Legal Institutions! said I, and prepared to sling a chair. Yet there were only twenty-eight class-hours to work with. And Jurisprudence is really both, and a good deal more. My guess is that any faculty will do well to turn the course over to two men, rather than one; but that the two – any two – will need a proper gestation-time to get their less rational ruffled exclusivities of Right Rightness a bit smoothed down. After Patterson had arrived at the conclusion that – wrong-headed as they were – there were yet some points in my outline which might not utterly corrupt the truth; and after I had simmered down to seeing that there were points in his which I could just barely bring myself to teach, each of us woke up to the discovery that he had learned a deal more about Jurisprudence than he had known before, and we began getting grateful to each other. It has been a much better course than either of us would have put on alone. And, in this field of so many choices, this field so rich for teacher and for student, my guess is that our experience offers a sound suggestion: two men have to expect not only less burden, each, but a rather lovely extra gain.

In sum, then, a compulsory third-year special course in Jurisprudence seems to me an obligation we owe to every man who is to be a lawyer. That he may try, on his own, to see Law, whole. That he may try, on his own, to make what he has been doing, and what he is to do, take on meaning, as a Whole. That he may enter into recognition that his profession is not apart from life, a thing of drudgery, but part of life, a thing of eternal service. That law may regain for him, for each of him, its rightful status as a liberal art, as a humanity, as the very focus and balance-wheel of men's lives together.

NOTE

This paper is the text of Llewellyn's contribution to The Round Table on Jurisprudence and Legal History at the 37th Annual Meeting of the Association of American Law Schools in 1939. An abbreviated version was published in 9 American Law School Review 590 (1940), together with contributions by Edwin Patterson and Walter B. Kennedy. The occasion took place in the year after Columbia Law School decided to require that every candidate entering for the LL.B degree should have successfully completed the course in Jurisprudence. Most of the shorter version is reprinted in Llewellyn *Jurisprudence: Realism in Theory and Practice* (1962). So far as one can tell this is the first time that the full text has been published. It is reproduced here by kind permission of Karl Llewellyn's literary executor.

Index

Abel, Richard, 71
Abortion Act 1967, 124
academic law, 1-6, 62-6; *see also* legal education; legal scholarship
accountability as legitimation principle, 100-1, 108, 109-10, 111
Ackerman, Bruce, 93, 95, 230
adjudication: and economic reasoning, 231-3; and interpretation, 116; theory of, in evidence scholarship, 69, 71, 73
administrative decision-making, 188-9
administrative law, 160, 165, 169-70, 171
Alderson, B., 219, 220
Allen, C. K., 3
alternative character of the norm, 200
Ames, James Barr, 46
Anderson, T., 75
Anson, Sir W., 23, 29, 47, 48, 50, 52
apprenticeship, 29, 30
Aquinas, St Thomas, 199, 204, 205, 206-7
Aristotle, 146
Atiyah, P. S., 1, 186-7
Atkin, Lord, 220
Attorney-General's reference, 195, 202
Austin, John: and Bentham, 37-8; on definition of law, 10, 13, 106, 199, 207; in history of jurisprudence, 2, 3, 35-6, 42-4, 54, 240; on legal education, 29; on natural law, 53; *Lectures on Jurisprudence*, 43; *The Province of Jurisprudence Determined*, 43; *The Uses of the Study of Jurisprudence*, 43
Austin, Sarah, 43

author as source of textual meaning, 120-1, 124, 133 n.50
authority, 8-9; of common law, 35; and content, 12-13; and custom, 19-20; for existence of rule, 13-14, 15-16; and legitimation, 98, 105; to manage, *see* managerial power; rules for use of, 16, 18, 23-4
autonomy, individual, 138-48, 151

Bacon, Sir Francis, 30, 102
Belsey, Catherine, 121
Bennion, F. A. R., 129
Bentham, Jeremy: on common law, 16-17, 21, 35, 199; and empiricism, 70; and English jurisprudence, 1, 2, 3, 37-42, 43, 63, 241, 244; on evidence, 66, 67, 68-9, 71, 72, 76; *Comment on the Commentaries*, 16; *Fragment*, 106; *Rationale of Judicial Evidence*, 69, 74-5
Berle, A., 167
Bingham, J., 9
Black, D., 71
Blackstone, W.: Bentham on, 39, 41; on common law, 19, 20, 21, 22; and definition of law, 10-11; on liberty, 48; on property, 87
Brougham, Lord H., 35
Brown, Jethro, 43
Bryce, J., 29, 31, 35, 42, 45
Buckland, W. W., 42, 52
'bundle-of-rights' conception of ownership, 87, 88